THE BOOK OF
HORSES
AND
Horse Care

THE BOOK OF
HORSES
AND
Horse Care

*An encyclopedia of horses,
and a comprehensive guide to
horse and pony care*

**J U D I T H
D R A P E R**

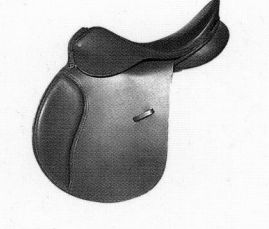

Photography by
Kit Houghton

SMITHMARK

For Boris, who helped

This edition published in 1996 by
Smithmark Publishers, a division of
U.S. Media Holdings, Inc.,
16 East 32nd Street,
New York, NY 10016

SMITHMARK books are available for bulk purchase for sales
promotion and for premium use. For details write or call the
manager of special sales, SMITHMARK Publishers Inc.,
16 East 32nd Street, New York, 10016; (212) 532-6600.

ISBN 0 7651 9785 5

Produced by Anness Publishing Limited
1 Boundary Row
London SE1 8HP

Publisher Joanna Lorenz
Senior editor Clare Nicholson
Project editor Marion Paull
Designer Michael Morey
Illustrator Rodney Paull

Printed and bound in Hong Kong

▮ PAGE ONE: **Shagya Arab**
▮ PAGE TWO: **An Arab horse**
▮ PAGE FOUR: **Mane combs and trimming scissors**
▮ PAGE FIVE: **Hoof picks**
▮ PAGE SIX: **Horses at the Catherston stud**

Contents

BREEDS OF THE WORLD

INTRODUCTION 9

HORSES 19

PONIES 129

TYPES 155

HORSE AND PONY CARE

BUYING A HORSE 171

KEEPING A HORSE 179

The Horse at Grass 181
The Stabled Horse 191

DAILY CARE 207

EQUIPMENT 227

GROOMING 241

INDEX 252

ACKNOWLEDGEMENTS 256

Breeds of
the World

Introduction

The lives of humans and horses have been bound together
for many thousands of years. Appreciated first as just another
source of food, the predecessors of the modern horse were
hunted like any other wild animal. In time there came a
steady process of domestication as nomadic peoples began to
herd horses in the same way as they did goats and other
animals. Ultimately, however, it was as a means of swift
transport that the horse really came into his own. Men learnt
to ride. Their whole lives were transformed. Horses became
their chief means of transportation, remaining so until well
into the twentieth century. Domestication, coupled with a
gradual increase in human population, signalled the end of
the truly wild horse. Today, even those horses which live in
herds on the few remaining extensive areas of suitable
grassland are not truly wild, for they are all "managed" by
humans to one degree or another. Nevertheless horses retain
much of the instinctive behaviour which enabled them to
exist without man's intervention and it is necessary to
understand what makes them "tick" if we are to enjoy our
continuing association with them.

The History of the Horse

The modern horse, *Equus caballus*, belongs to the family *Equidae*, which also includes asses and zebras. *Equidae* are placed in the order Perissodactyla, to which tapirs and rhinoceroses belong and which descended from the Condylarthra, a group of primitive, long extinct mammals which were the ancestors of all hoofed mammals.

Fossil remains have made it possible to trace at least some aspects of the evolution of the modern horse over a period of some sixty million years, indicating how it gradually adapted to changes in its environment. The known history of the modern horse starts with Eohippus, also called the Dawn Horse, which is known to have lived in North America during the Eocene epoch (fifty-four to thirty-eight million years ago). An animal no larger than a small dog, Eohippus was designed for life as a forest browser moving around on soft soil. It had four toes on its forefeet, three on its back feet and pads similar to a dog's. Its small, low-crowned teeth were

suited to eating leaves and other low, soft vegetation. It would probably have had a camouflage colouring to help it to escape predators. During the Oligocene epoch (thirty-seven to twenty-six million years

ago) first Mesohippus then Merychippus, showed distinct changes: the legs became longer, the back straighter (Eohippus had an arched back) and the whole animal larger. One toe disappeared on the forefoot, leaving three toes on both fore and hindfeet. The teeth also showed signs of change, the pre-molars becoming more like true molars.

In this slow process of evolution, the most significant change of all occurred during the Miocene epoch (twenty-five to seven million years ago) when forests gave

■ **PREVIOUS PAGE OPPOSITE**
A Cleveland Bay.

■ **PREVIOUS PAGE**
A Furioso.

■ **LEFT**
The zebra is one of the small group of animals belonging to the family *Equidae*.

■ **BELOW LEFT**
The Highland Pony probably resembles Pony Type 2 of pre-domestication times.

■ **BELOW RIGHT**
The wiry Akhal-Teke is thought to approximate to Horse Type 3.

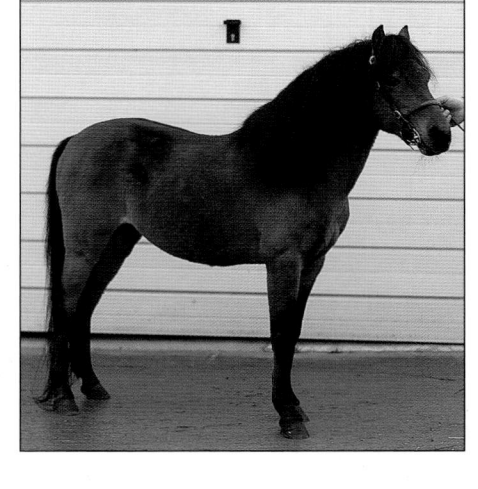

way to grassland and the horse's ancestors became plains dwellers. This significant change in environment called for teeth designed for grazing, as opposed to browsing, a longer neck to make grazing easier, longer legs to facilitate flight from predators and feet suitable for harder terrain. During this time the single toe, or hoof, began to evolve: the outer toes no longer touched the ground and the central toe became larger and stronger.

Then the history of the horse family becomes somewhat more complex, with various sub-families developing. Eventually, however, these became extinct and it was Pliohippus which provided the link in the chain from Eohippus to the modern Equus. Pliohippus evolved some ten to five million years ago and had long legs with a single hoof on each. Its direct successor, Equus, the genus of modern horse, finally emerged a million years ago.

During the Ice Ages of the Pleistocene epoch, Equus migrated via the land bridges which then existed to Europe, Asia and Africa. However, the disappearance of these land bridges (e.g. across what are now the Strait of Gibraltar and the Bering Strait) when the ice receded about 10,000 years ago meant that if an animal had become extinct in one continent, that

continent could not be repopulated – at least not without the help of man. This is exactly what happened in America: for some unexplained reason the horse disappeared. It was not seen again until European colonists reintroduced it thousands of years later.

All members of the modern *Equidae* family are swift runners with only one functional toe on each foot (the modern horse's ergot – the horny growth at the back of the fetlock – is believed to be the

vestiges of the pad of its ancestor, Eohippus). All live in herds and all have cheek teeth designed to grind plant-food.

Present-day horses and ponies are said to trace back to three distinct types, produced by variations in their natural environment. Northern Europe provided a slow-moving, heavy horse (*Equus silvaticus*) from which the world's heavy horse breeds are derived. Then there was the primitive Asiatic Wild Horse, survivors of which were found still living wild as late as 1881 (and called the Przewalski Horse); and finally the rather more refined Tarpan, from eastern Europe.

Later on, by the time that man began domesticating the horse, four sub-species had evolved: two pony types and two horse types. Pony Type 1 inhabited the north-west of Europe and resembled the modern Exmoor Pony. Pony Type 2, which was bigger and more heavily built, lived in northern Eurasia. The Highland Pony is probably the nearest modern-day equivalent. Horse Type 3 was a little bigger still, but much more lightweight in build and suited to hot climates. Its nearest equivalent is thought to be the Akhal-Teke. Horse Type 4, found in western Asia, was the smallest but the most refined and was the forerunner of the Caspian Pony.

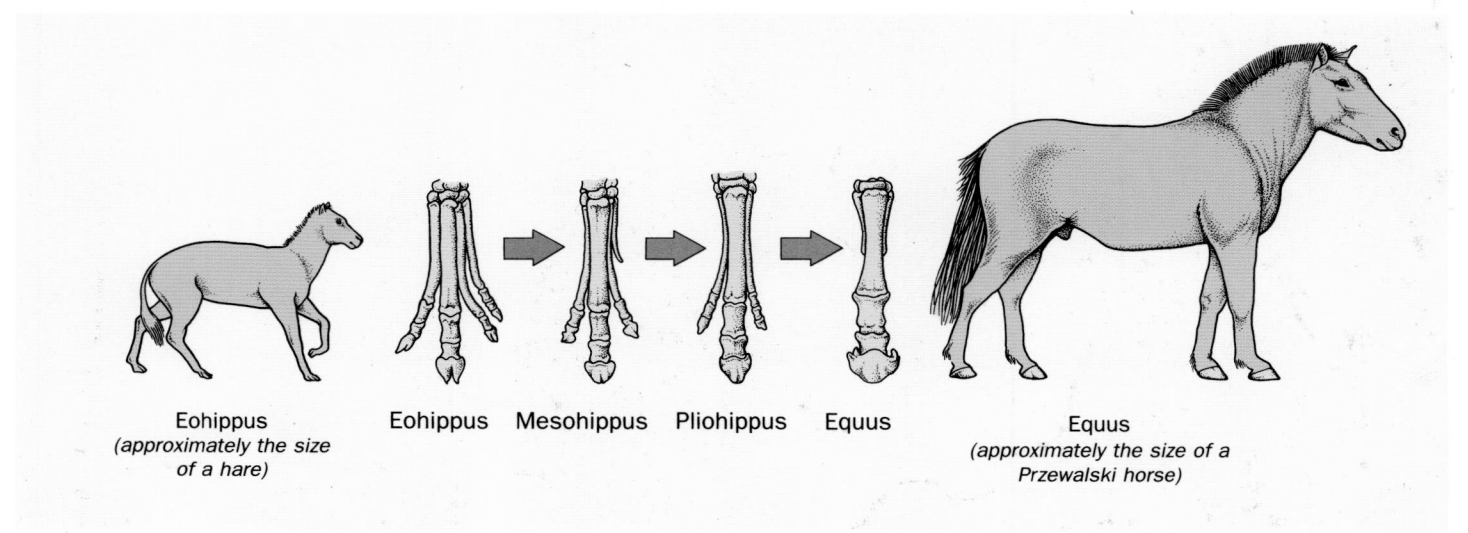

Eohippus
(approximately the size of a hare)

Eohippus Mesohippus Pliohippus Equus

Equus
(approximately the size of a Przewalski horse)

Horses in the Wild

The horse is a herbivore, that is, an eater of plants. Like all herbivores horses are basically grass eaters. In the wild the horse is a nomadic grazer and spends up to twenty hours out of every twenty-four grazing. When food is plentiful a wild horse thrives and puts on weight; when it is scarce, and weather conditions harsh, he loses condition. Nature, as usual, has arranged for foals to be born in the spring when the weather is mild and the grass lush – thus ensuring that the mares have a plentiful supply of food, which in turn ensures ample milk for the foals. Mares come into season every twenty-one days during the spring and summer, until around September or October, and the gestation period is approximately eleven months.

Horses are by nature herd animals. In the wild they live in social groups within a larger group (the herd), each small group comprising a stallion, some mares, their foals and yearlings and perhaps one or two two-year-olds. Depending on the power of the stallion, the total size of the group is usually in the region of a dozen. Young, timid stallions and old ones who no longer have any mares often live in bachelor groups – horses do not like to be alone. Just as family life is important to them, so is friendship. Horses indulge in mutual grooming with their teeth, they play together and relax and doze together. A stallion will groom a favourite mare even when she is not in season (grooming is also used to stimulate a mare sexually) and will play with the foals – though eventually he will drive out the more mature colts who must then either join a bachelor group or begin to collect their own band of mares.

Horses communicate with each other by a number of means, both vocal and physical. Their "vocabulary" includes neighing, nickering, squealing and, more rarely, roaring. A loud neigh enables a horse to make contact with another from whom it has been separated; a quieter, lower nicker may be used by a stallion to a mare, a mare to her foal or between friends as a greeting; squeals are signs of excitement and are used when horses are in close contact, particularly sexual contact; horses may emit loud roars and

■ LEFT
This Dartmoor Pony is typical of a number of breeds which, although they have been domesticated for a very long time, have retained the ability to thrive in semi-wild conditions.

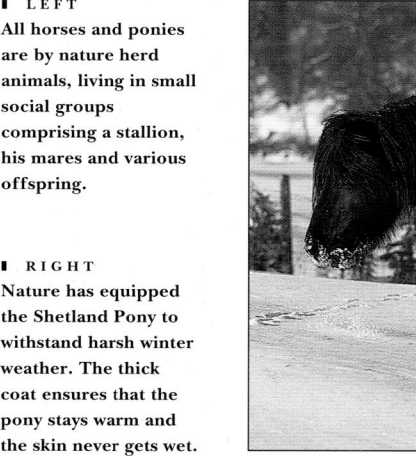

■ LEFT
Horses are constantly on the alert. These semi-feral Camargue mares are aware of everything going on around them.

screams during a fight that has serious intentions, as opposed to the sort of play-fighting indulged in by young colts, and a mare may well scream her disapproval at a stallion who pesters her when she is not ready to be mated.

Body posture is another means of communication. A relaxed horse looks relaxed: a hind foot resting, head lowered, eyes partly closed, lower lip drooping. An

excited stallion prances around, head tucked in, tail raised, his whole outline saying "look at me". A startled horse looks tense and alert, signs which indicate to its companions that there is cause for alarm.

Smell is also important to horses. Mares and foals recognize each other by smell. When meeting, horses will put their noses close together, often blowing down their nostrils, before deciding whether or not to be friends. Smell also plays a part in sexual communication – a stallion smells the vulva and urine of an in-season mare and can tell the difference between the dung of another stallion and that of a mare (he will urinate over a mare's dung but add his own dung to that left by a stallion).

A horse's ears, too, being tremendously mobile, say a good deal about what he is thinking – where his attention is focused,

what mood he is in. Drooping ears indicate that the horse is in a dozy state, alert ones that something has caught his attention; ears that are turned back may show that the horse's attention is focused behind him or they may indicate submission or fear; ears laid flat denote anger or fear.

Having eyes set on the sides of his head, the horse can see almost all round him, the only blind spots being immediately behind and a little way in front of his head – he can keep an approaching object in focus merely by turning his head slightly. The horse's sense of touch is enhanced by the whiskers on his muzzle which enable him to judge how far an object is from the end of his nose and may also be useful for assessing texture, for example when he is grazing.

The horse's long legs enable him to travel at speed, essential for an animal whose natural form of defence is to run away. Since he is not equipped to fight predators such as wolves, lions and snakes, his chief means of survival is flight. This helps to explain why domesticated horses often prefer to shelter from bad weather by standing by a hedge or wall rather than making use of a specially provided man-made building: horses feel safer in the open air where they can easily gallop off if anything frightens them.

■ LEFT
All horses and ponies are by nature herd animals, living in small social groups comprising a stallion, his mares and various offspring.

■ RIGHT
Nature has equipped the Shetland Pony to withstand harsh winter weather. The thick coat ensures that the pony stays warm and the skin never gets wet.

Conformation

Conformation, or the horse's overall make and shape, varies a good deal from breed to breed. What constitutes "ideal" conformation varies according to the work which the horse is required to perform. In spite of these necessary variations, however, certain guidelines can be followed when looking for desirable conformation. They relate to proportion: if a horse is correctly proportioned he will be better balanced, less prone to unsoundness and more able to perform his allotted tasks than a horse with less harmonious proportions. Indeed, many a horse with conformational defects has been condemned as "difficult" when it is simply his shape which prevents him from carrying out what his master requires.

A horse is deemed to have "correct" proportions when certain measurements are equal. For example: the length of the head, the depth of the body at the girth,

the distance from the point of the hock to the ground, the distance from the chestnut on the foreleg to the ground, the distance from the croup to the fold of the stifle and from the fold of the stifle to the point of the hock should all be the same.

The domesticated horse is required to work, which means that certain features of his conformation are of particular importance. If a horse is deep through the girth, that is from the top of the wither to below the elbow, then his lungs will have plenty of room to expand – essential for any working horse. The length of his back is also important, particularly for the ridden horse. Too long, and it will be inclined to weakness; too short, and it may restrict the action.

Starting at the front, it is important that the horse's head is in proportion to his overall size. An over-large, heavy head will upset the overall balance, putting

extra weight on the forehand, which already carries 60 per cent of the horse's total weight. Too small a head will also affect the balance. The upper and lower jaws should meet evenly at the front – if they do not this will inhibit the horse's ability to bite food such as grass. The nostrils should be large and wide, and large eyes are preferable to small ones, which experience has shown often denote a less than generous temperament. The set of the head is also important. If there is not sufficient clearance between the mandible (the lower jaw) and the atlas (the top bone in the neck), the horse will have difficulty in flexing at the poll, a requirement in the more collected gaits. There should be room for two fingers' width when the horse's head is raised.

In the riding horse the neck should be fairly long and curved. There should be no tendency to fleshiness around the

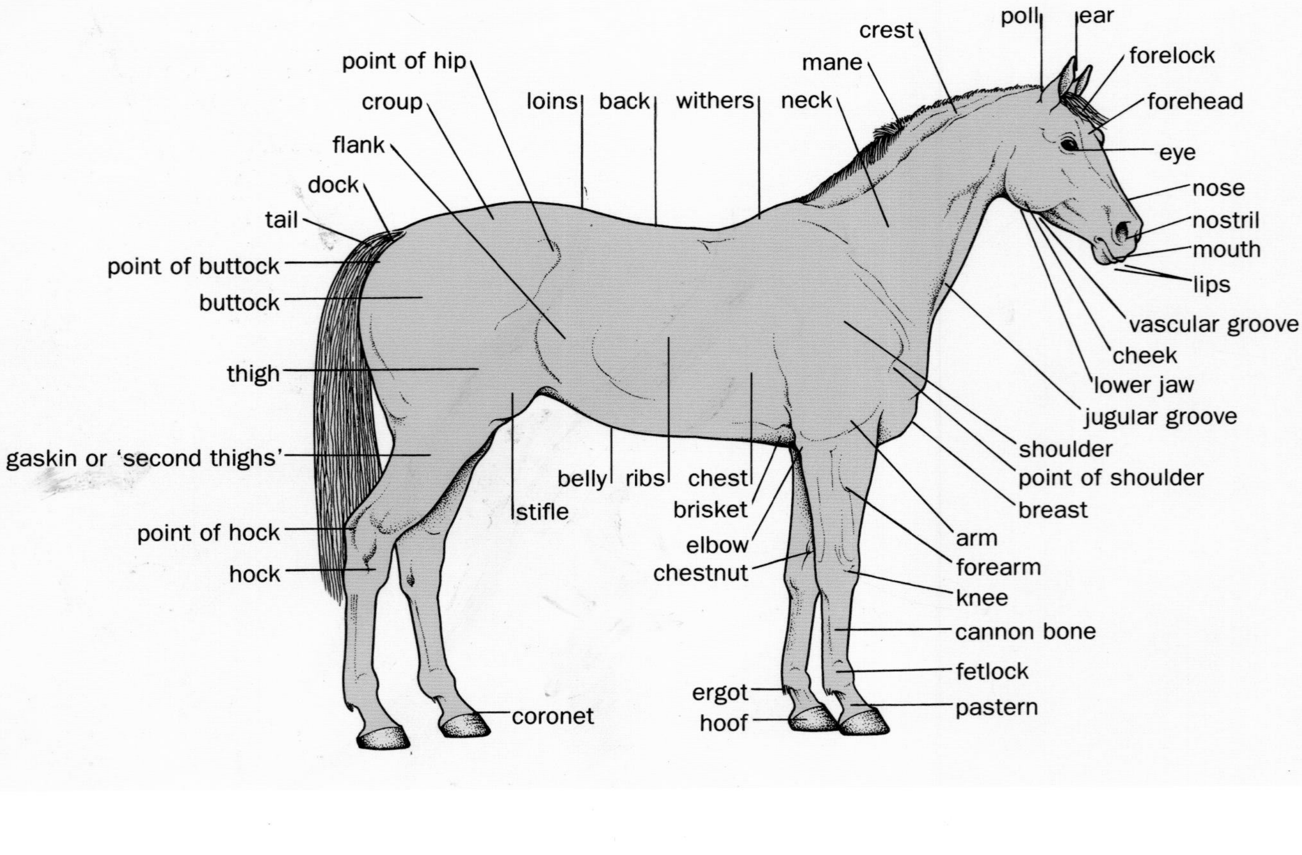

rounded and look like a matching pair.
"Boxy" upright feet are prone to jarring.
Large, flat feet may be more prone to
bruising of the sole and to corns. The
hindfeet, which bear less of the horse's
overall weight when he is stationary,
should be more oval in shape than the
forefeet. Viewed from the side the slope of
both fore and hindfeet should be a
continuation of the slope of the pastern.
The feet should point directly forwards.

throat, which again would restrict the
flexion of the head. This is particularly
important in the riding horse. A long neck
is associated with speed, a shorter one with
strength. Hence the heavy draught breeds
lack the length of neck seen, for instance,
in the Thoroughbred. The shoulder
should be well sloped (the angle of the
scapula gives the slope). Such
conformation enables the horse to take
longer strides than a straight shoulder,
which results in short, restricted action. A
straight shoulder may produce jarring,
which can be detrimental to the forelimb.
Horses with straight shoulders tend to give
an uncomfortable ride, too. The shoulder
should be muscular but not "loaded", i.e.
too heavy. The withers should be of a
good height and well defined. If they are
too high, it may be difficult to fit a saddle.
If they are poorly defined, it may be
difficult to keep a saddle in place. With
the draught horse, which must wear a
collar and for whom pulling power is
more important than extended paces, a
slightly straighter shoulder is acceptable.

The chest and body should be
reasonably broad, but not excessively so,
otherwise the horse's movement will be
affected. Narrowness in the chest, giving
the forelegs the appearance of "coming
out of one hole" is a serious fault, causing
the foreleg joints to brush against each
other. The back should rise slightly to the
croup, and be well muscled. Short, well-
muscled loins are essential: the lumbar

vertebrae have no support from the ribs,
yet it is the loins which transfer the thrust
from the engine (the hindquarters) to the
body. The croup of the fully grown horse
should be the same height as the withers
and should not be too sloping, a feature
which, combined with a low-set tail, is
usually a sign of weakness. Croup-high
horses throw extra weight on to the
forehand, thus putting more strain on
the forelimbs.

The horse's engine is in the back, that
is in the hindquarters. They should
therefore be strong and muscular. When
standing still the hindlegs should not be
stretched out behind him or tucked under
him – a line dropped vertically from the
point of the buttock to the ground should
touch the hock and run down the rear of
the cannon bone.

The forelegs should be straight and
strong, with long, muscular forearms and
large, flat knees. Short cannons indicate
strength and there should be a good
measurement of bone (the measurement
being taken around the cannon below the
knee). The amount of bone determines
the weight-carrying ability of the horse.
The amount of bone varies with the type
of horse but as a rough guide a
lightweight riding horse standing 16.2hh
should have a minimum of 8 inches
(20cm) of bone, a heavyweight horse of
the same height at least 9 inches (23cm).

The pasterns should be of medium
length and slope. The forefeet should be

COMMON CONFORMATIONAL DEFECTS

Back at the knee – where the knees, when viewed from the side, tend to extend backwards.

Calf knees – knees which are shallow from front to back.

Cow hocks – hocks which, when viewed from behind, turn inwards, as in a cow.

Ewe neck – where the top line of the neck is concave and the lower line convex.

Herring-gutted – where the horse has an upward slope from front to back on the underside of the belly.

Over at the knee – where the knees protrude forwards.

Pigeon toes – toes which turn inwards.

Roach back – where the spine has an exaggerated upward curve.

Sickle hocks – hocks which when viewed from the side have a concave line in front of the hocks and a slanting cannon bone.

Slab-sided – where the ribs are flat as opposed to "well-sprung".

Splay-footed – where the toes turn outwards.

Sway back – where the back has an exaggerated hollow.

Tied in below the knee – where the measurement of bone just below the knee is less than that farther down the cannon bone.

Colours and Markings

Equine coat colouring is controlled by numerous genes acting in combination to produce a multitude of variations in pigmentation. These genes, which are inherited, are located on paired structures known as chromosomes: the modern horse has 64 chromosomes, half of which are inherited from the sire and the other half from the dam. Some genes are dominant, others are recessive. For example, in horses chestnut is recessive to all other colours, bay is dominant to black, and grey is dominant to bay and black. The dominant greying gene can result in horses which are born with a dark coat turning progressively more grey as they

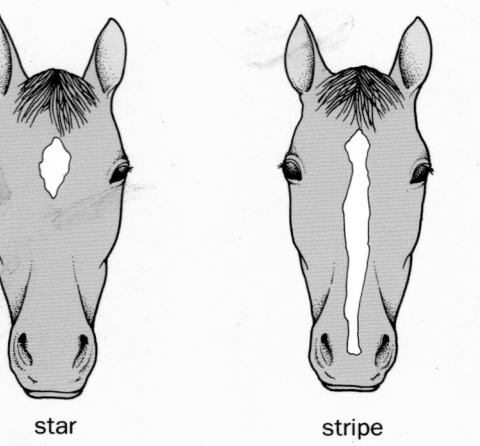

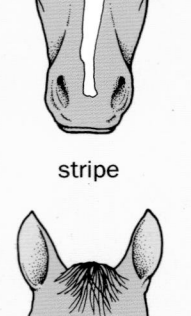

star

stripe

white face

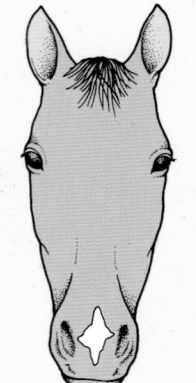

blaze

snip

interrupted stripe

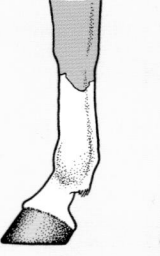

white to knee   mid-cannon   half-pastern   crown   coronet

FACIAL MARKINGS

These include: Star, stripe and interrupted stripe, snip, blaze, white face, white muzzle

LEG MARKINGS

For registration purposes leg markings are described in detail, using points of the anatomy: e.g. white to fetlock, white to knee, white to hock, etc.

Two less specific terms are also in popular use: sock (white colouring from the coronet up to the knee), stocking (white colouring from the coronet up to and over the knee or hock).

HOOF COLOURS

The horn of the hoofs can vary from blue or black to white and may be marked with dark stripes.

grow older. This is especially noticeable in the Lipizzaner, whose foals are born dark and, with rare exceptions, turn grey as they mature. Albinos occur where there is a congenital deficiency of colouring pigment. The hair is white, the skin pink and eyes often blue.

A horse is always described by its coat colouring, followed by other distinguishing features, where applicable, such as white markings and the colour of the mane and tail.

Some horses have more than one clearly defined coat colour. Broken or part-coloured horses such as piebalds and skewbalds (known as Pintos or Paint Horses in America) have irregular patches of two different colours while Spotted Horses show a variety of spotted markings. Black legs go with bay body colouring.

Horses' eyes are normally dark, although blue eyes also occur.

EQUINE COLOURS

Grey A mixture of black and white hairs throughout. The coat varies from light to iron (very dark). The skin is black.

Fleabitten Grey Grey coat flecked with brown specks.

Dappled Grey Light grey base coat with dark grey rings.

Bay Reddish coat with black mane, tail and "points" (i.e. limbs). The coat colour may vary from red to brown or yellowish.

Black All black except for occasional white marks on the legs and/or head.

Chestnut Varies from a pale golden colour to a rich, red gold. The mane and tail may be lighter or darker than the coat colour.

Liver Chestnut The darkest of the chestnut shades.

Sorrel A light-red chesnut.

Brown A mixture of black and brown hairs, with black limbs, mane and tail. A very dark brown horse may appear almost black.

Roan A body colour with white hairs interspersed, which lightens the overall effect.

Strawberry Roan Chestnut body colour with white hair giving a pinkish-red tinge.

Blue Roan Black or brown body colour with white hair giving a blue tinge.

Dun Light sandy-coloured coat with black mane and tail, often accompanied by a dark, dorsal eel-stripe extending from the line of the neck to the tail, and sometimes by "zebra markings" (stripes) on the withers and legs – the vestiges of a primitive form of camouflage. Dun can vary from yellow to "mouse", depending on the diffusion of pigment. The skin is black.

Palomino Gold coat with white mane and tail.

Spotted Small, more or less circular patches of hair of a different colour from the main body colour and distributed over various areas of the body.

Piebald Large, irregular patches of black and white.

Skewbald Large, irregular patches of white and any other colour except black.

Cream Cream-coloured coat with unpigmented skin (also known as cremello).

White Markings White markings on the face and legs and, occasionally, on the body, are a valuable means of distinguishing one horse from another and are therefore noted in detail on veterinary certificates and registration papers.

Brindle Brown or grey streaked or patched with a darker colour.

▌ OPPOSITE
ABOVE
The predominant coat colour of the Lipizzaner is grey, but foals are born dark and it takes several years for the coat to change to the typical "white" colouring associated with the breed.

▌ RIGHT
Spotted coat patterns have existed – and often been highly prized – throughout man's long relationship with the horse. Spotted horses are particularly associated with the Nez Percé Indians of North America.

Horses

There are more than 150 different breeds and types of horses in the world. The development of each of them has been influenced by man. Domestication resulted in selective breeding and, in many instances, more nutritious feeding, both of which led to an increase in the size or the quality (or both) of the horse. However, the biggest influencing factor was the work which humans required their particular horses to perform. Those who needed to move heavy loads bred for strength, while others in need of fast transportation bred for speed. The terms coldblood and warmblood (which have nothing to do with temperature) are used to describe horses. Coldblood refers to the heavy draught breeds which are believed to be descended from the prehistoric horse of northern Europe. Warmblood refers to the lighter, riding type of horse. Nowadays the term "warmblood" is used in connection with the horses being bred for competition riding. The breeds in this book are organized by continent, then sub-divided into countries within each continent.

"Wild" Horses

PRZEWALSKI HORSE

The horse no longer exists as a truly wild animal, although the Asiatic Wild Horse, believed to be one of the precursors of the domesticated horse, can still be seen in zoos in various parts of the world. The Asiatic Wild Horse (*Equus przewalskii przewalskii Poliakoff*) was "discovered" – or rather a small herd was – as recently as 1881 in the Tachin Schara Nuru Mountains on the edge of the Gobi desert by the Russian explorer Colonel N.M. Przewalski. Before that it was believed to have been extinct, over-hunted for its meat by Mongolian tribesmen. The Przewalski Horse, as it is widely known, differs genetically from the domesticated horse, having 66 chromosomes instead of 64. In appearance it has several "primitive" features: a large head, with the eyes set high up rather than to the side of the head as in the case of the modern horse; long ears; thick neck; heavy body with a dark dorsal strip and zebra markings on the legs. The Przewalski stands about 12–13hh and is always yellowish dun with a light-coloured nose and dark mane and

■ ABOVE
These Kaimanawa horses live in feral herds in New Zealand's North Island. Like the Brumbies of Australia they are unpopular with stockmen because they compete for food with domestic animals

■ PREVIOUS PAGE OPPOSITE
A Mustang.

■ PREVIOUS PAGE
A Trakehner.

■ LEFT
The Asiatic Wild Horse or Przewalski Horse is the only surviving race of the species from which domestic horses are descended. Its chromosome count differs from that of the domesticated horse.

INTERESTING FACTS

Free-ranging horses and ponies exist in
several parts of the world. In North America
there are the Mustangs and also two types of
island-based pony, the Sable Island, which
lives in small numbers on the windswept
island of that name off the coast of Nova
Scotia, and the Assateague, whose home is
off the coast of Maryland and Virginia. The
Sable Island Ponies, thought to be descended
from horses turned loose more than 200
years ago, are not managed, but the
Assateague Ponies are rounded up annually
and receive veterinary care. The population is
controlled as necessary. In Europe, the
Camargue horses lead a semi-wild existence
in southern France and several of Britain's
mountain and moorland pony breeds lead, to
a certain extent, free-ranging lives, as do
some of the horses bred in the former USSR.

tail. The mane, which grows upright, is
shed each spring and there is no forelock.
Intractable by nature – it cannot be
trained for riding – the Przewalski can
survive on a minimum of food and endure
extremes of heat and cold.

TARPAN

Eastern Europe and European Russia were
the home of the Tarpan, another horse
widely believed to have been an ancestor
of the modern horse. It survived in the
wild until the nineteenth century. One
authority claims that the last true Tarpan
in captivity died in 1919, in which case the
Tarpan which exists today, running semi-
wild in reserves in Poland, must be a
"reconstruction", almost certainly bred
from the Konik, which it strongly
resembled. Experiments with crossing
Przewalski stallions and Konik mares have
also produced an animal which looks very
like the original Tarpan. The Tarpan was
(and is) more lightly built than the
Przewalski, standing about 13hh and with

a brown or mouse dun coat, dark mane
and tail and, frequently, primitive dorsal
stripe and zebra markings.

BRUMBY

Australia's "wild" horse, the Brumby, is not
a true wild horse, equine animals having
been unknown in Australasia until the
arrival of European settlers a few hundred
years ago (the assumption being that
because there were no land bridges
linking the Americas with Australia,
Eohippus and its descendants had no
means of migrating there). The Brumbies
which live in feral herds in the Northern
Territory and, to a lesser extent, in central
Australia, are descended from settlers'
horses who wandered off into the bush,
producing offspring that grew up under
wild conditions. When rounded up and
broken in some Brumbies have, over the
years, been useful to man but today they
are generally regarded as a pest and are
culled because they compete for food with
domestic animals.
See also Camargue, Mustang, Sorraia.

▪ ABOVE LEFT
**The primitive looking
Konik pony is found in
Poland and is a
descendant of the
Tarpan. Crossed with
Przewalski stallions,
Konik mares produce
Tarpan "look-alikes".**

▪ LEFT
**The Sorraia pony,
which can be found
living in semi-feral
conditions in Portugal,
is believed to be of
ancient origin.**

Arab

The oldest and purest of all horse breeds, the Arab is considered by many people to be the most beautiful equine animal in the world. With its refined head and dished profile, expressive eyes, high spirits and unique, floating action, it is undoubtedly one of the most exquisite of creatures. Although it has certainly been bred with great care for many centuries, its exact origins are unclear. Depictions of horses

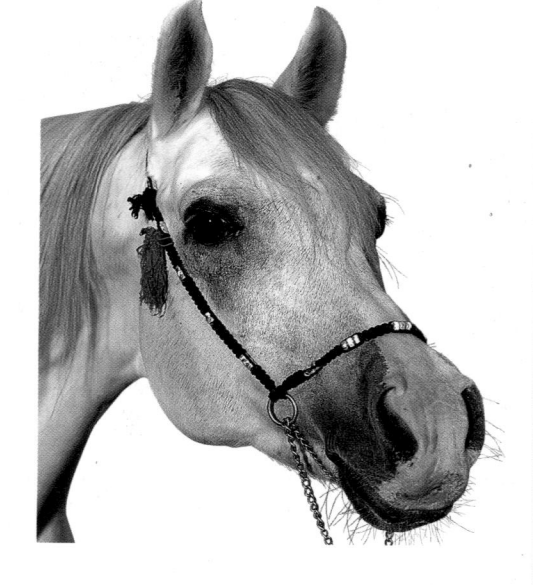

BREED DESCRIPTION

Height 14.2 – 15hh.

Colour Predominantly chestnut, grey, bay and black.

Conformation Small head with broad forehead, fine muzzle, concave profile, wide nostrils and small ears; deep, clearly defined jowl with the throat set into it in a distinctly arched curve; graceful, curving neck; long, sloping shoulders with well-defined withers; deep, roomy body with broad, deep chest and short, level back; high-set tail; hard, clean limbs with well-defined tendons and dense, fine bone; hard, well-shaped feet; fine, silky mane and tail.

INTERESTING FACTS

The unique outline of the Arab is determined by the formation of its skeleton, which differs from other equine breeds in several respects. The Arab has 17 ribs (other horses have 18); five lumbar vertebrae (other horses have six), and 16 tail vertebrae (other horses have 18).

in ancient art suggest that horses of Arab type lived in the Arabian peninsula as long ago as 2,000 – 3,000BC. Like the desert tribes with whom they have lived for so long, Arab horses became superbly well adapted to life in a harsh environment, having extreme powers of endurance, tremendous soundness and the ability to thrive on the most meagre of rations.

More than any other horse, it is the Arab which has influenced the development of equine

▌ TOP
Large eyes and nostrils are typical of the Arab. The short, refined head, with its dished profile, is one of the breed's most distinctive features.

▌ LEFT
The Arab's comparatively small size belies its weight-carrying ability. Standing no more than 15hh it will nevertheless carry a fully grown man with ease.

breeds throughout the world. This Arabian influence was initiated in the seventh and early eighth centuries AD when the followers of Islam spread across North Africa and into Spain. The horses they took with them were greatly superior to the native stock of other lands and so began a process of upgrading, through the introduction of Arab blood, that was to go on for many centuries and, indeed, still goes on today.

Pure-bred Arabian horses are now bred throughout the world. As well as appearing in the show ring, they are particularly suited to the sport of endurance riding. In recent times, too, there has been a resurgence of interest in Arab racing.

▮ ABOVE LEFT
The Arab horse often appears to float over the ground. This remarkable action, coupled with a gentle temperament, makes it a popular riding horse throughout the world.

▮ ABOVE RIGHT
The breed's legendary stamina makes it the perfect choice for endurance riding which at the top level involves covering a distance of 100 miles (161km) in a day.

▮ LEFT
With its elegance, spirit and exceptional looks, it is easy to see why the Arab is often considered to be the world's most beautiful horse.

Barb

The Barb comes from Morocco, Algeria and Tunisia – the coastal regions of these North African countries were formerly known as the Barbary Coast, "Barbary" meaning foreign or, more specifically, non-Christian lands. Opinions differ as to the Barb's origins, lack of documentary evidence making it impossible to do more than hazard an educated guess. According to one school of thought, the Barb may trace back to an isolated group of wild horses which survived the Ice Age. If that were true, it would make the Barb an even older breed than the Arab. Another theory links the Barb to the Akhal-Teke, the horse of the Turkmens.

Although it is unlikely that the breed's true origins will ever be revealed, what is certain is that the Barb has had more influence on the development of equine breeds throughout the world than any other horse except the Arab. As with the Arab, it was the spread of Islam which led to the forerunners of today's Barbs reaching Europe from the early eighth century onwards (the first Muslim army, seven thousand strong, landed in Spain in the spring of 711). Once established on the Iberian peninsula the Barb horse played a major role in the development of the Andalusian, which subsequently became one of the major influences in horse breeding all over the world. Among the many historical references to

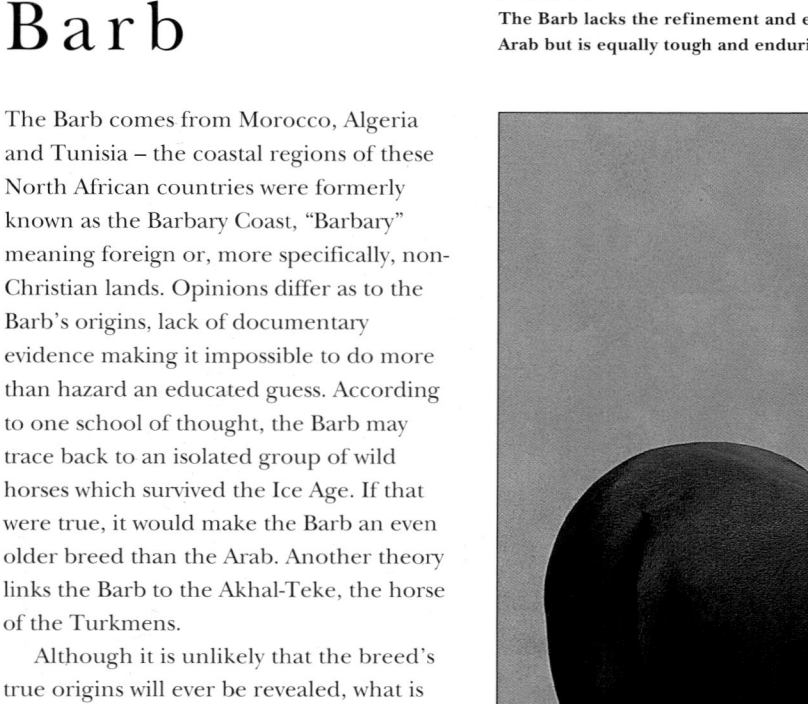

BELOW
The Barb lacks the refinement and elegance of the Arab but is equally tough and enduring.

BREED DESCRIPTION

Height Around 14.2 – 15.2hh.

Colour Predominantly grey, bay, brown and black.

Conformation Narrow head with convex profile; arched neck; flat shoulders with well-defined withers; short, strong body; sloping hindquarters with fairly low-set tail; rather slender, but strong, limbs; narrow, but hard, feet.

"Barbary" horses perhaps the most famous is Roan Barbary, belonging to the English king, Richard II (1367–1400). During the sixteenth century Henry VIII imported a number of Barbary horses into England and a century later the Barb played an important part in the evolution of the Thoroughbred. Elsewhere the influence of the Barb is still evident in the Argentinian Criollo and the American Mustang.

Despite its importance as a progenitor of other breeds, the Barb has achieved less widespread renown than the Arab, no doubt because it lacks the Arab's unique visual appeal, being much less refined and generally less impressive in appearance. Nevertheless it has the same boundless stamina and endurance, the same ability to thrive on meagre rations, the same sure-footedness – and an impressive turn of speed over short distances.

❚ BELOW
Dressed in ceremonial attire, Barb horses and their
Moroccan riders are a colourful sight at a modern
"Fantasia".

INTERESTING FACTS

The most well-known Barb horses of modern
times were those ridden by the Spahis, men
of the Algerian and Tunisian cavalry
regiments in the French army. The Spahis
originally came from Turkey but were
incorporated into their army by the French
when the latter occupied Algiers and Tunis.
Barb horses still feature in the exciting
present-day North African festivals recalling
these countries' military pasts.

❚ BELOW
In the dramatic rifle-firing charge seen at North
African festivals, Barb horses demonstrate their
impressive speed over a short distance.

Andalusian

As its name suggests, the Andalusian comes from the sun-baked region of southern Spain which is close to North Africa. While it is without doubt an ancient breed, its origins are uncertain. Whatever native horses existed in Spain when the Muslim invaders arrived in 711 – they may well have resembled the primitive Sorraian Pony still found today in Portugal – must surely have been crossed subsequently with the invaders' Barb horses, which were imported in such great numbers.

After the last Muslim state, Granada, had fallen to the Christians in 1492, Spain began to assume a new importance in the western world and so, too, did her horses. Taken to the Americas by the sixteenth-century

■ LEFT
The Andalusian's handsome head, a more refined version of the Barb, is as eye-catching and as distinctive in its own way as that of the Arab.

Conquistadores, Spanish horses provided the foundation stock for the majority of new breeds developed by the settlers. In Europe, meanwhile, the Spanish horse became the preferred mount of monarchs and of the great riding masters, including the Englishman, William Cavendish, Duke of Newcastle, who in the seventeenth century wrote that: "If well chosen it is the noblest horse in the world; the most beautiful that can be. He is of great spirit and of great courage and docile; has the proudest walk, the proudest trot...the loftiest gallop and is the lovingest and gentlest horse and fittest of all for a king in Day of Triumph." The Lipizzaner is a direct descendant of the Andalusian, while other famous European breeds influenced by Spanish blood include the Frederiksborg, the Friesian (which in turn

■ RIGHT
The Andalusian is not particularly tall but its compact, muscular frame is indicative of great strength.

BREED DESCRIPTION

Height 15 – 15.2hh.

Colour Predominantly grey (including "mulberry" – a dappled, purplish grey) and bay.

Conformation Handsome head with broad forehead and large, kind eyes; fairly long, thick but elegant neck; long, well-sloped shoulders with well-defined withers; short, strong body with broad chest and well-sprung ribs; very broad, strong, rounded hindquarters with rather low-set tail; medium length limbs, clean cut and elegant but strong; long and very luxuriant mane and tail.

■ LEFT
On point duty in present-day Barcelona. Thanks to its excellent temperament and willing nature, the Andalusian is an ideal all-purpose riding horse.

■ BELOW
Grey is one of the predominant Andalusian colours, along with bay. Spotted strains were once popular and were responsible for the founding of the Appaloosa breed in America.

INTERESTING FACTS

The Andalusian horse's survival down the centuries, which included some pretty turbulent times, was aided by the monastic orders, particularly the Carthusians, who became especially skilful at horse breeding. In times of danger, horses were moved from the great studs to remote monasteries for safe keeping. The Carthusians were instrumental in maintaining purity of line and produced animals of consistently high quality.

influenced the Oldenburg), the Holstein and the Connemara.

The Andalusian is one of the most elegant of horses. Possessing tremendous presence, lofty paces, agility and a gentle, willing nature, it makes an excellent all-round riding horse and is particularly well suited to the movements of the *haute école* (high school). It can also be seen to great effect taking part in the colourful annual *ferias*, or fairs, of its native Andalusia.

■ RIGHT
The breed's proud bearing and lofty action lend themselves perfectly to the movements of the *haute école*, or high school.

Thoroughbred

The life of man has been inextricably interwoven with that of the horse for more than 4,000 years but in all that time no achievement has excelled the "invention" of the Thoroughbred. Quite apart from being the world's supreme racehorse, the Thoroughbred has played a vital part in the upgrading of numerous old horse and pony breeds and in establishing as many new ones.

Henry VIII set the process in motion during the sixteenth century when he founded the famous Royal Paddocks at Hampton Court. His daughter, Elizabeth I, founded another stud at Tutbury, in Staffordshire. Both monarchs imported horses from Spain and Italy to cross with native stock. Under subsequent monarchs – James I, Charles I and Charles II – horse breeding and racing gained impetus. By the beginning of the seventeenth century regular race meetings were being staged at Newmarket, Chester, Doncaster and Lincoln. Many noblemen took up the

BREED DESCRIPTION

Height Variable. May be as small as 14.2hh or over 17hh. Average 16 – 16.2hh.

Colour All solid colours, the most common being bay, chestnut and brown. Also grey, black and roan. White markings are permissible.

Conformation Variable, but the best specimens have excellent conformation characterized by a refined, intelligent head; elegant neck; well-sloped shoulders; short, strong body with great depth through the girth; strong, muscular hindquarters with well -set tail; clean, hard legs with well let-down hocks and a minimum of 8 inches (20cm) of bone below the knee.

▍ **ABOVE RIGHT**
The head of the Thoroughbred is typically refined, with large eyes and nostrils. The dished profile so characteristic of its Arabian forebears is not found in the Thoroughbred.

▍ **RIGHT**
With its well-sloped shoulders, powerful hindquarters and long limbs, the Thoroughbred is the ultimate "racing machine". The deep girth ensures plenty of room for the heart and lungs.

■ RIGHT
The bigger, slower developing stamp of Thoroughbred often makes a first-rate steeplechaser. Chasing calls for courage, stamina and speed, qualities for which the Thoroughbred is renowned.

■ BELOW RIGHT
Thanks to carefully kept records (in the *General Stud Book*) dating back some two centuries, it is possible to trace the pedigree of this foal to one of the breed's handful of foundation sires.

■ BOTTOM
Thoroughbreds hurdling at speed at Cheltenham, spiritual home of the sport of jump racing. The Thoroughbred's athletic prowess makes it equally suitable for sports such as hunting and three-day eventing.

breeding of horses for racing, sending agents overseas to seek out good stallions. Records of the time repeatedly refer to Barb, Barbary, Arabian, Hobby and Galloway horses (the Irish Hobby and Scottish Galloway were famous "running"' horses of the day) – and it is on this blood that the modern Thoroughbred was founded.

The exact breeding of the Thorough-bred's forebears will never be known since horses often changed names when they

changed hands and the terms "Arabian", "Barb" and "Turk", were frequently used inaccurately. However, what is certain is that during the last quarter of the seventeenth century and the first quarter of the eighteenth, Englishmen or their agents bought a number of eastern stallions, crossed them with English mares of mixed pedigree and started a dynasty of great racehorses. The most famous of these stallions were the Byerley Turk, the Darley Arabian and the Godolphin Arabian, who are recognized as the founding fathers of the Thoroughbred. In 1791 *An Intro-duction to a General Stud Book* appeared and following the publication of several more preliminary editions, there came, in 1808, Volume I of the *General Stud Book*. A horse is classed as Thoroughbred if both its parents are entered in the *General Stud Book* (or in the equivalent official Thoroughbred stud books in other countries).

The Thoroughbred is a handsome horse, alert, spirited and full of presence. It has an easy, ground-covering stride at the gallop and possesses boundless courage and immense stamina, qualities which stand it in good stead on the racecourse, in the hunting field and in three-day eventing.

INTERESTING FACTS

The Byerley Turk was captured by Captain Byerley at Buda in the 1680s, ridden by him at the Battle of the Boyne and sent to England to stand at stud. His great-grandson Tartar sired Herod, one of the most important sires in Thoroughbred history. The Darley Arabian, foaled in 1700, was acquired by Thomas Darley and sent to England from the Syrian port of Aleppo. He was responsible for founding the Eclipse line – Eclipse was one of the greatest racehorses of all time. The Godolphin Arabian was foaled in the Yemen in 1724, exported to Tunis via Syria and later given by the Bey of Tunis to the King of France, who subsequently sold him to Edward Coke, from Derbyshire. He was eventually acquired by Lord Godolphin and was responsible for founding the Matchem line. The Herod, Eclipse and Matchem lines, plus the Highflyer (Highflyer was a son of Herod) are the four principal tail-male lines of the modern Thoroughbred.

Anglo-Arab

A more substantial horse than the pure-bred Arab, the Anglo-Arab is produced by mixing Arab and Thoroughbred blood. The Anglo-Arab can result from a first cross between a Thoroughbred stallion and an Arab mare or vice versa. It can also be produced by breeding Thoroughbred to Anglo-Arab or Arab to Anglo-Arab, or Anglo-Arab to Anglo-Arab. As a result of these different permutations, the amount of Arab blood varies a good deal. So, too, does the size and appearance of the horse. The biggest horses are often produced by using an Arab stallion on a Thoroughbred mare and the best examples of the Anglo-Arab will inherit the endurance and stamina of the Arab and the speed and scope of the Thoroughbred, but not the latter's rather high-strung temperament.

France has been a notable producer of Anglo-Arabs since the first half of the nineteenth century. The French Anglo-Arab traces back to two eastern stallions, Massoud (an Arab) and Aslam (which is said to be of Turkish origin). They were imported from Syria and crossed with three imported English Thoroughbred

BREED DESCRIPTION

Height Around 15.3 – 16.3hh.

Colour Usually chestnut, bay or brown.

Conformation Variable, but the best specimens tend towards good Thoroughbred conformation: intelligent head with straight profile, expressive eyes and alert ears; long neck with more prominent withers than the Arab; sloping shoulders; short, strong body – rather more sturdy than the Thoroughbred – with deep chest; somewhat long hindquarters; good, sound limbs; strong, well-shaped feet.

▮ TOP LEFT
The head of the Anglo-Arab is closer in appearance to that of the Thoroughbred than the Arab. The Anglo lacks the dished profile of the pure-bred.

▮ LEFT
The overall conformation is noticeably more Thoroughbred than Arab, although many Anglo-Arabs are more sturdily built than the average Thoroughbred.

The crossing of
Thoroughbred with
Arab blood has
produced some
outstanding
competition horses in
the Olympic
disciplines, including
dressage.

mares, Daer, Comus Mare and Selim
Mare. Their three daughters, Delphine,
Clovis and Danaë became the foundation
stock of France's first breed of sports
horse. At one time the Anglo-Arab was
much used in France by the military and
as a general riding and competition horse.
More recently it has been an influential
factor in the development of the modern
sports horse, the Selle Français.

BELOW
In recent years French Anglo-Arabs such as this one
have achieved great success in top-level three-day
eventing, holding their own against the best of the
Thoroughbreds and Warmbloods.

INTERESTING FACTS

Before the development of the Selle
Français, the French Anglo-Arab was highly
successful in the competitive disciplines,
particularly show jumping. Many of the
horses ridden by the dual Olympic champion
Pierre Jonquères d'Oriola were Anglo-Arabs,
the most famous being the little gelding
Marquis III (a very successful Grand Prix and
Nations' Cup horse) and Ali-Baba, on whom
d'Oriola won his first Olympic title at Helsinki
in 1952. More recently French Anglo-Arabs
have been successful performers with the
French three-day event team. They include
Twist la Beige (winner of the European
Championship in 1993) and Newport and
Newlot (both European team silver
medallists).

Noriker

Bred and developed over several thousand years in the mountain regions of Austria, the Noriker is an attractive looking light draught horse. Strong and hardy, this horse is noted particularly for its calm temperament, sound limbs and sure-footedness. These characteristics make it an ideal all-round work horse over difficult mountainous terrain.

As with most horses, despite its ancient origins there was no formal breeding programme until fairly recent times. The Prince-Archbishop of Salzburg is credited with forming a stud book some 400 years ago. It was then that standards were drawn up, for both mares and stallions, and stud farms established.

Because of its toughness and capacity for hard work the Noriker became popular throughout Europe. Different strains evolved, including the Bavarian, now known as the South German Coldblood and found in Upper and Lower Bavaria. Various colour lines, tracing back to Andalusian and Neapolitan horses, also had an influence on today's breed and were responsible for the dappled and brindle colourings.

BREED DESCRIPTION

Height Stallions 16 – 17hh.
Mares 15.3 – 17hh.

Colour Brown, chestnut, black, grey and brindle. White body markings are not acceptable. Too many or too large white markings on the head and limbs are not desirable.

Conformation Straight profile, wide nostrils, medium-sized eyes; medium-length neck with thick, curly mane; good sloping shoulders; broad, deep chest; medium-length, well-muscled back; long limbs with powerful forearms, large clean joints, well-muscled second thigh and good, sound feet.

INTERESTING FACTS

The breed takes its name from the ancient state of Noricum (during the Roman Empire Noricum was roughly approximate to present-day Austria). However, the Noriker can be traced back to pre-Roman times, when a heavy war horse was developed in Thessalonica. Horses of this type were taken to Noricum by the Romans. In due course they were crossed with other coldblooded horses of the region and became admirably adapted to the harsh conditions of their new environment.

▮ ABOVE
Most Norikers are brown but the breed embraces a wide range of coat colours, including this attractive dark chestnut with flaxen mane.

1880

▮ LEFT
The Noriker's sturdy build and good limbs and feet make it an ideal work horse in mountainous regions. Like most mountain breeds, it is a good mover, with a particularly active trot.

Belgian Draught

One of the world's finest and historically most important heavy horses, the Belgian Draught is an ancient breed, closely connected to the Ardennais. The Flanders Horse, as the breed was known during the Middle Ages, had an influence on the development of several other renowned "heavies", including the Shire, the Suffolk Punch and particularly the Clydesdale. Nowadays the Belgian Draught is also known as the Brabant, after its main breeding area in central Belgium.

Despite widespread mechanization, this gentle giant of a horse, known for its kind nature and willingness to work, can still be found in modest numbers in many areas of Belgium and is also much appreciated in North America.

Over the years breeders have managed to maintain the excellence of these horses by a policy of strict selection and some inbreeding. The result is a handsome individual – its short neck, strong shoulders, short limbs, deep-girthed body and huge hindquarters, coupled with the most amenable of temperaments, make it the ideal draught horse for work on the land and there is no finer sight in the equestrian world than a team of these magnificent animals hitched to a smart brewers' dray.

▌ A B O V E
The Belgian Draught is an impressive horse, combining great strength with a gentle temperament and willingness to work. Despite its size, it is economical to keep.

BREED DESCRIPTION

Height 16.2 – 17hh.

Colour Predominantly red-roan with black points, chestnut and sorrel. Bay, dun and grey also occur.

Conformation Small, rather plain head but with intelligent expression; short, muscular neck; massive shoulders; short, deep, compact body; rounded, powerful hindquarters; short, strong limbs with plenty of feather and well-shaped, medium-sized feet.

INTERESTING FACTS

Towards the end of the last century there were three recognized types of Brabant horse, each based on a different bloodline. Those from the celebrated stallion Orange I, known as the Gros de la Dendre line, were mainly bay in colour. A stallion called Bayard founded the Gris du Hainaut line, with its greys, red-roans and sorrels. A third line, the Colosses de la Méhaigne, descended from the bay stallion Jean I. Today the descendants of these bloodlines all come under the general title of Belgian Draught or Brabant.

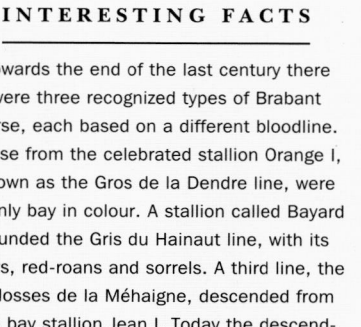

▌ A B O V E L E F T
The head is rather plain but the eyes have the kindly expression associated with so many of the heavy breeds.

▌ L E F T
Massive hindquarters are typical of the breed. These horses have docked tails.

Frederiksborg

The stud after which the Frederiksborg is named was founded by King Frederick II during the 1560s and was famous as a provider of quality horses to the courts of Europe. The stud's foundation stock came from Spain and was subsequently crossed with the Spanish horse's close relative, the Neapolitan. The horses thus produced were both elegant and spirited and well suited to the dual requirements of the day: as a mount for work in the manège and as a charger for the cavalry.

RIGHT
The Frederiksborg's somewhat plain head has a kind, intelligent look about it. Most examples of the breed, like this horse, are chestnut.

BREED DESCRIPTION

Height 15.3 – 16hh.

Colour Chestnut.

Conformation Intelligent, if somewhat plain, head; short, upright neck; strong but rather upright shoulders; strong back that tends to be long; high-set tail; good, strong feet.

The breed continued to develop through the introduction of eastern and British half-bred stallions and for several centuries the Frederiksborg was one of the most sought-after horses in Europe. Eventually, so numerous were the exports of the Frederiksborg from Denmark that stock became seriously depleted, with the result that during the first half of the nineteenth century the stud turned instead to Thoroughbred breeding. This venture was not a success and in 1871 the stud was dispersed. Fortunately, however, Frederiksborgs did not disappear altogether: private breeders went on producing them, mainly for use as light harness horses.

Frederiksborgs are still bred in Denmark, although recent demands for an outstanding sports horse have led to the development of a new horse, the Danish Warmblood, based mainly on Swedish, German and Polish stallions. Frederiksborg blood does occasionally appear in today's Danish Warmblood pedigrees, chiefly through the female line.

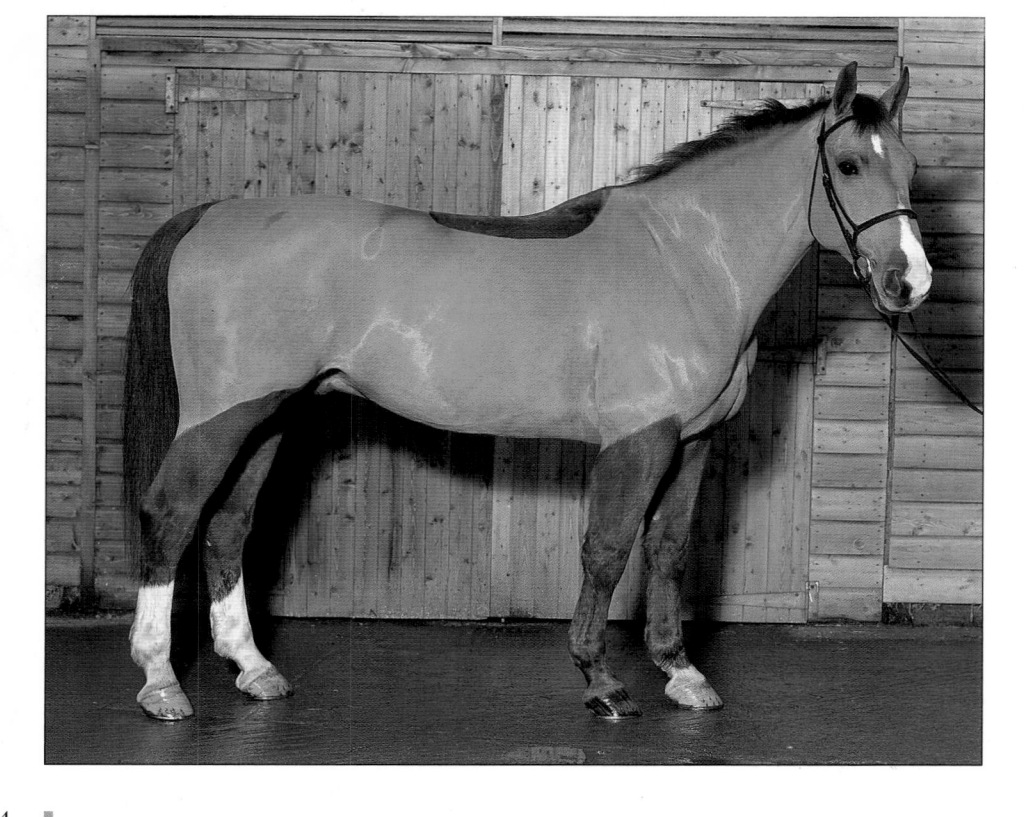

INTERESTING FACTS

The Frederiksborg played a significant part in the development of a much more well-known breed, the Lipizzaner, famous for its association with the Spanish Riding School in Vienna. The white stallion Pluto, from the Royal Danish Court Stud, was one of the six stallions on which the Lipizzaner breed is based. Pluto was foaled in 1765, the earliest of the six. More than two centuries later his descendants are still performing at the Spanish Riding School where they can be identified by the "Pluto" prefix to their names.

LEFT
The rather long back, short neck and upright shoulders are more typical of the light harness horse than the riding horse.

Jutland

Except for the feathering of its lower legs, Denmark's heavy horse bears an uncanny resemblance to the British breed, the Suffolk Punch. This resemblance is perhaps not so surprising, because the present-day Jutland was greatly influenced by the Suffolk blood introduced via the English stallion Oppenheim LXII, who stood at stud in Denmark during the 1860s.

The breed goes back much further than that, however. Heavy horses have been bred on the Jutland Peninsula for many centuries, certainly as far back as the twelfth century, when they were in great demand as war horses. Combining enormous strength with the most willing

BREED DESCRIPTION

Height 15 – 16hh.

Colour Predominantly dark chestnut with light mane and tail.

Conformation Heavy, rather plain head, but with kind expression; short, thick neck; strong, muscular shoulders; exceptionally deep body with broad chest; round, muscular hindquarters; short limbs with plenty of bone.

INTERESTING FACTS

The Jutland was an influential factor in the development of the Schleswig, a draught horse which takes its name from the northernmost region of Germany and which towards the end of the nineteenth century was in demand for pulling trams and buses. Infusions of Jutland blood from neighbouring Denmark were being used by German breeders well into this century. The Schleswig closely resembles the Jutland and the Suffolk, both in build and colour. However, the use of carefully selected Boulonnais and Breton stallions from France has led to the appearance of some greys and bays.

of natures, the Jutland horse made the ideal mount for the heavily armoured knights of the Middle Ages. Cleveland Bay and Yorkshire Coach Horse blood is said to have been used in the development of the Jutland, but it is unquestionably the Suffolk which has been the dominant factor, even to its chestnut colouring.

Mechanization has reduced the numbers of these attractive horses but some can still be seen, either at shows or pulling drays in the cities or, occasionally, working the land.

▮ ABOVE
In common with all heavy breeds, the handsome Jutland has been the victim of mechanization but a few are still working.

▮ LEFT
The Jutland is usually chestnut, a colour inherited through the Suffolk Punch element in its ancestry.

Danish Warmblood

The Danish Warmblood is one of a number of horses specifically developed for use in modern equestrian pursuits, particularly the competitive disciplines of dressage, show jumping and three-day eventing.

The Danes have a long tradition as horse breeders: their first organized studs date from the fourteenth century. However, the market for horses has changed enormously this century, and especially during the last few decades. In many countries the relentless march of mechanization has transformed the horse from an essential means of transport to a "leisure" animal. In the wake of this transformation the Danes found that their native breeds – the Frederiksborg and its cousin, the spotted Knabstrup (a popular circus horse) – were not going to measure up as competitive sports horses.

To remedy this deficiency, a breeding programme was set up in 1962 to produce a new type of Danish riding horse.

BREED DESCRIPTION

Height 15.3 – 16.3hh.

Colour All colours occur.

Conformation Quality head; long, well set-on neck; good shoulders with prominent withers; muscular back and loins; long croup; strong limbs with long forearms, well-defined joints and good bone.

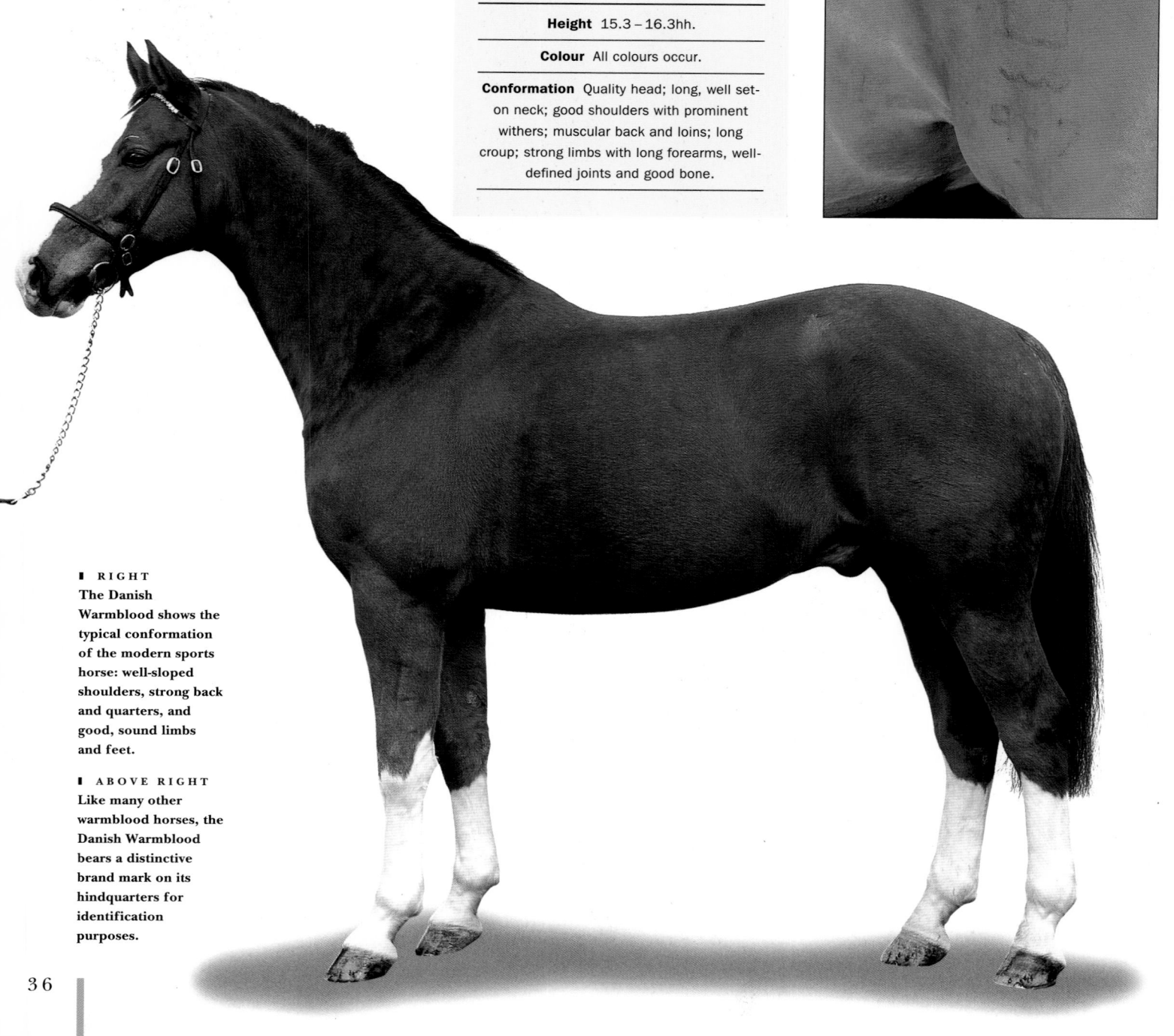

▌ RIGHT
The Danish Warmblood shows the typical conformation of the modern sports horse: well-sloped shoulders, strong back and quarters, and good, sound limbs and feet.

▌ ABOVE RIGHT
Like many other warmblood horses, the Danish Warmblood bears a distinctive brand mark on its hindquarters for identification purposes.

**Warmblood horses
have been specifically
developed for use in
competitive sports
such as show jumping.**

■ ABOVE RIGHT
**A good deal of
German blood has
been used in the
development of the
Danish Warmblood.
This is reflected in its
quality head.**

■ RIGHT
**Perhaps the most
famous of all Danish
Warmbloods is the
dressage stallion
Matador, winner of the
silver medal at the
1990 World Equestrian
Games.**

INTERESTING FACTS

Danish Warmbloods often excel at dressage,
and none more so than the attractive black
stallion Matador, who enchanted everyone
with his panache and exuberant personality.
Placed fifth in the Seoul Olympic Games in
1988, Matador was out of action for the
whole of the following season after a serious
operation for a life-threatening bout of colic.
In a spectacular comeback at the 1990
World Equestrian Games he finished runner-
up to the then reigning Olympic champion,
Rembrandt, making his rider
Kyra Kyrklund the first Finn to win a medal
in any equestrian sport at senior
championship level.

Carefully selected stallions, chiefly
Swedish, Trakehner, Hanoverian,
Holstein and Polish, were crossed with
the various local-bred mares to improve
the basic stamp of horse. Stringent
grading was introduced for both stallions
and mares to ensure that only the best
were granted entry to the stud books.
The breeding programme has been a
tremendous success. The resultant Danish
Warmblood is a handsome individual, well
proportioned and possessed of excellent
paces. It combines courage with a good
temperament and makes an outstanding
dressage horse.

Ariègeois

The Ariègeois, which lives in the Pyrenean mountains in the south-west of France, is a breed of great antiquity. It closely resembles the horses of southern Gaul described in Caesar's commentaries on

BREED DESCRIPTION

Height 13.1 – 14.3hh (the latter is rarely attained in its native habitat, although it may be on richer, lowland grazing).

Colour Solid black. Normally no white stockings or markings on the head, although the flank may be lightly flecked with white.

Conformation Light-boned, expressive head with flat forehead, straight profile, fairly short, hairy ears and bright, alert eyes with a gentle expression; fairly short, straight neck; rather straight shoulders; long but strong back and broad chest; round hindquarters with sloping croup; short, fairly slender limbs with a tendency to cow hocks; good, strong feet.

the Gallic Wars. Its home is the high valley of the Ariège river, from which it takes its name. Well adapted to the worst excesses of its mountain environment, it is impervious to cold and outstandingly sure-footed – ice-covered mountain trails hold no terrors for the little Ariègeois.

A versatile, hardy creature, the Ariègeois has for centuries been used as a packhorse, though it can just as easily function as a small riding horse or work the land on the steepest of hill farms, where modern machinery cannot venture.

INTERESTING FACTS

The coat of the Ariègeois acquires a distinctive reddish tinge in winter. It is fine in texture, unlike the mane and tail, which are harsh to the touch and extremely thick – nature's way of offering much-needed protection from the worst of the winter weather. The Ariègeois is less well suited to heat. In summer it will seek shelter from the sun during the hottest part of the day and come out to graze at night.

▌ TOP
Like all mountain breeds, the Ariègeois has very active paces. It has exceptionally strong hooves and is noted for its sure-footedness.

▌ LEFT
The Ariègeois has a fairly long, but nevertheless strong, back, a powerfully built neck and deep girth. The sloping croup and low-set tail are characteristic.

Norman Cob

The Norman Cob is a light draught horse, still in use on small farms in the La Manche region of Normandy. Normandy has long been famed for its horse breeding, notably at the historic studs of Le Pin (founded as a royal stud in the mid-seventeenth century) and Saint-Lô, where the ancestors of the modern Cob were bred.

Stocky and compact, like the English Cob after which it was named, the Norman Cob was developed as a distinct breed at the beginning of this century. It was at that time that the breeders of half-bred horses first began to distinguish between those animals suitable for use as riding horses, particularly for the army, and those of less quality and sturdier build, more suited to light draught work.

The Norman Cob, as the heavier type was subsequently named, became a popular workhorse, especially in the La Manche region – even the powerful Percheron failed to supplant it there.

Over the years there has been a tendency for the Norman Cob to become heavier, to cope with the work required of it, but although it is undoubtedly sturdy and muscular, it lacks the massive stature of the true heavy horse and has never lost the energetic action, particularly at trot, characteristic of the half-bred horse.

RIGHT
The Norman Cob has always been noted for its energetic action. The lively, free-moving trot is characteristic of the breed.

BELOW
The Norman Cob has the same kindly expression as the English Cob after which it is named.

BREED DESCRIPTION

Height 15.3 – 16.3hh.

Colour Chestnut, bay or bay-brown; occasionally red-roan or grey.

Conformation Overall strong, stocky build with short, well-proportioned limbs.

INTERESTING FACTS

The tail of the Norman Cob is still traditionally docked. Down the centuries this mutilation of horses' tails has been carried out for a variety of reasons: fashion, to prevent the tail becoming entangled with harness and equipment and, in ancient times, probably to serve some ritual purpose. It used to be the fashion to dock the tail of the English Cob, but the practice became illegal in Great Britain under the Docking and Nicking Act, 1948. Quite apart from the trauma of the operation, docking deprives the horse of a vital means of protection against flies.

LEFT
Strong and stockily built, the Norman Cob is a well-proportioned light draught horse. It lacks the massive proportions of the true heavy horse.

Camargue

The tough little Camargue, the native horse of the inhospitable wastes of the Rhône delta in southern France, was not recognized as a breed until January 1968 yet it is almost certainly of ancient origin. It bears a strong resemblance to the horses depicted in the cave paintings of Lascaux, dating from 15,000 BC. Moreover, the even older horse skeletons unearthed at Solutré in south-east France in the nineteenth century could well be those of the breed's forebears.

During its long occupation of the marshlands, the indigenous horse must

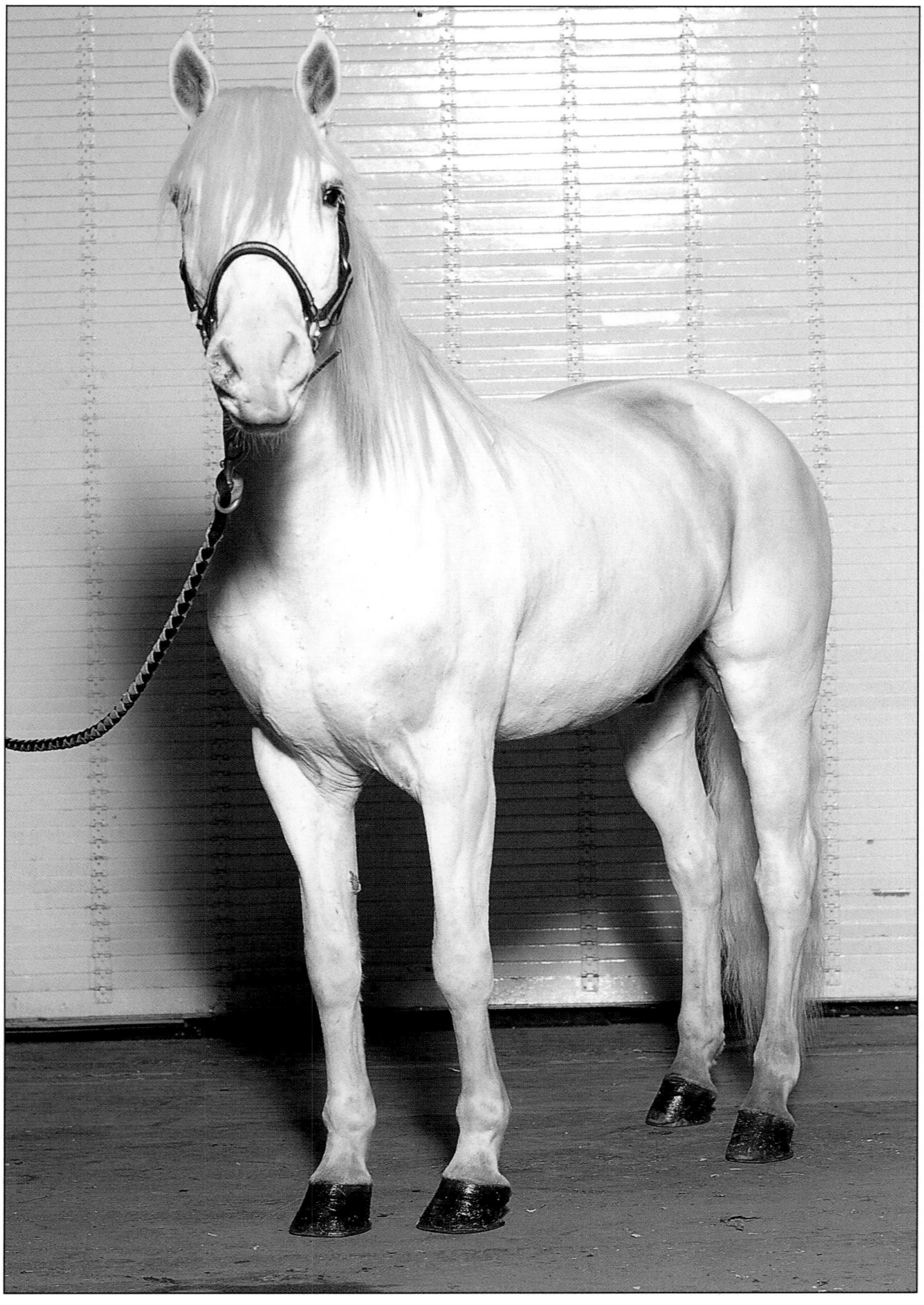

▮ BELOW LEFT
Small, strong and always grey, the Camargue has been an inspiration for artists and poets down the centuries.

▮ BELOW
The breed's ancient origins can be detected in the somewhat heavy, square head, which is reminiscent of that of the primitive horse.

have been influenced by influxes of North African blood, but it has retained certain characteristics of the primitive horse, particularly in its rather heavy, square head.

The horses have always played an integral part in the everyday life of the Camargue, providing the guardians, or herdsmen, with strong, sure-footed mounts for their work with the herds of fighting bulls traditionally raised in the area. Despite its relatively small size, the Camargue horse has the strength and courage to carry a grown man safely over the most treacherous wetland terrain.

The herds, or *manades*, of Camargue horses, each with its own stallion, enjoy a semi-wild existence, being rounded up annually for inspection, branding of young stock, selection of suitable breeding stock and gelding of non-breeding males. Although the practice of fencing off pastureland and draining large areas for the cultivation of crops has, over the years, reduced the need for herdsmen, the horses are still very much a feature of the area. They have taken on a new role as mounts for the increasing number of tourists to the Camargue, which is famed for its wealth of wildlife.

BREED DESCRIPTION

Height 13.1 – 14.1hh.

Colour Grey.

Conformation Rather large, square head with short, wide-set ears; short neck; short, upright shoulders; fairly short back and deep chest; muscular hindquarters with short, sloping croup and long, bushy tail; strong, well-formed limbs with big knees and very hard, sound feet.

INTERESTING FACTS

The half-wild Camargue horses have long held a romantic fascination for artists and writers. In his poem "Horses on the Camargue", Roy Campbell penned these typically evocative lines:

...in a shroud of silence like the dead,
I heard a sudden harmony of hooves,
And, turning, saw afar
A hundred snowy horses unconfined,
The silver runaways of Neptune's car
Racing, spray-curled, like waves before
*   the wind.*
Sons of the Mistral, fleet
As him with whose strong gusts they love
*   to flee,*
Who shod the flying thunders of their feet
And plumed them with the snortings of
*   the sea.*

▌ BELOW LEFT
Despite their semi-wild existence Camargue horses are perfectly amenable to training, as this French trick-riding expert demonstrates.

▌ BELOW
The inhospitable wastes of the Rhône delta have produced a breed renowned for its toughness, strength and sure-footedness.

▌ BOTTOM
Herding the fighting bulls reared in the region is the breed's traditional role. Despite its small size, the Camargue horse will carry a herdsman with great ease.

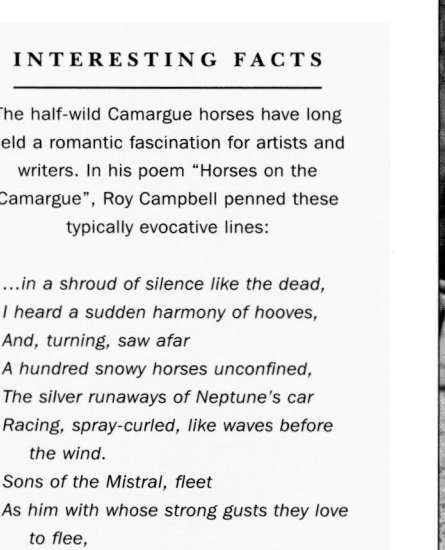

Ardennais

One of the world's premier heavy horses, the powerful but exceptionally docile Ardennais is of ancient origin and is named after its mountainous homeland region on the French–Belgian border.

The Ardennais used to be less massive – as late as the nineteenth century it was used not only for draught work but also for riding. Arab blood was introduced around 1810 and infusions of

BREED DESCRIPTION

Height 15 – 16hh.

Colour Roan, red-roan, iron grey, dark or liver chestnut and bay are the preferred colours. Bay-brown, light chestnut and palomino are admissible. Black, dappled grey and all other colours are inadmissible.

Conformation Straight profile with slightly prominent eye sockets, low, flat forehead, large expressive eyes, pricked ears and wide, open nostrils; medium-length neck, well set-on and generally arched; very strong shoulders; medium-heavy body with deep chest, rather short back and muscular loins; wide, rounded hindquarters; fairly short, strong and muscular limbs.

▌ BELOW
Massively built, but extremely docile, the bigger type of Ardennais makes the perfect partner for heavy agricultural work.

Thoroughbred, Percheron and Boulonnais were added later. These attempts to improve the breed were not a great success and were abandoned, but the Ardennais nevertheless continued to be a most useful animal. Its energy and stamina made it invaluable to the military during the Revolution, at the time of Empire and particularly during the ill-fated Russian campaign. During World

War I the Ardennais was in great demand as an artillery horse.

It was the requirements of agriculture and other heavy draught work which led to the development of a heavier stamp of horse and today, in addition to the original small Ardennais, two other types are recognized: a larger version of the Ardennais, known as the Auxois and the heavier, larger framed Ardennais du Nord (formerly known as the Trait du Nord), the result of using outcrosses to the Belgian Draught.

INTERESTING FACTS

In their writings some 2,000 years ago both the Greek historian Herodotus and the Roman emperor Julius Caesar made particular mention of the horses of north-eastern France, then known as northern Gaul, extolling their stamina and toughness. Skeletons unearthed in the region suggest that these horses stood 15hh – the height of the smaller type of Ardennais still seen today. These were the ancestors of the modern Ardennais.

❙ ABOVE
The Ardennais can still be found working on the land. Its ability to thrive on a minimum of feed makes it an economical proposition for the farmers of small holdings.

❙ BELOW
Roan is a very typical coat colouring of the breed. The eyes are invariably large, with an intelligent, gentle expression.

Selle Français

France has been well to the fore in the development of a modern sports horse, the Cheval de Selle Français (French Saddle Horse) being one of the great warmblood breeding success stories of the twentieth century. The term Selle Français came into use in December 1958 and the first stud book was published in 1965.

The French, with their great tradition of horse breeding, laid the foundations for their modern, quality riding horse as far back as the early nineteenth century, when many regions of the country began to import English Thoroughbred and half-

BREED DESCRIPTION

Height: Medium weight small, 15.3hh and under; medium, 15.3 – 16.1hh; large, over 16.1hh.

Height: Heavyweight small, under 16hh; large, 16hh and over. (The classification "medium" or "heavy" is based on the horse's weight-carrying ability, judged on conformation.)

Colour Predominantly chestnut, though all colours are permissible.

Conformation Refined head; long, elegant neck; sloping shoulders; strong body with well-sprung ribs; broad, powerful hindquarters; strong limbs with particularly powerful forearms, pronounced joints and good bone.

▌ ABOVE
A quality head, set on a long, elegant neck, is typical of the Selle Français. The breed is one of the world's most successful competition horses.

▌ RIGHT
English Thoroughbred and French Trotter blood provided the base for the Selle Français. Its harmonious proportions and overall appearance are very reminiscent of the Thoroughbred.

■ BELOW
Some Selle Français horses such as The Fellow (in
the red colours) have the speed to take on, and
beat, full Thoroughbreds on the racecourse.

■ BOTTOM LEFT
The breed excels at show jumping. This attractive
bay mare, Miss, won team and individual silver
medals at the 1994 World Equestrian Games.

■ BELOW
Some Selle Français horses such as The Fellow (in
the red colours) have the speed to take on, and
beat, full Thoroughbreds on the racecourse.

■ BOTTOM LEFT
The breed excels at show jumping. This attractive
bay mare, Miss, won team and individual silver
medals at the 1994 World Equestrian Games.

bred stallions to cross with their local, less
refined, mares (the chief exceptions were
the Limousin and south-west regions
which specialized in breeding Anglo-
Arabs). In Normandy, always a stronghold
of horse breeding, two important horses
evolved: a fast trotter, later to become the
French Trotter (many of the half-breds
imported from England came from
Norfolk Roadster stock) and the Anglo-
Norman. The vast majority of today's
Selle Français horses trace back to the
Anglo-Norman.

French Warmblood breeding differs
from that in neighbouring countries,
where the grading system is all-important.
Success in competition by stallions, mares
and their progeny or relatives forms the
basis for selection in France. It is a system
which, in a comparatively short space of
time, has produced a highly successful
competition horse, in appearance
reminiscent of the Thoroughbred (which
provided its most famous foundation
sires) and possessing the necessary spirit
to survive the cut and thrust of modern
competitive sports. The Selle Français
shines, above all, at show jumping where
its claims to fame include Jappeloup (1987
European and 1988 Olympic Champion),
Quito de Baussy (1990 World Champion),
I Love You (1983 World Cup winner) and
Galoubet (1982 world team gold
medallist).

■ BELOW
Thanks to the Thoroughbred blood in their veins,
Selle Français horses have the speed and stamina to
succeed in three-day eventing.

French Trotter

France – the country with the greatest tradition of trotting racing outside the United States – developed its own strain of trotter by crossing English Thoroughbreds, half-breds and Norfolk Roadsters with robust Norman mares. The process began in the early nineteenth century. The first French trotting races, which were ridden, not driven, took place in 1806 on the Champ de Mars in Paris. As the sport began to increase in popularity, purpose-built race tracks were opened, the first being at Cherbourg in the 1830s, and the breed developed and improved. In 1861 an Imperial decree gave official encouragement to the sport, leading to the formation of its first governing body.

The Anglo-Norman developed into a fine trotter and five important bloodlines became established: Conquérant, Normand, Lavater, Phaeton and Fuchsia.

BREED DESCRIPTION

Height Average about 16.2hh. The larger horses tend to make the best ridden trotters.

Colour All colours admissible. Chestnut, bay and brown are predominant with some roan. Grey is rare.

Conformation Well-sloped shoulders, giving good ground-covering action; short, strong body; immensely powerful, often sloping, hindquarters.

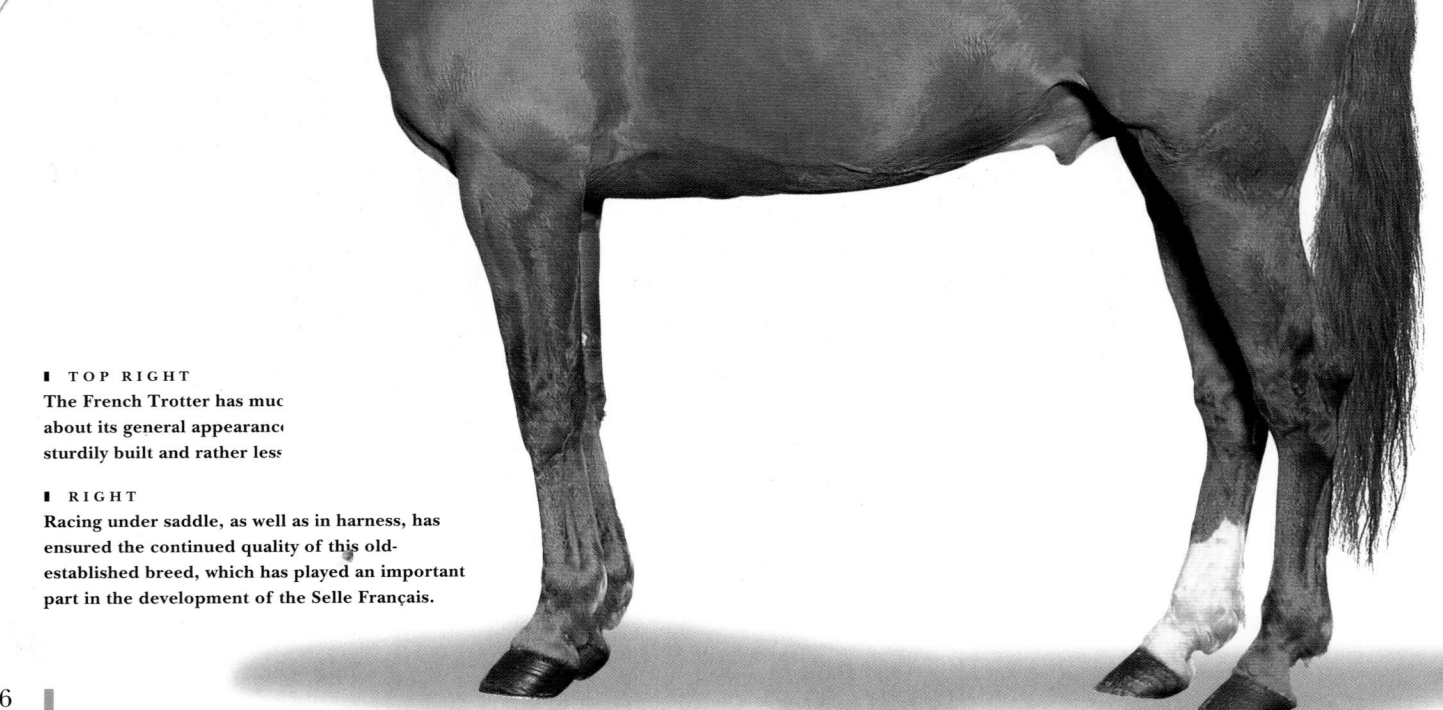

▮ TOP RIGHT
The French Trotter has muc
about its general appearanc
sturdily built and rather less

▮ RIGHT
Racing under saddle, as well as in harness, has ensured the continued quality of this old-established breed, which has played an important part in the development of the Selle Français.

■ LEFT
French Trotters are sometimes used in the sport of skijoring, in which the horse pulls its human partner on skis.

Conquérant and Normand were both by the English half-bred Young Rattler. This son of the Thoroughbred Rattler is sometimes called "the French Messenger" (Messenger being the foundation sire of the Standardbred) because of the enormous influence he has had on trotter breeding in France. Lavater was another example of the English connection, being by a Norfolk Roadster. The most prepotent of all the early stallions was Fuchsia. Foaled in 1883 he sired nearly 400 trotters and more than 100 of his sons

produced winners. Some Standardbred blood was introduced over the years to give the breed more speed but the Trotteur Français Stud Book was closed to non-French-bred horses in 1937 and has only been opened a fraction in recent years to allow a very limited number of carefully selected French/Standardbred crosses to be admitted.

The French have never totally given up ridden racing. Some ten per cent of today's trotting races staged in France are under saddle and they have an important effect on breeding. Because ridden trotters race under comparatively heavy weights they must accordingly be well built horses with good balance and level action. These quality horses have played a large part in maintaining the overall standard of the French Trotter.

■ ABOVE RIGHT
Powerful hindquarters are typical of the breed, the best examples of which can trot at speeds not much less than those of the galloping Thoroughbred.

■ RIGHT
Specially designed vehicles are used to replace the bike-wheel sulky for racing on snow. Unlike pacers, trotters always race without hobbles on their legs.

Percheron

The elegant, free-moving Percheron originated in La Perche, in the south of Normandy. Its ancestors were Arabian horses brought to Europe by the Moors. The oriental influence is believed to have begun following the defeat of the Moors by Charles Martel near Poitiers in AD 732, and was continued after the First Crusade in 1099, when Robert, Comte de Rotrou, imported more Arab horses into France. Much later, during the eighteenth century, Arab stallions at the Royal Stud at Le Pin were made available to breeders of Percherons to upgrade their stock. The

▌ LEFT
The Percheron has a fine head with prominent, alert eyes and wide, open nostrils.

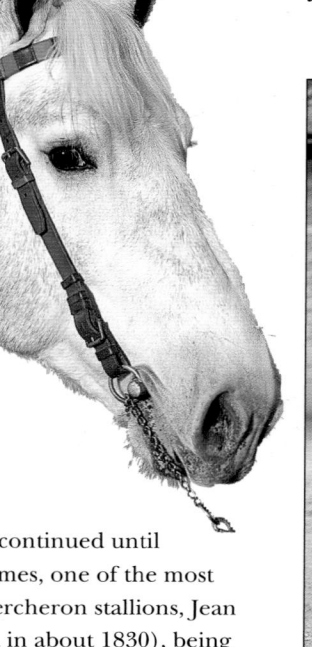

eastern influence continued until relatively recent times, one of the most important early Percheron stallions, Jean le Blanc (foaled in about 1830), being the son of the Arab stallion Gallipoly. The Percheron's great strength and courage, coupled with its sound limbs and

▌ ABOVE RIGHT
The breed is noted for its broad, deep chest, powerful forearms and excellent feet.

▌ RIGHT
Well-proportioned and clean-limbed (that is, without feather on the lower legs), the Percheron is an elegant horse possessed of surprisingly free-moving paces considering its great size.

One of the tallest horses on record was a Percheron named Dr Le Gear. Foaled in 1902, he stood 21hh or 7 feet (213.4m) at the withers and weighed just under 27cwt (1,370kg).

▌ FAR LEFT
The quality and excellent movement of the modern Percheron reflect the Arab influence on the breed.

▌ LEFT
Pause for a snack for a working horse. Percherons are so docile that they can be trained to work in a very short time.

▌ BELOW
Thanks to its good action and amenable temperament, the Percheron goes equally well under saddle and in harness.

longevity, made it tremendously popular in various fields: as a war horse, as a carriage horse and on the land. For some four decades during the late nineteenth and early twentieth centuries it was in great demand world wide, both for work purposes and as an improver of other heavy breeds. French breeders exported a great number of Percherons, which proved to be the most adaptable of horses whatever the climate. Many went to England, some to Australia (the Percheron is said to be the first heavy horse to be taken there) and South America, and the breed became particularly popular in North America, where the black coat colouring was preferred to the grey. American buyers also favoured a heavyweight horse which, together with the need elsewhere for big horses to work on the railways, encouraged the breeding of more massive animals. Despite its great size, however, the modern Percheron is very much a quality animal, retaining the long, low action of its ancestors.

BREED DESCRIPTION

Height 15.2 – 17hh. Average 16.1hh.

Colour Grey or black.

Conformation Fine head, with broad, square forehead, fine, long ears, prominent, alert eyes, straight profile and flat nose with wide, open nostrils; long, arched neck with fairly thick mane; sloping shoulders with prominent withers; broad, deep chest with fairly prominent sternum, short, straight back and loins with great depth through the girth and well-sprung ribs; long, sloping hindquarters; clean, sound limbs with prominent, powerful forearms and long, muscular thighs, large knees and hocks, small, strong fetlock joints and good, strong feet.

Breton

Short-legged and heavily built, the Breton is a surprisingly active heavy horse, with an especially lively trot: characteristics that testify to its Norfolk Roadster and, even further back, Arab ancestry. Like so many southern European horse breeders, those in Brittany used horses brought back from the Middle East by the Crusaders to cross with their more plebeian native stock adding, in more recent times, infusions of blood from England and a number of continental countries – the latter not always with successful results.

Down the centuries there has always been more than one type of Breton horse. Two were identified in the Middle Ages, the Sommier and the Roussin. The Sommier was descended from stock bred mainly in the north of Brittany and was used for pack and agricultural work. The Roussin, a much lighter stamp of animal, was found in the south and some central parts of the region and was a popular

■ BELOW
Chestnut is the most usual colour for the Breton. The beautiful, kind eyes are set in a wide, somewhat square head.

saddle horse, noted for its comfortable, ambling gait.

Although the Breton is no longer thought of as a saddle horse, it does still come in different types – a large and small draught, and a coach-horse type known as the Postier, which is built on less massive lines than the draught horse. The Postier owes its lighter conformation and brilliant paces to infusions of Norfolk Roadster blood from England during the nineteenth century.

An early-maturing animal, the Breton is highly regarded in the French meat trade for the high yield and quality of meat it produces. However, it is still also valued as a draught animal and some Bretons can still be seen working on the land, particularly in the vineyards.

INTERESTING FACTS

The Breton is a hardy, adaptable animal and a most willing worker. Because of its ability to work in hot climates, it has been used for upgrading purposes by breeders in Italy, Spain and even as far afield as Japan.

BREED DESCRIPTION

Height 15 – 16.1hh.

Colour Mainly chestnut; some red roan, bay and grey; black rarely occurs.

Conformation Squarish head with straight profile, open nostrils, bright eyes and small, fairly low-set ears; short, strong and slightly arched neck; rather short but sloping shoulders; short, broad and strong body with well-sprung ribs; very powerful hindquarters; short, strong limbs with very muscular thighs and forearms.

■ RIGHT
Stocky and short-legged, the Breton is nevertheless a very active mover and has been used over the years as a warhorse, draught horse, pack-horse, coach horse – and even a riding horse.

Boulonnais

The gentle Boulonnais, the most elegant of all the heavy horse breeds, traces back to Roman times. It is a native of north-west France and, like the Percheron, was greatly influenced by oriental blood. The Arab influence occurred more than once. First there was the arrival of the Roman armies, with their horses of eastern origin, who massed on the French coast before invading Britain. Then there were the Crusaders, who brought more eastern horses back with them. Two great noblemen in particular, Robert, Comte d'Artois and Eustache, Comte de Boulogne, are credited with importing Arab horses for use in their stables at this time. There was a slight change of direction during the fourteenth century, when Mecklenburg blood from Germany was introduced in order to breed a sturdier animal capable of carrying knights with their new, plated armour.

The term Boulonnais dates from the seventeenth century and reflects the main breeding region of that name on the north French coast. Sadly, the number of Boulonnais horses was seriously depleted during World War I because their chief breeding grounds were right at the heart of the battle zone. World War II had a second serious impact on the breed just as it was recovering. These two setbacks, plus the rapid spread of mechanization following World War II all but signalled the death blow of this fine horse. Fortunately it did survive, thanks to the efforts of a few dedicated enthusiasts, and although the meat trade features as one of the prime outlets for breeders, some Boulonnais horses may still be seen working small farms, where they can prove more effective and economical than tractors. Despite its size and substantial build, it is still possible to detect traces of the breed's Arab ancestry both in the small, refined head, with its large, expressive eyes, and in its outgoing nature.

LEFT
Famous for its gentle nature, the Boulonnais is the most elegant of the heavy horse breeds.

BREED DESCRIPTION

Height 15.3 – 16.3hh.

Colour All shades of grey.

Conformation Elegant head, short and broad overall, with straight profile, wide forehead, slightly prominent eye sockets, strong, rounded, widely spaced jowls, large, bright eyes, small, erect ears, open nostrils and small mouth (in mares the head is slightly longer and less heavy); thick, often arched, neck with thick mane; muscular shoulders with fairly prominent withers; broad, straight back, broad chest and well-sprung ribs; round, muscular hindquarters with fairly high-set, thick tail; strong limbs with very prominent muscular projections in the forearms and thighs, short, thick cannons, large, flat joints and no feather.

INTERESTING FACTS

Two types of Boulonnais evolved: a large, heavy version for use in agriculture and industry, and a smaller, lighter horse suitable for less strenuous work on small-holdings and in light draught work. At one time the small type was known as the *maréeur* or *mareyeur* (fish merchant) because it was used for the transportation of fish from Boulogne to Paris. Nowadays the small type is used in agriculture, the meat trade favouring the larger animal.

BELOW
Boulonnais horses are branded with an anchor on the neck, reflecting their maritime homeland.

Trakehner

Of all the warmbloods, the Trakehner is the closest in appearance to the Thoroughbred. Organized breeding of this attractive riding horse began in 1732, when Friedrich Wilhelm I of Prussia established the Royal Trakehner Stud Administration in East Prussia (now part of Poland). A great deal of Thoroughbred and Arab blood was used to upgrade the local horses. These were descendants of the tough little Schweiken breed known to the Teutonic knights who colonized the region during the early thirteenth century. The Schweiken was a descendant of the Konik pony, which traces back to the primitive Tarpan.

Towards the end of the eighteenth century a determined effort was made to improve the Trakehner, or East Prussian, as it was also known. Inferior breeding stock at the Royal Stud was drastically weeded out, a process which led to the swift development of the Trakehner. It was soon much in demand, first as a carriage horse and subsequently as an army remount.

Renowned for its twin qualities of elegance and toughness, the Trakehner flourished for nearly two centuries – until the disastrous upheaval of World War II. During the autumn and winter of 1944 the breed suffered catastrophic losses as desperate efforts were made to evacuate the horses before the arrival of the advancing Russian troops. Of the

thousands of Trakehners, many of them mares with foals at foot, who set off on the 900 mile (1,450km) journey west across Europe, few survived. Before their flight there were more than 25,000 horses registered in the East Prussian stud book. A mere 1,200 or so made it to the West

▌ ABOVE RIGHT
The Trakehner is noted for its refined head. Large eyes and a small, tapered muzzle enhance the overall impression of quality.

▌ RIGHT
The Trakehner's elegant outline owes much to the Thoroughbred influence. The Trakehner, in its turn, has been used in the development of the Dutch, Danish and Swedish Warmbloods.

BREED DESCRIPTION

Height Average 16 – 16.2hh.

Colour Any solid colour.

Conformation Refined head with large eyes and small muzzle; elegant, tapering neck; well-sloped shoulders; strong, medium-length body, well ribbed-up; well-rounded hindquarters; hard limbs with short cannons and excellent, sound feet.

INTERESTING FACTS

One of the most famous examples of the Trakehner is the show jumper Abdullah, a handsome grey stallion who competed for the United States. Ridden by Conrad Homfeld, he won a team gold medal and the individual silver at the 1984 Olympic Games and was victorious in the World Cup the following year. Abdullah was originally exported *in utero* to Canada and was foaled in 1970. After his retirement from competition he was used for breeding in many countries, thanks to the use of frozen semen.

LEFT
Like the Thoroughbred, the Trakehner is possessed of courage and stamina, qualities which make it suitable for tough sports such as carriage driving.

BELOW LEFT
The powers of endurance which helped the breed survive the harsh times of World War II stand the breed in good stead in the modern sport of eventing.

BELOW
The show-jumping stallion Abdullah demonstrated the breed's fine qualities to great advantage when winning a team gold medal at the 1984 Olympic Games.

and many of these failed to survive in the very harsh economic conditions of post-war Germany.

Incredibly, thanks to the dedicated efforts of the keepers of the original stud book, the Trakehner did not die out. The surviving equine evacuees were tracked down and re-registered in West Germany and, as breeding resumed and numbers increased, the Trakehner began to take its place in the modern equestrian world. Valued for its good conformation and action, its spirited temperament and its endurance, it has found favour both as a competition horse and as an improver of other warmbloods.

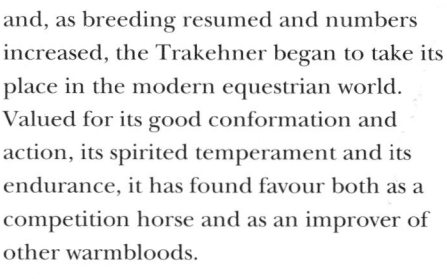

Hanoverian

George II, Elector of Hanover and King of England, was instrumental in the establishment of this famous German warmblood, thanks to the foundation of the state stud at Celle in 1735. The aim was to provide local people with the services of good quality stallions at nominal fees, the original horses being Holsteins of predominantly Andalusian and Neapolitan blood. Thanks to the later

▌ LEFT
Previously bred as an all-purpose work horse, the modern Hanoverian has been refined for use in equestrian sports.

BREED DESCRIPTION

Height 15.3 – 16.2hh.

Colour All solid colours.

Conformation Medium-sized head, clean cut and expressive, with large, lively eyes and good free cheek bones; long, fine neck; large, sloping shoulders with pronounced withers; strong, deep body; muscular hindquarters with well set-on tail; well-muscled limbs with large, pronounced joints and well-formed, hard hooves.

▌ ABOVE RIGHT
Thoroughbreds and Trakehners were used in the development of the present-day Hanoverian. Their influence can be seen in the breed's clean-cut head.

▌ RIGHT
The Hanoverian is noted more for its strength than its speed, hence the many successes of its representatives in dressage and show jumping.

INTERESTING FACTS

A great many Hanoverians have become household names as show jumpers, among them Dollar Girl (1995 World Cup winner with Nick Skelton), Top Gun (1992 Olympic team gold medallist with Jan Tops), Walzerkönig (1988 Olympic team gold medallist with Franke Sloothaak), Deister (three times European Champion with Paul Schockemöhle), Tigre (1978 world team gold medallist with Caroline Bradley), Simona (1974 World Champion with Hartwig Steenken) and Ferdl (1960 Olympic team gold medallist ridden by Paul Schockemöhle's brother, Alwin).

▌ LEFT
Hanoverians have found favour throughout the world as show jumpers. Amadeus Z, bred in Belgium, is seen competing for Holland at the 1994 World Equestrian Games.

importation of English horses, including Thoroughbreds, the Hanoverian gradually began to show more quality, the aim being to produce a good all-purpose animal that was capable of working on the land but also suitable for ridden work and for use as a light carriage horse.

In common with so many other horse-breeding enterprises, the development of the Hanoverian at Celle was adversely affected by war. By the end of the eighteenth century the stud had over 100 stallions, but by 1816, after the Napoleonic wars, a mere thirty remained. To help make up for these losses, more outside blood was brought in, especially Thoroughbred. But the time came when the breed was tending to become too light for the work required of it and this influence was accordingly reduced.

After World War II, however, the Hanoverian had to be adapted to a new way of life if the breed was to survive and Thoroughbred blood was again introduced, along with Trakehner, to produce a warmblood suited to the demands of the leisure-horse market.

The modern Hanoverian is lighter and less coarse than of old and is noted for its good, honest temperament. In common with other German warmbloods, stallions are only licensed if they pass the required veterinary inspection and, after licensing, must pass ridden performance tests. Hanoverians are among the world's most sought-after sports horses, their strength and athleticism making them especially suitable for dressage and show jumping.

▌ LEFT
Dressage is the other sport at which the Hanoverian excels. With its great strength and true, energetic action, it is well suited to this demanding discipline.

Holstein

The Holstein is probably the oldest of the German warmbloods, dating back several centuries. As early as the seventeenth century horses bred in the region were much in demand in France, Denmark and Italy. The old Holstein horses contained mixed blood, including German, Neapolitan, Spanish and oriental. During the nineteenth century they were crossed with Yorkshire Coach Horses, a policy which helped give the breed a distinctive high knee action, great presence and an exceptionally tractable nature. Holsteins became renowned for being tough but handsome carriage horses and subsequently as army remounts.

The Traventhall Stud, founded by the Prussians in 1867 in Schleswig-Holstein, is considered the modern Holstein's birthplace. However, this stud is no longer in operation and the breeds main base is now at Elmshorn.

To produce a stamp of horse suitable for today's requirements, some Thoroughbred blood was used in the period after World War II, which resulted in a lighter type of horse with less high, "carriage-horse" action and a better shoulder. Although the infusions of Thoroughbred blood may have made the Holstein rather more excitable than it was

▌ ABOVE
This handsome head, with its alert, intelligent expression, is typical of the Holstein.

▌ LEFT
Formerly bred for use as a carriage horse and army remount, the Holstein was upgraded into a better-quality animal through the introduction of a certain amount of Thoroughbred blood.

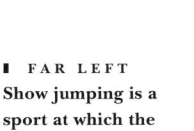

■ FAR LEFT
Show jumping is a
sport at which the
Holstein, with its
intelligent and bold
character, has excelled
for many years.

INTERESTING FACTS

One of the most celebrated Holstein horses of all time was the big bay gelding Meteor, the only show jumper to have won a medal at three Olympic Games. Foaled in 1943, he won the individual bronze medal at the 1952 Games and four years later helped Germany win the team gold in Stockholm, where he finished fourth individually. In Rome in 1960, at the age of 17, he won a second team gold medal and finished sixth in the individual contest. Ridden by Fritz Thiedemann, an exceptionally talented all-round horseman, Meteor was an outstanding ambassador for the Holstein breed. He died in 1966 and is buried at Elmshorn, the breed's headquarters.

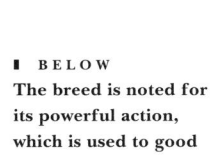

■ BELOW
The breed is noted for
its powerful action,
which is used to good
effect in Grand Prix
dressage.

of old, it has, generally speaking, retained its good temperament. Its intelligence and boldness make it a first-rate mount for top-level dressage and show jumping.

Holstein horses are not bred in such quantity as some other warmbloods nor is their breeding area particularly large. Possibly as a result, there is less variation in overall type.

■ BELOW
Originally prized as
tough, active carriage
horses, Holsteins can
still be seen in harness
in the competitive
discipline of four-in-
hand driving.

BREED DESCRIPTION

Height Approximately 16 – 17hh.

Colour All colours permissible. Bay with black points and brown predominate. Grey is quite common, chestnut less so.

Conformation Expressive head, well set-on and in proportion to the size of the horse, with big, bright eyes; long, muscular and slightly arched neck; long, sloping shoulders; strong back, deep, wide chest and muscular loins; strong, muscular hindquarters with well-muscled thighs, stifles and gaskins; short, strong cannon bones, flat knees, big, clean hocks, medium-length pasterns and good, hard feet.

Oldenburg

The Oldenburg, Germany's heaviest type of warmblood, was originally developed as a coach horse and was based on the old Friesian horses bred in the region between the River Weser and the Netherlands. The breed takes its name from Count Anton Gunther von Oldenburg (1603–67), who played a leading part in its development, crossing stallions from Italy and Spain with the native stock. Later breeders introduced Thoroughbred, Cleveland Bay, Hanoverian and Norman blood. The result was a big upstanding horse, measuring a good 17hh, and fairly heavily built. Unlike most large animals, however, it matured early which undoubtedly popularized it as a work horse.

▌ LEFT
The Oldenburg was originally bred as a coach horse. It is the heaviest of the German Warmbloods.

BREED DESCRIPTION

Height Approximately 16 – 17hh.

Colour Predominantly brown, black and bay.

Conformation Rather plain head, occasionally with a Roman nose; fairly long, very strong neck; sloping, muscular shoulders; powerfully built body with deep chest; strong hindquarters with high-set tail; fairly short limbs with large joints and plenty of bone.

▌ LEFT
Careful breeding has helped eradicate coach-horse characteristics such as upright shoulders and a long back, though some modern Oldenburgs retain the rather high knee action of their forebears.

■ LEFT
The German rider
Franke Sloothaak on
his way to becoming
World Show Jumping
Champion in 1994.
His mount is the
Oldenburg mare,
Weihaiwej.

As coach horses gave way to motorized transport in the early twentieth century, breeders had of necessity to change the type of the Oldenburg and look more to the production of a general-purpose farm horse. More recently, further infusions of Thoroughbred blood, and some Selle Français, have produced a horse which is considerably finer than its coaching ancestors and well able to hold its own in the competitive sports, working equally well under saddle or in harness. The Oldenburg still tends to be a big individual compared with other warmbloods but many of the coach-horse characteristics, such as an upright shoulder and long back, have been eliminated. The knee action still tends to be a little on the high side.

Oldenburg horses are exported to many countries and have proved particularly popular in the United States.

■ BELOW
From coach horse to dressage horse: refinement of the breed has been brought about through the introduction of Thoroughbred and Selle Français blood, making the present-day Oldenburg an outstanding sports horse.

INTERESTING FACTS

Olympic Bonfire, an Oldenburg gelding foaled in 1983, won the World Dressage Freestyle to Music Championship in 1994 when ridden by the leading Dutch rider, Anky van Grunsven.

Westphalian

Closely related to the Hanoverian, the Westphalian is bred in the region of Nordrhein-Westfalen, in the north-west of Germany. Its main breeding centre, Warendorf, is famous for being the home of German equestrianism (the National Federation is based there). The area has a long tradition of horse breeding. It is known that in the early nineteenth century East Prussian stallions were made available to local mare owners to enable them to upgrade their stock. Over the years various outcrosses were made, involving Oldenburg, Hanoverian, Friesian, Anglo-Norman and trotter blood and it was not until this century that breeders finally settled for just one influence: the Hanoverian. Today's Westphalian shares the bloodlines of the present-day Hanoverian, although there are also several important ones which have developed specifically in the Westphalia region.

BREED DESCRIPTION

Height 15.3 – 16.2hh.

Colour All solid colours.

Conformation Intelligent head with good width between the eyes; well-shaped neck; deep, broad body; powerful hindquarters, although they can be a little flat.

▮ ABOVE
The Westphalian has the same clean-cut good looks as the Hanoverian, with whom it shares a common ancestry.

▮ RIGHT
The conformation is typical of that of the modern sports horse: a good length of neck, deep body and powerful hindquarters. It tends to be a little longer in the leg than the Hanoverian.

INTERESTING FACTS

Famous Westphalian horses include Rembrandt (Olympic dressage champion in 1988 and 1992, ridden by Nicole Uphoff-Becker); Ahlerich (Olympic dressage champion in 1984, ridden by Reiner Klimke); Fire (winner of the World Show Jumping Championship in 1982, ridden by Norbert Koof) and Roman (winner of the World Show Jumping Championship in 1978, ridden by Gerd Wiltfang). Rembrandt, one of the most handsome representatives of the breed, was the first horse in the history of the Olympic Games to win two individual gold medals for dressage. He was European champion in 1989 and also took the individual title at the first World Equestrian Games, held in Stockholm in 1990.

▌ ABOVE RIGHT
Two Step is a Westphalian who has found fame as a show jumper. Originally named Polydektes, he is by Polydor, one of the breed's most successful sires of competition horses.

▌ RIGHT
Ahlerich was one of the breed's most outstanding performers in the world of dressage. He crowned a gloriously successful Grand Prix career with victory at the 1984 Olympic Games in Los Angeles.

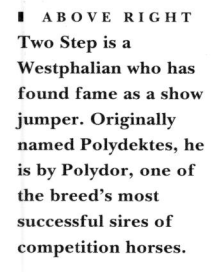

Schleswig

A sturdy, compact heavy horse, the Schleswig comes from the northernmost region of Germany, Schleswig-Holstein, which borders on to Denmark and which was, indeed, at various times actually part of that country. It is not surprising, therefore, that the Schleswig bears a marked resemblance to the Jutland, the Danish heavy breed to which it is closely related. The Schleswig was developed during the second half of the nineteenth century as a medium-sized draught horse. Infusions of lighter blood, including Yorkshire Coach Horse and Thoroughbred, were made towards the end of the century but these had no lasting effect on the breed. Popular as a tram and bus horse, and for use on the land and in forestry, the breed survived World War I (during which its homeland was under Danish rule) although it was seriously depleted in both numbers and quality. The subsequent introduction of Breton and Boulonnais blood from

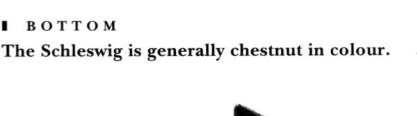

BREED DESCRIPTION

Height 15.2 – 16hh.

Colour Predominantly chestnut, occasionally bay or grey.

Conformation Large, rather plain head, but with a kind eye; short, crested neck; very powerful shoulders; rather long body, though with good depth through the girth; well-muscled hindquarters; short, strong limbs with some feather.

France proved highly successful. The Schleswig recovered and flourished in large numbers until the years immediately following World War II. In time, however, mechanization took its usual toll, and numbers dwindled drastically. In recent years some of the surviving Schleswigs have been bred back to Jutlands, in order to increase the breed's size.

INTERESTING FACTS

The attractive Schleswig horse, which often has a flaxen mane and tail, is extremely powerfully built and weighs in the region of 1,766lb (800kg).

South German

This strong and agile heavy horse is descended from the Austrian Noriker, which was introduced into Bavaria, in southern Germany, towards the end of the nineteenth century. With a view to improving and developing their own stamp of horse, breeders in Upper Bavaria added some Holstein and Oldenburg blood, while those in Lower Bavaria experimented with an extraordinary variety of outcrosses, from Oldenburg and Cleveland Bay to Clydesdale and Belgian Draught. In time, however, German breeders reverted to using the original Noriker blood for upgrading purposes. Originally called the Pinzgauer Noriker, after the region in Salzburg province from which that particular strain of the Austrian heavy horse came, the German version of the breed became known as the South German Heavy Horse. Today it is bred mainly in Bavaria and Baden Wurtemburg. It still resembles the Noriker, although it is inclined to stand a little less tall. It is a

▌ BELOW
The South German Coldblood has a large head and, typically, a docile expression.

▌ BOTTOM
The South German resembles the Noriker but is a little smaller.

well-proportioned horse, with a calm, docile temperament, and can be seen in parades and at shows as well as, occasionally, at work in agriculture.

INTERESTING FACTS

The South German heavy horse is a popular attraction at shows. As well as being used by trick riders, it takes part in races – which it clearly enjoys!

BREED DESCRIPTION

Height Around 15.3hh.

Colour Brown, bay and chestnut.

Conformation Rather large head, with kind eye; short, strong neck; powerful shoulders; strong back with deep girth; good limbs with a little feather.

Cleveland Bay

A race of bay-coloured horses was being bred, primarily for pack work, in the north east of England as far back as mediaeval times. It was the preferred means of transport of the chapmen, or travelling salesmen of the day, and was accordingly known as the Chapman Horse. Taking the Chapman Horse as their base, seventeenth-century breeders used some of the Andalusian and Barb stallions that were being brought into the country at that time to produce a fine coach horse, renowned for its active paces and great stamina. This became known as the Cleveland Bay after the area where it was chiefly bred. As roads improved, and a faster type of coach horse became necessary, some Thoroughbred blood was introduced, usually by means of putting half-bred stallions to Cleveland mares. This lighter, faster version of the Cleveland Bay was called the Yorkshire Coach Horse. It had its own breed society, founded in 1886, and stud book. But the coming of motorized transport signalled the demise of coach horses everywhere and the Yorkshire breed was no exception.

▮ ABOVE
The Cleveland Bay is the descendant of a race of bay-coloured horses bred in north-eastern England since medieval times.

▮ LEFT
A handsome, upstanding stamp of horse, the Cleveland Bay produces excellent hunters when crossed with the Thoroughbred.

■ LEFT AND FAR LEFT
Cleveland Bay horses at the Royal Mews in London testify to the interest taken in the preservation of this historic breed by Queen Elizabeth II.

Its stud book was finally closed in 1936, by which time the breed had virtually died out. Fortunately the Cleveland Bay survived, albeit in small numbers. Crossed with the Thoroughbred, the breed produces fine upstanding heavyweight hunters and excellent carriage horses. The Cleveland Bay has a true, straight and free action (high action is not characteristic of the breed), moves freely from the shoulder and covers the ground well. As well as making an excellent hunter and carriage horse, the Cleveland Bay, when crossed with the Thoroughbred, has also produced some first-rate show jumpers.

BREED DESCRIPTION

Height 16 – 16.2hh, though height does not disqualify an otherwise good animal.

Colour Bay with black points.

Conformation Bold head, not too small, with large, well-set, kind eyes and large, fine ears; long, lean neck; deep, sloping, muscular shoulders; deep, wide body, with muscular loins, powerful hindquarters and well set-on tail; clean limbs (without feather), with muscular forearms, thighs and second thighs, large knees and hocks, and strong, sloping pasterns; good, sound feet.

INTERESTING FACTS

The survival of the Cleveland Bay was aided in no small measure by Queen Elizabeth II. A colt named Mulgrave Supreme, due to be sent to the United States, was bought by the Queen, subsequently broken to saddle and to harness and then made available to breeders of Cleveland Bays, both pure- and part-bred, throughout Britain. This tremendously successful promotional exercise sparked off renewed enthusiasm among breeders. Prince Philip further enhanced the breed's profile by driving, for many years, teams of pure- and part-bred Cleveland Bays at international level.

■ RIGHT
For many years HRH The Duke of Edinburgh drove a team of Cleveland Bays in international four-in-hand events. They have excellent ground-covering action, well suited to work both in harness and under saddle.

Hackney

The Hackney, with its high-stepping action, is a native of England though it is prized the world over as a carriage horse, especially in the show ring. The Hackney horse originated in the late seventeenth and early eighteenth centuries and is a descendant of the famous English trotting horses of the time, the Yorkshire Trotter and the Norfolk Roadster. These horses had a common ancestor, a horse known as the Original Shales, who was foaled in 1755 and was by the Thoroughbred Blaze out of a mare described as a "hackney". Blaze was by Flying Childers, generally recognized as being the first great racehorse. Blaze and his progeny, notably his two sons, Driver and Scot Shales, had a considerable influence on the development of the trotters of eastern England. Despite their shared ancestry, the horses bred in Yorkshire and Norfolk developed somewhat different characteristics – those of Yorkshire origin tended to have more quality than those from Norfolk, which were more cob-like in appearance – but these regional

BREED DESCRIPTION

Height Hackney pony not exceeding 14hh. Hackney horse 15 – 15.3hh.

Colour Usually dark brown, black, bay or chestnut.

Conformation Small, convex head with small muzzle, large eyes and small ears; fairly long, well-formed neck; powerful shoulders and low withers; compact body, with great depth of chest; short legs with strong, well let-down hocks and well-shaped feet.

INTERESTING FACTS

The derivation of the word hackney is doubtful but it is thought to come from the Old French *haquenée*, "an ambling horse or mare, especially for ladies to ride on", and may be related to the Old Spanish and Portuguese *facanea* and Spanish *hacanea*. In the fourteenth century the word was latinized in England as *hakeneius*.

▪ LEFT
Hackneys are popular
in show rings
throughout the world.
Here they are being
driven in an unusual
three-horse
combination known as
a unicorn, comprising
two wheelers and a
leader.

distinctions later disappeared.

The Hackney pony was developed
during the second half of the eighteenth
century – earlier use of the term "Hackney
ponies" almost certainly referred to small
part-bred Hackney horses. It was the very
enterprising Westmorland breeder,
Christopher Wyndham Wilson, a
remarkable man whose achievements
included inventing the silo to store winter
feed for farm animals, who was largely

responsible for the development of the
true Hackney pony. Wilson used a variety
of pony breeds, especially the Fell, as his
foundation mares, crossing them with a
good-looking Hackney horse named Sir
George, who was sired in 1866 and stood
less than 14hh. His policy of inbreeding to
the prepotent Sir George enabled Wilson
to achieve his aim of developing a
Hackney with real pony characteristics and
in due course other breeders followed his

lead. The original height limit for ponies,
as recommended by the Hackney Horse
Society, was 14.2hh but this was
subsequently reduced to 14hh. The high-
stepping action for which the Hackney is
renowned was not developed until the
second half of the nineteenth century,
when it became the fashion to drive
elegant, showy carriage horses. It is partly
inherited, partly taught and can be
enhanced by training.

▪ RIGHT
In classes for single
turnouts the Hackney
is harnessed to a
lightweight vehicle
with pneumatic tyres.

▪ OPPOSITE
The Hackney has a
compact body,
powerful shoulders
and a deep chest. The
limbs are strong and
the feet invariably well
formed.

Shire

England's most magnificent looking heavy horse is descended from the mediaeval warhorse known as the Great Horse, which was later given the name of the English Black. It was developed by crossing imported Flanders and Friesian horses with native stock to produce first a military mount and subsequently a farm and general draught horse. The introduction of the term "blacks" for these heavy horses is attributed to Oliver Cromwell, and was probably used originally to describe the imported Friesians, which are always black in colour. The main breeding areas of the

BREED DESCRIPTION

Height Stallions 16.2 – 17.2hh. Mares 16 – 17hh.

Colour Black, brown, bay or grey.

Conformation Lean head (neither too large nor too small), wide between the eyes, slightly Roman nose, large, prominent eyes with docile expression, and long, lean, sharp, sensitive ears; fairly long, slightly arched neck; deep, oblique shoulders, wide enough to support a collar; short, strong, muscular back, broad chest and wide, sweeping, muscular hindquarters with well let-down thighs; clean, hard limbs with 11–12 inches (28–30cm) of bone and broad, deep, flat hocks, set at the correct angle for leverage; fine, straight, silky feather; deep, solid feet with thick walls and open coronets.

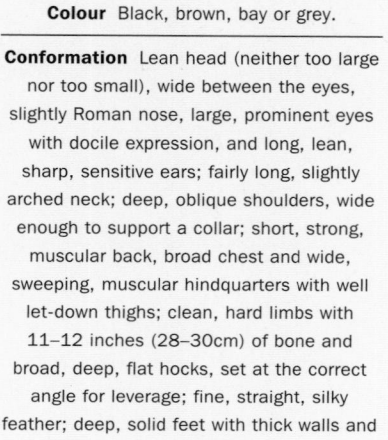

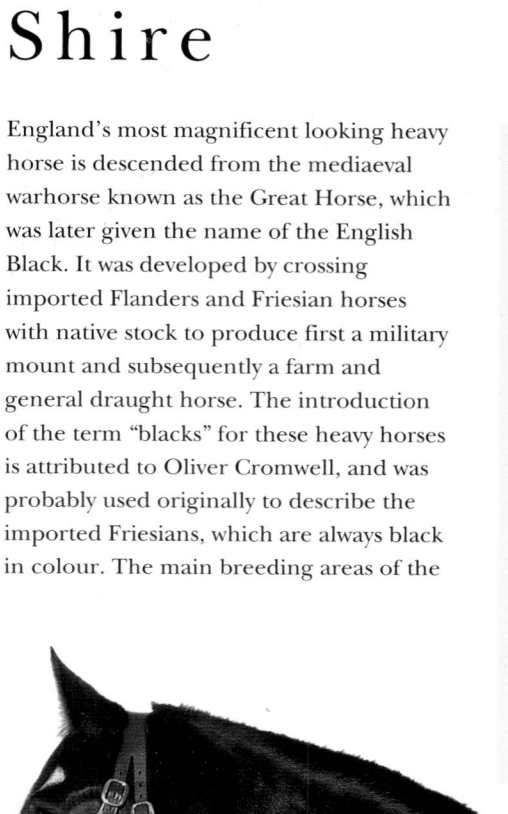

▌ ABOVE RIGHT
The Roman nose, long, sharp ears, large eyes and docile expression are typical of the Shire, the archetypal "gentle giant".

▌ RIGHT
The magnificent Shire is descended from the medieval warhorse known as the Great Horse. It weighs in excess of 20cwt (1,016kg).

■ RIGHT
A team of twenty Shires makes a magnificent sight at an English horse show, admirably displaying the breed's tractable nature.

■ BELOW
A foal dozes in the summer sun. While Shires will never be seen in the same numbers as in olden times, the breed has enough enthusiasts to ensure its future.

INTERESTING FACTS

One of the earliest records of a Shire stallion standing at stud is of the horse known as the Packington Blind Horse. He was named after the village of Packington, near Ashby-de-la-Zouche, where he lived between 1755 and 1770. This horse, and horses said to be his progeny, had a significant influence on the breed during its formative years.

English Black were the Fen country and the Midland shires of Leicestershire, Lincolnshire, Derbyshire and Staffordshire, from which the breed eventually took its name. In the early days the breed displayed regional variations, horses bred in the Fens tending to be bigger, heavier and somewhat coarser than those from the "Shires". Those from Derbyshire and Leicestershire were predominantly black, while Staffordshire horses were more often brown.

It was not until the late nineteenth century that the breeding of these horses became formalized, as a result of the publication of the first stud book. In 1878 a breed society was set up under the title of the Old English Cart Horse Society. The name was changed in 1884 to the Shire Horse Society and the breed has been known as the Shire ever since.

Following the formation of the breed society, the Shire went from strength to strength, competing with great success in the leading agricultural shows of the time and attracting the interest of foreign buyers. Shire horses were soon being exported as far afield as North and South America, Russia and Australia. They also became an indispensable part of daily life in Britain. With their qualities of strength, stamina, soundness and good temperament, these gentle giants could be seen ploughing the land, hauling timber and pulling farm wagons, railway vans, brewers' drays and coal carts. Although mechanization took its customary toll, a Shire "revival" began in the 1960s and today these wonderful horses can again be seen at shows, ploughing the land and, not least, pulling brewers' drays on short-haul routes in cities.

■ LEFT AND ABOVE
Shires hitched to brewers' drays are a popular sight at many British horse and agricultural shows. Some are still used for short-haul work in inner cities, where they are more economical than motorized transport.

Suffolk

Britain's oldest heavy breed, the Suffolk or Suffolk Punch, is named after the East Anglian county where it has been bred since the sixteenth century. Little is known of its origins, but as far back as 1506 there is an historical reference to a distinctive type of Suffolk horse. The Suffolk was developed as a farm horse and with its tremendously strong shoulders and clean legs (i.e. free of feather) it is ideally suited to working on the very heavy clay soils of East Anglia.

The breed is unique in that all Suffolks trace back to a single stallion, known as Crisp's Horse of Ufford, foaled in 1760.

■ LEFT
This mare shows the typical broad forehead and full, bright eyes of the Suffolk. All Suffolks are chesnut in colour – traditionally spelt without the middle "t".

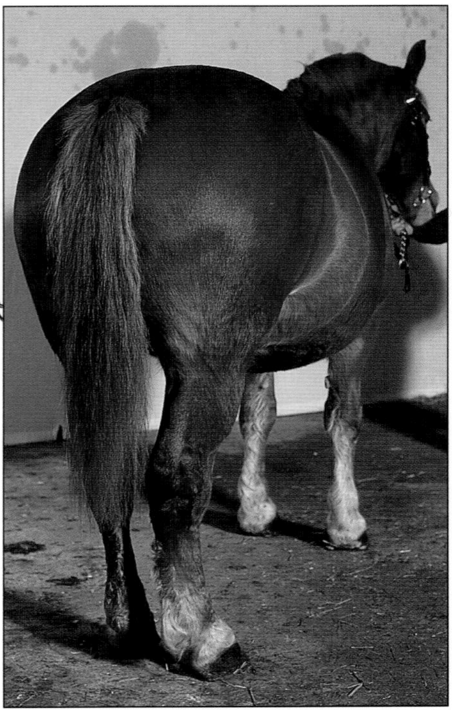

■ BELOW
Although there is plenty of width between the forelegs, the hindfeet are set close together. Such conformation prevents the horse damaging crops when working in the fields.

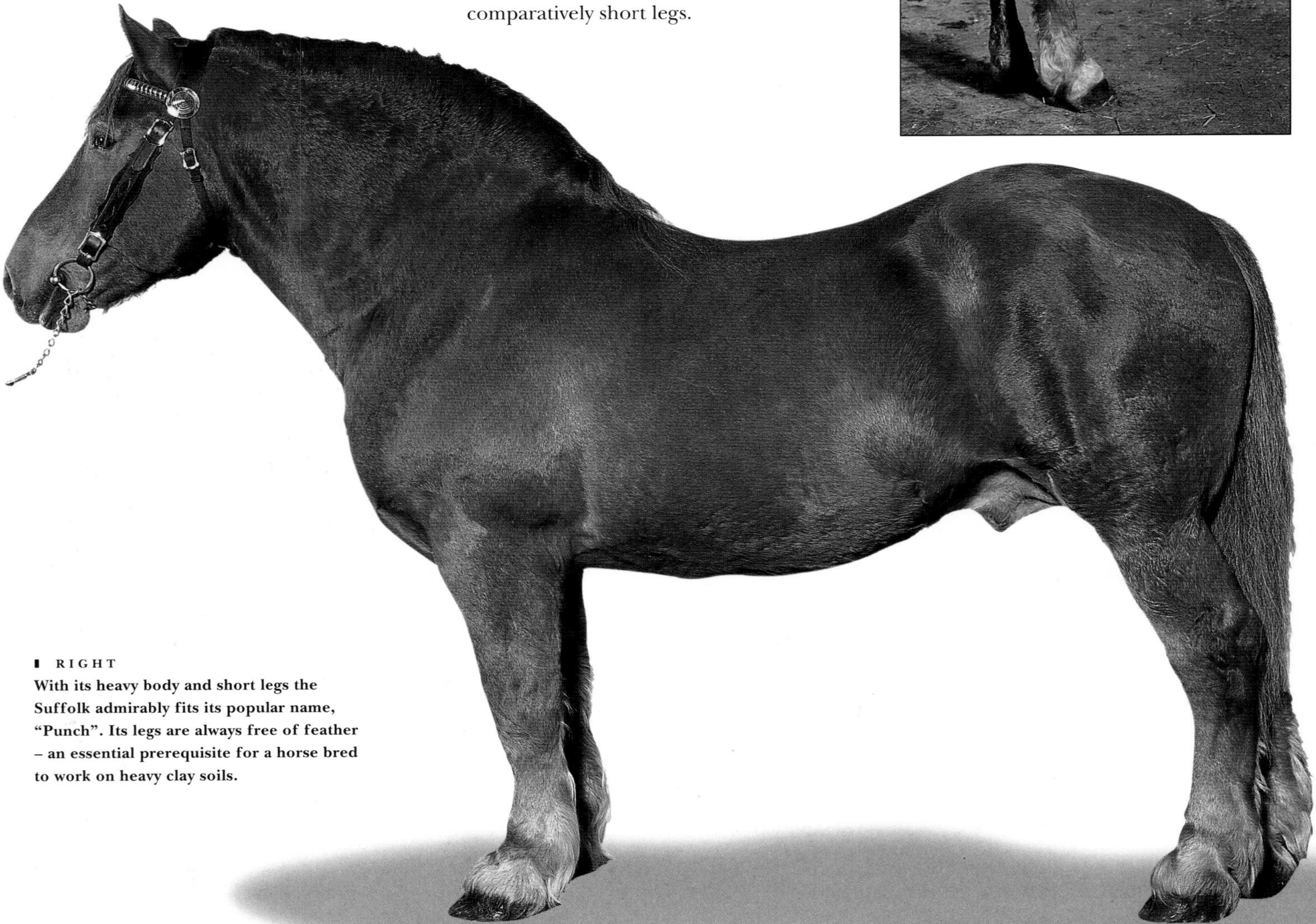

This purity is manifested in the fact that it always breeds true to colour: all Suffolks are "chesnut" (traditionally spelt without the first "t"). Quite apart from its coat colour, the Suffolk is quite unmistakable in appearance, having a heavy body set on comparatively short legs.

■ RIGHT
With its heavy body and short legs the Suffolk admirably fits its popular name, "Punch". Its legs are always free of feather – an essential prerequisite for a horse bred to work on heavy clay soils.

BREED DESCRIPTION

Height 16 – 16.3hh.

Colour Always "chestnut", of which seven shades are recognized, ranging from a pale mealy tone to a very dark, almost brown, shade. The most common is a bright reddish shade. A little white may occur on the face and the mane and tail are sometimes pale in colour.

Conformation Quite large head, with broad forehead; deep, tapering neck; long, muscular shoulders; deep, well-rounded body with strong quarters and well-set tail; fairly short, straight limbs with plenty of bone, sloping pasterns and no coarse hair; hard, sound, medium-sized feet.

INTERESTING FACTS

The ability of the Suffolk to thrive on less rations than other working heavy horses is well illustrated by the experiences of one farmer who, during the early part of this century, compared the feed requirements of two dozen cross-bred farm horses which he used for several years on one farm, and those of twenty-five Suffolks which he used for a similar period on another. While all the horses ate the same quantities of bulk food – hay, mangolds and chaff – the cross-breds each required 75lb (34kg) of corn per week, increasing by some 14–21lbs (6.4-9.5kg) per week as they grew older, while the Suffolks, even the older ones, kept their condition on a regular 50lb (22.7kg) per week.

Despite its size the Suffolk is a remarkably economical horse to keep, thriving and working on comparatively small rations. It matures early – Suffolks can be put to light work at two years of age and go into full work at three. It has an exceptionally amenable temperament and it is noted for its great soundness and longevity – it is common for horses to be in use and mares to be producing foals into their late teens and Suffolks often live until they are nearly thirty. The Suffolk's remarkable qualities combined to make it one of the most popular agricultural and draught horses of all time and, not surprisingly, its popularity spread abroad. There have been Suffolks in the United States for many years and representatives of the breed have also been exported to Australia, Africa, Russia and Pakistan (where they were used to produce army horses). Like the Shire, the Suffolk survived the coming of mechanization and can still be seen occasionally working the land, pulling drays and at shows, principally in eastern England.

▌ **ABOVE RIGHT**
A pair of present-day Suffolks drawing a vehicle of yesteryear.

▌ **RIGHT**
Suffolks can still be seen at their traditional work, ploughing. Early maturing, sound, long-lived and economical to feed, the breed possesses all the attributes so vital in a draught horse in the days before mechanization.

Clydesdale

■ OPPOSITE PAGE
The brisk, ground-covering paces of the Clydesdale make it eminently suitable for both agricultural and heavy haulage work.

Scotland's breed of heavy horse, as its name suggests, originated in that area of Lanarkshire through which the Clyde river runs. Today's Clydesdale, which developed more recently than the other British heavy breeds, began to evolve during the second half of the eighteenth century when imported Flemish stallions were used to improve the stock, descended from pack animals, of local farmers. Before that, during the early part of the century, a breeder named Paterson of Lochlyoch had begun to produce horses which, by all accounts, bore a distinct resemblance to the modern Clydesdale, certainly as far as colour was concerned. The stallion Glancer, to whom many Clydesdales can be traced back, was out of a mare known as Lampit's Mare, who was believed to be a

BREED DESCRIPTION

Height Stallions 17.1 – 18hh. Mares 16.3 – 17.2hh

Colour Bay, brown or black. Chestnut is rare. Often with a good deal of white on the face and legs, which may run up on to the body, particularly as flashes on the stomach.

Conformation Strong, intelligent head, with broad forehead, wide muzzle, large nostrils, bright, clear eyes and big ears; long, well-arched neck; sloping shoulders with high withers; short back with well-sprung ribs and muscular hindquarters; straight limbs with forelegs set well under the shoulders, long pasterns and a fair amount of fine feather; round, open feet.

■ ABOVE
Large, kind eyes and big ears give these Clydesdales the gentle, sensible expression typical of the breed. Unlike the Shire, the Clydesdale never has a Roman nose.

■ LEFT
Although the Clydesdale is closely related to the Shire, it has a number of distinguishing features, the most readily discernible of which is the large amount of white often seen on the limbs and extending up to the lower parts of the body.

Wearing traditional Scottish harness decorations, the Clydesdale makes a fine sight in the show ring.

INTERESTING FACTS

One of the most famous and influential stallions in the development of the Clydesdale was a dark brown horse named Prince of Wales, foaled in Ayrshire in 1866. He was a mixture of English and Scottish blood and had outstanding action. His stud fee of £40, by no means a small sum for those days, was well worth paying – young horses sired by him fetched anywhere from £2,000 to £3,000.

descendant of the Lochlyoch horses.

Shire blood was used in the breed's development – indeed the two leading Clydesdale breeders during the second half of the nineteenth century, Lawrence Drew and David Riddell, believed the Clydesdale and the Shire to be of the same origin, and regularly interbred the two.

The Clydesdale Horse Society was formed in 1877 and the first stud book was published the following year. By this time interest in the breed had spread to other countries and Clydesdales were soon

being exported, often in large numbers, to work the vast wheatlands of North America; others went to Australia, South America and Russia. It was, without doubt, the Clydesdale's docile nature combined with elegance and great activity that endeared it to heavy horse enthusiasts all over the world. Describing his action, the breed society says that the inside of every shoe should be made visible to anyone walking behind. The Clydesdale is an exceptionally sound horse, great emphasis having always been placed on good limbs and feet.

■ RIGHT
Many Clydesdales were exported to North America to work in agriculture. Their descendants can still be seen, though in rather different roles. This team is being used to haul the starting stalls at Santa Anita Racetrack.

Furioso

Hungary has long enjoyed a world-wide reputation as a horse-breeding country and as a producer of fine horsemen. The famous stud farm at Mezöhegyes, founded in 1784 by the Emperor Josef II, quickly became established as one of the great breeding centres of Europe. One of the most important breeds developed there was the Furioso, which was produced by crossing Thoroughbreds with mainly Hungarian mares. The chief influences were the English Thoroughbred stallion, Furioso, after whom the breed was named and who was acquired by Mezöhegyes in 1841, and another English horse, North Star, who was imported during the 1850s. Using these two bloodlines Mezöhegyes began producing quality carriage horses and good, heavyweight riding horses. For a time these two bloodlines were kept separate, with North Star proving a particularly successful sire of harness racehorses. He was descended from the

BREED DESCRIPTION

Height About 16hh.

Colour Any solid colour.

Conformation Fine head (denoting its Thoroughbred ancestry); well-sloped shoulders; strong back; good strong limbs and feet.

1793 Derby winner, Waxy (a grandson of the great Eclipse), and is said to trace back to Norfolk Roadster blood, which could account for his progeny's success in harness. Towards the end of the nineteenth century the North Star and Furioso strains were merged, after which the Furioso became the dominant force.

INTERESTING FACTS

The Csikos horse herders of Hungary are renowned for their trick-riding skills. Their breathtaking displays, often performed with Furioso horses, are famous all over the world.

▌ TOP
The present-day Furioso is a quality all-purpose riding horse, built on somewhat heavier lines than its Thoroughbred ancestors.

▌ LEFT
Large herds of horses, including the Furioso, have traditionally been raised on the grasslands of Hungary.

Nonius

Like the Furioso, the more heavily built Nonius evolved at the Mezöhegyes stud farm founded by the Emperor Josef II. The breed's foundation sire was an Anglo-Norman horse by the name of Nonius Senior. He was foaled in 1810, captured in

BREED DESCRIPTION

Height Large type 15.3 – 16.2hh. Small type 14.3 – 15.3hh.

Colour Predominantly bay, with some black, brown and chestnut.

Conformation Attractive, honest head; sloping shoulders; broad, strong back; strong hindquarters; sound limbs.

France by the Austrians in 1814 and installed at Mezöhegyes in 1816. Nonius was said to be by a half-bred English stallion out of a Norman mare and almost certainly had Norfolk Roadster blood in him. He was by all accounts not the most prepossessing individual and would have won no prizes for conformation, but during his sixteen years at stud he became a tremendously successful sire. Mated with mares of various breeds, including Arab, Lipizzaner, Spanish and Turkish, as well as Hungarian, he produced good quality horses, the best of which were mated back to him. In this way a distinctive type emerged – to be known as the Nonius.

During the 1860s, infusions of Thoroughbred blood were made, a policy which led to the development of two different types of Nonius: one, a large horse suited to light agricultural work and as a carriage horse, the other, a smaller, finer animal suitable for riding. In more recent times, as the need for farm horses diminished, the larger type of Nonius was used mainly for driving, a skill at which Hungarian horsemen have long excelled. Both types of Nonius combine active paces with a calm, willing temperament.

BELOW
The head, though lacking refinement, reflects the breed's kind, tractable nature.

BELOW
Thoroughbred, Norman and Norfolk Roadster blood all played a part in the development of the Nonius. Today's sturdily built individuals make good all-round riding and driving horses.

INTERESTING FACTS

There are two distinct types of harness used for driving purposes. These Nonius horses are wearing breast harness. For pulling heavy loads horses wear collars to enable them to use the full strength of their shoulders.

Hungarian Half-bred

The Hungarians began producing
leisure and sports horses during the
1960s, continuing their tradition of
breeding fine horses. They imported
Hanoverians and Holsteins to cross with
the Furioso and the Gidran in order to
develop an animal suited to modern
requirements. The Gidran, which to all
intents and purposes is the Hungarian
Anglo-Arab, can be traced back to an
Arabian stallion known as Gidran Senior,
imported into Hungary in 1816. Gidran's
son, Gidran II, bred from a Spanish mare,
became the foundation sire of the type
which bears his name.

Initially a variety of mares were
used, but later Thoroughbred blood
was introduced and, subsequently,
more Arab blood. This breeding policy

BREED DESCRIPTION

Height 15.3 – 16hh.

Colour Any solid colour.

Conformation Variable, but usually well
proportioned with good, sloping shoulders
and strong hindquarters.

▮ ABOVE LEFT
**Intelligent and spirited, the Hungarian
Half-bred has Arab, Thoroughbred,
Hanoverian, Holstein and native Hungarian
blood in its veins.**

▮ LEFT
**The breed was developed to meet the need
for a modern competition horse. Good
overall conformation and strong, sound
limbs and feet are therefore essential.**

INTERESTING FACTS

The Hungarian Half-bred has a good temperament which lends itself to training for a wide variety of activities – as this daring trick riding display proves.

LEFT
Speed, stamina and a ground-covering stride make the half-bred a suitable partner for the tough sport of three-day eventing.

BELOW
Hungarian Half-breds have achieved their greatest competition successes in the gruelling sport of four-in-hand driving. They have been exported to many countries for this purpose.

resulted in a quality horse with a good, ground-covering gallop. The breed was developed at Hungary's chief studs – the old-established one at Mezöhegyes; the Kisber, named after the Hungarian-bred horse who won the British Derby in 1876, and the Kecskemet, which is famous for its cross-bred driving horses, based on Lipizzaner and trotter blood.

Hungarian Half-breds have achieved outstanding success in the sport of inter-national four-in-hand driving, where they have competed not just in the hands of the traditionally dashing and skilful Hungarian drivers but also for a number of other European nations, notably Switzerland and Britain.

Shagya

The Shagya is a strain of Arabian horse bred in Hungary and descended from a stallion of the same name. Shagya was a Syrian-bred horse, foaled in 1830 and imported to the Hungarian stud at Babolna some six years later. Shagya was used to cover quality mares which, although they were of mixed blood (including Hungarian, Thoroughbred and Spanish, as well as Arabian) were distinctly "eastern" in overall appearance. By employing the practice of inbreeding, the Babolna Stud produced the distinctive type of Arab horse seen today. The Shagya is rather taller and has a noticeably bigger frame than other Arabs (Shagya himself

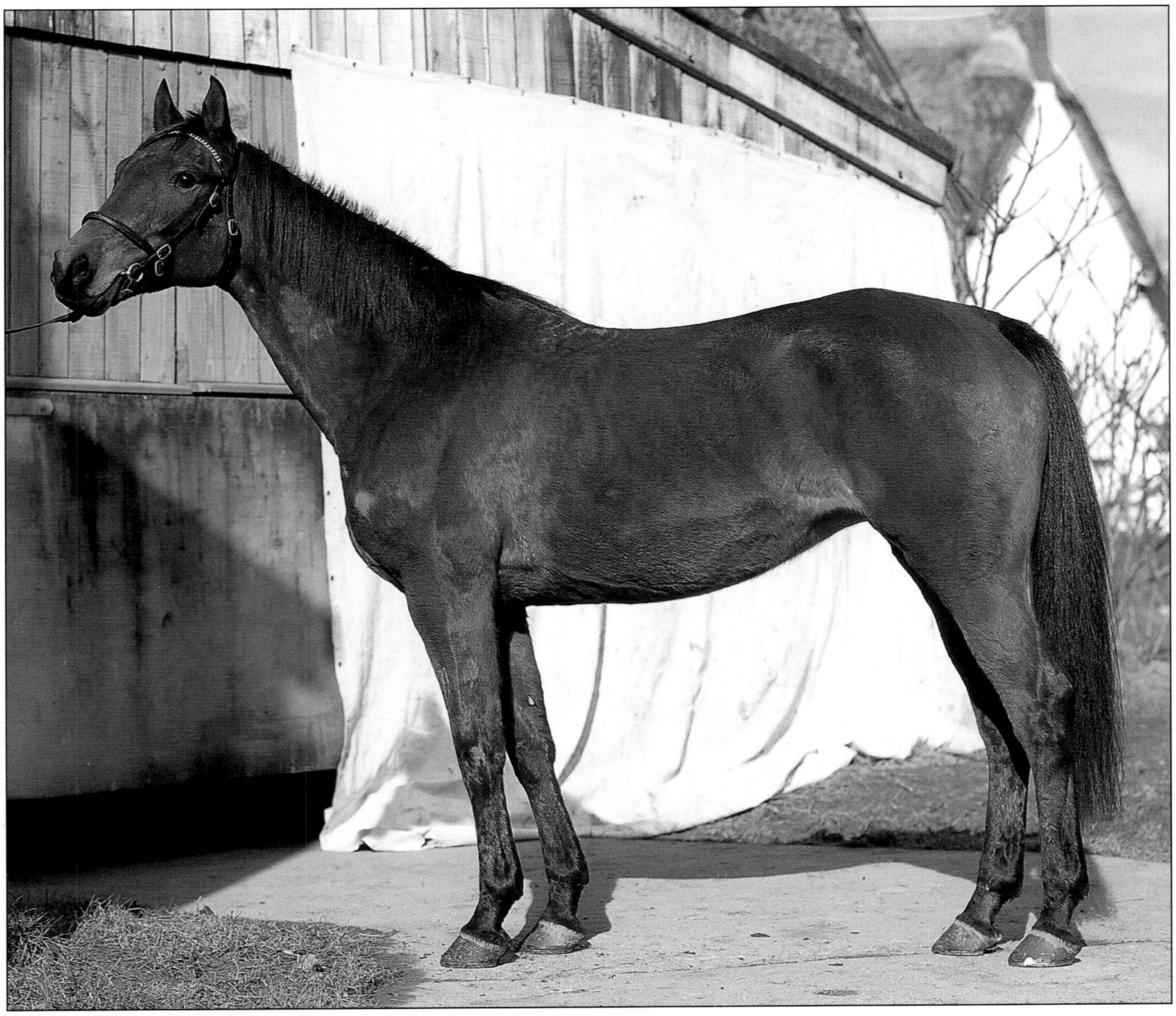

■ ABOVE LEFT
The wide-set eyes and tapered muzzle, with its large nostrils, are typical of the Shagya.

■ LEFT
The Shagya tends to have a rather more substantial frame than the pure-bred Arab, though its overall outline is very similar.

INTERESTING FACTS

The Babolna Stud, home of the Shagya Arab, was founded in 1789 by the Emperor Joseph II. Hungary has one of the oldest traditions of organized horse breeding in the world, its first recorded stud (founded by Prince Arpad, who died in 907) dating back more than 1,000 years. During the mid-eighteenth century horse breeding began to slip into a gradual decline and it was Joseph II who was largely responsible for revitalizing it. He founded the Veterinary College in Budapest, decreed the building of the famous Mezőhegyes stud farm in 1785 and subsequently Babolna, thus paving the way for the golden age that Hungarian horses enjoyed during the nineteenth century.

BREED DESCRIPTION

Height 14 – 15hh.

Colour Predominantly grey but all other Arab colours occur.

Conformation Refined head, with dished profile, small, tapered muzzle and large eyes; elegant, curved neck; sloping shoulders; short, slightly concave back with strong loins, level croup and high-set tail; good, strong limbs with especially good, well-formed feet.

was a little taller than normal for an Arab, standing over 15.2hh). But the overall appearance, with its beautiful, dished face, large eyes, short back and high-set tail, are all characteristic of the pure-bred Arab. Combining toughness with elegance, the Shagya was bred as a riding horse and found favour as a cavalry mount in the days before mechanization. Nowadays it is bred for leisure riding and is exported to a number of countries.

▪ **ABOVE**
Mares and foals at the Babolna Stud in Hungary, home of the Shagya Arab. Babolna was founded by Royal decree more than 200 years ago.

▪ **BELOW**
Grey is the breed's predominant colour, although all other Arab colours also occur. Shagya Arabs often stand a little taller than their pure-bred relatives.

Icelandic

■ BELOW
The tremendously thick mane and forelock give
much needed protection against the severe weather
conditions of the northern winters.

■ BOTTOM
Stocky and compact, with short, strong limbs and
notably hard, sound feet, the Icelandic horse is
perfectly adapted to its harsh environment.

The little Icelandic horse is probably
the purest horse breed in the world. Its
ancestors were taken to Iceland by ninth-
century settlers, travelling from western
Norway and the north of Britain. They
were small, sturdy horses who adapted well
to the rigorous Icelandic climate. Later
some imports were made of eastern
horses, but these had such a detrimental
effect upon the original stock that in
AD 930 the Althing (parliament) passed a
law forbidding the import of further
horses. Although this law seems to have
been flouted occasionally, for the last 800
years there have been no infusions of
outside blood. As a result the Icelandic

horse has changed little since the age of
the Vikings.

It is an outstandingly tough, weather-
resistant little horse (although it stands no
more than 13.2hh it is always referred to
by the Icelanders as a horse, not a pony).
A strong swimmer – there were no bridges
over Iceland's numerous turbulent rivers
until the beginning of this century – it is
also remarkably sure-footed. It can be seen
carrying a full-grown man at speed, with
ease and safety, over mountainous terrain
during the traditional autumn sheep
round-ups.

Some Icelandic horses are noted for
their keen sense of direction and

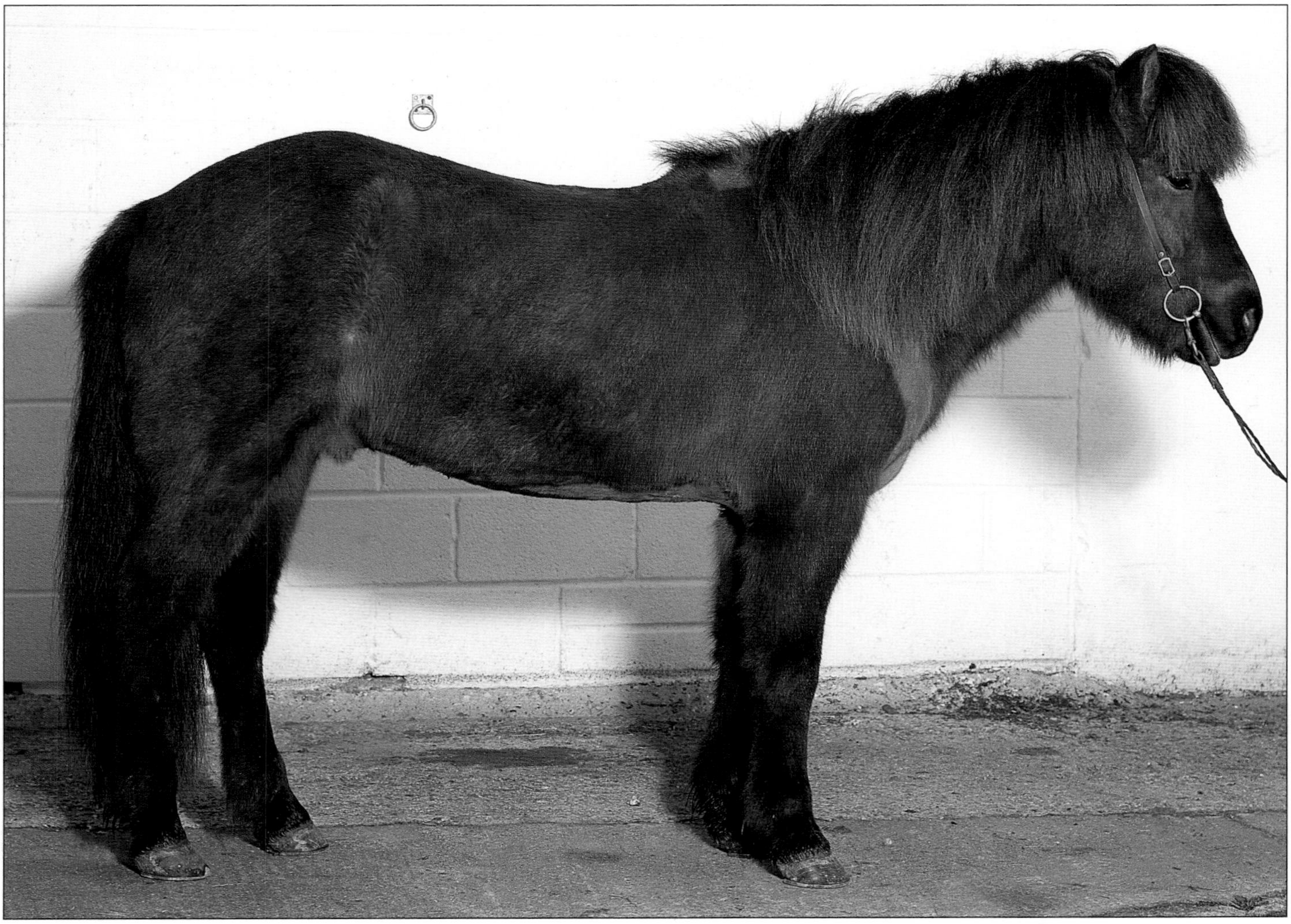

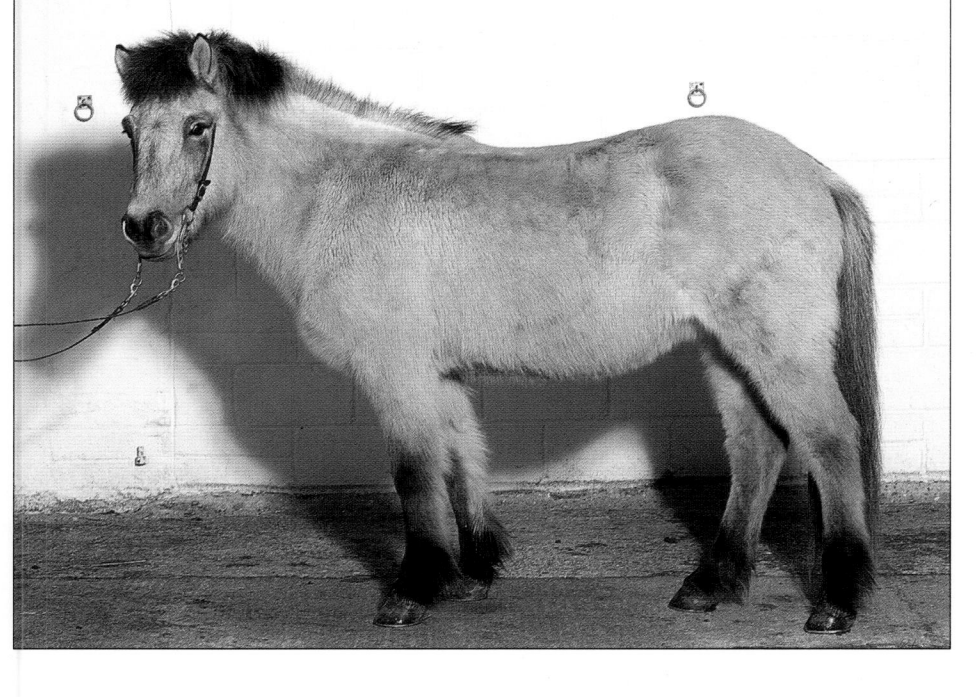

BREED DESCRIPTION

Height 12.3 – 13.2hh.

Colour Any.

Conformation Fairly heavy head; short, well-carried neck; compact body with short back and deep girth; sloping, wedge-shaped, very strong, muscular hindquarters; strong limbs with short cannons and strong hocks; strong, well-shaped feet.

extraordinary homing instinct. After the annual round-up, while sheep are penned and sorted into each farmer's flock, horses are often turned loose and will set off alone down the valleys to their homes. There are also many recorded instances of horses that have been sold to another part of the country travelling for weeks to return to their original homes.

While some local selection of breeding stock probably took place from time to time, it was not until 1879 that Iceland undertook a practical selective breeding programme. It was begun in Skagafjördur, the country's most famous horse-breeding area. Conformation is naturally taken into account, but it is the quality of the horse's gaits which is of prime importance. These are: the fetgangur (walk), the brökk (trot – used when crossing rough country), the stökk (gallop), the skeid (lateral pace – used to cover short distances at high speed) and the tölt (a running walk used to cover broken ground). The tölt is a gait of four equal beats – the sequence being near hind, near fore, off hind, off fore – with which the horse achieves great speed.

■ BELOW
Notwithstanding its diminutive size, the breed
is immensely strong and fast. It is a popular
all-round riding horse in many countries outside
its native Iceland.

INTERESTING FACTS

In days gone by horse fights were a popular form of entertainment in Iceland. Playing on the natural instinct of stallions to fight each other for possession of a mare, Icelanders would set two specially trained stallions against one another, using goads to urge them on. This pastime was so dangerous that it was a common occurrence for handlers to be injured or even killed.

Irish Draught

Irish horses are renowned for being the best hunters in the world and none more so than those produced by crossing the Thoroughbred with the versatile Irish Draught. Although there are no early formal records or stud books, Ireland's light draught horse is known to trace back many centuries, to the time when Norman horses were introduced to Ireland and crossed with the native animals, which at

that time were small of stature. Later infusions of Andalusian – and, probably, eastern – blood helped improve the overall quality (and height) of the Irish horses. The result was

very much an all-round horse, totally suited to the Irish country way of life: capable of working on the small Irish farms but active enough to be harnessed to a trap or to carry a rider safely across country. The modern Irish Draught is generally accepted to have evolved from the crossing of imported Thoroughbred stallions with the best of these country-bred mares. The numbers of these splendid horses declined in Ireland following the famine of 1847 and some heavy horses were introduced from Britain, but this tended to lead to a coarsening of the Irish Draught. To save the best of the remaining stock, in the early years of this century a scheme of subsidies was introduced by the government, for approved stallions of Irish Draught and hunter type. As a result the active, clean-legged general-purpose

RIGHT
Substance and plenty of bone are the hallmarks of the modern Irish Draught. The conformation should incorporate all the features of the correctly built riding horse.

BREED DESCRIPTION

Height Stallions 16hh and over. Mares 15.2hh and over.

Colour All solid colours.

Conformation Small, intelligent head; sloping shoulders; strong body with deep chest and oval rib cage; powerful hindquarters; strong limbs with plenty of flat bone and no feather.

■ LEFT
As a safe conveyance across the most testing of hunting countries, there is nothing to beat the Irish Draught and the Irish Draught/ Thoroughbred cross.

■ BELOW LEFT
The international show jumper Mill Pearl: a good example of the Irish Draught cross with the ability to perform at the highest level.

■ BELOW
The breed possesses good, natural balance and the action is straight and true.

Irish Draught horse survived and in 1917 the Department of Agriculture introduced "a scheme to establish a Book for Horses of the Irish Draught type", in which 375 mares and 44 stallions were entered as being suitable and sound. The Irish Draught Horse Society was formed in 1976.

The excellence of Irish-bred horses owes much to the limestone pastures on which they are raised. The mineral-rich land contributes to the growth of strong bone and the production of good, up-standing animals. Today's Irish Draught has plenty of substance but is also an attractive looking, well-balanced, quality horse, with straight, athletic action. It is noted for its intelligence and kind temperament. It has an inherent ability to cross the most testing of hunting country with total assurance and because of its jumping prowess is a successful producer of top-level show jumpers.

INTERESTING FACTS

Since World War II many of the world's leading show-jumping horses have been Irish bred, with a fair percentage being by registered Irish Draught stallions. One of the most famous names in show-jumping breeding is King of Diamonds, an Irish Draught who sired many famous horses, including Special Envoy – who has jumped with great success for Brazil, ridden first by Nelson Pessoa then by his son Rodrigo – and Mill Pearl, ridden by the United States Olympic champion Joe Fargis.

Maremmano

Maremmano horses are bred in Tuscany and are the traditional mounts of the *butteri*, or cattlemen. Maremma, a coastal tract on the Tyrrhenian Sea extending from Piombino to Orbetello, is a former marshland which was drained in ancient times but later reverted to being an unhealthy wasteland. Drainage was reintroduced earlier this century and the area is now used as pastureland.

The origins of the Maremmano horses are obscure but it is likely that they are descended from the Neapolitan horses (founded on Arab, Barb and Spanish

■ RIGHT
The Maremmano is a strong horse possessed of a quiet temperament, and although not particularly speedy it makes a useful all-round riding horse.

blood) made famous in the sixteenth century by Federico Grisone. Grisone was the founder of the Neapolitan riding academy and regarded as the first of the great classical riding masters after the

Greek, Xenophon (c. 430–350 BC). A good deal of outcrossing took place later – some involving imported English horses, including the Norfolk Roadster – so that the horses which became known as the

■ RIGHT
The Maremmano is a strong horse possessed of a quiet temperament, and although not particularly speedy it makes a useful all-round riding horse.

■ LEFT
Maremmano horses vary a good deal in type and conformation. This horse is much more refined than many examples of the breed, with an especially elegant head.

▮ BELOW
A Maremmano wearing the traditional tack of the *buttero*, or Italian cowboy. Its toughness and reliability make the breed an ideal mount for working with cattle.

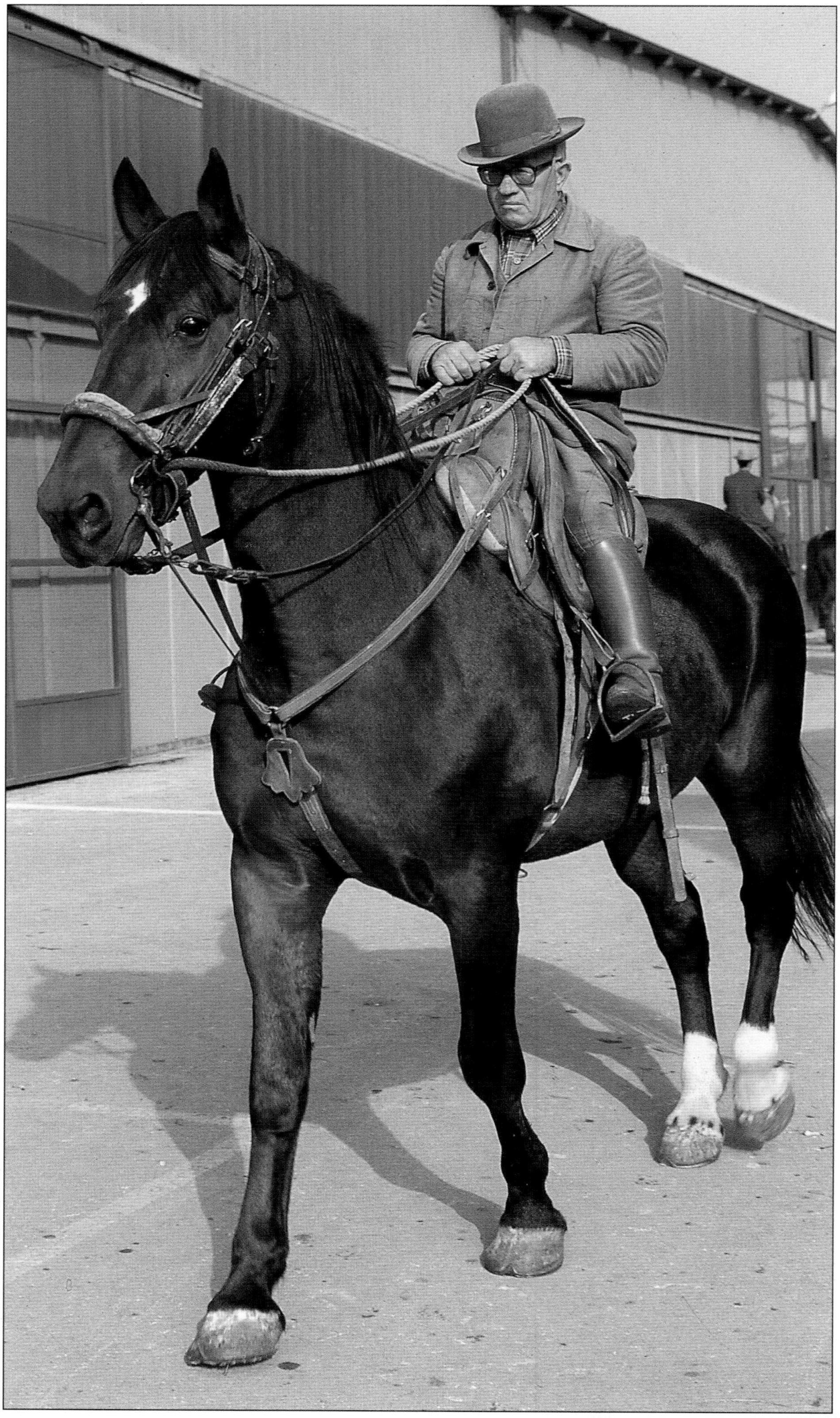

BREED DESCRIPTION

Height Variable, usually around 15.3hh.

Colour Any solid colour.

Conformation Variable. Overall appearance somewhat coarse, with rather upright shoulders, flat withers and low-set tail, though conformational improvements are being made through the introduction of Thoroughbred blood.

Maremmano were something of a mixture and of no fixed type. By no means the most beautiful looking of horses, nor the speediest, they are nevertheless good, honest workers, combining strength and toughness with a calm temperament. Amenable by nature and economical to feed, they have proved useful as army and police horses, as well as in agriculture – they are strong enough to perform light draught work – and cattle herding.

INTERESTING FACTS

During the seventeenth century Italy became one of the world leaders for horse breeding. Most famous of all was the Neapolitan, of which the Maremmano is possibly a descendant.

Murgese

Originating from the Orfano plain and the hill districts near Gravina, the original Murgese horse can be traced back at least 500 years. During the late fifteenth and early sixteenth centuries the governor of the port of Monopoli, which for some years belonged to the Venetian Republic, kept a stock of Murgese stallions and several hundred brood mares in order to provide remounts for the cavalry. However, somewhere down the years the breed died out and the modern version dates only from the 1920s.

The Murgese is basically a light draught horse, though inferior in quality to the Irish Draught and showing no great uniformity of type. It can be ridden, but a better stamp of riding horse is produced by putting a Murgese mare to a Thoroughbred or warmblood stallion, the latter giving the progeny more quality, and paces better suited to a saddle horse.

BREED DESCRIPTION

Height 15 – 16hh.

Colour Usually chestnut, though other solid colours occur.

Conformation Variable. Overall appearance suggests a light draught horse. The head tends to be plain, though with an honest expression, and the hindquarters rather poor, with a low-set tail.

▌ **ABOVE**
Although basically best suited to light draught work, the Murgese can make a useful riding horse. This example of the breed has been fully trained as a police horse.

▌ **TOP LEFT**
Although the predominant coat colouring is chestnut, some dark colours do occur.

▌ **LEFT**
The Murgese is Italy's breed of light draught horse. However, it lacks definitive type and the overall quality of the light draught horse of Ireland.

■ BOTTOM LEFT
The head is small with a straight profile. The eyes
are large and bright, the ears small and mobile.

■ BELOW
Chestnut coat colouring with a flaxen mane and tail
is typical of this attractive breed. It has inherited
the active paces of the Breton, which had an
important influence on its development.

Italian Heavy Draught

Italy's premier heavy horse, the Italian
Heavy Draught – also known as the
Agricultural Heavy Horse – bears a distinct
resemblance to the handsome Breton,
which has had an important influence
upon its development. The Italian Heavy
Draught originated at Ferrara in the north
of the country during the second half of
the nineteenth century, when Neapolitan
blood was crossed with Arab and Hackney

BREED DESCRIPTION

Height Stallions 15 – 16hh.
Mares 14 – 15hh.

Colour Predominantly chestnut with flaxen
mane and tail. Occasionally dark bay.

Conformation Square head with broad
forehead, large eyes and nostrils and small,
mobile ears; muscular, slightly arched neck;
well-sloped shoulders; deep chest, short,
strong back with broad, slightly sloping
croup; short strong limbs with muscular
forearms and large joints, short pasterns and
large, well-shaped feet.

to produce an active, lightweight
workhorse. In due course the need arose
both for a heavier agricultural animal and
a heavy artillery horse, and breeders
accordingly began introducing new blood,
notably Boulonnais. Then, in the 1920s,
pure-bred Breton stallions were used to
establish the stamp of horse now known as
the Italian Heavy Draught.

An attractive looking horse, stocky and
muscular in build, the Italian Heavy
Draught is noted for its conformation and
active paces. It is capable of maintaining a
good speed even when pulling heavy
loads. The limbs are short and very strong
with well-developed muscles and large
joints. Although the need for draught
horses has decreased in Italy, as elsewhere,
the Italian Heavy Draught can still be seen
at work on some of the smaller farms, and
is also used for meat production.

INTERESTING FACTS

A stud book for Italian Draught Horses was
opened in 1961. Horses accepted for
registration are branded on the nearside of
the hindquarters with the breed mark, a
five-runged ladder within a shield.

Friesian

The Friesian is one of Europe's oldest horses and down the centuries it has had an influence on a number of other breeds, notably the Oldenburg in Germany and Britain's Fell and Dales ponies. The breed's homeland is Friesland, in the

■ LEFT
The Friesian's friendly disposition is evident in its kind but alert expression. The rather long head is set on a well-arched neck.

north of the Netherlands. The remains of an ancient coldblood type of heavy horse have been unearthed there, from which the modern Friesian is believed to be descended. Eastern blood, introduced into the Netherlands during the time of

BREED DESCRIPTION

Height 15 – 16hh.

Colour Always black.

Conformation Rather long head, with short ears and alert expression; elegant, arched neck with long, flowing mane; powerful shoulders; strong, compact body with strong, sloping hindquarters and rather low-set, very full, tail; short, strong limbs with good bone and a fair amount of feather.

■ RIGHT
Excellent overall conformation is the hallmark of the breed. The body is compact, the limbs strong and the feet hard and sound.

LEFT
An attractive turnout
much appreciated
throughout its native
land: a Friesian driven
to a traditional high-
wheeled gig.

BELOW
Appreciation of
Friesians is not
restricted to Holland.
This handsome team
was pictured in a busy
London street.

INTERESTING FACTS

The Friesians' noble bearing makes them
ideal for ceremonial occasions. These
horses were part of a six-strong team pulling
the Dutch Royal Carriage at the opening
ceremony of the 1994 World Equestrian
Games in The Hague.

the Crusades, had an influence on the development of the Friesian, as did the Andalusian during the Eighty Years' War, when the Netherlands were occupied by the Spanish. The Friesian horse which thus developed was an active all-rounder, suitable for work on the land but, because of its ability to trot at speed, also useful as a harness horse and for riding.

During the nineteenth century, when trotting became extremely popular, breeders sought to improve the Friesian's already active, high-stepping trot, by outcrossing to trotters. This led to the Friesian becoming lighter in build and less useful as a farm horse. By the beginning of World War I its numbers were seriously depleted and the decline continued between the wars. However, lack of fuel during World War II led to a revival in the breed's fortunes as farmers once again turned to it for draught work.

During the second half of this century there has been a resurgence of interest in the breed and it is now very popular as a carriage horse. A well-balanced horse with proud bearing, the Friesian looks exceptionally attractive when pulling a traditional high-wheeled Friesian gig. The breed is noted for its kind temperament.

Gelderland

A number of different breeds went into the making of the Gelderland, which comes from the region of the same name in the central Netherlands and was developed during the nineteenth century. Native mares were crossed with, among others, English, French, German, Hungarian and Polish stallions to produce a good stamp of dual-purpose horse, one that was big and strong enough to do farm work or pull a carriage but not so heavy that it could not be used for riding. Hackney blood was also used in a

■ LEFT
Strong and active, the Gelderland makes an excellent carriage horse and has also played a part in the development of Holland's remarkably successful competition horse, the Dutch Warmblood.

breeding programme that was noted for its well-founded principles of selection, only horses that had proved themselves to be good, sound workers being used at stud. As mechanization spread, and horses were needed less for use on the land, breeders introduced Thoroughbred blood to lighten the Gelderland.

A typical carriage type of horse, the modern Gelderland, with its excellent

shoulders and good, free action, has been used successfully in the sport of four-in-hand driving and has also provided one of the main bases for the production of the Netherlands' sports horse, the Dutch Warmblood.

INTERESTING FACTS

The Gelderland is one of two types of all-purpose horse developed in the Netherlands, the other being its northern neighbour, the Gröningen. The Gröningen is somewhat heavier than the Gelderland. It has Friesian and Oldenburg blood in its ancestry, as well as some Suffolk Punch. Like the Gelderland, it has played an important part in the development of the Dutch Warmblood.

■ RIGHT
Good shoulders are a characteristic of Gelderland conformation, ensuring free movement at all paces.

BREED DESCRIPTION

Height About 16hh.

Colour Predominantly chestnut, sometimes bay or grey.

Conformation Rather plain, sensible looking head, with a tendency to a convex profile; strong neck; good shoulders, with fairly low withers; fairly long but strong body with good depth through the girth; powerful hindquarters with high-set tail; short, strong limbs with good, sound feet.

Dutch Warmblood

The production of the Netherlands' highly successful leisure and competition horse began with the selection of the best Gelderland and Gröningen mares, who were then mated with Thoroughbred stallions. The latter, also carefully selected, were imported from all over the world, including Britain, Ireland, France and the United States. Many of these came from the best racing lines, a fact which was to prove highly beneficial: as time went on Dutch breeders found that the stallions

BREED DESCRIPTION

Height 16 – 17hh.

Colour Any solid colour, with bay and brown the most usual.

Conformation Quality head, with alert, intelligent expression; good, sloping shoulders with pronounced withers; strong back and hindquarters; good, sound limbs, with plenty of bone and short cannons; good, sound feet.

who produced the best warmbloods had themselves enjoyed successful racing careers. In addition to Thoroughbreds, some Trakehner stallions were used in the early years, and a number of Holstein mares were imported and put to Gelderland or Gröningen stallions. Later on warmbloods of the type which the Dutch breeders were seeking to develop, such as the Holstein and Selle Français, were introduced into the breeding programme, and a dash of Hanoverian and Westphalian blood was added. At the same time there was a gradual decrease in the amount of Gelderland and Gröningen blood used. The result is a riding horse of harmonious proportions, with straight, true action, an easy, ground-covering stride at all paces and a good temperament.

■ LEFT
Milton is a grandson of the Trakehner Marco Polo, one of the most influential Dutch Warmblood stallions.

INTERESTING FACTS

One of the most important stallions in the breeding of Dutch Warmbloods was the Trakehner Marco Polo (1965–1976). By the Thoroughbred Poet, he was only small but he produced some top-class show jumpers. They included Marius, who was ridden with great international success by Britain's Caroline Bradley. In Britain Marius combined his competitive career with stud duties and had the distinction of siring Milton, the world's most successful show jumper.

Dutch breeders use a highly efficient, performance-based selection system to produce their horses and, despite its relative newness, the Dutch Warmblood has already demonstrated the correctness of their approach by achieving success at top international level in dressage, show jumping and carriage driving. Dutch Warmbloods have been used in the establishment of other warmblood strains, too, notably in Britain, the United States, Australia and New Zealand.

■ LEFT
The Dutch Warmblood is a quality horse possessed of a good temperament. The correct proportions of its conformation result in excellent action, thus ensuring its suitability for modern competitive sports.

Lusitano

As its appearance suggests, the Portuguese Lusitano is a close relative of the Andalusian in neighbouring Spain. Indeed, until quite recent times the horses bred on the Iberian peninsula were regarded as being one and the same. It was not until the early years of the twentieth century that the two countries decided to establish independent stud books.

Since opening their own stud book the Portuguese have made great strides in monitoring and improving their breeding programme. They have been diligent in preserving the Lusitano's greatly admired qualities of strength and courage. These attributes led to the breed being very highly esteemed as a warhorse (the best Iberian horses have always been bred along the long frontier between

Portugal and Spain where endless battles were fought).

These same qualities also make the Lusitano an ideal mount for the demanding sport of mounted bullfighting. In Portugal, where it is considered a disgrace for a horse to be injured during a bullfight, the horses are extremely well

trained, using their inherent powers of acceleration and manoeuvrability to evade the bull.

As they have proved down the centuries, Lusitano horses are most amenable to training. Intelligent, gentle and affectionate, they work hard and enthusiastically. Possessed of good natural

BREED DESCRIPTION

Height Generally 15.1 – 15.3hh. Some horses reach over 16hh.

Colour Often grey or bay, but any true colour is found, including dun and chestnut.

Conformation Long, noble head, typically with a convex profile, finely curved nose and large, generous eyes; powerful, arched neck, deep at the base and set at a slightly wide angle to the shoulders, giving the impression of being fairly upright; powerful shoulders; short-coupled body with deep rib cage, broad, powerful loins, gently sloping croup and rather low-set tail; fine, clean legs with excellent dense bone; abundant silky mane and tail.

▪ **ABOVE LEFT**
This noble head and powerful, arched neck are characteristic of the Lusitano. The breed is also noted for its silky mane and tail.

▪ **LEFT**
The overall outline of the Lusitano is virtually the same as that of its close relative, the Andalusian.

■ BELOW
The bay colouring of this mare at the Alter Stud is typical of the Alter Real Lusitanos.

■ BOTTOM
Portugal's horses are renowned for their muscular strength, great impulsion and elevated paces.

INTERESTING FACTS

The Lusitano horse gives an exceptionally smooth, comfortable ride. Agile and intelligent, it makes the ideal mount for the mounted bullfighter.

■ BELOW
The bay colouring of this mare at the Alter Stud is typical of the Alter Real Lusitanos.

balance and with agile, elevated paces, they give a smooth comfortable ride. With their proud bearing and tremendous joie de vivre they have, not surprisingly, always excelled at high school work. However, it is not only in the manège that the breed excels. More and more Lusitanos are proving themselves well suited to modern sports such as show jumping and carriage driving. People who work with them testify to the great understanding which quickly develops between horse and human.

ALTER REAL

The Alter Real is not a distinct breed but an offshoot of the Lusitano. It takes its name from the town of Alter do Chão, in the Portuguese province of Alentejo, the world "real" meaning royal in Portuguese. The royal stud founded at Alter supplied the royal manège in Lisbon with high-school and carriage horses. The stud flourished for many years, producing a fine line of horses which were valued not

only in Portugal but all over the Peninsula. However, the stud's progress suffered serious interruption on a number of occasions, notably during the Peninsular War, and the Alter Real horses went into decline. Attempts to resurrect the strain towards the end of the nineteenth century by importing English, Norman and German blood were not successful, nor was a subsequent attempt, using Arab horses. Through the introduction of Andalusian blood at the end of the century, the Alter Real Lusitanos were finally re-established but after the fall of the monarchy in the early twentieth century, many horses were sold or destroyed. The Alter Real line would have died out but for the efforts of the d'Andrade family, who during the early 1940s saved two stallions and a handful of mares and instigated a breeding programme. Today the Alter Stud is state run and again produces horses for high school work. The Alter Real is essentially a Lusitano, although it is always bay, brown or black in colour.

Bashkir

The small Bashkir horse comes from the southern foothills of the Ural mountains, taking its name from the region of Bashkirsky where it is kept in herds. It goes equally well in harness and under saddle and for centuries has been used as a pack and general work horse as well as a supplier of meat and milk. Stockily built,

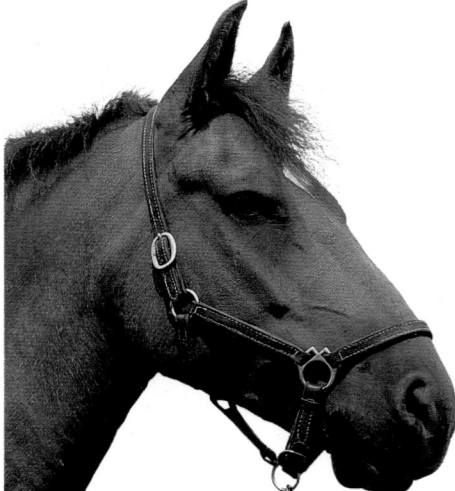

BREED DESCRIPTION

Height 13.3 – 14hh.

Colour Predominantly bay, chestnut and brown.

Conformation Massive head; short, fleshy neck; low withers; wide, deep body with broad, straight back; comparatively short legs with substantial bone; good, hard feet.

with a thick coat, mane and tail, it can survive in the open in temperatures as low as -22° to -40° Fahrenheit (-30° to -40° C). It is able to withstand ferocious blizzard conditions and will dig through snow a metre deep to find food. Furthermore, its tremendously hard feet enable it to work without being shod. The Bashkir is undoubtedly one of the hardiest breeds of horse or pony in the world.

A type of Bashkir also exists in the north-west of the United States, prompting the theory that these horses' ancestors travelled over the former land-bridge between Asia and North America (now the Bering Strait). The horse, however, is generally believed to have become extinct on the North American continent as long ago as the Ice Age and was not reintroduced until Spanish explorers of the modern era "discovered" the land. It is therefore much more likely that the Bashkir was introduced from Russia in fairly recent times.

INTERESTING FACTS

Bashkir mares are renowned for their milk yields. During the lactation period of some seven to eight months, a mare will produce upwards of 330 gallons (1,500 litres). In a number of areas of the former USSR horses are still run in herds and their milk is used to produce the fermented liquor known as kumis, which is both drunk by the local herdsmen and bottled on a large scale for consumption elsewhere.

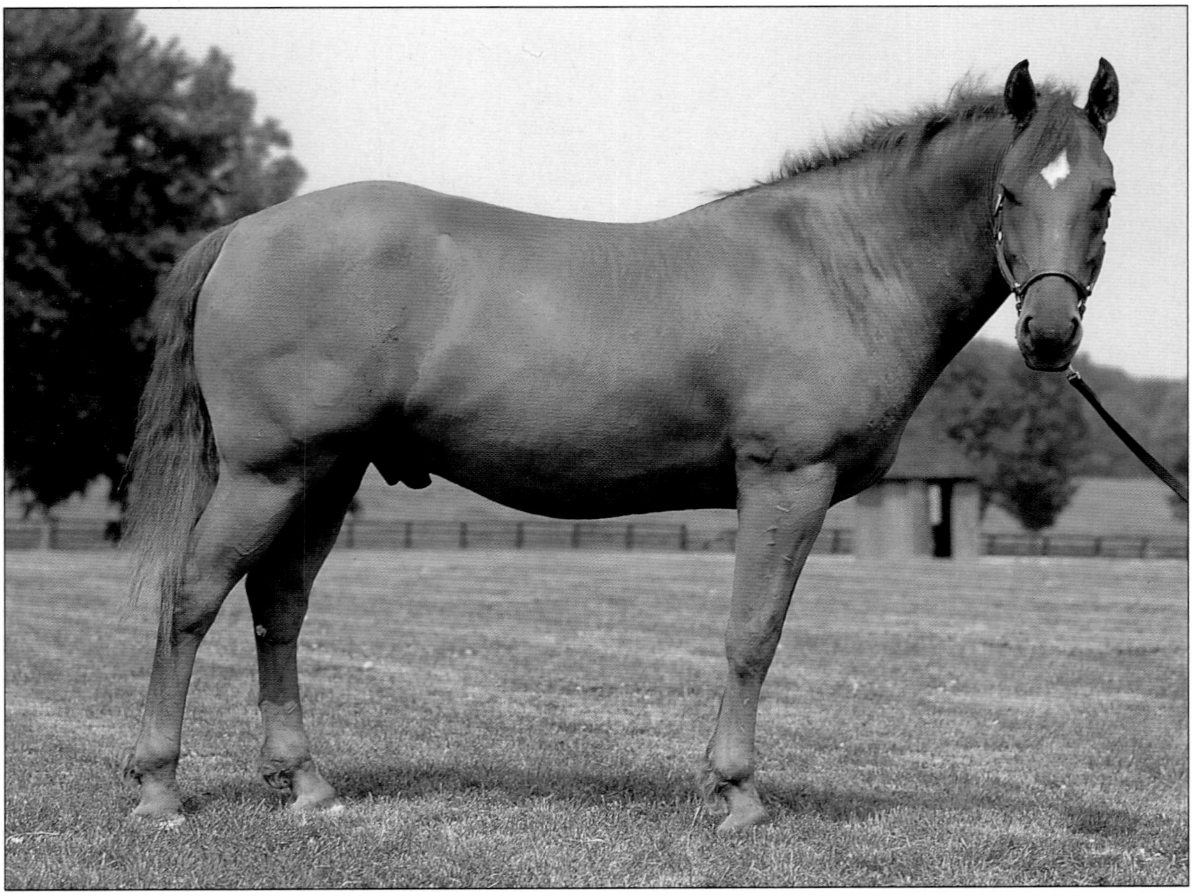

ABOVE LEFT
The Bashkir's head is heavily built and set on a short, fleshy neck. The chest is broad.

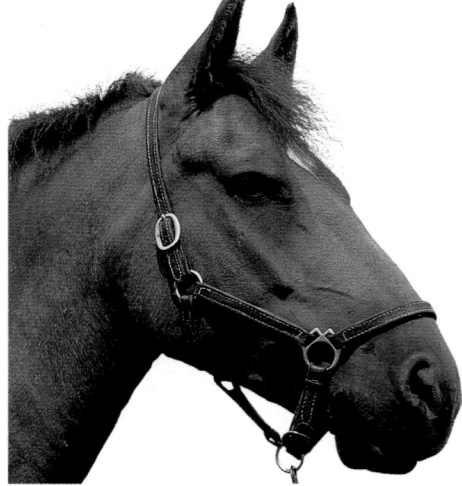

LEFT
With its stocky build, short strong limbs and exceptionally hard feet, the Bashkir is well equipped for life in a harsh environment – though, as this picture shows, it also thrives in less rigorous surroundings.

Don

INTERESTING FACTS

The Don Cossacks were famous for their dashing horsemanship. Riding with short stirrups (a style not adopted in western Europe until much later), they would surprise their foes through the sheer rapidity of their movements. The French General Morand described how they "spring from a state of rest to the full gallop, and at that gallop they make a dead halt: their horses second their skill and seem only part of themselves." They operated in swarms, harassing the enemy rather than charging them, and were particularly skilled in picking off stragglers. With their equally agile horses, they were especially useful for reconnaissance and raiding work.

Don horses were made famous by the Don Cossacks, who between 1812 and 1814 helped drive Napoleon's invading troops from Russia. The Cossacks' horses were descended from those of the nomadic steppe people and were of mixed blood. Early influences would have included the Nagai from Mongolia, the Karabakh (a type of light riding horse), the Turkmen and the Persian Arab. During the nineteenth century infusions of Orlov and Thoroughbred blood were made and outcrosses were also made to the part-bred Arab horses produced at the Strelets Stud in the Ukraine. All these crosses, used to upgrade the old Cossack strain, ceased at the beginning of this century, since when no more outside blood has been used in the breeding of Don horses.

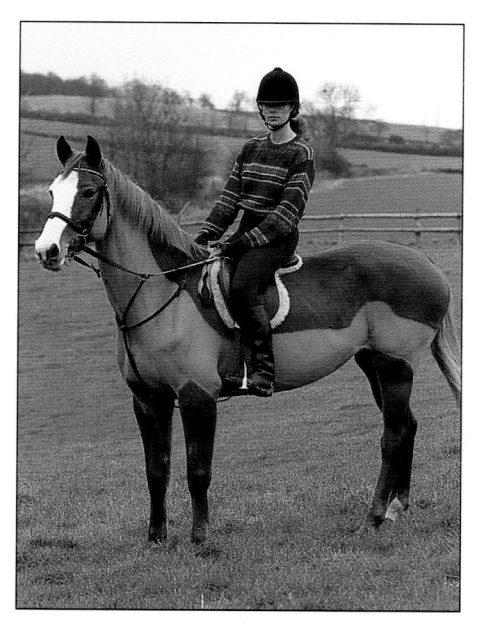

Like most Russian breeds, the Don was traditionally reared in herds on the vast expanses of the steppes, and accordingly developed into a tough individual, capable of thriving with minimal help from humans. It was ideally suited to its original role as an army remount while nowadays it is used for general riding purposes.

Various inherent conformational defects tend to limit the quality of its paces but its strong constitution makes it a suitable mount for endurance riding.

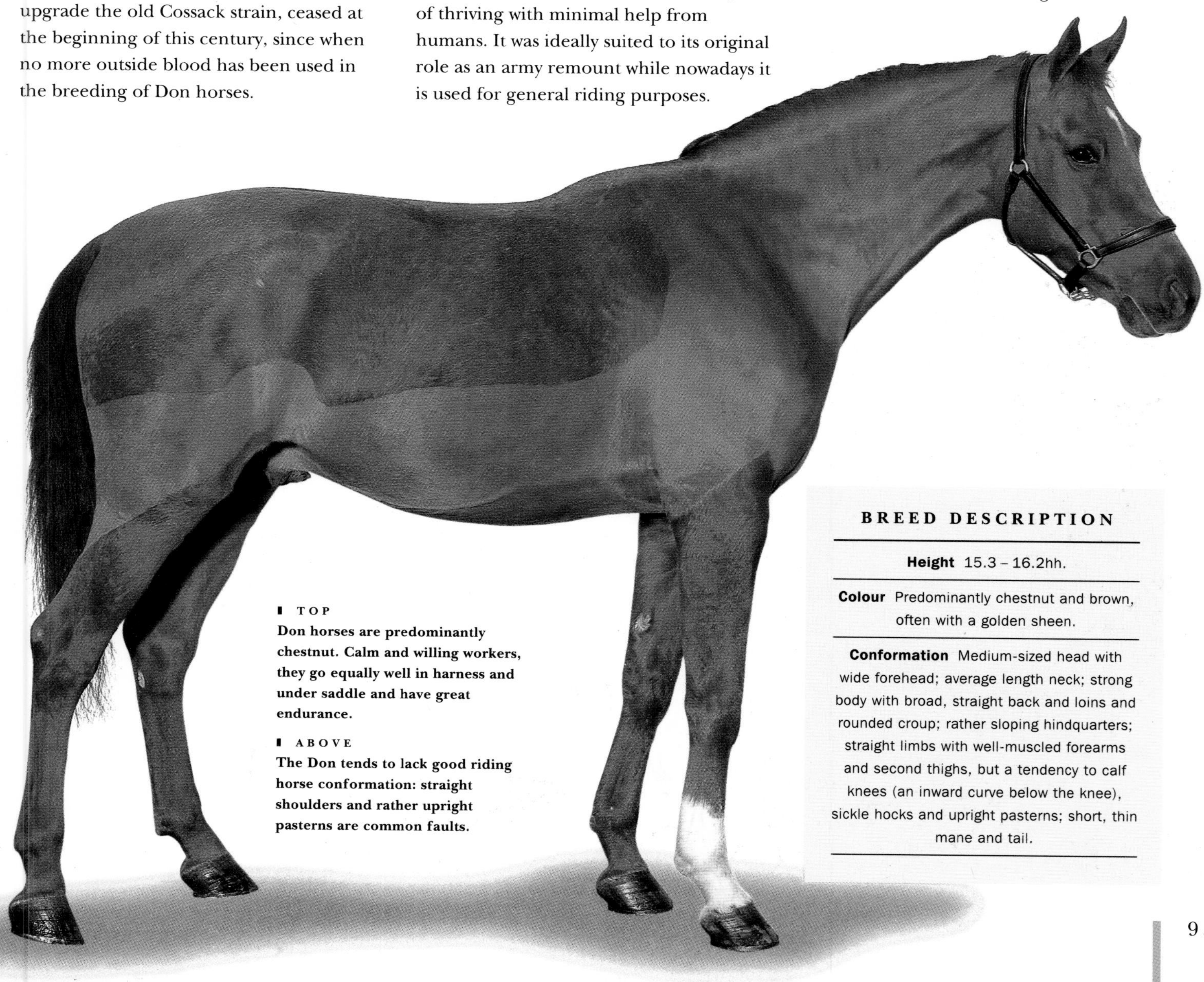

TOP
Don horses are predominantly chestnut. Calm and willing workers, they go equally well in harness and under saddle and have great endurance.

ABOVE
The Don tends to lack good riding horse conformation: straight shoulders and rather upright pasterns are common faults.

BREED DESCRIPTION

Height 15.3 – 16.2hh.

Colour Predominantly chestnut and brown, often with a golden sheen.

Conformation Medium-sized head with wide forehead; average length neck; strong body with broad, straight back and loins and rounded croup; rather sloping hindquarters; straight limbs with well-muscled forearms and second thighs, but a tendency to calf knees (an inward curve below the knee), sickle hocks and upright pasterns; short, thin mane and tail.

Budenny

A breed of relatively recent origin, the Budenny was created by crossing Don and Chernomor mares with Thoroughbred stallions (the Chernomor was the horse used by Cossacks who settled in the Kuban during the eighteenth century and was similar to the Don, though somewhat smaller and lighter in build). The chief purpose was to produce a good army remount, possessed of great endurance. Breeding was centred in the Rostov region, using a process of careful selection. The best mares were bred to the

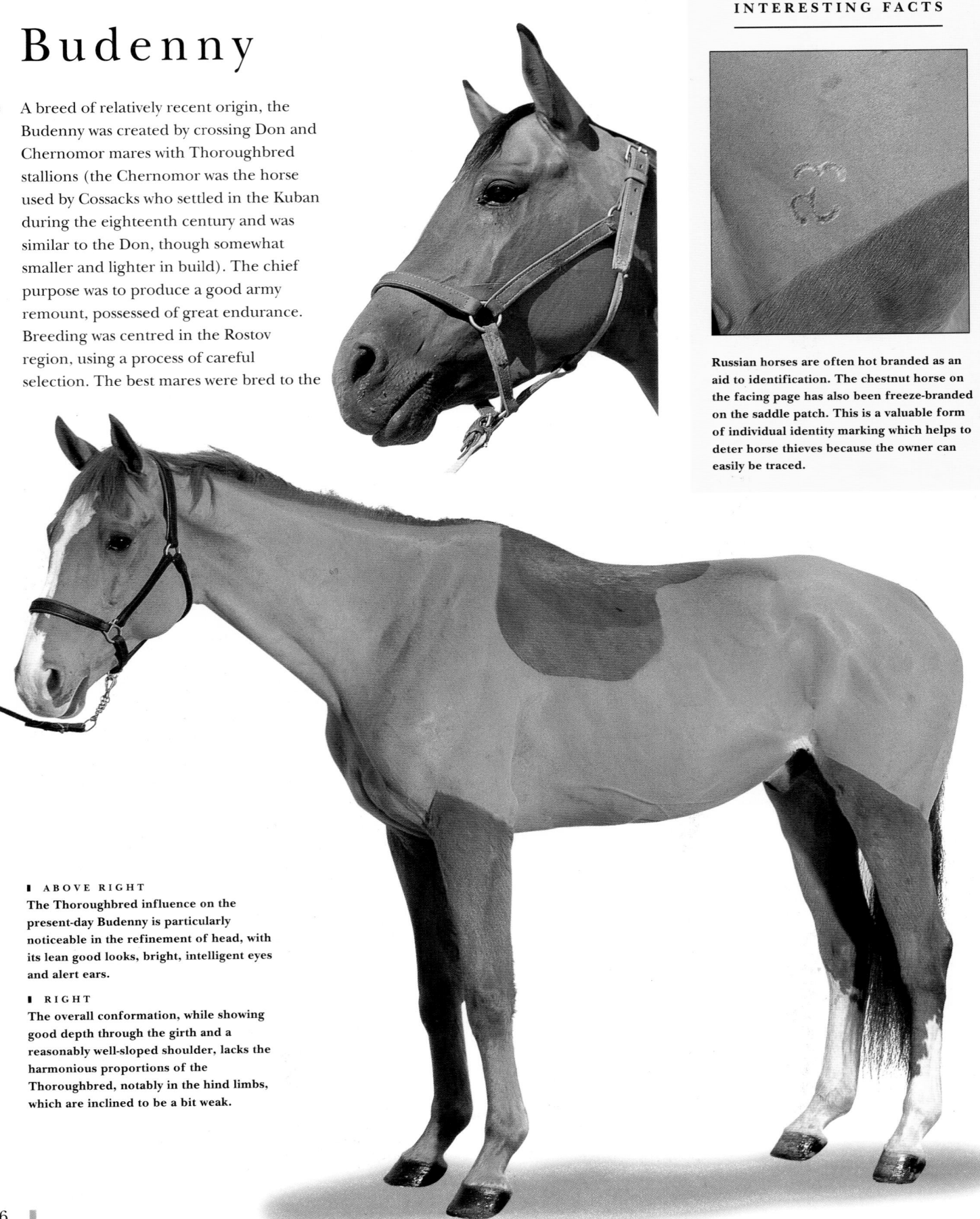

Russian horses are often hot branded as an aid to identification. The chestnut horse on the facing page has also been freeze-branded on the saddle patch. This is a valuable form of individual identity marking which helps to deter horse thieves because the owner can easily be traced.

▪ **ABOVE RIGHT**
The Thoroughbred influence on the present-day Budenny is particularly noticeable in the refinement of head, with its lean good looks, bright, intelligent eyes and alert ears.

▪ **RIGHT**
The overall conformation, while showing good depth through the girth and a reasonably well-sloped shoulder, lacks the harmonious proportions of the Thoroughbred, notably in the hind limbs, which are inclined to be a bit weak.

best Anglo-Don stallions. The brood mares were both well fed and, unusually in Russian horse breeding at the time, stabled during the worst of the winter weather, thus ensuring that they produced better, healthier foals than they might otherwise have done if forced to burn up their resources merely on keeping themselves warm. The young stock were tested on the racecourse between two and four years of age.

The robust constitution of the Don horse and the excellent action of the Thoroughbred proved to be a good combination and as a result the Rostov military stud farm was soon turning out an

BREED DESCRIPTION

Height 16hh.

Colour Predominantly chestnut, some bay and brown. The coats of some Budenny horses have a golden sheen (a throwback to the Chernomor and Don horses).

Conformation Well-proportioned head with straight or slightly concave profile; long, straight neck; reasonably well-sloped shoulders with high withers; comparatively heavy body with short, straight back and long croup; fine, straight limbs, though with a tendency to small joints and rather weak hindlegs; usually well-shaped feet.

upstanding horse, with a tractable nature, which proved suitable for both riding and light draught work. Named the Budenny, it was officially recognized as a breed in 1949.

As the need for army remounts ceased and interest turned to pleasure riding and sport, more Thoroughbred was added to improve the Budenny. Although the Thoroughbred influence is quite evident in the overall light build, the Budenny has a noticeably heavier body while the legs tend to be a bit light on bone. Today the breed is used as a general purpose riding horse, especially in the sports of show jumping, dressage and steeplechasing.

▌ RIGHT
The predominant Budenny coat colouring is chestnut. Some horses have a striking golden sheen.

Kabardin

Sure-footedness and a well-developed sense of self-preservation are the hallmarks of the Kabardin and little wonder, for its home is the northern Caucasus, where it has for centuries been accustomed to carrying men over the toughest mountain terrain. It traces back

BREED DESCRIPTION

Height 15 – 15.2hh.

Colour Predominantly bay, dark bay and black, usually without distinguishing markings.

Conformation Long head, often with Roman-nosed profile, with sharp, mobile ears; well-muscled, medium-long neck; fairly straight shoulders and low withers; strong body, with short, straight back and short, often concave loins; strong limbs, with generally good joints, good bone and short, strong cannons, although the hindlegs tend to be sickle-shaped; good, strong feet; usually long, full mane and tail.

■ RIGHT
Having evolved in the mountains, Kabardin horses are very athletic and well balanced. They make good jumpers.

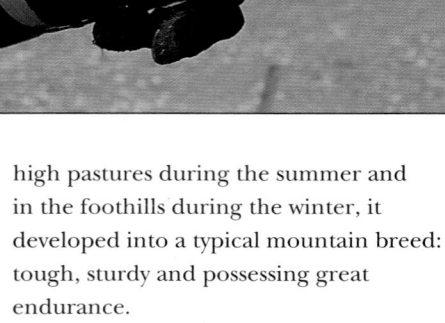

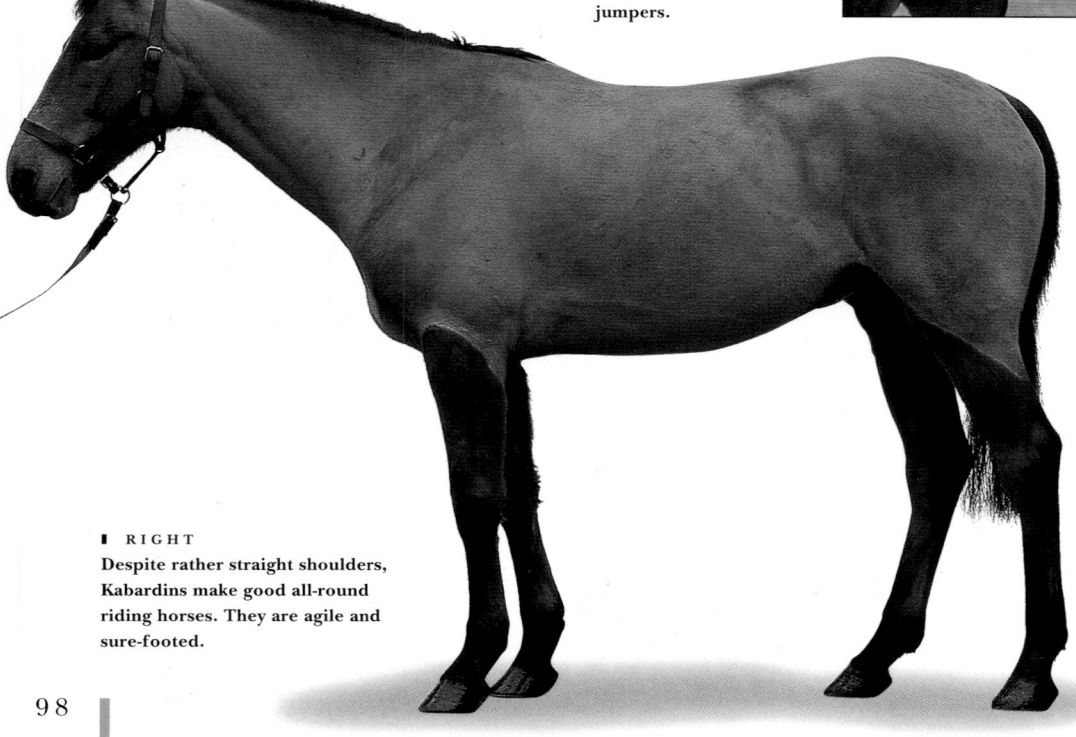

to the sixteenth century and is derived from the horses of the steppe tribes who were crossed with Turkmen, Persian and Karabakh horses. Originally the Kabardin was itself fairly small. Raised in herds, which were (and still are) grazed on the high pastures during the summer and in the foothills during the winter, it developed into a typical mountain breed: tough, sturdy and possessing great endurance.

The numbers of Kabardin horses were seriously depleted as a result of the Revolution and it was during the 1920s, when efforts were made to re-establish the breed, that a bigger stamp of horse began to be produced, one suitable as an army remount and for agricultural work. The Malokarachaev and Malkin Studs became the producers of the best modern Kabardin horses, which are used to improve stock in neighbouring areas as well as for general riding and driving purposes.

Tersk

Like the Kabardin, the Tersk comes from the northern Caucasus, though it is a breed of more recent origin, having been developed from 1921 onwards at the Tersk and Stavropol Studs.

The Tersk is based on Strelets horses, the part-bred Arabs which were formerly bred at the Strelets Stud in the Ukraine. The Strelets was produced by crossing

BREED DESCRIPTION

Height Stallions 15hh. Mares 14.3hh.

Colour Predominantly light grey or "white" with a silvery sheen.

Conformation Fine head with large, expressive eyes and medium-length, mobile ears; medium-length neck set high on well-sloped shoulders; strong body with deep chest, wide back and muscular loins; fine legs with well-defined tendons; fine mane and tail.

INTERESTING FACTS

Nowadays most of the world's Tersk horses are produced at the Stavropol Stud. Stavropol is in the northern Caucasus between the Black Sea and the Caspian Sea.

█ BELOW
Tersk horses are invariably refined and elegant. Their predominantly light grey colouring adds to their attraction.

█ BOTTOM
The breed shows unmistakable signs of its Arab ancestry though it is usually a little taller than the pure-bred Arab.

pure-bred Arabs with, among others, high quality Orlovs and Anglo-Arabs (some Thoroughbred blood was also used, though this was not a dominant factor).

The result was a horse with a distinctly Arabian look about it but one which was bigger built than the pure-breds.

By the 1920s there were very few Strelets in existence. The few that did remain, including two stallions, were taken to the Tersk Stud in an attempt to increase their numbers. The mares were put to pure-bred Arab stallions; and various cross-bred mares, including Strelets x Kabardin and Arab x Don, were covered by the Strelets stallions. After some thirty years the new type, known as the Tersk, became fixed. It has inherited the general appearance of the Arab, though it stands a little taller, and also its elegant paces. A handsome horse, usually grey in colour, it combines a kind temperament with tremendous energy, attributes which have made it a favourite in circuses and also as a sports horse.

Orlov Trotter

The Orlov shares with the Standardbred and the French Trotter the distinction of being one of the world's foremost breeds of trotting horse. Indeed, before the development of the Standardbred it was probably the most famous of all trotters. Although the Orlov is less well known now outside its native land than the other two members of the triumvirate, it nevertheless plays an important role both in Russian harness racing and in the upgrading of other Russian breeds.

The Orlov takes its name from Count Alexis Orlov (1737–1809), founder of the Orlov Stud near Moscow. The Count imported from Greece a grey Arab stallion called Smetanka. Despite Smetanka's short stud career, he was to prove highly influential in the development of this popular breed. Smetanka's grey son

Polkan, bred out of a Danish mare and foaled in 1784, produced Bars I, who became the foundation sire of the Orlov Trotter.

The breed was developed by Count Orlov and his stud manager V.I. Shishkin at the then newly founded Khrenov Stud in the province of Voronezh

▌ LEFT
The head of the Orlov Trotter is inclined to be coarse and rather small.

BREED DESCRIPTION

Height Stallions 16hh. Mares 15.3hh.

Colour Predominantly grey. Bay and black are commonly found. Chestnut is rare.

Conformation Small, often somewhat coarse head; long, often swan-shaped, neck set high on the withers; long, straight back with muscular loins and broad, powerful croup; fine, squarely set legs with a minimum of 8 inches (20cm) of bone below the knee.

▌ LEFT
Most fast-trotting horses are fairly long in the back and the Orlov is no exception. The good measurement of bone below the knee denotes its strength.

INTERESTING FACTS

Count Alexis Orlov, the breed's founder, was a soldier famous for his courage and audacity. In 1762 he played a part in the assassination of Peter III. The Count's older brother, Grigorei, who distinguished himself during the Seven Years' War, had attracted the attention of Peter's wife, soon to become Catherine II. However, having helped place her on the throne, Grigorei found himself ousted from the Empress's favour by his fellow conspirator, the handsome Prince Potemkin. Alexis is reputed to have knocked out Potemkin's eye – and turned to horse breeding as a diversion from affairs at court!

RIGHT
The Russian Trotter is part Orlov, part Standardbred. It is faster on the racetrack than the Orlov.

to which the stock from the Moscow stud was transferred in 1788. Bars I was used to breed from Arab, Dutch and Danish mares as well as half-breds imported from England. Inbreeding back to Bars I was practised extensively. During the early part of the nineteenth century the breed continued to improve thanks to the systematic training and racing of trotters in Russia.

Later, as the Standardbred began to demonstrate its supremacy on the racetrack, the Russians started importing horses from America to cross with the Orlov. The resultant half-breed, subsequently known as the Russian Trotter, proved faster than the Orlov. Imports of Standardbreds ceased at the outbreak of World War I but in recent times the traffic has resumed to maintain the speed of the Russian Trotter.

BELOW
As well as being raced in their native country, Orlovs are well suited to the modern sport of four-in-hand driving. They are exported for this purpose.

BELOW
This horse, hitched to a training vehicle, demonstrates the Orlov's tremendously powerful action.

Vladimir Heavy Draught

The Clydesdale played a significant part in the development of the Vladimir, a heavy draught horse created in the provinces of Vladimir and Ivanovo, to the north-east of Moscow. During the early years of this century stallions of various heavy breeds were imported from Britain and France to cross with the local mares of the region in order to produce a good-quality heavy work horse. Among the most influential of the foundation stallions were the Clydesdales Lord James, Border Brand, both imported in 1910, and Glen Albin (1923). Shire stallions were also used, though to a lesser extent, and some Cleveland Bay, Suffolk, Ardennais and

Percheron blood is also said to have been introduced. The experiment met with success, the result being a powerfully built heavy horse, well suited to all types of heavy agricultural and draught work. Named the Vladimir Heavy Draught, it was recognized as a breed in 1946.

Its docile nature makes it easy to handle, while its active paces – no doubt inherited from its Clydesdale forebears – mean that despite its massive build it can be used to pull the famous Russian troikas. Another bonus is its early maturity: the Vladimir is so well developed by the age of three that it can start work and also be used at stud, where the stallions are noted

■ OPPOSITE ABOVE
**The Vladimir Heavy Draught combines great
strength with the most docile of natures – note this
horse's kindly expression.**

■ OPPOSITE BELOW
**Clydesdale blood was used with great success in the
development of this breed, which is renowned for
its powerful build and active paces.**

BREED DESCRIPTION

Height Stallions 16.1hh. Mares 15.3hh.

Colour Predominantly bay, also black
and chestnut with white markings on head
and legs.

Conformation Large, long head with convex
profile; long, muscular neck; pronounced
withers; wide chest, rather long, broad back
and long, broad, sloping croup; long limbs;
some horses carry feather.

for their good fertility rate. Minus points
include, in some horses, a rather long
back, which is not conducive to strength,
and a flat-sided rib cage (the reverse of
"well sprung" or rounded ribs, which
enable the lungs to work to maximum
efficiency). The Vladimir is the largest of
the Russian heavy breeds. Stallions have a
girth of some 6 feet 9 inches (207cm) and
weigh in the region of 1,688lb (758kg).
Mares are only a little smaller, with a girth
of 6 feet 5 inches (196cm) and a weight of
1,507lb (685kg).

INTERESTING FACTS

Other heavy horses in the former USSR
include the Russian Heavy Draught, founded
a century or so ago, and based largely on
the Ardennais, and the Soviet Heavy
Draught, which was founded by crossing
Belgian Heavy Draught stallions with local
harness-type mares. Both were registered as
breeds in 1952. The Russian Heavy Draught
is quick to mature and remarkably long lived.
It was formerly known as the
"Russian Ardennes".

LATVIAN

The Latvian is a powerfully built harness
horse renowned for its weight-pulling
ability. It is of recent origin, dating only
from the early 1920s when local mares
were crossed with German, English and
French horses to produce an all-round
worker possessed of strength, stamina
and good, active paces. There are two
distinct types of Latvian horse: a heavy
harness type which is based largely on
Oldenburg, Norfolk Roadster and
Anglo-Norman outcrosses and a lighter
version which has a preponderance of
Hanoverian blood.

Latvian horses have good overall
conformation and great freedom of
movement. Stallions stand up to 16.2hh,
mares up to 16hh. Black is the
predominant colour of the heavier type,
while most of the lighter weight horses
are chestnut.

The Latvian harness horse was
recognized as a breed in 1952 and
although some outcrosses to Oldenburg
and Hanoverian horses have been made
since, these have been on a fairly limited
scale. The breed is especially noted for
its placid temperament which, together
with its strength and energy, make it a
popular working animal.

North Swedish

Forestry is the chief area of employment for the North Swedish horse, a small, compact, agile draught horse ideally suited to moving timber in confined spaces, over difficult terrain and often in inclement weather conditions.

The breed is descended from the ancient native work horse of Sweden which was influenced by the Døle horses from neighbouring Norway. At some time during the nineteenth century, outcrosses were made to horses of lighter build from outside Scandinavia but towards the end of the century there was a move to produce a heavier stamp of horse, more suited to pulling the heavier types of machinery which were then becoming available. Consequently stallions from larger breeds, such as the Clydesdale, were imported.

BREED DESCRIPTION

Height Stallions around 15.2hh. Mares around 15hh.

Colour Any solid colour.

Conformation Fairly large head with longish ears; short, crested neck; strong, sloping shoulders; rather long, but deep, strong back; rounded hindquarters with sloping croup; short, strong limbs with good bone; the mane and tail are usually very abundant.

The possibility of the old Swedish horse dying out altogether as a result of these crosses prompted interested parties to form an association to save it, the aim being to breed from the old-type stock still found in the remoter parts of the north of the country, using Døle stallions. Government support during the early years of the twentieth century aided this aim and during the 1920s performance testing was introduced as a means of selection, something which is still used today. Horses are tested for their draught aptitude as well as draught efficiency. The former test involves pulling a sled laden with logs, the judges awarding points according to the horse's performance and its condition after the work. For the efficiency test the horse is hitched to a wagon and its actual pulling power is measured by a dynamometer.

Lumbering is an area where heavy horses can prove more efficient and more cost effective than mechanized transport, and the North Swedish Horse continues to thrive in its traditional environment.

▌ LEFT
Small and compact, the North Swedish horse is particularly strong through the neck and shoulders. Its short limbs have plenty of bone.

INTERESTING FACTS

North Swedish horses make good all-round draught animals. They are, however, most often associated with agricultural work and, more especially, forestry. They begin work as three-year-olds and within a couple of years are sufficiently mature to be capable of working an eight-hour day. Stallions weigh anything from 1,440 to 1,655lb (650–750kg) and mares 1,200 to 1,545lb (550–700kg).

Swedish Warmblood

Sweden has been renowned for its fine riding and carriage horses for many centuries, so it is not surprising that the Swedish Warmblood should have had such an impact on present-day competitive sports, particularly top-level dressage.

The Skåne province of what is now southern Sweden (the area had previously been under Danish rule) was noted for its horse breeding as long ago as the twelfth century, when Archbishop Absalon raised remounts there for his cavalry. Then in the mid-seventeenth century, Charles X of Sweden founded the Royal Stud at Flyinge, to the north-east of Malmo, to supply horses for the royal stables and the

army. Down the years horses from a wide variety of breeds were used at the stud to produce a quality cavalry horse. They included Holsteins, Hanoverians, East Prussians, Frederiksborgs, Arabs,

Thoroughbreds and Oldenburgs, with the East Prussian and Hanoverian blood being particularly influential.

Officers of the Swedish cavalry mounted on Swedish horses enjoyed tremendous success in all three equestrian disciplines (dressage, show jumping and three-day eventing) at Olympic level both before and after World War I. The Swiss army bought many Swedish horses after World War II, a number of whom found fame in the dressage world. When mechanization signalled the demise of the cavalry horse it was a natural progression for the Swedes to channel their horse-breeding efforts towards leisure and

■ LEFT
This handsome head is typical of the Swedish Warmblood, which is noted for its intelligence and pleasant disposition.

■ BOTTOM
Although overall conformation varies, most examples of the breed have a long, elegant neck and well-proportioned limbs and hindquarters.

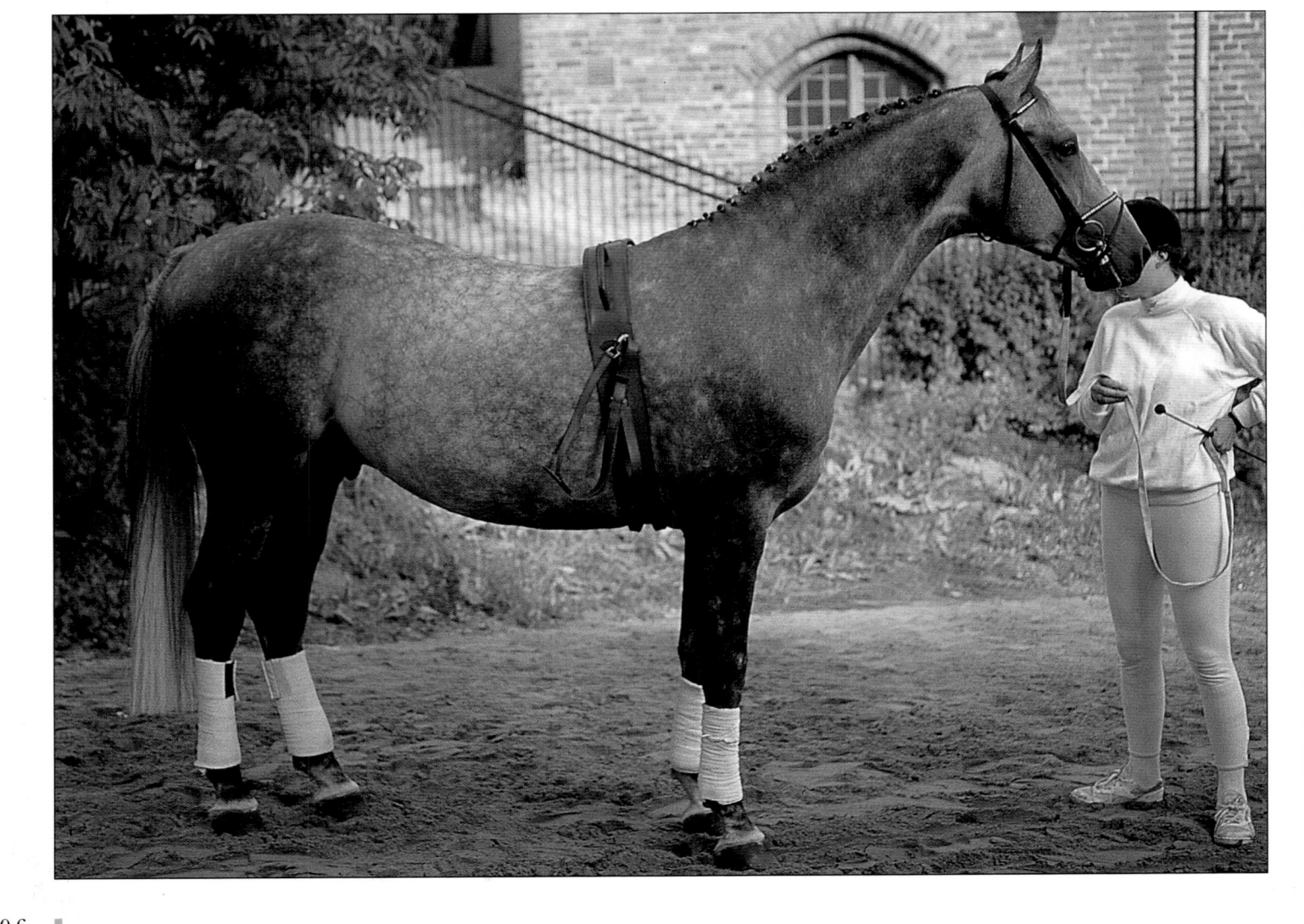

■ RIGHT
Warmblood mares with their foals put on a fine show to an appreciative crowd during the 1990 World Equestrian Games in Stockholm.

■ BOTTOM LEFT
Thanks to infusions of outside blood, including Thoroughbred, the breed has become a good all-round sports horse.

■ BOTTOM RIGHT
Swedish Warmbloods have traditionally excelled at the demanding discipline of Grand Prix dressage.

BREED DESCRIPTION

Height 15 – 17hh.

Colour Any solid colour.

Conformation Variable, but usually a handsome head, with wide forehead and kind, intelligent eyes; long neck; shoulders sometimes tend to be rather straight, depending on the bloodline; well-proportioned body, hindquarters and limbs.

INTERESTING FACTS

Swedish-bred dressage horses which have found fame at the Olympic Games include Piaff, winner of the individual gold medal in Munich in 1972, when ridden by the West German, Liselott Linsenhoff. Piaff's sire was Gaspari, who competed for Sweden in the 1960 Games in Rome, where another Swedish horse, Wald, won the individual silver medal in the hands of the Swiss rider, Gustav Fischer. In Tokyo in 1964 Fischer's compatriot, Henri Chammartin, was the individual gold medallist on yet another Swedish horse, Woermann. Also Swedish bred was Gauguin de Lully, winner of the individual bronze medal at the Seoul Games in 1988, again competing for Switzerland.

competition. There was no doubting the Swedish Warmblood's prowess as a dressage horse and in recent times top jumping blood has been introduced from France, Germany and Holland. Carefully selected Thoroughbred stallions have also been used on warmblood mares.

To maintain the excellence of the breed, in terms of both conformation and temperament, Swedish Warmblood stallions are graded and must pass a performance test, veterinary examination and assessment of type, conformation and action. There is also a system of progeny testing, the results of which are available to mare owners seeking a suitable stallion.

Akhal-Teke

One of the most striking looking horses anywhere in the world, the Akhal-Teke, or Turkmen, has been bred for some 3,000 years in the desert oases of Turkmenistan, a region to the north of Iran and to the east of the Caspian Sea. Although the Turkmen people probably introduced a certain amount of Arabian and Persian blood at some stage, its isolated homeland has kept the Akhal-Teke freer from outside influences than many riding

LEFT
The Akhal-Teke's head is always very fine, with large expressive eyes and beautifully shaped ears.

BELOW
The luminous sheen on the coat of this horse is typical of the breed, as is the lean overall appearance.

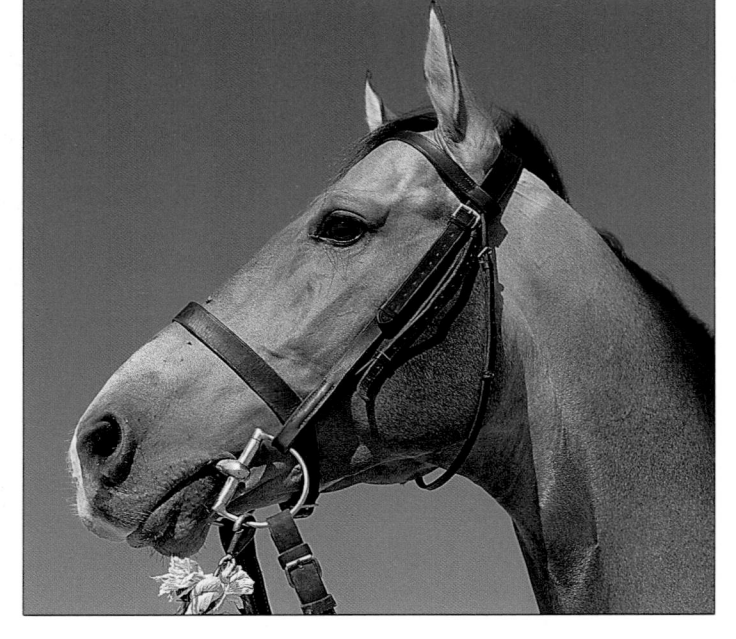

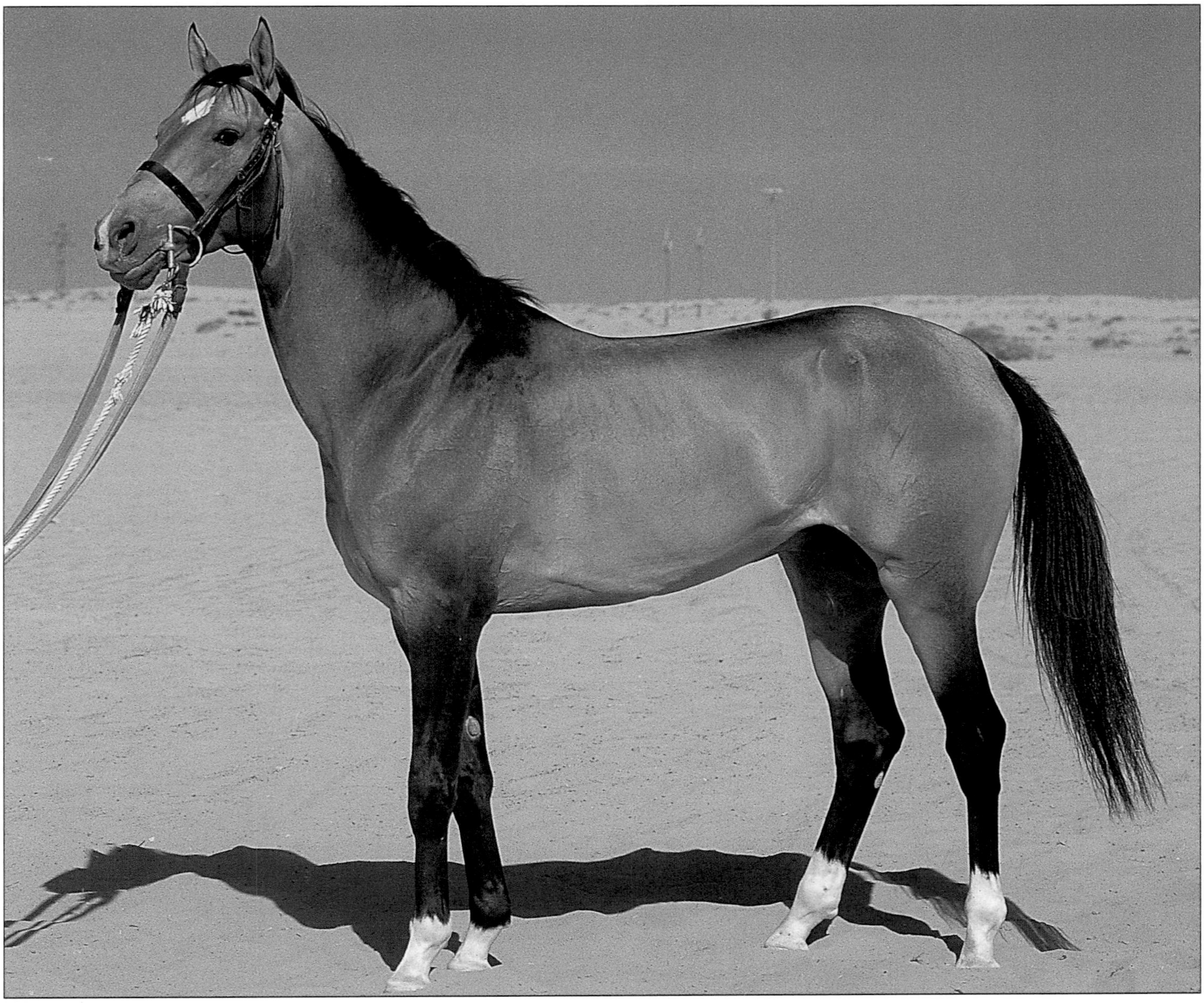

▌ RIGHT
Akhal-Tekes make good all-round riding horses, their legendary stamina making them excellent mounts for competitive endurance riding.

▌ BOTTOM RIGHT
Despite being raised for centuries in desert conditions, the breed adapts perfectly well to life in the much less rigorous climate of western Europe.

BREED DESCRIPTION

Height 15.1 – 15.2hh.

Colour Bay and chestnut, often with a remarkable golden sheen; also grey and black.

Conformation Very fine head with wide nostrils, large, expressive eyes and long, beautifully shaped ears; long, straight and often thin neck set high on the shoulders; sloping shoulder with high withers; long, often weak back, shallow rib cage and a tendency to poor loins, lacking in muscle; narrow hindquarters but with muscular croup and long, muscular thighs; strong, straight forelegs with long forearm, and long hindlegs which tend to be sickle shaped with cow hocks; small but hard feet; sparse mane and tail; thin skin.

horses. Raised to withstand the extreme conditions of the desert – fiercely hot days alternating with cold nights – the Akhal-Teke developed into a tough, lean horse, whose undoubted conformational defects are offset by its fast paces, stamina and tremendous hardiness. This hardiness owes much to the rigorous lifestyle imposed upon it over many centuries. The traditional Turkmen method of horse management did not included stabling. The animals were wrapped in felt, with only their heads uncovered, and kept on tethers. Their diet included meagre amounts of dry lucerne, barley and some mutton fat. Foals were weaned very young and the horses raced as yearlings. Nowadays Akhal-Tekes are kept along more modern lines, out at grass by day and stabled by night. They are still raced, though not until they are two- or three-year-olds, as is the custom in the Thoroughbred racing world.

Spirited and athletic, they are used for general riding purposes, including show jumping and dressage, and at stud in the development of other riding horse breeds. Their phenomenal stamina also makes them the ideal mount for endurance rides, since they are capable of covering great distances, in extremes of temperature, on the most modest of rations. One of the most celebrated of all endurance rides took place in 1935, when Akhal-Teke horses travelled from Ashkabad to Moscow (their journey included crossing the Karakum desert), completing a distance of 2,580 miles (4,152km) in 84 days.

INTERESTING FACTS

The Akhal-Teke used to be renowned for its devotion to its rider – which is not surprising if one tale told about the Turkmen training techniques is true. According to this story, a young horse would be kept alone in a pit or enclosure. Stones would be thrown at it by everyone but the owner. Only he would treat it kindly and offer it food. Thus the horse learnt to trust only one man and to fear all others. This could account for the breed's sometimes difficult temperament.

Morgan

The American Morgan horse is highly unusual in that it can be traced back to just one stallion, the extraordinary little Justin Morgan, who stood a mere 14hh but who excelled in weight-pulling contests and races, both under saddle and in harness.

Justin Morgan was probably foaled in 1789 and was originally named Figure, later taking the name of his first recorded owner, Thomas Justin Morgan, who came from farming stock in Vermont but who was also a music teacher and church composer. How Justin Morgan was bred has never been satisfactorily resolved because of the lack of recorded evidence. Plausible claims have been made for Thoroughbred, Arab, Welsh Cob and Dutch ancestry. What is beyond dispute is that despite his small stature – he weighed no more than 850lb (386kg) – Justin Morgan proved himself a remarkably strong work horse, and he undoubtedly

■ LEFT
The head of the Morgan is expressive, with large, prominent eyes and shapely ears set rather wide apart. Mares may have slightly longer ears than stallions.

worked extremely hard for a succession of owners. He was used for ploughing, as a harness horse and in woodland clearance and was never beaten in log-hauling matches against rivals weighing nearly half as much again.

He was, moreover, a wonderfully prepotent sire, passing on to his progeny all his own remarkable attributes of strength, endurance, speed and, not least, his gentle temperament. Three of his sons were to have a particular influence on

the development of the breed of which he was the founder: Sherman Morgan, foaled around 1808, Woodbury Morgan (1816) and Bulrush Morgan (1812). The Sherman Morgan line was noted for its excellent harness horses and had an important influence on the foundation of other breeds in the US: the Quarter Horse, Saddlebred, Standardbred and Tennessee Walker. The Woodbury Morgans were much in demand as saddle and parade

■ LEFT
The top line of the Morgan is distinctive. The gentle curve from the poll to the back gives the impression of the neck sitting on top of the withers rather than in front of them.

BREED DESCRIPTION

Height 14.1 – 15.2hh with some individuals over or under.

Colour Bay, chestnut, brown or black. No white markings permitted above the knee or hock, except on the face.

Conformation Expressive head, with straight or slightly dished profile, broad forehead, large eyes and short, alert ears; slightly arched neck; sloping shoulders and well-defined withers; compact, deep body, with short back, well-sprung ribs, broad loins and deep flank; well-muscled hindquarters with high-set tail; straight, sound legs, with short cannons, flat bone and sufficiently long, sloping pasterns to provide light, springy step; good, sound feet with dense horn; full, soft mane and tail.

horses, while the Bulrush Morgans were noted for their trotting speed.

Like so many other breeds, the Morgan horse went into decline with the coming of motorized transport, but thanks to the efforts of enthusiastic members of the Morgan Horse Club, founded in 1909, the breed survived. Today there is a thriving population of Morgan horses in the United States plus recognized breed clubs in Canada, Britain, Australia, Spain, New Zealand, Germany, Italy and Sweden. The Morgan is kept as a show horse and is also to be seen competing in a variety of spheres, such as cutting horse, stock horse and reining horse classes, hunter-jumper division, dressage and roadster and carriage driving competitions.

INTERESTING FACTS

A Morgan horse named Comanche, the mount of Captain Myles Keogh, was the only non-Indian survivor of the Battle of the Little Big Horn in 1876. He recovered from his many wounds and lived to the ripe old age of 29.

❚ **ABOVE**
The versatile Morgan horse is equally at home in harness and under saddle.

❚ **LEFT**
Morgan horses are well up to carrying the weight of adult riders. The action is straight and springy.

Quarter Horse

The Quarter Horse, as its name implies, excels at racing over a short distance – a quarter of a mile to be precise. It traces back to the horses taken to America by the Spanish Conquistadores. During the seventeenth and eighteenth centuries the waves of English settlers in the eastern states used the local Spanish-based stock to cross with their own, imported horses to produce a good, all-round work horse, suitable for every type of ridden work, for tilling the land and for work in harness. Tough and stocky, these horses became the settlers' "right-hand men". Spreading westward, they became indispensable during the great days of cattle herding

when the chief requirement was for a totally dependable mount, one which was athletic and fearless working among cattle. In time these horses developed an innate "cow sense" and could anticipate the movements of a steer, stopping and turning at breakneck speed.

It was the Englishman's growing enthusiasm for racing which led to these all-purpose horses being raced in impromptu contests: on the road, in a clearing, anywhere where a couple of

▌ ABOVE LEFT
The head of the Quarter Horse is short and wide with large, intelligent eyes, alert ears and a small muzzle.

▌ ABOVE RIGHT
The chest is broad and deep, and the forelegs wide set. The muscling on the insides of the forearms gives the appearance of a well-defined inverted V.

▌ RIGHT
The breed is noted for its strong, close-coupled back and deep girth. Well-muscled hindquarters and strong, low-set hocks give the horse its tremendous acceleration.

BREED DESCRIPTION

Height 14.3 – 16hh for mature stallions and mares.

Colour Any solid colour.

Conformation Short, wide head, with small muzzle, large, wide-set, intelligent eyes and medium-length, alert ears; fairly long, flexible neck; sloping shoulders and well-defined withers; compact body with broad chest, deep girth, short back, well-sprung ribs and powerful loins; broad, deep, heavy and well-muscled hindquarters with long, gently sloped croup; good limbs, with short cannons, broad, flat, low-set hocks, muscular thighs and gaskins and medium-length pasterns; oblong feet with deep, open heels.

horses could be galloped upsides for a few hundred yards. The Quarter Horse, as it was dubbed, developed immensely powerful hindquarters, which could propel it into a flat-out gallop virtually from a standing start, and the speed to sprint over short distances. Eventually, however, as Thoroughbred racing became established, interest in Quarter Horse racing dwindled. Still later, when mechanization brought about a lessening of the horse's importance in ranching, the Quarter Horse, in common with riding horses all over the world, became a leisure riding horse.

Today the Quarter Horse enjoys great popularity in Western-style competitions such as barrel racing, in rodeos and, once again, in racing over short distances. Thanks to a revival of interest in the latter sport, Quarter Horses now compete on proper tracks for big purses.

INTERESTING FACTS

The American Quarter Horse Association was formed in 1940. Its registry is now the largest of any breed in the world, with more than two million horses listed.

ABOVE
Quarter Horses have an innate "cow sense" and are able to anticipate the movements of a steer.

BELOW LEFT
The Quarter Horse makes an ideal mount for traditional Western sports.

BELOW RIGHT
The breed is well known for its pleasant disposition and gentleness and as a result is used in a wide variety of activities.

Saddlebred

Formerly known as the Kentucky Saddler, the elegant Saddlebred was developed by the early nineteenth-century settlers in the southern states of North America. To meet their requirements for a quality utility horse, the plantation owners interbred horses of various kinds, including the Narragansett Pacer (a speedy strain of pacing horse from Rhode Island) and the Thoroughbred. The end result was a good-looking animal who gave an exceptionally comfortable ride – essential for long hours spent in the saddle on crop-inspection tours – but was equally well suited to pulling a carriage. In 1891 a group of leading breeders established the American Saddle Horse Breeders' Association and a Saddle Horse Registry was set up.

BREED DESCRIPTION

Height 15 – 17hh; average about 15.3hh.

Colour Usually chestnut, bay, brown, black or grey; also palomino, spotted and occasionally roan.

Conformation Well-shaped head with large eyes set well apart, small, alert ears and wide nostrils; long, arched neck; sloping shoulders with sharp withers; short, strong back; well-muscled hindquarters with level croup and high-set tail; straight, strong limbs with long, sloping pasterns; good, sound hooves, open at the heels.

Blessed with the most amiable disposition, intelligence, speed and natural balance, the Saddlebred could (and still can) be used for all manner of different purposes, including working with cattle. Not surprisingly it has made the transition from work horse to pleasure

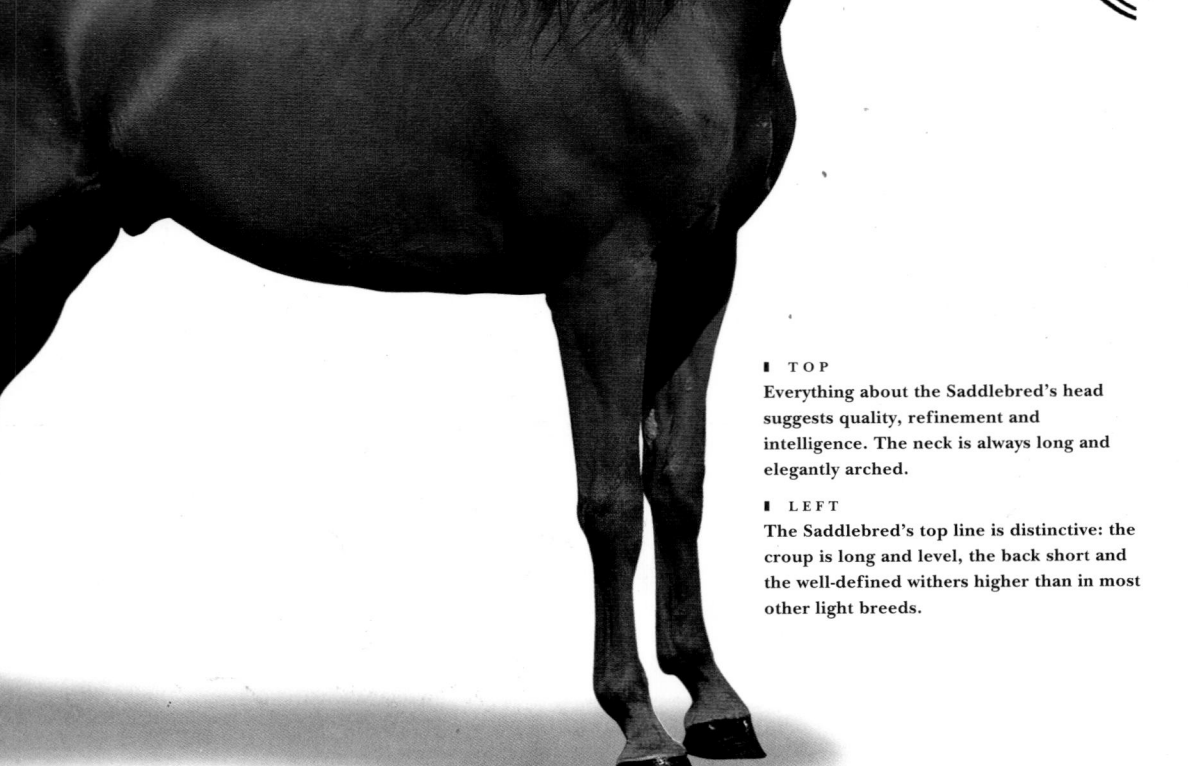

▎ TOP
Everything about the Saddlebred's head suggests quality, refinement and intelligence. The neck is always long and elegantly arched.

▎ LEFT
The Saddlebred's top line is distinctive: the croup is long and level, the back short and the well-defined withers higher than in most other light breeds.

■ LEFT
Long, well-sloped
pasterns contribute to
the comfortable paces
for which the breed is
famous.

■ BELOW
As well as being
popular riding horses,
Saddlebreds go equally
well in harness. The
peculiar tail carriage is
not natural, being
achieved through an
operation and
maintained by keeping
the tail in a device
known as a tail set
when the horse is
stabled.

horse with no difficulty whatsoever and
can be seen today competing in show
classes under saddle and in harness.

In the show ring, ridden Saddlebreds
are classified either as three-gaited or five-
gaited. The three-gaited horses are shown
at walk, trot and canter. The walk is
springy, the trot has high action and the
canter is slow, smooth and rhythmic. The
five-gaited horses show these three paces
plus two others: the slow gait and the rack.
The slow gait is a high-stepping, four-beat
gait executed in a slow, restrained manner.
The rack is a fast, flashy, four-beat gait in
which each foot strikes the ground at equal
intervals and which is free from any lateral
movement or pacing. The practice of
growing the feet unnaturally long (to
enhance the action), and operating on the
tail to make it unnaturally high set,
developed for the show ring.

Outside the artificial confines of the
show ring, in its handsome natural state,
the Saddlebred makes an excellent all-
round riding horse – easy to train, fast,
possessing great stamina and having a
good jump, too.

INTERESTING FACTS

In their natural state the Saddlebred's
strong hooves are well formed. For showing
purposes they are grown to an unnatural
length and shod with heavy shoes.

Standardbred

The American Standardbred is to harness racing what the English Thoroughbred is to flat racing and steeplechasing. During the past century or more, every country where harness racing flourishes has imported Standardbred horses to upgrade its own trotters and pacers.

BREED DESCRIPTION

Height 14 – 16hh.

Colour All solid colours, predominantly bay, brown, black and chestnut.

Conformation The Standardbred is a powerfully built horse, of rather less quality and refinement than the Thoroughbred and somewhat longer in the body and shorter in the leg. The shoulders are long and sloping and the croup invariably high.

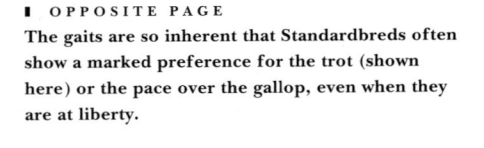

▌ OPPOSITE PAGE
The gaits are so inherent that Standardbreds often show a marked preference for the trot (shown here) or the pace over the gallop, even when they are at liberty.

Strangely enough the foundation sire of the Standardbred was a horse who only ever raced at the gallop: the English Thoroughbred, Messenger. A grey tracing back to the Darley Arabian, Messenger was foaled in 1780 and raced on the flat for three seasons, winning eight of his fourteen starts. Exported to Philadelphia in May 1788, he stood at stud in America for twenty years, covering mainly Thoroughbred mares to start with then, after racing was suppressed in New York, all types of non-Thoroughbreds. Some of his descendants became fine flat

▌ ABOVE
The head of the Standardbred is not exactly refined but the overall aspect is workmanlike and the expression sensible.

▌ LEFT
In comparison with that other great racehorse, the Thoroughbred, the breed is rather long in the back and short in the leg. The shoulders are invariably long and well sloped, giving the horse the necessary freedom of movement.

racehorses but it was his ability to throw good trotting stock (not so much his immediate progeny as their descendants) that earned him lasting fame. His great grandson, Hambletonian, became a prolific sire of trotters and Hambletonian's four sons, George Wilkes, Dictator, Happy Medium and Electioneer, founded the sire lines responsible for virtually all harness racehorses in the USA today. Hambletonian was out of the Charles Kent Mare, who was inbred to Messenger, and descended, through her sire, Bellfounder, from the famous Norfolk Trotter, Old Shales.

In addition to the dominant Messenger line, two other important influences on

the early development of the Standardbred were the Clays (descendants of a Barb stallion imported from Tripoli in 1820) and the Morgan horse. Neither produced important families within the breed but both are believed to have helped establish its characteristic gait.

The first register of trotters was published in 1871 and the term "Standardbred" was introduced eight years later when a set of qualifications was drawn up for the admission of horses into the register. The original "standard", from which the breed takes its name, was judged to be the ability of a horse to cover a mile (1.6km) in 2 minutes 30 seconds (as trotters and pacers improved, this time

had to be reduced). Standardbreds race either at the pace (a lateral gait) or the trot (a diagonal pace). Up until the last couple of decades of the nineteenth century, trotters were more popular than the marginally faster pacers, but this is not so today.

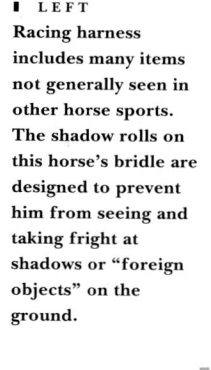

▌ ABOVE
Although the pace is one of the breed's natural gaits it is usual for pacing racehorses to wear hobbles to encourage them to maintain the lateral movement.

▌ LEFT
Racing harness includes many items not generally seen in other horse sports. The shadow rolls on this horse's bridle are designed to prevent him from seeing and taking fright at shadows or "foreign objects" on the ground.

Missouri Fox Trotter

Although a stud book for the Missouri Fox Trotting Horse was not opened until 1948, the breed began to evolve in the early part of the nineteenth century. Settlers travelling westwards across the Mississippi river from Kentucky, Tennessee and Virginia took with them a variety of horses, including Thoroughbreds, eastern-bred stock and Morgans, and then interbred them to produce a horse suited to the conditions of their new home in the Ozark Hills region of Missouri.

The chief requirement, especially of doctors, sheriffs, stock raisers and the like, was for a horse that could be ridden for long periods, often over rough terrain, with a minimum of fatigue either to horse or rider. The answer was found in the gait known as the fox trot, in which the horse walks with its forelegs but trots behind. The Fox Trotter does not put its hindfeet down with the jarring action characteristic of the

BREED DESCRIPTION

Height 14–16hh.

Colour Any. Most commonly sorrel and chestnut sorrel with white markings.

Conformation Neat, clean, intelligent head with pointed, well-shaped ears, large, bright eyes and a tapered muzzle; graceful neck, in proportion to length of body; well-sloped, muscular shoulders; deep, strong body with deep, full chest and short, strong back; strong, muscular limbs; strong, well-made feet.

▌ ABOVE
This neat, intelligent looking head, with its bright eyes and well-shaped ears, is typical of the Missouri Fox Trotter.

▌ RIGHT
The body is deep, the back short and the overall impression one of compactness. Well-sloped shoulders ensure good riding action.

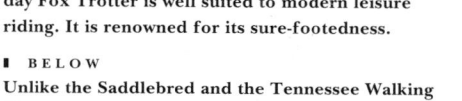

INTERESTING FACTS

In the fox trot the horse's hindfeet disfigure
the tracks of the forefeet, that is the hindfeet
touch the front tracks and slide forward. The
horse should travel in a collected manner,
with animation, rhythm and style. The horse's
tail is slightly elevated and moves in a
bobbing rhythm with the gait. The flat-foot
walk should also be performed with style and
animation. It is an animated four-beat gait in
which the horse overstrides its front track
with the hindfeet. The typical canter of the
Fox Trotter is collected, with the head and
tail slightly elevated.

■ BELOW LEFT
Originally bred as a means of transport, the present-
day Fox Trotter is well suited to modern leisure
riding. It is renowned for its sure-footedness.

■ BELOW
Unlike the Saddlebred and the Tennessee Walking
Horse, the Missouri Fox Trotter is shown with
normal-length feet. Artificial appliances such as
weights and tail sets are forbidden.

normal trot, but slides them along under
him. The result is a smooth, comfortable
gait at which the horse can travel for
extended periods without tiring. The
ability to walk in front and trot behind is
inherited but it can also be enhanced with
training. The overall quality of the Fox

show classes in which it is judged 40 per
cent for the fox trot, 20 per cent for the
flat foot walk, 20 per cent for the canter
and 20 per cent for conformation, the only
exceptions being two-year-olds, who are
judged 50 per cent for fox trot, 25 per cent
for walk and 25 per cent for conformation.

Trotter was improved over the years
through infusions of Saddlebred and
Tennessee Walker blood and today the
breed is noted for its compact, muscular
build and its sure-footedness.

Having become obsolete as a means of
transport, the Fox Trotter is now used as a
pleasure horse, being ideally suited to trail
(long-distance) riding. It is also ridden in

Tennessee Walking Horse

The Tennessee Walking Horse traces back to the Narragansett Pacer and, like the Saddlebred and the Missouri Fox Trotter, it was developed as an exceptionally comfortable riding horse with gaits not found in other breeds. Originally known as the Southern Plantation Walking Horse or Tennessee Pacer, it was an invaluable mode of transport for planters carrying out crop inspections, being fast, robust, comfortable under saddle and having a most tractable temperament.

The foundation sire was a horse named Black Allan, who arrived in Tennessee in

LEFT
The Tennessee Walking Horse is customarily ridden in a plain bit with long shanks and on a single rein which is held with a light hand and flexed wrist.

BELOW
The Walking Horse has the substance of the Standardbred and the style of the Saddlebred which are two of the breeds on which it is based.

1903. Black Allan's sire came from a line of Standardbred trotters, while his dam was a Morgan. Black Allan was crossed with the Tennessee Pacers of the time to produce the forerunners of the modern Walking Horse. Saddlebred blood was also introduced, the most important influence being that of Giovanni, who in 1914 was brought from Kentucky to stand at stud in Tennessee. By adding Saddlebred blood, breeders succeeded in producing a better quality, more refined, animal. Today's Walking Horse, which might be decribed as a somewhat more powerful version of

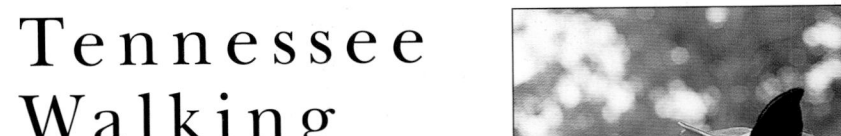

BREED DESCRIPTION

Height Average 15 .2hh.

Colour Any. Black and solid colours are most popular.

Conformation Intelligent but rather plain head; strong, arched neck; well-sloped shoulders; powerful body with broad chest; strong hindquarters; clean, hard limbs.

the Saddlebred, is therefore an amalgam of Thoroughbred, Standardbred, Morgan and Saddlebred blood. The Tennessee Walking Horse Breeders' Association was formed in Lewisburg, Tennessee, in 1935 and the Walking Horse was finally recognized as a breed in 1947.

Walking horses are fine all-round riding horses, their inherently kind nature making them especially suitable for novice riders. They are also popular horses in the show ring.

INTERESTING FACTS

The Tennessee Walking Horse's distinctive gaits – the flat-foot walk, the running walk and the canter – are inherited. Small foals can be seen performing the running walk beside their dams. Both walks are a loose, four-beat gait, with high action in front. As it moves, the horse nods its head in rhythm with the rise and fall of the hoofs, and the hindfeet overstride the tracks left by the front feet. The flat-foot walk should be loose, bold and square with plenty of shoulder motion. There should be a noticeable difference in the tempo between the two walks. The canter has a distinctive "rocking chair" motion.

∎ LEFT
The breed's unique gaits are inherited – young foals are seen to "walk" alongside their mothers with the ease of older horses – but are encouraged with artificial aids applied to the forefeet.

∎ FAR LEFT
An impressive collection of Walking Horse trophies won in America, where the breed is a popular show-ring attraction.

∎ BELOW
The exaggerated outline of the show horse is produced in part by the extra-long forefeet. The rider sits way behind the normal saddle position (on what is generally held to be the weakest part of the horse's back).

Mustang

Mustangs, the "wild" horses of North America, are descended from the horses taken to the New World by the sixteenth-century Conquistadores. As Spanish colonizers began moving north from Mexico into what is now Texas, so the Indian tribes with whom they came into contact began to have their first experience of horses. Initially, the Indians were inclined to kill and eat any horses they captured from the settlers. In time, however, as they began to realize the value of the horse as a means of transport, they learnt how to handle and ride them.

By the second half of the seventeenth century, some tribes were taking horses from the Spaniards and using them in mounted raids against the newcomers – during which they would acquire more horses. So began the gradual spread of the horse to other tribes (either by trading or by theft) and the movement of the horse

■ LEFT
This Mustang shows unmistakable signs of its Spanish ancestry in its attractive head and luxurious growth of silky mane.

BREED DESCRIPTION

Height 13.2 – 15hh.

Colour Any.

Conformation Because of its mixed ancestry (the original Spanish stock was progressively diluted as a wide variety of settlers' horses, who either became lost or were abandoned, joined and interbred with the wild herds) there is a good deal of variation. The best are sturdily built with strong, clean limbs and feet.

northwards. Many of the horses who subsequently ran "wild" would have done so after getting loose during skirmishes between Indians and Spaniards. Others, perhaps those who were lame or needed resting, were probably turned loose, their owners intending to round them up later. Some domestic horses put out to graze on the range simply wandered off. Gradually these horses joined together to form feral

herds, which flourished in the wide open spaces of the Great Plains. By the late eighteenth and early nineteenth centuries there were huge numbers of "wild" horses grazing the plains – one authority estimates the number to have been as high as two million.

The turning point for the Mustang, as these feral horses became known, was the westward spread of civilization. Many were

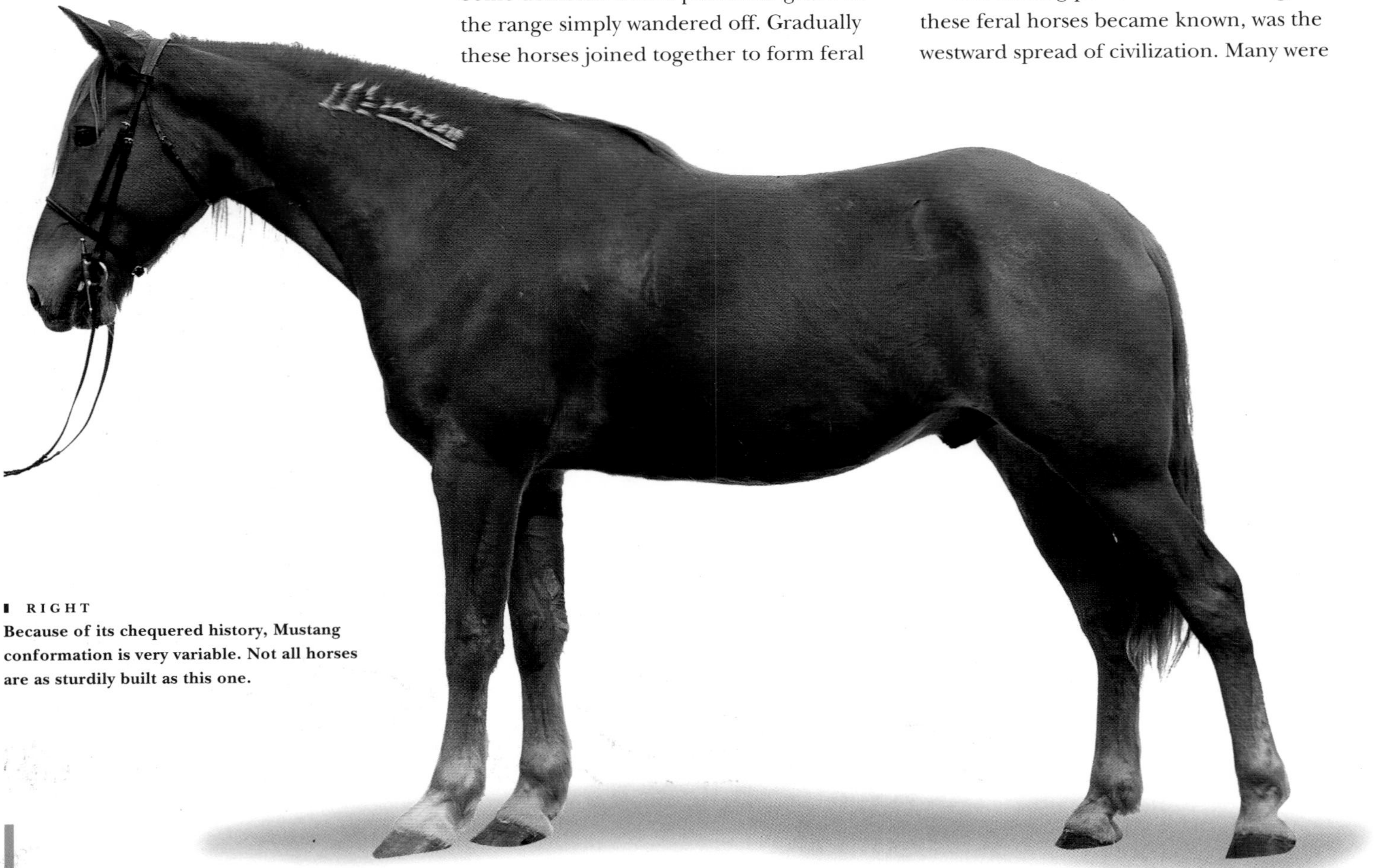

■ RIGHT
Because of its chequered history, Mustang conformation is very variable. Not all horses are as sturdily built as this one.

█ LEFT
Centuries of living in a feral state led to the
development of a tough, enduring type of animal.

INTERESTING FACTS

The term mustang probably comes from the
Spanish word *mesteno*, from *mesta*, meaning
an association of graziers or stock raisers. In
thirteenth-century Spain *mestas* were
organizations of sheep owners. Stray sheep
were called *mestenos*, meaning "belonging to
the *mesta*". Some etymologists think that
mustang comes from the word *mestengo*, a
later form of *mostrenco*, from the verb
mostrar, to show or exhibit. Stray sheep,
sometimes referred to as *mostrencos*, were
shown in public to give the owner the chance
to claim them. But according to the wild-
horse authority J. Frank Dobie, English-
speaking people in the American south-west
did not know the word *mostrenco*. Dobie
dates the introduction of the term Mustang
to the early nineteenth century.

killed, others were rounded up for use as
draught animals, some were used for
cross-breeding. Large numbers were used
as army remounts in the Boer War. During
the twentieth century still more have been
killed for the meat and pet food trades.

Public pressure led to the introduction,
in 1971, of an act giving protection to wild
horses in the United States and there are
several ranges where they still live, albeit
in much reduced numbers. Domesticated
Mustangs often make good riding horses.
Because of their inherent toughness, they
are well suited to endurance rides.

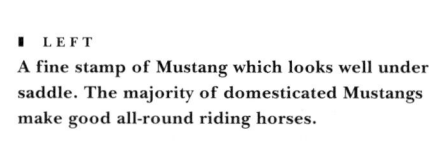

█ LEFT
A fine stamp of Mustang which looks well under
saddle. The majority of domesticated Mustangs
make good all-round riding horses.

█ RIGHT
Decorated in
traditional style, these
horses reflect their
links with the Indian
tribes who came to rely
on the horses first
introduced into
America by the
Conquistadores.

Australian Stock Horse

Horses were not indigenous to Australia and the modern Stock Horse is descended from the first imported animals, shipped over in small numbers from South Africa during the latter part of the eighteenth century. The precise breeding of these early imports is not known but they were probably of mainly Arab and Barb blood. It was not long before regular voyages began between Europe and Australia, each ship with its quota of horses aboard, and so Australia's equine population steadily grew.

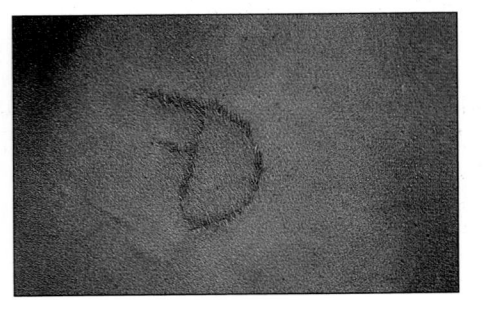

BREED DESCRIPTION

Height 15 – 16.3hh.

Colour Any solid colour.

Conformation There is considerable variation, but the best types are similar to the Thoroughbred, with particularly good sound limbs and feet.

Tough horses were needed to help settlers explore their rugged new home and, not surprisingly, Thoroughbreds and Arabs were the most popular imports. Thoroughbreds were required, too, to satisfy the growing interest of the settlers in racing, a sport which rapidly gained popularity from the early years of the nineteenth century onwards.

The horse which evolved for everyday use was a tough all-rounder: hardy, reliable, of good temperament, able to work in harness or under saddle, to plough the land, clear timber, and herd cattle and sheep. Until 1971, when the term Stock Horse was introduced, it was known as the "Waler" (after New South Wales). Walers were renowned for their stamina, courage and soundness and were accordingly highly prized by the cavalry.

The present-day Stock Horse is the descendant of the Waler. It has almost certainly been influenced by a number of breeds other than the Thoroughbred and Arab – Quarter Horses, various ponies and heavy breeds such as the Clydesdale and Suffolk Punch were all imported into Australia over the years and some out-crosses would have been made – but the Stock Horse is essentially a quality riding horse. Still in demand for cattle herding, at which it excels, it can also be seen taking part in rodeos and is suitable for general riding purposes, including competitive sports.

▌ LEFT
There is as yet no set type within the breed. This striking-looking horse shows unmistakable signs of his eastern ancestry.

▌ BELOW
The breed was and still is a cattle-herding horse par excellence: tough, enduring, sound and good-natured.

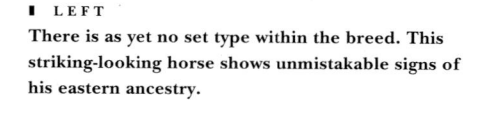

INTERESTING FACTS

Regal Realm is one of a long line of Australian Stock Horses to compete successfully at the highest level. Ridden by Lucinda Green he won the individual gold medal at the World Three-Day Event Championships in 1982, helping Britain to take the team title. The following year he was runner-up in the European Championships, winning a team silver medal. At the Los Angeles Olympic Games in 1984 he won another team silver and finished in sixth place individually. A year later he was a member of the victorious British team in the European Championships. When he retired from international competition he returned to his native land.

▌ OPPOSITE ABOVE LEFT
The head resembles that of the Thoroughbred, which is one of the major influences in the development of the Australian Stock Horse.

▌ OPPOSITE ABOVE RIGHT
It is usual to brand Stock Horses for identification purposes. This brand is on the horse's shoulder.

▌ OPPOSITE BELOW
Many Stock Horses show the refinement and good overall conformation of the Thoroughbred. They have as a result produced some good sports horses.

Criollo

A descendant of the horses taken to South America by the sixteenth-century Spanish Conquistadores, the Criollo comes from Argentina and is one of the toughest breeds of horse in the world. Its hardiness is the result of many years of natural selection. Some of the Spanish horses and their descendants formed feral herds on the pampas, where the extremes of climate – intensely dry, hot summers and severe winters – would have proved intolerable to all but the sturdiest individuals. Those that survived adapted to their harsh environment remarkably well, no doubt helped by the fact that they were descended from Andalusian and Barb horses, both breeds noted for their endurance. The Criollo, as it became known, even developed a coat colour – Criollos are predominantly dun – which helped render it inconspicuous against

■ **BELOW**
Originally the mount of the gauchos, or cowboys, of South America, the Criollo has achieved world-wide fame in the world of polo.

■ **BOTTOM**
The sturdy, compact Criollo is one of the world's toughest horses, with strong short limbs, plenty of bone below the knee and exceptionally sound feet.

BREED DESCRIPTION

Height Around 14 – 15hh.

Colour Usually dun with dark points and often with a dorsal stripe.

Conformation Medium-sized head, with wide-set eyes and alert ears; muscular neck; short, deep body with well-sprung ribs; short, strong limbs with plenty of bone and good, sound feet.

the dry pastureland of its habitat.

The Criollo became the favoured mount of the gauchos, the cowboys of the pampas, and an indispensable riding and packhorse for settlers in the huge and frequently inhospitable countries of South America. It can be found throughout the continent and although there are some variations, the result of adaptation to differences in habitat and climate, wherever it is bred it retains its basic qualities of stamina and soundness. Crossed with the Thoroughbred, the Criollo produces a fine polo pony, the Thoroughbred blood providing the extra speed required in the modern game.

INTERESTING FACTS

The most famous example of the Criollo's extraordinary powers of endurance was "Tschiffely's Ride", a journey undertaken by the Swiss-born traveller and writer Aimé Felix Tschiffely (1895–1954). In 1925, together with two Criollos – the 16-year-old Mancha, and the 15-year-old Gata – Tschiffely set off from Buenos Aires to ride to Washington D.C. in the United States. Alternately riding one horse and leading the other as a packhorse, he completed the journey, over some of the most arduous terrain in the world, in two and a half years. The horses were then shipped back to South America, where they spent their retirement, Gata living to the age of 36 and Mancha to 40.

Peruvian Paso

The Paso (meaning "step") is another breed which owes its origins to the Barb and Andalusian horses introduced to South America by the Spaniards. The first horses to arrive in Peru were taken there in 1532 by Francisco Pizarro (c.1478–1541).

The Paso's characteristic lateral gait is thought to have been inherited from the Spanish "jennet", which was a riding horse akin to the old English ambler. The lateral movement has been preserved down the centuries; the Paso usually demonstrates a preference for it over the canter. The paso is unlike any other lateral gait in that the horse's forelegs arc out to the side as he moves. With his hindlegs he takes long, straight strides, carrying his hindquarters

BREED DESCRIPTION

Height 14 – 15.2hh.

Colour Any, but predominantly bay and chestnut.

Conformation Intelligent looking head; fairly short, muscular neck; strong shoulders; strong body with broad, deep chest; strong, rounded hindquarters; short, strong limbs and excellent feet.

low, with his hocks well under him. This combination of flowing foreleg movement and powerfully driving hindlegs gives a particularly smooth ride. The Paso is said to be able to reach speeds of up to 15mph (24kph) and to maintain the lateral gait over rough terrain for extended periods without tiring.

Fairly small and stockily built, the Paso is noted for its sure-footedness, its ability to thrive on meagre rations and its kind nature. It makes an ideal ranch and long-distance riding horse.

▌ RIGHT
Horse and rider make an attractive, workmanlike picture in their traditional Peruvian tack and costume. The Paso is up to carrying a good deal of weight.

▌ ABOVE
Compact and well-muscled, with powerful hindquarters and short, strong limbs, the Peruvian Paso is a tremendously strong individual.

▌ LEFT
The Paso's long silky mane (and tail) is reminiscent of that of its Spanish ancestors, introduced into South America during the sixteenth century.

INTERESTING FACTS

The Peruvian Paso is not the only horse to show a natural preference for a lateral gait but the curious outward arcing of the forelegs, which move rather like the arms of a swimmer, is unique to the breed.

Ponies

Broadly speaking a pony is a small horse, "small" usually meaning no higher at the withers than about 14.2hh (a hand is 4 inches). However, not all small horses can be classified as ponies. Arab horses, for example, often stand below 15hh but they are very much horses, with the proportions and characteristics of the horse. An unusually small Thoroughbred is certainly not a pony and the remarkable little Caspian, although it is classified as a pony, actually resembles a miniature horse.

True ponies have very distinct pony characteristics, which include a proportionately short length of leg in relationship to the depth of the body. True ponies are perhaps best exemplified by the Mountain and Moorland breeds of Britain and Ireland, remarkable animals which have existed in the comparative isolation of their island home for thousands of years. These ponies, which are now divided into nine distinct breeds, are possessed of extraordinary strength in relation to their size. Fashioned by a harsh environment, they are tough, sure-footed, able to exist on minimum rations and have an inherent sagacity often lacking in their larger cousins.

Haflinger

Austria's attractive Haflinger pony is named after the village of Hafling in the southern Tirol, the region where it was first bred hundreds of years ago. Its ancestors were indigenous mountain

BREED DESCRIPTION

Height Around 14hh.

Colour Chestnut with flaxen mane and tail.

Conformation Intelligent looking head, with large eyes, small ears and slightly dished profile; sloping shoulders; strong, deep body with fairly long back and muscular loins; powerful hindquarters; strong limbs and excellent feet.

■ PREVIOUS PAGE
OPPOSITE
Exmoor ponies.

■ PREVIOUS PAGE
A Norwegian Fjord
pony.

■ LEFT
The "Hungarian Post" – Haflinger style! The breed combines strength with very active paces and can be trained to perform in a wide range of equestrian activities.

■ BELOW LEFT
Haflingers are true all-rounders, equally adept at work in harness and under saddle. This handsome team was photographed in Switzerland.

■ BELOW
The Haflinger's good temperament is easily discerned in this attractive head, with its large, kind eyes and alert expression.

horses and ponies which were upgraded with Arabian blood. All modern Haflingers trace back to a half-bred horse named El Bedavi XXII – who was bred in Austria and was a great grandson of the Arabian stallion, El Bedavi – and to El Bedavi XXII's son, Folie.

Over the years inbreeding has resulted in a pony of very definite type: small, but powerfully built, always chestnut in colour, hardy and sure-footed as befits a mountain

pony, and with the active paces of its Arab forebears.

With its amenable nature, the Haflinger makes an excellent all-round riding and driving pony. Before mechanization it was in great demand for agricultural work and as a pack-pony. Nowadays many Haflingers are used for leisure riding. The breed has been exported to a number of countries, and is especially popular in Germany and Switzerland. It is noted for its longevity.

INTERESTING FACTS

Haflingers which are entered in the breed's stud book are traditionally branded. The brand mark is the alpine flower, the edelweiss, at the centre of which is placed the letter "H".

Sorraia

Formerly used for farm work and general riding purposes, the primitive looking Sorraia survives today mainly in small feral groups. Its homeland is in Portugal in the region between the rivers Sor and Raia, tributaries of the Sorraia, which flows into the Tagus estuary from the south.

The Sorraia pony is believed to be descended from the Asian Wild Horse and the Tarpan. It bears a remarkable likeness to the latter, with its small stature and large head. The Sorraia's colouring, predominantly dun, often with an eel-stripe and zebra markings on the legs, is also typical of the primitive equine type.

The Sorraia does not have the best conformation in the world. It is, however, an extremely tough individual, able to exist on poor forage and to withstand extremes of climate. The shoulders tend to be upright, the hindquarters weak and the limbs rather long and lacking in bone, though the feet are hard and sound.

■ LEFT
Dun is the predominant colour of the Sorraia, Portugal's small, semi-feral pony. The breed is of ancient origin and is exceptionally hardy.

■ BELOW
In build and overall outline the Sorraia is not unlike the primitive Tarpan. Some selective breeding is carried out in order to preserve the original form.

BREED DESCRIPTION

Height 12 – 13hh.

Colour Predominantly dun, with black eel-stripe down the centre of the back and frequently with zebra markings on the legs and occasionally on the body; also grey.

Conformation Large, primitive looking head with convex profile; straight shoulders; poor hindquarters with low-set tail; long limbs, lacking in bone.

INTERESTING FACTS

The Sorraia is believed to be related to the Garrano, the pony of northern Portugal. The Garrano shows more quality than the Sorraia, the result of infusions of Arab blood. Although small, the Garrano is inherently hardy, and has been used for all types of farm work, as a pack-pony and for hauling timber.

Exmoor

The Exmoor is the oldest of Britain's Mountain and Moorland breeds and one of the oldest equine breeds in the world. This attractive pony has inhabited the wild moorland area of west Somerset and north Devon in the south-west of England for many centuries. Ponies of Exmoor type were certainly known during Roman times and may well have existed as far back as the Bronze Age, when they would have been used for pulling chariots. Mention is made of Exmoor ponies and their owners in the Domesday Book of 1085.

The remoteness of its habitat has meant that the Exmoor pony has been subjected to very little in the way of

"improvement" through the introduction of outside blood. The rigours of life on the moor have produced a tremendously hardy pony, strong enough to carry an adult rider in spite of the fact that the ponies stand no higher than 12.3hh.

The Exmoor Pony Society was founded in 1921 to improve and encourage the breeding of Exmoor ponies of the

traditional moorland type. By carrying out rigorous inspections, it ensures that no pony lacking true Exmoor type is registered as a pure-bred. When ponies are passed for registration, they are branded on the shoulder with the

BREED DESCRIPTION

Height Stallions and geldings not exceeding 12.3hh. Mares not exceeding 12.2hh.

Colour Bay, brown or dun with black points. No white markings anywhere.

Conformation Clean-cut face with wide forehead, large, prominent eyes, wide nostrils and clean throat; good length of rein; well laid-back shoulders; strong body with deep, wide chest, well-sprung ribs and broad, level back; clean, short limbs and neat, hard feet.

▌ TOP
The Exmoor's attractive head, notable for its large eyes, small, mobile ears and intelligent expression, is full of true pony character.

▌ RIGHT
The Exmoor is a fine stamp of pony: hard and strong, vigorous, alert and symmetrical in appearance. Its general poise indicates its good natural balance.

Society's star brand. Beneath this the pony's herd number appears, while on the nearside hindquarter there is the pony's own number within that herd.

Herds of ponies still run "wild" on the moor, although they are rounded up annually for inspection. The Exmoor's robust build and constitution make it an excellent riding pony and they are also used in the sport of driving.

INTERESTING FACTS

The most instantly recognizable features of the Exmoor are its mealy coloured muzzle and its large, prominent eyes. The latter are termed "toad" eyes because of their heavy top lids. The eyebrows are surrounded by light, buff-coloured hair.

■ ABOVE
Correctly handled and schooled, the Exmoor, for all its great strength, makes a good riding pony for a small child.

■ LEFT
The breed's inherent athleticism makes it a good all-round performance pony for an older child.

Dartmoor

BREED DESCRIPTION

Height Not exceeding 12.2hh.

Colour Bay, black or brown preferred, but no colours are barred except skewbald and piebald. Excessive white markings discouraged.

Conformation Small, well set-on head with small, alert ears; strong, medium length neck, not too heavy, stallions to have a moderate crest; strong back and loins; strong, muscular hindquarters with full, high-set tail; hard, well-shaped feet.

Unlike its neighbour, the Exmoor, the Dartmoor Pony has been influenced by a number of breeds over the many centuries during which ponies have run free on the high moorland of Devon, in south-west England. Ponies are thought to have lived on the moor during Saxon times. Later the important trade route which existed between Exeter and Plymouth would have been travelled by horses of many different types, some of which would almost certainly have had an influence on the native stock. Arabs and Barbs, brought back by Crusaders, are also believed to have found their way onto the moor.

Climate and the hardships of existing in such a wild region would have ensured that the animals roaming the moors achieved a certain degree of uniformity, particularly with regard to size. During the Industrial Revolution the requirements of the mining industry prompted a new development: the crossing of Dartmoor Ponies with the much smaller Shetland, in order to produce animals suited to working underground. This proved to be a highly retrograde step as far as the Dartmoor Pony was concerned. The type of riding-quality pony that had evolved began to deteriorate. In order to set matters right, new blood had to be introduced, including Welsh Mountain Pony, Polo Pony and Hackney.

The first stud book for Dartmoors was opened in 1899 and the height limits for

■ LEFT
Strength and active paces make the Dartmoor a
good harness pony.

INTERESTING FACTS

There was a steady decline in the numbers of
ponies of true Dartmoor type after World War II
and many of those found on the moor were
only poor quality cross-breds. However, in
1988 the Dartmoor Pony Society Moor
Scheme was set up in order to encourage
farmers with unregistered pure-bred type
ponies to offer them for registration and to
provide them with the services of pedigree
stallions. The aim is to establish a pool of
pure-bred ponies – hardy enough to thrive on
the moor – to which breeders can then go for
true native pony characteristics. Suitable
mares from the moor are put in large enclosed
areas known as newtakes together with a
pedigree stallion. Their female progeny are
inspected and those which pass muster are
entered in a supplementary register of the
stud book. In due course these ponies will also
be mated to a fully registered stallion, and so
on until their descendants, on inspection, can
be admitted to the full stud book.

■ RIGHT
**Dartmoors have a
calm temperament
and make good mounts
for children.**

■ OPPOSITE TOP
**The Dartmoor's neat,
well set-on head with
its small, alert ears,
shows true native pony
character.**

■ OPPOSITE
BOTTOM
**The best examples of
the breed combine
quality with great
hardiness.**

■ BELOW
**Although Dartmoor ponies declined in number and
quality after World War II, in recent times measures
have been introduced to ensure the preservation of
a pool of hardy pure-breds.**

stallions was given as 14hh and for mares
13.2hh. It was more than twenty years
before this was reduced to the present
12.2hh. Hackney blood was prominent in
a number of the foundation stallions.
However, the most influential sire of those
early years was undoubtedly The Leat, who
was by a pure-bred Arab (Dwarka, who
stood 14.1hh) out of a Dartmoor mare.
Standing 12.2hh, The Leat was a beautiful
looking pony with excellent conformation.
During his short stud career only a
handful of his progeny were registered,
but many of the best present-day ponies
trace back to him.

At its best the Dartmoor is a hardy,
quality riding pony with smooth, low, free
action. Its sound constitution, intelligence
and excellent, calm temperament, make it
an ideal pony for a child.

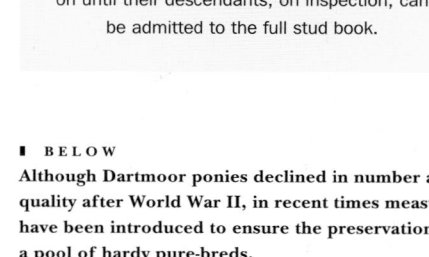

Welsh Mountain

The rugged landscape of Wales is home to four distinct equine breeds: two ponies, designated Section A and Section B in the Welsh Pony and Cob Society Stud Book, and two cobs, designated Section C and Section D.

At the base of all Welsh breeding is the beautiful Welsh Mountain Pony, Section A, which has thrived for many centuries in the tough environment of its native land

▌ ABOVE
The eastern influence is clearly visible in the beautiful head, with its big eyes, wide nostrils and dished profile.

▌ LEFT
The Section B is larger than the Welsh Mountain Pony but the best examples have the same true pony character. The action is straight, quick and free.

▌ BELOW
Section A ponies like this one were used in the development of the Australian Pony, which is based on Welsh and Arab blood.

BREED DESCRIPTION

Height Not exceeding 12hh.

Colour Predominantly grey, though bay, chestnut and palomino occur and any solid colour is permitted.

Conformation Small, clean-cut head, tapering to the muzzle, with bold eyes, small, pointed ears and prominent, open nostrils; lengthy, well-carried neck; long, sloping shoulders; strong, muscular back with deep girth, well-sprung ribs and strong loins; lengthy, fine hindquarters with tail well set on and carried gaily; good, strong limbs, with long, strong forearm, well-developed knee, large, flat hocks and well-shaped feet, of dense, hard horn.

and is considered by many people to be the most beautiful of all ponies. The development of the breed is obscure, but it goes back at least to the times of the Romans, who crossed horses of eastern origin with the native Welsh stock. In more recent times, particularly during the eighteenth century, some Thoroughbred, Arab and Barb blood was introduced.

The modern Welsh Mountain Pony is courageous and spirited, yet kindly, and makes a superb child's riding pony. It is also an outstanding performer in the increasingly popular sport of carriage driving. It has evolved as a supremely hardy individual, able to endure harsh weather conditions and to thrive on sparse rations. It has been used to improve other breeds, including the New Forest, and also in the development of the British Riding Pony. The Welsh Mountain Pony is popular in many countries outside its native Wales. It has been exported to Europe, the United States, New Zealand and Australia.

INTERESTING FACTS

The Welsh Pony (Section B) is larger than the Mountain Pony, though it retains the true pony characteristics. Arab, small Thoroughbred and small Welsh Cob stallions were crossed with Mountain Pony mares to develop this quality riding pony, which stands up to 13.2hh. Formerly used for shepherding and hunting, Welsh Ponies are now much in demand as children's riding ponies.

New Forest

Wild horses are known to have existed in the New Forest, in southern England, as far back as the time of Canute (c. 995–1035). The exact origins of today's New Forest Pony are, however, unknown although it has certainly been influenced down the years by a variety of other breeds. During the eighteenth century the Thoroughbred stallion Marske, the sire of the great racehorse Eclipse, was used for a time to

BREED DESCRIPTION

Height 13.3 – 14.2hh.

Colour Any colour except skewbald, piebald, or blue-eyed cream.

Conformation Rather large head; fairly short neck; well-sloped shoulders; deep body; strong hindquarters; straight limbs with plenty of bone and good hard, round feet.

serve New Forest mares and in the mid-nineteenth century an Arab stallion belonging to Queen Victoria was allowed to run with the herds. Hackney blood was also introduced. While these infusions of outside blood added to the pony's size, they were detrimental when it came to the preservation of true pony substance and to rectify the situation, outcrosses were made to stallions of other native breeds, including Dales, Dartmoor, Exmoor, Fell, Highland and, later, Welsh Mountain.

Today's New Forest Ponies, like many Exmoor and Welsh Mountain Ponies, still roam freely in their native habitat. Life in the Forest can be hard, the food supply often meagre and low in quality. This tough environment has produced a hardy, sure-footed animal. The pony's action is free, active and straight and its good temperament makes it easy to train. As a result they make excellent all-round riding and driving ponies. They are popular not only in their native country but also in mainland Europe, North America, Australia and New Zealand.

▌ TOP
The best type of New Forest Pony is strongly built and possesses good, well-sloped riding shoulders, powerful hindquarters and strong, sound limbs

▌ ABOVE LEFT
The New Forest's head indicates the breed's typically calm, tractable temperament.

INTERESTING FACTS

The ponies are owned by the New Forest Commoners, who carry out an annual "drift" or round-up in order to select those which are to be sold. The remaining breeding stock is then returned to the Forest.

Welsh Cob

The Welsh Cob (designated Section D in the Welsh Pony and Cob Society Stud Book) is derived from the Welsh Mountain Pony, of which it is, in essence, a larger version. It traces back at least to the twelfth century when eastern-type horses were brought back by the Crusaders and crossed with the local ponies. Subsequently infusions of Yorkshire Coach Horse, Norfolk Roadster and Arab blood were made.

Tough, sound, spirited and courageous, yet with an amenable temperament, the

▮ ABOVE
The action is straight, free and forceful. The whole foreleg is extended from the shoulders and as far forward as possible in all paces, with the hocks well flexed, producing powerful leverage.

▮ RIGHT
The Welsh Cob Section D is described by the breed society as the embodiment of strength and hardiness.

BREED DESCRIPTION

Height Above 13.2hh – usually 14.2 – 15.2hh.

Colour Any, except piebald and skewbald.

Conformation Quality, pony head with bold, widely set eyes and neat, well-set ears; long, well-carried neck; strong, well laid-back shoulders; strong, deep, muscular body; muscular hindquarters; short, powerful limbs with long, strong forearms, strong, muscular second thighs, large, flat joints and well-shaped feet.

INTERESTING FACTS

By crossing Welsh Mountain Pony mares with small Welsh Cobs breeders produced the Welsh Pony of Cob Type (Section C in the Stud Book), a smaller version of the Cob and a marvellous all-round riding and driving pony. It shares all the characteristics of its larger cousin, but does not stand over 13.2hh. Like the Cob, it was formerly much used by hill farmers and also to transport slate from the mines of North Wales. After World War II it was in danger of becoming extinct, but its numbers have since recovered and nowadays it enjoys popularity as a trekking pony, a small hunter and as a driving pony.

▍ RIGHT
A popular attraction in the show ring, the Welsh Cob is also a good hunter and a marvellous all-round performer in competitive sports.

▍ RIGHT
A quality head, depth through the girth and strong limbs, with an abundance of flat bone, are prerequisites of this sturdy breed.

Welsh Cob was traditionally used for all manner of heavy work on the hill farms, being equally at home in harness and under saddle. It was also formerly much in demand by the army, particularly for pulling guns and other heavy equipment. Possessed of active paces and great stamina, the Welsh Cob is renowned above all for its spectacular trotting action, inherited no doubt from the Norfolk Roadster. Indeed, up until 1918, when stallion licensing was introduced, breeding stock was selected by means of trotting matches. Nowadays, not surprisingly, the breed enjoys notable success in the sport of carriage driving.

Unique among the British Mountain and Moorland breeds, the Cob has no upper height limit, but whatever its size it should retain true pony characteristics – its quality head testifying to its Welsh Mountain Pony ancestry. When crossed with the Thoroughbred (particularly the second cross) the Welsh Cob produces excellent competition horses.

Highland

One of the strongest and heaviest of Britain's Mountain and Moorland breeds, the Highland Pony comes from the Highlands of Scotland and the islands off the west coast. Ponies are believed to have inhabited the region many thousands of years ago. The modern Highland Pony, sure-footed, hardy and long-lived, evolved as a result of various outcrosses, particularly Arab and Clydesdale. The Dukes of Atholl, influential breeders of Highland Ponies for several centuries, almost certainly introduced eastern blood as early as the sixteenth century.

Until fairly recently the breed was divided into two types: a more substantial mainland type, which stood up to 14.2hh,

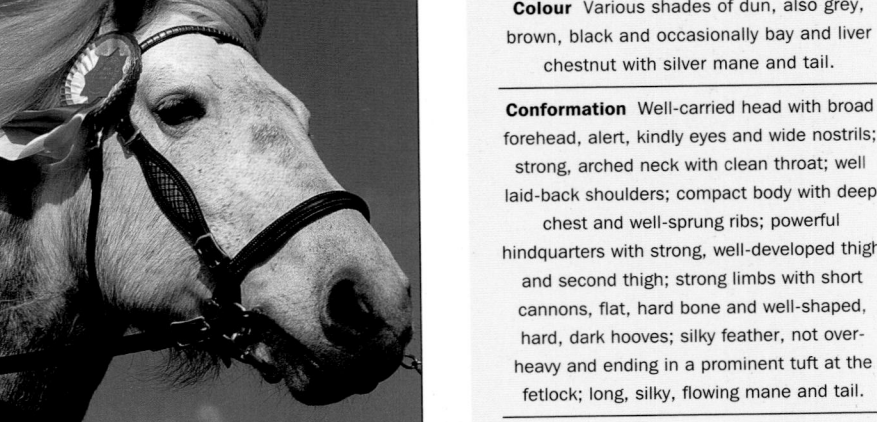

and the lighter, somewhat smaller Western Isles type. Although the Highland Pony Society, founded in 1923, no longer recognizes these distinctions, differences in type can still be discerned to some extent.

BREED DESCRIPTION

Height 13 – 14.2hh.

Colour Various shades of dun, also grey, brown, black and occasionally bay and liver chestnut with silver mane and tail.

Conformation Well-carried head with broad forehead, alert, kindly eyes and wide nostrils; strong, arched neck with clean throat; well laid-back shoulders; compact body with deep chest and well-sprung ribs; powerful hindquarters with strong, well-developed thigh and second thigh; strong limbs with short cannons, flat, hard bone and well-shaped, hard, dark hooves; silky feather, not over-heavy and ending in a prominent tuft at the fetlock; long, silky, flowing mane and tail.

The Highland is a strong, sturdily built pony, a real all-round worker which in its time has carried men to war, been the mount of shepherds, worked in harness, hauled timber, taken deer-stalkers into the hills and carried the shot stags – weighing

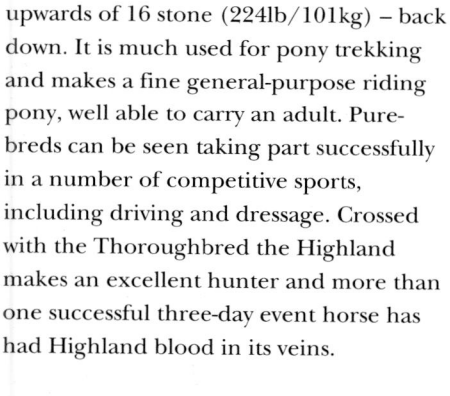

■ LEFT
The Highland Pony is a willing worker. It is still used on Scottish estates to carry game panniers and to cart shot stags.

upwards of 16 stone (224lb/101kg) – back down. It is much used for pony trekking and makes a fine general-purpose riding pony, well able to carry an adult. Pure-breds can be seen taking part successfully in a number of competitive sports, including driving and dressage. Crossed with the Thoroughbred the Highland makes an excellent hunter and more than one successful three-day event horse has had Highland blood in its veins.

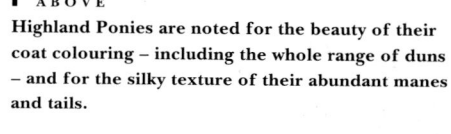

INTERESTING FACTS

One of the most striking features of the Highland is its colouring, particularly the various shades of dun: yellow, golden, mouse, cream and fox (yellow dun is believed to have been the breed's original colour). Most ponies show at least one of the characteristics of the primitive horse, i.e. a dorsal eel-stripe and zebra markings on the legs. These markings testify to the antiquity of the breed.

■ ABOVE
Highland Ponies are noted for the beauty of their coat colouring – including the whole range of duns – and for the silky texture of their abundant manes and tails.

■ BELOW
Versatility is one of the most valuable characteristics of the breed, which will haul timber as easily as it will carry a rider to hounds or go in harness.

■ OPPOSITE TOP
The Highland Pony's head is broad between the eyes, short from eyes to muzzle and well-carried on a strong, arched neck. The eyes have a kind expression.

■ OPPOSITE
Moulded by its harsh natural environment, the breed is strong, hardy, long lived and economical to feed. It is eminently sure-footed over the most treacherous terrain.

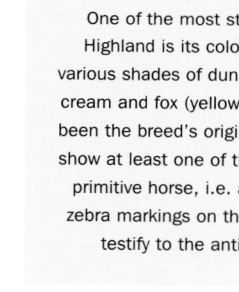

Shetland

Named after the remote group of islands situated to the far north-east of mainland Scotland and in the same northern latitude as south Greenland, the Shetland Pony is the smallest of the British native breeds. Its origins are uncertain but there have certainly been ponies in the Shetlands for many centuries and it may

BREED DESCRIPTION

Height Not exceeding 40 inches (102cm) at three years or under. Not exceeding 42 inches (107cm) at four years or over.

Colour Any colour except spotted.

Conformation Small, well-carried head with broad forehead, bold, dark, intelligent eyes, small, erect ears and broad muzzle with wide open nostrils; strong, deep body with short back and muscular loins; broad, strong hindquarters; strong limbs, with good, flat bone and short cannons; tough, round, well-shaped feet.

▮ LEFT
The Shetland's profuse growth of mane and tail afford valuable protection from the severe weather of its northern homeland.

well trace back to far more distant times.

Small of stature, it is nevertheless immensely strong – one of the strongest equine animals, in relation to size, in the world. Wonderfully well adapted to the vagaries of the islands' northern climate and the poor quality grazing, the Shetland is inherently hardy. Its action is free and straight, with a characteristic lift to its joints – the result of centuries of traversing rough, rocky or heather-covered terrain. An integral part of the lives of the

islanders, the ponies have traditionally been used both under saddle and as pack animals, carrying everything from grain to peat for fuel. They were formerly much in demand for coal mining, their small size and great strength making them perfect for work underground. Breeding flourished, though there was little attempt at selective breeding before the middle of the nineteenth century.

The Shetland has also found favour far from its native islands as a children's riding pony. It can be strong-willed but it is intelligent and responds to correct handling. With its active paces and manoeuvrability, it makes a particularly good driving pony and can be seen competing right up to international level.

▮ LEFT
Short-legged and stocky, the breed is noted for its great strength in relation to its diminutive size.

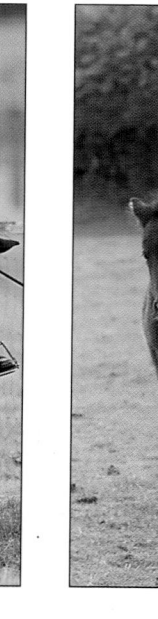

▌ ABOVE
Shetland Ponies can be wilful, but in the hands of a
competent child they make good riding ponies.

▌ RIGHT
Centuries of living on rough, rock-strewn terrain
have made the ponies both active and sure-footed.
Their feet are well-shaped and extremely hard.

INTERESTING FACTS

In winter the Shetland Pony grows a double
coat as protection against the inclement
climate of its native home. The coat has
"guard hairs", which shed rain and keep the
pony's skin completely dry, however severe
the weather. The mane and tail are profuse.

Dales

The Dales Pony comes from the Upper Dales (river valleys) of the eastern side of the Pennine Hills in northern England. It shares the same ancestors as its slightly larger neighbour, the Fell Pony, whose traditional home is on the western side of the Pennines. These ponies are believed to be descended from horses of the Roman period, when Friesians were introduced into northern England – this could have been the source of the Dales' predominantly black colouring. In more recent times various outcrosses are said to have been made, Norfolk Roadster among them. Some Welsh Cob blood was used during the nineteenth century and also Clydesdale. Despite the introduction of the latter, the Dales has retained its pony character, as can be seen in its neat head with its small, mobile ears.

The Dales is noted for its tremendously active paces and its great strength in relation to its size. At one time it played a vital part in lead mining, working both under- and overground, carrying loads of lead ore to the sea ports. It was also much

BREED DESCRIPTION

Height Not exceeding 14.2hh.

Colour Predominantly black, also bay, brown and, occasionally, grey.

Conformation Small, neat head, with wide forehead, bright eyes and small, erect ears; well-sloped shoulders; strong, deep body with short back, well-sprung ribs and strong loins; well-developed hindquarters; strong limbs with short straight cannons, good, clean joints and broad, very hard, well-shaped feet; fine, silky feather at the heel.

INTERESTING FACTS

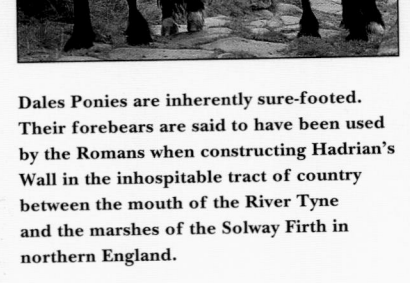

Dales Ponies are inherently sure-footed. Their forebears are said to have been used by the Romans when constructing Hadrian's Wall in the inhospitable tract of country between the mouth of the River Tyne and the marshes of the Solway Firth in northern England.

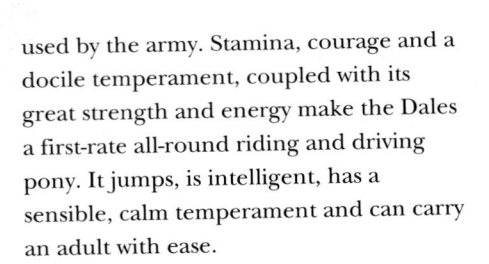

used by the army. Stamina, courage and a docile temperament, coupled with its great strength and energy make the Dales a first-rate all-round riding and driving pony. It jumps, is intelligent, has a sensible, calm temperament and can carry an adult with ease.

■ TOP
There have been native ponies on either side of the Pennines and in the Scottish borders for many centuries. They trace back in part to the Scottish Galloway although the Dales' black colouring probably comes from the influence of Friesian blood.

■ LEFT
The breed is particularly renowned for its strong limbs, good bone and excellent feet.

Fell

Like its relative, the Dales, the Fell Pony is believed to be descended from the Friesian which was brought to northern England during Roman times. Down the centuries it, too, was almost certainly influenced by the now extinct Galloway, the mount of border reivers (raiders, particularly cattle thieves) who needed a strong, fast, sure-footed horse for their nefarious purposes.

BREED DESCRIPTION

Height Not exceeding 14hh.

Colour Black, brown, bay and grey, preferably with no white markings, though a star or a little white on the foot is allowed.

Conformation Small, well set-on head with broad forehead, bright, prominent eye, small, neat ears, large nostrils and fine throat and jaws; strong neck but not too heavy, giving a good length of rein; good, sloping shoulders; strong, deep body with muscular loins; strong hindquarters with well set-on tail; strong limbs with plenty of good flat bone below the knee and well-formed feet with characteristic blue horn.

INTERESTING FACTS

HRH The Duke of Edinburgh competes in trials with a team of HM The Queen's Fell Ponies. With their lively trot and great stamina they are well suited to the marathon phase, run over a distance of 16 miles.

The Fell has evolved as a somewhat smaller, lighter pony than the Dales (official recognition of a distinction between the two did not come until 1916, when the Dales Pony Improvement Society and the Fell Pony Society were formed). The Fell is, nevertheless, enormously strong and, like the Dales, was used as a pack-pony. During the eighteenth century it transported lead, coal and iron ore to the coast, carrying up to 16 stone (224lb/101kg) at a time in panniers. Some were used in pack-trains to carry produce such as wool as far as London.

The Fell is noted for its good paces, having a fast, active walk and a swift trot. Now that it is no longer in demand for pack work, shepherding and general farm work, it has become a popular all-round pleasure pony. It makes an excellent mount for trekking, goes superbly across country, both under saddle and in harness, and has the paces to do well in pure dressage.

▌ ABOVE
Fell ponies are native to the western side of the Pennines. They are slightly smaller than their near neighbours, the Dales, but have the same inherent toughness and active paces.

▌ BELOW
The Fell makes a first-class riding pony. These ponies, pictured at a breed performance show, were competing in show jumping and mounted games as well as in show classes.

Connemara

Elegant, hardy, intelligent, possessed of tremendous agility and jumping prowess, the Connemara is arguably the best performance pony in the world. It is Ireland's only indigenous breed; it takes its name from the wild, rocky region on the western seaboard of Ireland where ponies have existed, in one form or another, since ancient times.

How this paragon among ponies developed is unclear. One theory is that it is descended from Barb and Spanish horses introduced into the west of Ireland as early as the sixth century BC, when the Celts overran the whole of Europe. These horses would then have been crossed with the indigenous stock. Also, during subsequent centuries of trade between the west coast of Ireland and the Iberian peninsula it is highly likely that quantities of horses would have been imported. The breed undoubtedly does show signs of Spanish and eastern blood to this day. The suggestion that the Connemara is descended from horses of the Spanish Armada that swam ashore after being shipwrecked in 1588 is nowadays dismissed by most experts as mere fancy!

Arab stallions are known to have been imported by landowners during the middle of the nineteenth century, but it is impossible to say what influence, if any, they had on the Connemara. During the latter part of the century, however, Welsh

BREED DESCRIPTION

Height Not exceeding 14.2hh.

Colour Predominantly grey but also brown, dun, black and occasionally chestnut and roan.

Conformation Short head, often with slightly dished profile, with broad forehead, dark, full eyes, small ears; long, arched neck giving good length of rein; well-sloped shoulders; deep, compact body; strong hindquarters with high-set tail; good strong limbs with short cannons and plenty of bone below the knee; strong, sound feet.

■ RIGHT
Excellent conformation - notably the well-sloped shoulders - make the Connemara a superb riding pony, possessed of strength, free-going movement and superb balance.

■ ABOVE
Connemaras in their natural habitat of western Ireland.

blood was certainly introduced and did play a part: one of the Welsh stallions, Prince Llewellyn, sired Dynamite out of a native mare. Dynamite in turn sired Cannon Ball (foaled in 1904), who is the first stallion listed in the Connemara Stud Book. Other attempts to "improve" the breed included the use of Thoroughbred, Hackney and Clydesdale blood.

Finally, in 1923, the Connemara Pony Breeders' Society was founded in Galway. It had the backing of the Department of Agriculture and the intention was to improve the breed from within, by seeking out the best type of mare and an appropriate number of similar quality stallions to use as foundation stock. The result of these efforts is an outstanding, quality pony of fixed type, courageous but sensible, able to excel in virtually all sports, from show jumping and three-day eventing to dressage and driving. When crossed with the Thoroughbred it produces a top-class performance horse.

■ BELOW
Traditional pony power: carting seaweed in Galway.

■ ABOVE
As a ridden pony the Connemara cannot be bettered. Spirited but sensible, courageous but kind, it is an ideal mount for children and adults alike.

Fjord

Norway's unusual looking Fjord Pony is believed to have inhabited Norway and probably other parts of Scandinavia since prehistoric times. At a quick glance it is not unlike the Przewalski's Horse (the Asiatic Wild Horse) in appearance, though the head is much less heavy and "primitive", being more pony-like in size and shape. Ponies resembling the Fjord are depicted in Viking art. They can be seen fighting, a pastime which was also popular in Iceland and which may have been engaged in for sport, as a form of performance testing or, probably, a combination of both.

Hundreds if not thousands of years spent in a mountainous habitat have

produced a pony that is perfectly adapted to its environment. Sturdy and muscular, the Fjord has short, strong legs with good joints and hard, sound feet. Down the centuries its inherent sure-footedness, strength, soundness and tremendous stamina have made it an invaluable

helpmate to farmers. Used to coping with severe weather conditions and undaunted by the most rugged terrain, it also proved the perfect pack-pony for use on mountain trails.

Nowadays the Fjord Pony can be found in a number of countries outside Scandinavia, including Germany, Denmark and England. It makes a good general-purpose riding pony and also goes well in harness.

BREED DESCRIPTION

Height 13 – 14hh.

Colour Most shades of dun with a black dorsal eel-stripe and, often, zebra markings on the legs.

Conformation Pony-type head with broad forehead and small ears; muscular neck; strong, deep body; fairly low-set tail; short, strong limbs with good joints, short cannons and plenty of bone; hard, sound feet.

■ LEFT
Although its natural environment is the mountains, the adaptable Fjord can be found in many other types of country, where it is valued both for its attractive appearance and its performance ability.

■ OPPOSITE TOP
The Fjord has a true pony head, with small ears, large, wide-set eyes and a small muzzle which is lighter in colour than the rest of the coat.

■ OPPOSITE
The pony's stocky build testifies to its great strength. Deep through the girth and with a particularly muscular neck and strong legs, it is a great little worker in areas not accessible to machines.

■ LEFT
The striking colouring of the mane and tail, with their black and silver hair, is unique to the Fjord Pony.

■ RIGHT
Fjords make excellent driving ponies. They have a kind, willing temperament but are active movers and, like all mountain breeds, exceptionally sure-footed.

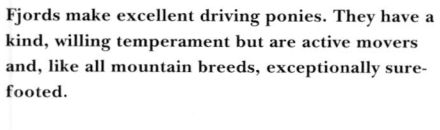

INTERESTING FACTS

One of the most distinctive features of the Fjord Pony is its unusual mane and tail colouring. Both mane and tail have black hairs in the centre, with silver on the outside. The stiff mane is traditionally cut in a curve with the dark inner hair standing higher than the outer silver hair.

Caspian

In 1965 an exciting discovery was made in northern Iran, in a remote, mountainous region not far from the Caspian Sea. Some three dozen miniature horses, no taller than a small pony but with the outward characteristics of a diminutive horse, were found. Detailed scientific examination revealed that these little horses had certain physical characteristics that did not match those of other horses: an extra full-sized molar on each side of the upper jaw; a scapula that was a different shape from that usually found in equine animals, and a slightly different formation of the three parietal bones in the head.

The Caspian Pony, as it has become known, is believed to be the direct descendant of the earliest equine animals that roamed the region around 3,000 BC. Bones have been excavated in Iran that point to the existence in the area of a very similar small horse at that period, a seal in the British Museum shows King Darius riding in a chariot drawn by horses of

Caspian type, and other artefacts of the period exist depicting similar small horses. It is thought possible that the Caspian is a far-off ancestor of the Arabian.

For many centuries the Caspian was mysteriously "lost". After its re-discovery a careful breeding programme was set up at studs in order to safeguard its future. Caspian Ponies can now be found in a number of European countries as well as Australia, New Zealand and the United States.

BREED DESCRIPTION

Height 10 – 12hh.

Colour Bay, grey and chestnut, with occasional white markings on head and legs.

Conformation Short, fine head with large eyes, vaulted forehead, fine tapering muzzle with large, low-set nostrils and very short ears; graceful neck; sloping shoulders; slim body with straight back and high-set tail; slim limbs but with dense, strong bone and little or no feathering at the fetlock; neat, oval, unusually strong hoofs.

The Caspian is extremely hardy, and possesses great speed and endurance as well as a kind temperament. It has dense bone and exceptionally hard, tough feet, which do not require shoeing. It makes a good riding pony and despite its small size has remarkable jumping ability.

▌ TOP
The skin on the Caspian's short, refined head is particularly fine. The ears should be no more than 4½ inches (11.5cm) long.

▌ ABOVE
On account of its small size the breed is described as a pony, although it has all the attributes of a miniature horse.

INTERESTING FACTS

Despite its lack of height, the Caspian has wonderful natural action; it can keep up with a horse at walk, trot and canter. Even at this early age the foal shows tremendous length of stride.

Riding Pony

Any pony which can be ridden is, technically, a "riding pony" but the Riding Pony which has been developed in Britain for showing purposes has evolved into a very definite type. It is essentially a child's hack, the equivalent of the adult rider's Thoroughbred show hack. It is not, therefore, surprising that small Thoroughbreds have been used in its development. Together with the Arab, the Thoroughbred was crossed with native ponies, particularly the Welsh and the Dartmoor, to produce ponies of great quality and excellent conformation. The best examples, while resembling the Thoroughbred in miniature, will not have lost the bone and substance of the native ponies and should certainly look like ponies, not small horses.

Since it is by definition a child's mount, the Riding Pony must have a sensible nature and be safe for children to ride; but since it is also a show pony, it must have presence and the long, low, graceful action of the Thoroughbred. The perfect combination of these elements, together with the retention of true pony character, is the challenge faced by all breeders of Riding Ponies. Riding Ponies may be entered in the National Pony Society Stud Book.

INTERESTING FACTS

In the show ring, as well as the height divisions there are classes for ponies ridden side-saddle, for pairs of ponies and for novice ponies. Ponies are judged on their paces, conformation and manners but are not required to jump.

BREED DESCRIPTION

Height Show class divisions – up to 12.2hh, 12.2 – 13.2hh and 13.2 – 14.2hh.

Colour Any whole colour; white markings are permissible.

Conformation Fine, quality head, with large, well-spaced eyes and small ears; fairly long neck; good sloping shoulders with clearly defined withers; medium length back, deep through the girth; well-muscled hindquarters with well set-on tail; clean, hard limbs with flat joints, short cannons and well let-down hocks; good, sound feet of equal size; no feather.

Pony of the Americas

This breed of spotted pony originated in the 1950s, the foundation sire, Black Hand, being the result of a mating between a Shetland pony stallion and an Appaloosa mare. Black Hand was the equivalent of a miniature Appaloosa. Interest in this concept of a spotted pony soon spread and the Pony of the Americas, as it became known, is now a popular all-round riding pony throughout the United States and also in Canada. It has its own breed society and stud book.

The Pony of the Americas stands no more than 13.2hh and must have one of the recognized Appaloosa colourings. It should be well proportioned, with substance, style and refinement – something like a miniature cross between a Quarter Horse and an Arabian. The pony's paces should be smooth and the action straight and free. The Pony of the Americas is a versatile performer. It is shown in Western pleasure and performance classes, as well as under English saddles and in harness. It has a kind nature and makes an ideal all-round riding pony for children.

▌ ABOVE
The head is clean cut and the pony has a kind eye, which reflects its docile, friendly nature.

▌ BELOW
In overall appearance the Pony of the Americas is not unlike the Quarter Horse, but with more refinement.

Leslie Boomhower, of Mason City, Iowa, was responsible for the mating of Shetland to Appaloosa which produced the breed's foundation sire.

BREED DESCRIPTION

Height 11.2–13.2hh.

Colour Normal Appaloosa markings – leopard, snowflake, blanket, frost, marble.

Conformation Clean-cut head, sometimes with slightly dished profile, with large, kind, prominent eyes and medium-sized, alert ears; slightly arched neck; deep, sloping shoulders with prominent withers; round, full-ribbed, heavily muscled body with well-sprung ribs and short back and loins; muscular hindquarters with long, level croup; strong limbs, with good clean joints; wide, well-shaped feet.

American Shetland

Shetland Ponies were first imported into America during the 1880s and quickly became popular. In 1890, when the American Shetland Pony Club was formed, there were over two hundred listed American breeders – Buffalo Bill Cody featuring prominently among them. Today there are large numbers of American Shetlands but, although they retain the name "Shetland", they do not bear a great deal of resemblance to the native "Sheltie" of Britain's Shetland Isles.

The American Shetland is the result of crossing pure-bred Shetlands with Hackney Ponies, with the addition of a little Arab and Thoroughbred blood. In appearance it is more like a Hackney than a British native pony. It is more refined than the true Shetland, being somewhat narrower and longer in the body and with longer, more slender limbs. The head, too, has lost the true pony character. Its high, extravagant action, which testifies to the infusion of Hackney blood, makes the American Shetland a popular harness pony.

BREED DESCRIPTION

Height Up to around 42 inches (103cm).

Colour Any.

Conformation Fairly long head with straight or slightly dished profile; long, graceful neck with pronounced withers; sloping shoulders; short, strong body and hindquarters; fairly long limbs.

■ LEFT
The American Shetland usually stands a couple of inches (5cm) taller than the true Shetland. The same range of colours occurs as in the original Scottish breed.

INTERESTING FACTS

The high-stepping action produced through the infusions of Hackney blood, has resulted in a pony well suited to harness classes. As with the American gaited horses, the action is enhanced by means of growing the feet longer than normal. Shetlands compete in classes for singles, pairs and tandems as well as in draught harness and under saddle.

■ ABOVE
Due to the addition of Hackney, Arab and Thoroughbred blood, the American Shetland has lost, in varying degrees, the true native pony character of its British ancestors.

Types

Horses and ponies with unusual or exotic coat colours and patterns have occurred throughout history and have usually been highly prized by man, regardless of their breeding. In recent times registers or stud books have been opened in some countries for the most popular of these colour types – in fact some now qualify for the title "breeds". The term "breed" is used to describe horses who have been bred selectively over a period of time and who have, as a result, developed fixed characteristics. Horses belonging to a particular breed have their pedigrees recorded in a stud book. The term "type" describes a horse bred for a particular purpose, such as hunting. Any number of permutations can be (and are) used to produce a horse suitable for riding to hounds and hunters cannot therefore be described as a breed. Horse and pony types, although few in number compared with the established breeds, nevertheless have an important role to play in the world of leisure riding.

Palomino

Throughout history man has prized horses with golden-coloured coats. Horses with this striking colouring are depicted in works of art, often dating back many centuries, from Asia, Japan and a number of European countries. Golden horses are referred to in Homer's *The Iliad* and in Norse legend. In Spain Queen Isabella,

sponsor of Columbus, encouraged their breeding, as a result of which they are often referred to in that country as "Isabellas".

There are various suggestions as to the derivation of the word Palomino, now used to describe golden horses. The most likely is that it comes from Juan de Palomino, who received a horse of this colouring from Cortès. Other theories are that it comes from the name of a Spanish grape or from the word *paloma*, meaning dove. Palomino colouring features in a number of breeds, therefore the term Palomino refers to a colour type, not a specific breed.

BREED DESCRIPTION

Height The registry of the Palomino Horse Breeders of America (PHBA) admits horses standing between 14 and 17hh.

Colour Body colour of a newly minted gold coin, with variations from light to dark. The skin is usually grey, black, brown or motley, without underlying pink skin or spots except on the face or legs. Black, hazel or brown eyes. White mane and tail with not more than 15 per cent dark, sorrel or chestnut hairs. Dorsal stripe and zebra stripes not permitted.

Conformation To be eligible for registration with the PHBA a Palomino must show refinement of head, bone, and general structure appropriate to the breeds recognized by the PHBA and be suitable for carrying Western or English equipment. It must show no pony or draught horse characteristics.

■ **PREVIOUS PAGE OPPOSITE**
A Paint horse with totiano markings.

■ **PREVIOUS PAGE**
Typical Palomino colouring.

■ **ABOVE**
Palominos always have a white mane and tail. For registration purposes the head must be of true riding horse proportions, with no pony or draught characteristics.

■ **LEFT**
This Quarter Horse is an admirable example of the requirements of the PHBA, which call for a body colour "of a newly minted gold coin".

RIGHT
Palominos, like this English pony, are found all over the world and do not have to be of any particular breed to qualify for registration as such.

BELOW RIGHT
Golden-coloured horses have been prized throughout history and in all parts of the world. These two were photographed in France.

cremello. Cross a Palomino with a sorrel and the chances are still only 50 per cent – and any Palomino colouring that is achieved may be too poor to be eligible for most Palomino societies. Cross a Palomino with any other colour and the chances of producing a Palomino foal diminish.

Despite the uncertainties involved in breeding for colour, Palomino horses retain their age-old appeal. Being good all-round riding horses – conformation should never be sacrificed for the sake of colour – they can be seen taking part in all kinds of activities, from cutting horse events to trail riding.

They may occur in many parts of the world, but Palomino horses are particularly associated with North America, where they were introduced by the Spanish Conquistadores. The origin of this type of colouring is uncertain but it is thought to have come from the Arab – though it is not found nowadays in the pure-bred Arabian horse. One of the intriguing, if frustrating, aspects of Palomino horses is that they do not "breed true", in other words there is no sure-fire way of ensuring Palomino colouring in a foal. It is all a question of genetics and the genetics of equine coat colouring is a complicated subject, involving dominant and recessive genes. Put simply, mate a Palomino to a Palomino and there is only a 50 per cent chance of a Palomino foal. There is a 25 per cent chance that the foal will be sorrel (a bright chestnut) and the same chance of the result being a pseudo-albino, known as a

Appaloosa

The spotted coat colouring of the American Appaloosa traces back to stock imported by the Spanish Conquistadores. Spotted horses became particularly prized by the Nez Percé Indian tribe who lived in the region that is now northern Idaho, north-east Oregon and south-east Washington. The word Appaloosa is derived from Palouse country, an area named after the Palouse river.

The Nez Percé are said to be the first Indian tribe to have practised systematic breeding of horses. Following the defeat of the Indians by the US army during the latter half of the nineteenth century, the horses which escaped slaughter became

■ LEFT
The eye-catching markings of the American Appaloosa are derived from Spanish stock imported by the Conquistadores.

■ BELOW LEFT
The Appaloosa is a compact, muscular stamp of horse. The sparse mane and tail hair are characteristic of the breed.

scattered. It was not until the 1920s that efforts were made to re-establish the Appaloosa horse, using the descendants of those which survived as a basis. In 1938 the Appaloosa Horse Club was founded in Oregon. Its objectives were to collect records and historical data relating to the origin of the Appaloosa, to preserve, improve and standardize the breed and to set up a register for approved animals.

The re-establishment of the Appaloosa has been a great success and today the breed is widely used in all types of Western riding, for endurance riding and in the show ring in both hunter and jumper classes. Appaloosas are mainly associated

BREED DESCRIPTION

Height Around 14.2 – 15.2hh.

Colour Spotted. The skin is mottled (especially noticeable around the nostrils and genitalia).

Conformation The Appaloosa is a compact stamp of horse with a well-shaped neck, short, strong back, powerful hindquarters and strong limbs with extremely good, hard feet.

INTERESTING FACTS

In America gaited spotted horses, that is those who show the ability to perform an intermediate gait other than the trot (such as the rack, foxtrot, running walk or pace) are termed Walkaloosas. To qualify for registration with the Walkaloosa Horse Association, which was founded in 1983, a horse must meet one of three criteria: either be the progeny of a registered Walkaloosa stallion and mare, or show Appaloosa colouring and demonstrate an intermediate gait other than trot, or be the product of verifiable Appaloosa (colour) and Paso, Foxtrotter or Tennessee Walker blood. The Walkaloosa's colouring is typical of that found in the Appaloosa, including white sclera round the eyes. Coat patterns include, but are not limited to, leopard, blanket and snowflake. The Walkaloosa, like the Appaloosa, is noted for its kind, sensible nature and makes an outstanding pleasure and trail horse.

▌ LEFT
This horse and rider, decked out in traditional style, recall the time when spotted horses were the preferred mounts of the Nez Percé Indians.

▌ FAR LEFT
Spotted horses are popular in many countries outside the United States. There is a thriving Appaloosa society in Britain – this horse was photographed at the Royal Windsor Horse Show.

with the United States but they are also found in many other countries.

There are five main Appaloosa coat patterns: leopard – white colouring over the loins and hips with dark, round or egg-shaped spots; snowflake – dark spots all over a white body but usually dominant over the hips; blanket – white area over the hips without dark spots in the white; marble – mottled all over the body; frost – white specks with a dark background. Other distinguishing features include white sclera round the eyes and, often, vertical black and white stripes on the hooves. The mane and tail tend to be quite sparse.

▌ LEFT
Noted for its strong limbs and the excellence of its feet, the Appaloosa makes a good endurance riding horse.

Paint Horse

Horses with broken coloured coats (also known as piebalds and skewbalds) are found all over the world, though they are particularly associated with the North American Indian.

In America a horse with this type of colouring may be registered either as a Paint Horse or as a Pinto, depending on the horse meeting certain criteria. The American Paint Horse Association was founded in 1962 to provide a register for horses with individual, colourful patterns of contrasting light and dark hair and skin, and distinctive stock-type conformation. To qualify for registration with the APHA

horses must be bred from registered American Paint Horses, registered American Quarter Horses or registered Thoroughbreds and must meet a minimum colour requirement. A horse with a predominantly solid-coloured coat must have a definite "natural" Paint marking, which is defined as an area of solid white hair with some underlying,

unpigmented skin. A horse with a mainly white hair coat must have a contrasting area of colour with some underlying, pigmented skin. The contrasting areas should be visible at the time the foal is born and at the time of registration.

The APHA maintains two registries, the Regular and the Breeding Stock. To be eligible for inclusion in the Regular

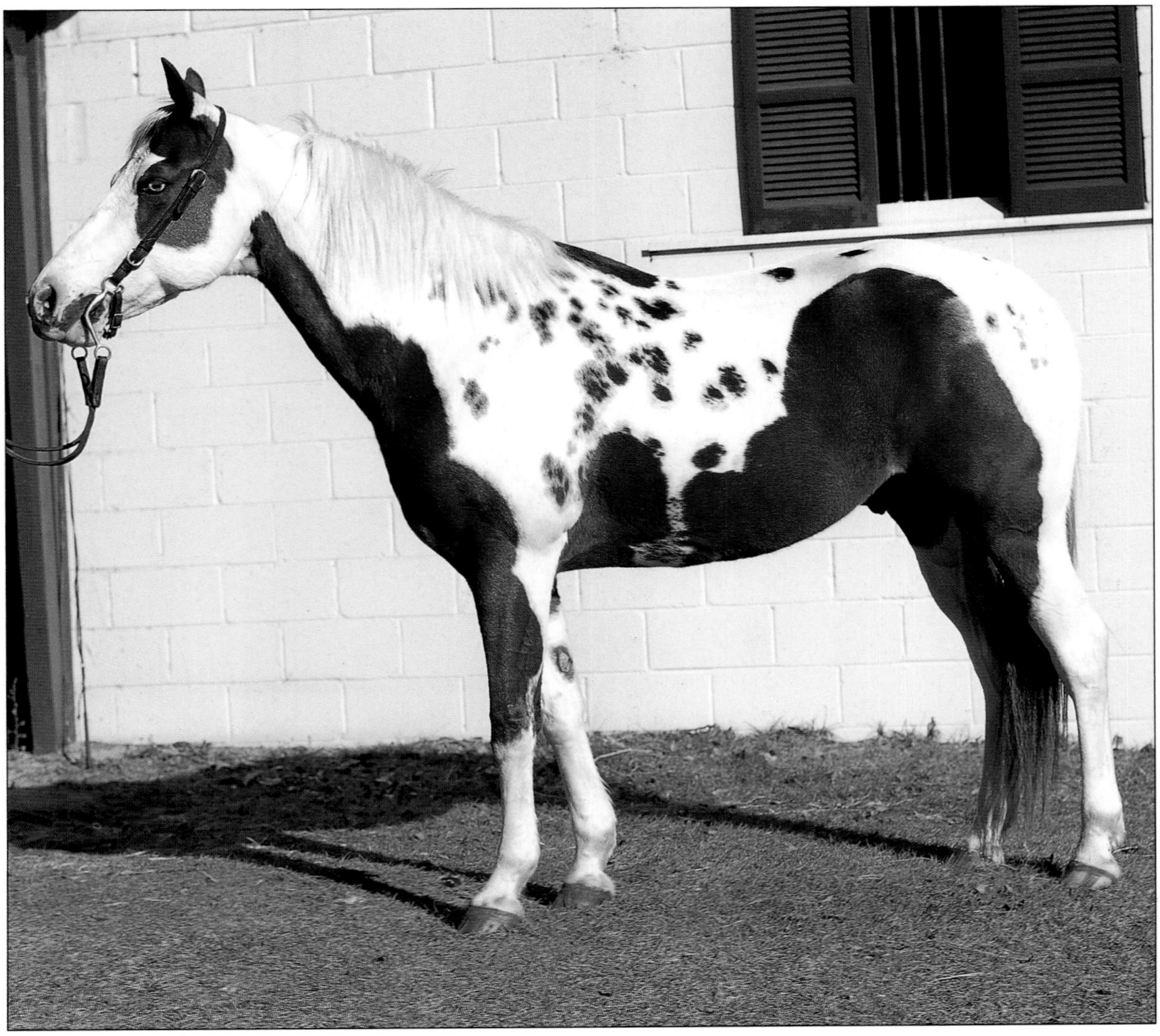

BREED DESCRIPTION

Because horses of various breeds are eligible for registration as Paint Horses, there is accordingly a degree of variation in the height and overall size. However, all American Paint Horses have distinct stock-type conformation. This may be generally defined as an animal whose bone and muscle construction make it highly adaptable to ranch work. It will be both versatile and athletic.

▎ TOP LEFT
This Paint horse has tobiano markings: dark colouring on the flanks, a "shield" down the neck and chest and white legs.

▎ OPPOSITE
Paint horses have always been associated with the American West. The horse on the left is an overo with a bald face.

▎ LEFT
The characteristic shape and build of the Paint horse is that of the stock horse: good overall riding horse conformation and a sturdy, compact appearance.

▌ BELOW
Like the Paint horse, the Pinto has overo or tobiano colouring (this horse is a tobiano). For registration purposes, Pintos are divided by conformation type.

Registry the foal must have at least one "natural" Paint marking which is a minimum of 2 inches (5cm) in diameter. If a horse does not meet the required colour requirement but meets the other registration requirements (for example a solid-coloured foal resulting from a mating between two registered American Paint Horses), it may be entered in the Breeding Stock Registry.

The spectrum of coat colours in the Paint Horse encompasses all of the tones known in the horse world. The patterns range from almost total colour with a minimal amount of white to almost total white with minimal colour. The patterns are distinguished by the location of colour on the horse, the two major ones being overo and tobiano.

Overo horses have the following characteristics: the white usually will not cross the back of the horse between the withers and the tail; generally at least one and often all four legs will be dark; generally the white is irregular, rather scattered or splashy, and is often referred to as calico; head markings are often bald-faced, apron-faced or bonnet-faced; the tail is usually one colour.

Tobiano horses have the following characteristics: the dark colour will usually cover one or both flanks; generally all four legs will be white, at least below the hocks and knees; generally the spots are regular and distinct as ovals or round patterns which extend down over the neck and chest, giving the appearance of a shield; head markings are like those of a solid-coloured horse – solid colour or with a blaze, stripe, star or snip; the tail usually displays two colours.

Horses with overo and tobiano characteristics are called toveros.

INTERESTING FACTS

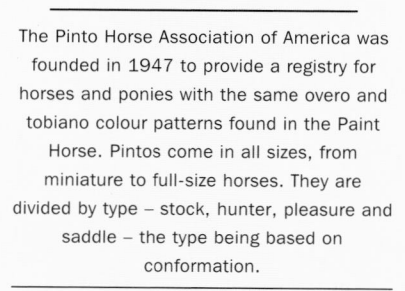

The Pinto Horse Association of America was founded in 1947 to provide a registry for horses and ponies with the same overo and tobiano colour patterns found in the Paint Horse. Pintos come in all sizes, from miniature to full-size horses. They are divided by type – stock, hunter, pleasure and saddle – the type being based on conformation.

Stock Type Horse – of predominantly Quarter Horse breeding and conformation (horses which are double registered as Paint generally fall into this category). Conformation is that generally associated with a Western breed of horse. Pony – Western type, displaying conformation similar to the Quarter Horse.

Hunter Type Horse – of predominantly Thoroughbred/Jockey Club breeding (a few Paint Horses fit this category). Conformation is that generally associated with an English riding horse. Pony – reflects conformation associated with the Thoroughbred horse and Connemara pony.

Pleasure Type Horse – of predominantly Arabian or Morgan breeding. Pony – reflects carriage and conformation associated with the Arabian, Morgan or Welsh Pony.

Saddle Type Horse – of predominantly Saddlebred or Tennessee Walking Horse breeding, displaying the high head carriage and animation. Pony – reflects conformation and action of the American Shetland and Hackney Pony.

For registration in the Colour Division a Pinto must have noticeable white markings on the body, not including the head and legs. Those areas must be large enough to show Pinto breeding and colour pattern. A dark cheek or cap, or spotted face on a white horse, is a marking common to the Pinto. An all-white horse with a coloured area on the head and on the body is a Pinto, as is a solid coloured animal with a spot on the body; but the amount of colour, its location, the bloodlines of the parents and the sex and age of the animal determine whether it may be registered in the Colour Division or in the Breeding Stock Division.

Knabstrup

Spotted horses have been known – and have often been highly prized – since ancient times. They can be seen in early Chinese art and there were spotted strains of the Noriker (Austria's old-established light draught breed) and the Spanish horses which were so influential in the development of many of the world's modern breeds. Denmark's once-famous Knabstrup is of Spanish ancestry and dates back to the time of the Napoleonic Wars. At that time a spotted mare named Flaebehoppen was acquired by a butcher called Flaebe (hence her name). Flaebehoppen, an exceptionally fast mare possessed of great endurance, was bred by her next owner, Judge Lunn, to Frederiksborg horses and founded a line of spotted horses. Named the Knabstrup, after Lunn's estate, this strain was rather less substantial than the Frederiksborg but

BREED DESCRIPTION

Height Around 15.2 – 16hh.

Colour Mainly white, with brown or black spots of varying size over the body, head and legs.

Conformation Variable, but the best examples have reasonably good overall conformation, with a kind, intelligent head. The mane and tail are usually sparse, as in the majority of spotted horses.

INTERESTING FACTS

The breed's remarkable talents as a circus horse were demonstrated in America not so long ago when a centre-ring attraction consisted of a large Bengal tiger riding a Knabstrup horse. The horse wore protective harness – in case the big cat slipped and decided to hang on with his claws!

was tough and sound and, because of its attractive markings, became popular as a circus horse. Subsequent crossings back to the Frederiksborg reduced the number of pure-bred Knabstrup horses but examples of the breed are still to be found, though not in anywhere near the numbers of the American Appaloosa.

▌ TOP LEFT
The mottled skin colouring of the lips and muzzle, so typical of all spotted horses, can be clearly seen on this Knabstrup.

▌ LEFT
The characteristic white body hair with all-over dark spots, together with its intelligent, kind nature, made the Knabstrup a popular circus horse.

Spotted Pony

Spotted Ponies are known to have existed in Britain, and especially in Wales and the West Country, for many centuries. The Romans are said to have brought spotted horses into the country and some of the ancestors of today's Spotted Ponies would have been imported Spanish horses. The creation of a breed society for these striking looking animals is, however, of very recent origin. A British register for spotted horses and ponies was created in 1947 and then in 1976 the organizing society was split, with ponies up to 14.2hh coming under the aegis of the British Spotted Pony Society and larger animals being entered in the British Appaloosa registers.

To qualify for registration ponies must display some of the following features: white sclera round the eye; mottled skin – this part-dark, part-pink skin is usually most evident around the genitals, lips, muzzle, eyes and inside the ears; and striped hooves. If ponies are of solid colour but have proven spotted breeding,

BREED DESCRIPTION

Height Not exceeding 14.2hh.

Colour Leopard (spots of any colour on white or light background); few spot leopard (white base coat with few spots); snowflake (white spots on dark base coat); blanket (area of white over hips and hindquarters, with or without spots, any base colour).

Conformation Quality pony head with big, bold eyes set well apart, small, neat, well-placed ears, prominent, open nostrils and clean, well-defined throat; good length of neck, moderately lean in mares, inclined to be more cresty in stallions (slightly heavier neck allowed in cob type); good, strong, sloping shoulders, well laid back, with well-defined withers; strong, muscular body with deep girth and well-sprung ribs; lengthy, strong, well-muscled hindquarters with well set-on tail (slightly finer hindquarters in riding type); good limbs, with long, strong forearms, well-developed knee, well let-down hocks, short cannons; well-shaped, dense hooves.

INTERESTING FACTS

As with all colour types, breeding for spots is a question of genetics. Some ponies which have spotted coats when young may lose their spots as they grow older. They are known as "faders". Fading is caused by the dominant grey gene. Raised spots, that is ones that stand out above the rest of the pony's coat, rarely fade. The colour of the foal's coat cannot be used as a guide to the adult pony's colouring, since the colour often changes with the first change of coat.

they are eligible for entry in a separate register but they should preferably show some breed characteristics. Piebald and skewbald ponies are not eligible, nor are their progeny.

Spotted Ponies may be of small, riding or cob type, but all should show true pony character and must have bone, substance and active paces. They make good all-round performance ponies, both under saddle and in harness, and there is growing interest in ridden and in-hand show classes. British Spotted Ponies have been exported to Australia, North America and several European countries, including France, Germany and Holland. Indeed, the demand from overseas has led to so many good mares and stallions being exported that the breed society has now introduced performance and sire-rating awards in order to encourage breeders to keep more of the best stock at home.

▌ TOP LEFT
The British Spotted Pony has the large, expressive eyes, neat, mobile ears and open nostrils that are characteristic of all good types of pony.

▌ LEFT
Versatile and strong, the British Spotted Pony makes a good all-round riding pony and has also been used with great success in four-in-hand driving.

Hunter

As its name implies, a hunter is a horse used for riding to hounds. It is a type, not a breed, and there is no fixed "recipe" for producing a hunter. It is, however, generally accepted that the finest hunters are bred in Ireland, Britain and, to some extent, the United States.

The type of horse required for hunting varies according to the nature of the country hunted – a big, quality Thoroughbred type may be perfect for galloping and jumping over the grassland of the English "shires", but will be less than ideal for areas of heavy plough or trappy hill country, where boldness and speed are less important than steadiness and sure-footedness. Whatever the exact type of horse required, however, a hunter must have correct conformation, without which he is unlikely to stand up to the

hard work required of him. He must be well balanced and give a comfortable ride. He needs to be agile and fearless but also well mannered and controllable. He must have the necessary speed to keep up with hounds and the stamina to see him through a long day of physical exertion, often twice a week during the hunting season. He must also have jumping ability,

the exact degree depending on the type of country hunted.

The Irish hunter is often produced by crossing the Thoroughbred with the Irish Draught, while many of the best British hunters have an element of native pony blood, again laced with Thoroughbred. There is no fixed height and in hunter showing classes in Britain and Ireland the horses are divided according to their weight-carrying ability.

■ ABOVE LEFT
In the show hunter, the judge is looking for as near perfect conformation as possible. The horse must also give a good ride and be well mannered.

■ LEFT
Depth through the girth is essential to allow for expansion of the lungs. Well-sloped shoulders ensure free-going action. The horse's weight-carrying ability is determined by its overall build and the amount of bone (measured round the cannon, below the knee).

BREED DESCRIPTION

Height From 14.2hh upwards.

Colour Any.

Conformation Well set-on head and neck, giving good length of rein; well-sloped shoulders; strong, shortish back with well-sprung ribs and great depth through the girth; strong loins; powerful hindquarters; strong limbs with large joints and plenty of bone; strong, well-shaped feet.

Cob

The cob is a short-legged "stuffy" type of small horse, stocky in appearance and capable of carrying a heavyweight rider. Its kind, unflappable, willing nature and impeccable manners, coupled with its weight-carrying ability, make it an ideal mount for a heavyweight elderly rider – or indeed for anyone who is not particularly athletic.

As with the hunter, there is no set formula for breeding a cob. Many of the best are produced by chance, although Irish Draught blood is often used with great success, particularly when mixed with Thoroughbred. The cob's sturdy, muscular proportions are not designed for great speed, but it should none the less have active paces and be able to gallop and to jump well.

At one time the cob was used as an all-purpose horse, performing equally well in harness and under saddle. Nowadays it is most often seen as a riding horse – the best make excellent hunters.
Under British Show Hack and Cob Association

■ **ABOVE RIGHT**
Good conformation ensures that the cob possesses tremendous freedom of movement despite its chunky proportions.

■ **RIGHT**
The overall impression of this most workmanlike of horses should be one of intelligence, calmness and reliability.

In the show ring cobs are judged like hunters and are expected to show that they can gallop. The judge rides each exhibit in turn to assess the quality of ride they give.

rules, cobs are exhibited in two weight classes: as lightweights, capable of carrying up to 14 stone (196lb/89kg) and as heavyweights, capable of carrying over 14 stone. There are also working cob classes, in which the horses must jump a working hunter-type course of fences.

The cob's mane is traditionally hogged (cut short). It used to be the custom to dock the tail of cobs but this cruel practice was made illegal in Britain under the Docking and Nicking Act, 1948.

TYPE DESCRIPTION

Height Up to about 15.3hh (in show classes not over 15.1hh).

Colour Any.

Conformation Intelligent looking head, with no suggestion of coarseness; fairly short, arched neck; strong, sloping shoulders; broad, deep body with short back and powerful loins; strong, well-muscled hindquarters; short, strong limbs with plenty of bone; broad, open feet.

Hack

In Britain the hack is a supremely elegant, refined type of show horse – although the word "hack" is also used to describe any horse suitable for general riding purposes (as opposed to competitive sports, such as eventing or hunting).

The term hack goes back to the days before the motorization of transport, when "park hacks" were used by the most fashionable people of the day for leisure riding, notably in London's Rotten Row, in Hyde Park. In appearance and manners the park hack was impeccable, thus complementing its elegant, well turned-out rider. In the hunting world riders formerly made use of the "covert hack", a quality horse with less substance than a hunter, to take them to the meet – their grooms having ridden the hunters on beforehand at a leisurely pace to conserve their energy for the day ahead.

◼ ABOVE
Gaiety and lightness of movement are essential attributes of the show hack.

Today's show hack is nearer to the park hack and is usually Thoroughbred, or near Thoroughbred. It is judged on conformation, presence, action, training, ride and manners – it should give a comfortable ride and its manners should be faultless. During judging, horses are usually required to give a solo show, designed to demonstrate the horse's correct training and obedience. It should include walk, trot and canter on both reins and a good halt, with the horse standing still on a loose rein.

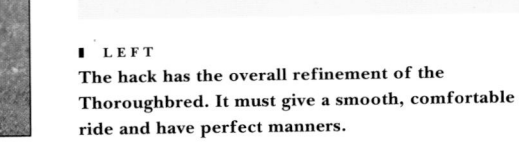

TYPE DESCRIPTION

Height 14.2 – 15.3hh.

Colour Any solid colour.

Conformation Small, quality head; elegant neck; well-sloped shoulders with prominent withers; strong body with deep girth and well-sprung ribs; well-rounded hindquarters; good, sound limbs with at least 8 inches (20cm) of bone; good, sound feet.

INTERESTING FACTS

Hacks are shown in two height classes: small hack, for horses exceeding 14.2hh but not exceeding 15hh, and large hack, for horses exceeding 15hh but not exceeding 15.3hh. There are also classes for ladies' hacks (14.2 – 15.3hh) in which horses are shown under side-saddle.

◼ LEFT
The hack has the overall refinement of the Thoroughbred. It must give a smooth, comfortable ride and have perfect manners.

Polo Pony

The ancient game of polo is believed to have originated in Persia some 2,500 years ago. It was subsequently played in India, the Far East and Tibet, reaching the western world – England and then North and South America – during the nineteenth century. Any pony used in the game is technically a polo pony but the modern polo pony has evolved as a definite type. Many of the best animals are bred in Argentina or at least are descended from Argentinian stock.

By the beginning of the twentieth century the sport was well established in Argentina, where breeders produced suitable mounts by crossing their Criollo horses with imported Welsh ponies. After the 14.2hh height limit for polo ponies was abolished in 1919 the Argentinians began introducing English Thoroughbred blood, which produced animals of greater quality and with more speed.

The polo pony must be capable of short bursts of speed but does not require the long stride of a racehorse. Far more important is a smooth action, which makes the rider's job of hitting the ball easier, the ability to accelerate and decelerate quickly, and to make fast turns. The essential qualities of the polo pony are courage, stamina and natural balance.

▐ RIGHT
Whatever their height, polo ponies are always referred to as "ponies", not horses.

INTERESTING FACTS

Between the two World Wars some of the best polo players were to be found in India, where the game was popular both with members of the native aristocracy and in the Indian army. The game there was immortalized by Rudyard Kipling (1865–1936) in *The Maltese Cat*, the story of an inter-regimental match seen through the eyes of the equine participants. A flea-bitten grey, brilliantly quick on his feet, "The Cat" knows more about "playing the game" than most humans!

▐ FOLLOWING PAGE
Mares and foals at grass in Kentucky.

▐ LEFT
A typically intelligent looking Argentinian polo pony. It is customary to hog the mane to prevent the hair obstructing the player's stick.

TYPE DESCRIPTION

Height Around 15.1hh.

Colour Any.

Conformation Variable, the chief requirements being: fairly long, well-muscled neck; sloping shoulders with well-defined withers; strong, deep body with fairly short back and well-sprung ribs; well-rounded, muscular hindquarters; strong limbs with short cannons, good joints and plenty of bone; well-shaped, round feet.

Horse and
Pony Care

Buying a Horse

Everyone who takes part in sport on a regular basis reaches the stage when they want their own equipment. Whether it is a tennis racquet, a fencing foil, a pair of skis or a yacht, owning rather than hiring makes life easier on two counts: the equipment will be available whenever it is required and, most importantly, the owner's performance will almost certainly improve because that equipment will have been selected with their skills and limitations in mind. Riders, however, are faced with a problem not encountered by other sportsmen: their most important piece of equipment is not a man-made object which, to varying degrees, can be tailored to fit individual needs. The horse is a living creature, with a mind, will and personality of his own. He is an expensive animal both to buy and to keep. Choosing the right one is not always easy; choosing the wrong one can be disastrous, both for an owner's bank balance and for his or her confidence. The prospective horse owner should proceed with caution and the rewards will be great.

Choosing the Right Horse

Before you buy a horse make an honest assessment of your riding ability, bearing in mind that most people tend to over-estimate their skill. Talented, experienced riders get the best from all sorts of horses, even those with difficult temperaments. They can school and bring on the young horse, improve the poorly educated older one and ensure that the well-trained performer is used to the best effect. A novice rider, who has only just mastered the basics of horsemanship, can do none of these things and should choose a mount accordingly. The novice needs a correctly schooled, well-mannered mount with a kind disposition, one who will look after his rider. The term "schoolmaster" is aptly used to describe these equine paragons.

For the majority of people cost is one of the most important factors and the purchase price will be determined by a number of things: the type, size and conformation of the horse or pony; its age; its temperament and manners; its performance capabilities (either proven or potential) and its level of schooling.

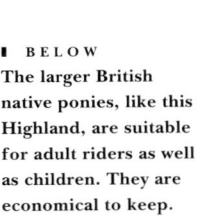

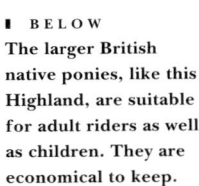

■ **RIGHT**
The majority of warmbloods, specifically developed as sports horses, make fine show jumpers. This horse is a Holstein.

■ **BELOW**
The larger British native ponies, like this Highland, are suitable for adult riders as well as children. They are economical to keep.

■ **PREVIOUS PAGE OPPOSITE**
A Dartmoor pony: a suitable ride for a child.

■ **PREVIOUS PAGE**
A Karbardin horse: ideal for endurance riding.

■ **LEFT**
With the right horse, the experience of ownership will be enjoyable and rewarding for both horse and rider.

Generally speaking, an unbroken two- or three-year-old will be cheaper than a four- or five-year-old which has already received some schooling; after that the horse gradually increases in value until it reaches the age of about ten. Once into its teens, it will tend to decrease in value.

Apart from price, your choice of horse or pony will be determined by your size and weight; your riding ability; your stabling/grazing facilities; the amount of

time you have to look after it, and the use to which you intend to put it. For example, there is no point in spending a lot of money on a flighty Thoroughbred if you are a nervous rider who wants to do no more than go for quiet hacks; similarly, a pure-bred Arab is not going to take you to the top in the show-jumping world. As to size, much depends on your own build – someone with long legs will certainly be more comfortable on a big horse than someone with short legs and vice versa, and it is usually easier to ride well if you are neither under- nor over-horsed. Temperament and manners are a vital consideration, too. Nervous riders need placid (though not lazy) mounts if they are not to be frightened and put off riding altogether, while a bolder rider will be able to cope with, and enjoy, a more spirited ride.

■ BELOW
If quiet hacks out are your aim, make sure you don't choose the horse who is too spirited.

■ RIGHT
For endurance riding, choose a horse with proven stamina. Arabs and part-bred Arabs are particularly suited to the higher levels of this sport.

■ BOTTOM
Experienced riders will be able to school young horses, but novice riders should learn on a more experienced horse.

Unless you are planning to become involved in an activity which requires a specific breed – such as a particular category of showing – you will have a wide variety of breeds and types to choose from. Always bear in mind, however, your intended use for the horse: for endurance riding he will need great stamina; for eventing, stamina plus speed; for dressage, excellent movement. While stallions often excel in the last named discipline and are increasingly seen in other types of equine competition as well, they do require more expert handling than geldings and mares, and are not suitable for the novice horse owner. Mares can be more moody and take rather more understanding than geldings (very often, though, a good competition mare is very good indeed). They do, of course, come into season regularly during the summer months and this can be a problem.

If you have good stabling and grazing facilities, you can keep any type or breed without a problem. Lack of stabling will tend to determine what you can or cannot buy, particularly if you live in a region where the winters are cold and wet and/or the summers excessively hot. A British native pony will do perfectly well living out all year round, provided supplementary feed is given in winter, as necessary. A thin-skinned Thoroughbred, on the other hand, may not thrive unless he has the shelter of a stable, at least at night. If you wish to keep your horse at peak fitness for competition work or hunting, you will certainly need the use of a stable.

Then there is the question of how much time you can devote to looking after your horse. If you have a full-time job, and limited time for weekday exercising, life will be easier for you and your horse if he can live out or at least be turned out during the day.

If you are not planning to do a lot of strenuous competition work, then age need not be too much of a factor, though of course the older the animal the more work he is likely to have done and the more wear and tear there will have been on his legs and body by the time you buy him. However, for general riding purposes horses and ponies often go on well into their late teens and even early twenties. A young horse will, of course, have many more useful years ahead of him and will be easier to sell on for a good price. However, young horses are not suitable for the novice rider, who will be unable to give them the necessary schooling.

Where to Buy

There are various ways to buy a horse. These include at a public sale, through a dealer, from a private vendor advertising in the equestrian or local press, or perhaps from the riding school where you have been taking lessons.

The novice rider is generally advised not to buy at a public sale. The problem is not that all sales are conducted by less than reputable people – that is certainly not the case – but that everything takes place so quickly and there may not be sufficient opportunity for the purchaser to ride the horse. Buying in this way calls for an expert, practised eye and it is incumbent upon the purchaser to be observant. For instance, if a horse offered for sale has an obvious physical defect, the onus is on the purchaser to see it – a subsequent plea of ignorance will not be accepted. On the other hand the horse must correspond to its description – a horse described as a show jumper must be able to jump – and the buyer is entitled to return it if this proves not to be the case (or, if necessary, to sue for damages).

Dealers are businessmen with a reputation to maintain and are unlikely to try to sell you a bad lot. Your local riding school may be able to put you in touch with one or, failing that, you may see them advertising in the equestrian press. The advantages of buying through a dealer are that you will almost certainly have the choice of several horses and there should be plenty of opportunity to see them being handled and to ride them yourself. Some dealers may also allow you to try the horse at home and, if you have a horse to sell, may offer part-exchange terms.

Buying from a private vendor – and there are always a great many advertising in the equestrian and farming press as well as in local newspapers – may seem the simplest way of acquiring a horse but it is not necessarily the safest. Here the rule is *caveat emptor* (let the buyer beware), a common law maxim warning you that you cannot claim that your purchase is defective if you have not obtained express guarantees from the vendor. Many of the horses and ponies described in the "For Sale" columns are up for sale for perfectly genuine reasons but others may not be. It is easy to compose an advertisement praising their good points but omitting their shortcomings. Just because a horse is good to box and shoe does not mean that he is quiet to clip or sensible in traffic. The brilliant jumper may refuse to go into a horsebox or trailer. The otherwise perfect equine specimen may, when you get him home, persist in jumping out of his paddock, refuse to be caught, or chew his stable, his rugs, his bandages – or all three. Often it is not so much what the advertisement does say but what it omits to say, so you must be prepared to ask the right questions.

If you have been attending a good riding school, the proprietor should be able to advise on the purchase of a horse or pony and may well have one on the premises which would suit you. The advantage here is that the instructor will have a good knowledge of your skills and limitations as a rider.

▌ LEFT
There are plenty of horses available from private vendors. Be sure to find out as much as possible about the horse.

▌ LEFT
Buying horses from sales is best left to the experts because everything happens so quickly.

Trying a Horse

▮ BELOW
When trying a horse, ride him at different paces
and have a jump if you wish.

When you learn of a horse which you think may suit your purpose, the first step is to make an appointment to see it and try it. Always take a more knowledgeable person along with you both to offer expert advice and to act as a witness to any sale. If you have no one who will do this as a friend, it is worth paying for an expert opinion.

Explain to the vendor exactly what you want to use the horse for and ask specific questions: is the horse good to box, clip, shoe, catch, in traffic, etc. Ask to see the horse led up outside and pay close attention to how he behaves while he is having his rugs removed and his bridle put on. Note the bit which is being used. Cast an eye around the inside of the stable and the door for signs of kick marks or chewing. It may be that this is not the horse's usual box but if it is, such signs could indicate a behavioural problem. Ask to see the horse stood up outside and view him from both sides to assess his conformation before having him walked and trotted up. Make sure that he is trotted up on a loose rein both away from you and towards you (leading a horse on a short rein can help to cover up defective action).

Before you ride him, watch the vendor put him through his paces to see how he goes with a familiar rider. Then ask your expert adviser to try him. If the vendor failed to ask the horse to do certain things, such as strike off on a particular leg at canter, it may be that there is a problem, and your adviser (who should have noticed even if you have not) can look into the matter. Finally, ride the horse yourself. Does he feel right for you: not too big, not too wide, not too narrow? Is there a good length of rein? Put him through his paces, have a jump if you wish, take him out on the road to make sure he is safe in traffic and generally try to get the feel of him.

It is not easy in a relatively short time to assess whether this is the horse you really

want to have on a long-term basis, so if possible arrange to have him at home on trial, say for a week. This will enable you to get to know his character, to ride him in more relaxed circumstances and also to get to know more about his general behaviour: is he well mannered in the stable, is he good in the company of other horses, will he willingly go away from other horses, is he safe in the company of dogs and in all traffic (not just cars) and so on. However well he suits you from the riding point of view, it is important that you should actually like him, too.

If you do decide to have a horse on trial, make sure that the arrangements are agreed and set down in writing – you will be responsible for feed, vet's bills and so on and will be liable for negligence.

Horses sold at public sales usually come with a warranty or warranties. A warranty is a statement of fact made before or during

a transaction – for example a horse may be "warranted sound". Privately sold horses do not always come with a warranty and if you ask the vendor for one and he or she declines, then you may have grounds for suspicion (on the other hand, in these days of increasing litigation, the vendor may simply be being extra cautious). When in doubt, consult your expert equestrian adviser and, if necessary, a solicitor. The law does give some protection to buyers of horses, as in the case of other merchandise, the big difference being that the horse is a living creature and therefore far less predictable than, say, a television or a refrigerator or a motor car.

When you do find the horse of your dreams and decide to purchase, buy him "subject to a veterinary certificate" and ask your own veterinary surgeon (not the vendor's) to carry out the inspection.

Vetting

If possible, you should be present when your veterinary surgeon carries out his examination of your proposed purchase so that he can discuss the horse with you.

The examination will begin with a preliminary visual inspection. The vet can deduce a good deal from the general attitude of the horse when approached: his stance might show signs of lameness; the condition of his stable could indicate behavioural problems such as box-walking (constant pacing round and round the stable), assuming that the vendor has not switched the horse to another box to hide the evidence; his head carriage can indicate problems of balance or vision; how he reacts to being handled will be indicative of his temperament.

The vet will take in the horse's general state of health, noting any discharges from the nose or eyes, the condition of his skin; and the presence of lesions, or heat in a

tendon or joint. He will also examine the eyes and heart.

Once outside his stable, the horse will be stood up squarely on flat ground while the vet makes a detailed appraisal of his conformation. This is followed by a manual examination of the entire horse:

the head, including the mouth and teeth, the neck, ribs, sternum, back, abdomen and the limbs. Once the horse has been examined at rest he will be walked and then trotted in hand both away from the vet and towards him to enable him to detect any signs of lameness. Turning the horse to either side on a tight circle, backing him for a few strides and lungeing him at trot on a hard, flat surface are other tests which may reveal problems of unsoundness.

Flexion tests may be carried out on the limbs, particularly if there is a suspicion of lameness. However, opinion differs on these flexion tests, as they can actually induce lameness if they are used with sufficient force.

■ ABOVE LEFT
Vetting includes a manual examination of the entire horse.

■ LEFT
The vet will check the horse's heart and respiratory rates both at rest and after exercise.

■ BELOW
During the vetting procedure the horse will be warmed up under saddle, then given a gallop. Fast work sometimes produces signs of an old lameness problem.

To test the horse's wind and heart he is tacked up, warmed up gently at walk, trot and canter and then given a gallop. The vet will note whether the horse dips its back when the saddle is put on and the rider mounts. Some horses habitually do this, in others it may be a sign of back problems. After exercise the vet will listen to the lungs for any signs of abnormal respiration and to the heart for any irregularity. After the horse has been cooled off he will be rested for half an hour, after which he will be trotted out again in hand. If the horse is suffering from muscular or arthritic problems, which might disappear while the horse is warm, they may well reappear after this period of rest. Signs of old lameness might also appear after fast exercise. A further examination of the heart and respiration may also be made. The vet will then complete the certificate.

The certificate includes a detailed identification of the horse, the vet's report and his opinion as to its suitability for purchase, bearing in mind the use for which it is required. It is important to remember that the certificate is not a guarantee, but an opinion expressed by a qualified person. The certificate means that the horse has been found to be free of certain disorders at the time of examination. It does not and cannot mean that the horse is and will remain completely free from disease – vets are certainly not clairvoyant. Nor does the certificate guarantee that the horse is free from so-called stable "vices" such as crib-biting or weaving. If you would like a written warranty to this effect, you must obtain it from the vendor.

Keeping a Horse

Horse ownership is a big responsibility and should not be entered into lightly. Certainly no one should consider it unless they have the necessary facilities and have first mastered the rudiments of horse care. These include a knowledge of feeding, grooming, general stable management and basic first aid. All horses and ponies need safe accommodation and daily attention – they cannot be set aside on a Sunday afternoon and forgotten about until the following weekend. Unlike small domesticated animals, who share their owners' home, they need large facilities of their own, maintenance of which takes time and money. Depending on the work required of them and their breed or type, horses can either be kept at grass or stabled, or a combination of the two (known as the combined system). The owner will therefore need access to grazing, a stable, a weatherproof storage area for feed, bedding and tools and somewhere secure to keep tack and other equipment.

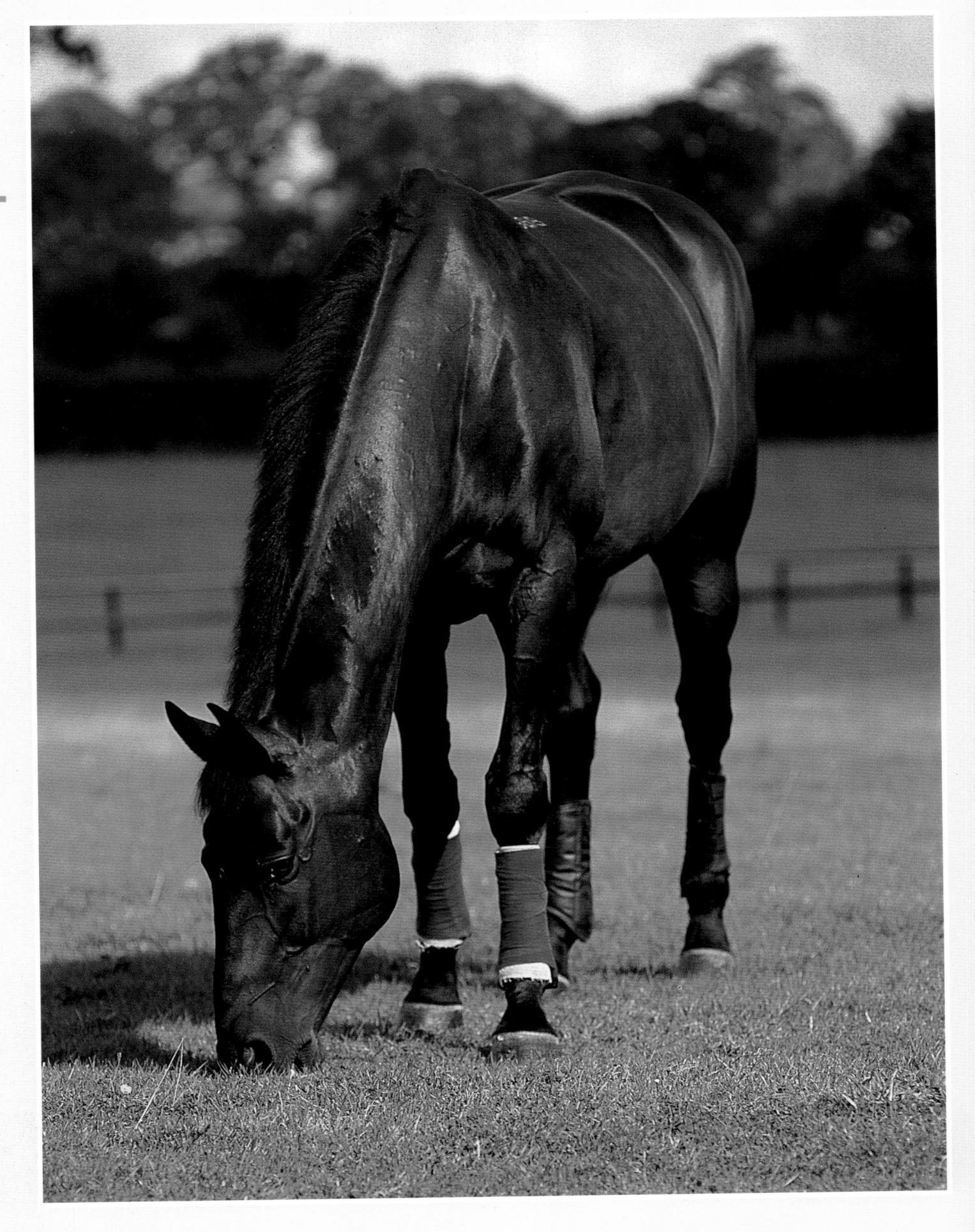

THE HORSE AT GRASS

The horse is by nature a nomadic, grazing animal, so it is far more natural – and less stressful – to keep him in a paddock than in a stable. However, a fenced paddock, no matter how large, is still an unnatural environment for a horse and certain precautions must be taken if the horse is to be safe and secure.

■ **PREVIOUS PAGE OPPOSITE** Stabled horses need constant care and attention.
■ **PREVIOUS PAGE** Most small ponies are quite hardy and can live outside all year round.
■ **OPPOSITE** Fit horses who spend part of the day at grass should wear bandages and boots to guard against injury.
■ **ABOVE** Brood mares grazing in a well-fenced paddock.

Fencing

All fields used for grazing horses must be securely and safely fenced. Since it is the horse's nature to roam, if he sees a gap he will certainly go for it. Similarly, if there is anything on which the horse can injure himself, he will find it – the domesticated horse is notoriously accident prone.

Undoubtedly the most effective (but unfortunately also the most expensive) fencing is good **wooden post and rail**. It is sturdy, long lasting and looks attractive. The wooden support posts, which should be 4 inches (10cm) square, must be driven well into the ground since horses like to rub against fencing, particularly when they are changing their coats. For a 4 foot (1.2m) fence the posts should be no less than 6 feet 6 inches (2m) in length. The fence should be constructed of good-quality wood and treated with non-toxic preservative to give protection against the weather and to discourage horses from chewing it. The top rail should be level with the top of the posts, which should be cut on a slope to allow rain to run off. Where possible the rails should be attached to the inner side of the posts. This prevents the horse banging into the

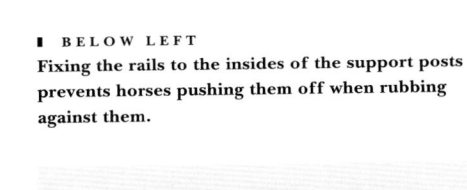

■ LEFT
Provided they are sufficiently high to deter the horse from jumping out, well-maintained stone walls are effective barriers.

■ BELOW LEFT
Fixing the rails to the insides of the support posts prevents horses pushing them off when rubbing against them.

SAFETY CHECKLIST

- ☛ Make regular checks of all field boundaries.
- ☛ Repair any broken sections of boundary immediately.
- ☛ Keep wire fencing taut at all times.
- ☛ Set the lowest strand of a wire fence 18 inches (46cm) above the ground.
- ☛ Block off gaps in hedges with stout fencing – never use loose strands of wire.
- ☛ Never use pig or sheep netting – horses tend to put their feet through the squares of wire and can become caught up.
- ☛ Never use sheep posts, with sharp, upward pointing ends.
- ☛ Fence off potential danger areas, such as treacherous ground or ditches.
- ☛ When using electric fencing, ensure that it is visible – to humans as well as horses – by tying strips of strong plastic (for example, from feed or fertilizer bags) at intervals along the wire.
- ☛ Avoid metal or concrete fence posts – they will do far more damage than wooden ones should a horse collide with them.

■ OPPOSITE TOP
Good-quality wooden
post and rail fencing
makes the perfect
horse-proof boundary
and looks attractive.

■ LEFT
Electric fencing can be very useful, especially for
dividing paddocks into smaller sections. Horses
quickly learn to respect it.

■ BOTTOM
Curved fencing with no right-angled corners is
safest for horses.

■ BELOW RIGHT
Rusty metal, barbed
wire and concrete
posts are potentially
lethal to horses.
Sections of poor
fencing like this
should be replaced.

Electric fencing has its uses, especially
for temporarily dividing one area of a field
from another, for example when resting
one section of grazing.

Stone walls will also contain horses very
well, provided they are sturdy and high
enough – all boundaries should be a
minimum of 4 feet (1.2m) high, otherwise
horses might try to jump out. Like a
hedge, a wall will afford some protection
against the weather.

Modern **plastic fencing**, which comes
in a variety of colours, may not look as
"natural" as wood but it does have certain
advantages: horses do not chew it, it does
not rot and it will absorb impact without
causing injury. Like wire, it should be correctly strained on strong, wooden posts.

Whatever the fencing used, right-
angled or sharp corners should be avoided
in paddocks where horses are kept.
Rounding the corners of the field makes it
less likely for a horse to injure himself
when galloping about, either by coming to
an abrupt halt (with the possibility of
jarring the legs) or actually crashing into
the boundary. Acute corners can also be
traps for a timid horse who might find
himself literally "cornered" by a more
aggressive companion.

posts when galloping about and also
prevents him from pushing a rail off if he
leans or rubs against it.

A tall, thick **hedge,** provided it is
without poisonous trees or shrubs, can
also make a good boundary. Beech and
hazel are particularly suitable since horses
will not eat them. Unlike a fence, a hedge
provides horses with shelter in bad
weather. It will, however, require regular
trimming to keep it in good order – if
gaps begin to appear they must be
fenced off.

Probably the best boundary of all is a
combination of the two: a good dense
hedge with a post and rail fence running
immediately in front of it.

Cheaper, less attractive but equally
effective fencing can be constructed with
wire mesh. The mesh must have small, V-
shaped openings so that there is no
possibility of a horse catching his foot in
the holes. Mesh fencing needs to be
erected professionally to prevent sagging.
It is also likely to stretch when leant on.

Plain wire fencing will provide a good
horseproof barrier so long as it is well
constructed. It should consist of four or
five strands of wire attached to stout
wooden posts, with strainers at the corners
to keep them taut. An alternative, and one
which makes the fence more easily visible
to the horse, is to use a wooden rail in
place of the top strand of wire. The
strands of wire should be some 12 inches
(30cm) apart and the placing of the lowest
strand is particularly important. It should
be about 18 inches (46cm) above the
ground. Any lower and the horse may put

a leg through the strands and become
caught up; any higher and he may be
tempted to put his head underneath.
Plain wire is more suitable than barbed
wire. If the latter cannot be avoided, it
must be kept absolutely taut – loose
barbed wire can cause dreadful injuries if
any part of the horse becomes caught up
in it. Horses can also cut themselves if they
rub against the barbs.

Gates

Good access to fields is most important. Gateways must be wide enough to allow not only horses to pass through safely but also large machinery (such as a tractor and harrow) which will be required from time to time to keep the pasture in good condition. For safety's sake it is better for gates to be situated away from busy roads. Wooden and metal gates are both suitable for horse paddocks. All gates should have cross bars for added strength.

It is best to have a gate hung by an expert to ensure that it does not sag, drag on the ground or swing. Gates must open easily otherwise a horse could try to push his way out while you are still struggling to open it. The safest way to hang a gate is so that it opens inwards into the field. This

❚ BELOW
Gate posts must be strong. Gates should be securely fastened at both ends with sturdy chains and padlocks.

will prevent a horse pushing it open as soon as you unfasten the catch. A wooden gate should be heavy and solidly built and, like fencing, should be treated with preservative. Galvanized metal gates will

❚ BOTTOM
This broken gate is totally unsuitable for a paddock. Rusty metal may cause serious injuries and flimsy barriers encourage horses to escape.

require regular painting. Gateposts need to be very strong and should be set about 3 feet (90cm) into the ground with concrete to keep them firm. They will require strong hinges and a horse-proof catch, that is one that the horse cannot unfasten with his teeth. All catches should be easy for a person to open with one hand. There should be no protruding hooks or other fastenings on which the horse could injure himself.

Horse stealing is not uncommon and so it is vital to secure all gates. Use heavy-duty chain with a strong padlock and fit one to BOTH ends of the gate so that would-be thieves cannot simply lift the gate off its hinges. Avoid climbing over gates as it tends to weaken them. If you must, always climb over the hinge end and do it quickly.

During wet weather the ground in gateways quickly becomes poached by horses being taken in and out on a daily basis or simply pacing up and down waiting to be fed. If possible, gates should be situated on well-drained ground, and not in a muddy hollow.

Shelters

In the wild, horses make use of natural shelter such as trees, banks or rocks for protection from extremes of wind, wet or heat or to escape from flies. For horses kept in the confines of a paddock it is essential to provide an equivalent form of protection. Most domesticated horses retain their natural instinct to shelter beside a good, thick hedge or under a tree rather than going inside a confining man-made structure. But not all paddocks have hedges and trees and so a wooden shelter may be the only alternative.

Since horses are happiest when kept in company with others of their kind, a field shelter needs to be large enough to accommodate the number of horses that graze together, without risk of squabbling and overcrowding. It should be positioned on well-drained ground. If this is not possible, the floor and the area around the shelter may need a hard surface, such as concrete. The shelter should be built with its back to the prevailing wind. It must be strongly constructed and treated with preservative. The roof must be sufficiently high to give horses plenty of head room (thus avoiding possible injury) and should slope towards the back so that rainwater runs away from the entrance. Open-fronted shelters are the safest, because it is easy for a horse to escape should he be bullied by a companion. Any fixtures and fittings, such as mangers, hay racks, etc., must be strongly made and fitted at a good height from the ground, again to prevent injury. They should be checked regularly and repaired as necessary, as should the whole shelter.

Some types of smaller field shelter are designed with a bottom door which, when closed, converts the shelter into a stable.

This can be very useful if you have no other stabling but sometimes need to keep your horse or pony inside. It can also be used as an isolation box in the event of the horse contracting a contagious illness.

A less costly type of shelter may be provided by means of a wooden screen, erected in conjunction with the fencing. Windbreak screens need to be about 6 feet 6 inches (2m) high and can either be straight or double-sided, using a corner of the field. Multi-angled screens, affording protection from different directions, can be built free-standing in the open away from the fencing.

▌ TOP
A well-designed wooden field shelter with high, sloping roof, wide front opening and strong kicking boards.

▌ LEFT
This small shelter, with its narrow opening, is suitable for a single horse. With the addition of a door it could convert into a stable for emergency use if necessary.

185

Poisonous Plants, Shrubs and Trees

There are a good many plants, shrubs and trees which are poisonous to horses and ponies. Some, such as the **buttercup**, which are poisonous if eaten in large quantities when fresh, are not particularly palatable. On the other hand horses will readily eat yew, all parts of which are lethal. A quantity as small as 1lb (0.5kg) can kill a horse. All paddocks should be rigorously checked for dangerous plants before horses are put out to graze and regularly checked thereafter – remember that however well you tend your own grazing it can still be contaminated by seeds blowing from neighbouring land.

One of the most dangerous plants of all is **ragwort**, which is tall and easily recognized by its bright yellow flowers. Ragwort

SAFETY CHECKLIST

☛ Learn to recognize poisonous plants and trees.

☛ Before putting a horse in a new paddock, make a thorough check of grassland and hedges for signs of poisonous vegetation.

☛ Dig up and burn poisonous plants.

☛ Fence off any poisonous trees which cannot be removed – make sure they are well out of reach of horses or ponies.

☛ Make regular checks of all paddocks and hedges – remember that poisonous plants can spread from neighbouring land.

☛ Never leave poisonous plants which have been dug up lying about in the paddock – many plants, notably ragwort, are far more palatable to horses when wilted or dead.

☛ Practise good pasture management: a good, dense sward of grass helps prevent poisonous plants from seeding.

☛ If there are poisonous trees in the vicinity, keep an eye open for fallen twigs or branches – particularly during windy weather.

☛ If paddocks adjoin gardens, make regular checks for cuttings dumped over the fence by their owners – they may contain poisonous plants.

☛ After using chemical weedkillers keep horses off the grass for several weeks and at least until there has been a good downpour of rain.

contains alkaloids which poison the liver and the effects are cumulative: small doses eaten over a long period of time are just as lethal as a large amount eaten in a short time. There is no specific treatment for ragwort poisoning and the effects are usually fatal.

Ragwort can be eliminated by spraying – the best time is between late April and late May, before the flower shoots develop and while young plants are just becoming established. Or it can be dug up, though this can be hard work. All the roots must

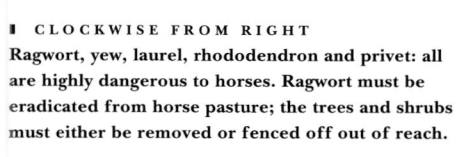

CLOCKWISE FROM RIGHT
Ragwort, yew, laurel, rhododendron and privet: all
are highly dangerous to horses. Ragwort must be
eradicated from horse pasture; the trees and shrubs
must either be removed or fenced off out of reach.

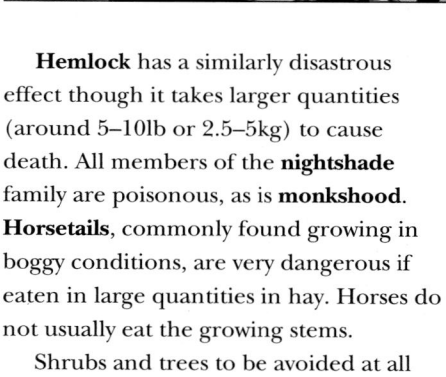

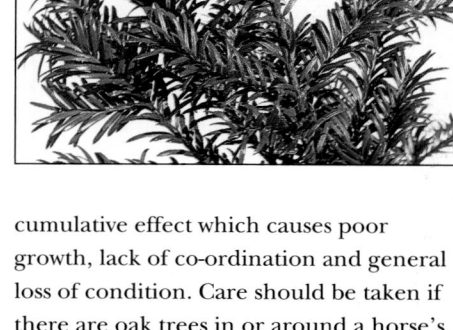

be removed from the ground and the
flower heads should be burnt. Attempting
to control ragwort by cutting it when it is
in flower to prevent the production of
seeds is unlikely to solve the problem since
the plants will often grow more vigorously
the following year. If a paddock is really
badly infested with the plant, the best
solution is to plough the land and reseed
it. The better the grassland management
the less opportunity there will be for
ragwort to become established. The
denser the sward of grass the less likely
ragwort is to seed.

Foxgloves, which like ragwort become
more palatable when they are dried in hay
than when fresh, are also lethal to horses.
As little as ¼lb (100g) may prove fatal.
Symptoms of foxglove poisoning include
convulsions and difficulty in breathing. A
horse will die in a matter of hours.

Hemlock has a similarly disastrous
effect though it takes larger quantities
(around 5–10lb or 2.5–5kg) to cause
death. All members of the **nightshade**
family are poisonous, as is **monkshood**.
Horsetails, commonly found growing in
boggy conditions, are very dangerous if
eaten in large quantities in hay. Horses do
not usually eat the growing stems.

Shrubs and trees to be avoided at all
cost include **rhododendron** (small
quantities cause death through failure of
the respiratory system), **oleander**,
laburnum (especially the seeds), **box,
privet** and **laurel**. All parts of **yew**, living or
dead, are lethal in small quantities – again
there is no known antidote. **Meadow
saffron** contains a poison which may take
time to build up in the system, by which
time the horse is beyond help, and the
poisons present in **bracken** also have a

cumulative effect which causes poor
growth, lack of co-ordination and general
loss of condition. Care should be taken if
there are oak trees in or around a horse's
paddock. The crop of **acorns** varies from
year to year. If they are eaten in large
quantities, they can be harmful. They
should be raked up and removed.

**Plants, shrubs and trees which are
poisonous to horses include:**

Bracken, buttercup, flax, foxglove, hemlock,
horsetail, lupin, meadow saffron,
nightshade, purple milk vetch, ragwort, St
John's wort, yellow star thistle

Box, laurel, oleander, privet, rhododendron

Buckthorn, laburnum, magnolia, yew

Acorns

Water

Horses and ponies kept at grass must have constant access to a clean supply of water. A natural supply of running water, such as a stream or river, is ideal but nowadays it is all too likely that it may be polluted. If it is not, then horses and ponies may be allowed free access provided the bottom is gravel (if it is sandy the horse may ingest sand with the water).

The approach to the drinking area must be clean, fairly flat and safe. Steep banks are not suitable since the horses will slip and slide down and the bank will eventually collapse. If the stream is narrow, this could arrest the flow of water. Any fencing that crosses the stream or river must be checked regularly to ensure that horses cannot escape from their paddock by wandering off along the waterway. Streams which are not free flowing in summer are not suitable, since the water will tend to become stagnant. Horses should never be allowed access to polluted rivers, stagnant ponds or boggy areas: these should be securely fenced off.

The alternative to running water is a man-made container. A galvanized water trough, purpose-built, fed by mains water and controlled by a ballcock provides an efficient water supply, although there is

always the problem of pipes freezing in winter. The feed pipe needs to be buried to a suitable depth and the length of pipe which is above ground will need to be well lagged. It is essential that the ballcock is enclosed so that horses cannot damage it.

If mains water is not available, troughs can be filled by hosepipe or, if convenient, by bucket. Troughs such as this with static water will require baling out every week and refilling. Smaller containers, such as old stone sinks, plastic tubs and buckets can also be used but they will need more frequent filling. The advantage of small, lightweight containers is that they are easy to clean and they can be moved about to different areas of the field to prevent wear and tear on the ground. The disadvantage is that they are easily knocked over.

Standing a bucket or tub in an old car tyre is one solution to this problem.

Water troughs are best positioned parallel to a fence. Horses drink a lot so the approach to a trough will be in constant use. It should be hard – it may be necessary to lay concrete or hard core.

SAFETY CHECKLIST

- Check your horse's water supply every day.

- Bale out and clean all water containers regularly.

- During severe weather be prepared to break ice on water two or three times a day.

- Fence off all sources of stagnant water.

- Never place a water trough in the corner of a field where a horse may be trapped by one of its companions.

- Never place a water trough under deciduous trees or near a hedge where leaves, twigs and seeds can foul it.

- Avoid placing troughs in the middle of fields where they can become a source of injury.

- Recess water troughs into the line of the fence to minimize projections and the risk of injury.

- Never place a water trough slightly in front of a fence so that a horse could trap his leg between it and the fence.

- Avoid using containers such as old baths that have rough edges or dangerous projections.

Grass Management

Careful management is required if a paddock is to withstand the horse's close-biting method of grazing and the constant wear and tear inflicted by his feet. Poor quality grazing quickly becomes "horse sick" – barren areas alternate with patches of intrusive, unpalatable weeds such as nettles, docks and thistles – and without a good grass sward it will also become badly poached in wet weather. Even good quality grazing will deteriorate if it is not given the right attention.

The ideal pasture is one that has been sown with seed selected and mixed specifically with horses in mind. A good basic mixture would contain 50 per cent of perennial rye grass, 25 per cent of creeping red fescue and 25 per cent of a mixture including crested dog's tail, meadow grass and a little wild white clover. Timothy should also be included if you intend to take hay from the paddock.

Rye grass grows well in most conditions although on poor, light soils it will decline after a few years if it is not fertilized. Two different types should be included in the mix. Creeping red fescue is particularly useful in difficult conditions (it is often used on sports grounds) and again two different types should be included. Smooth-stalked meadow grass will grow in dry, sandy soils while the rough-stalked variety, which horses find very palatable, thrives in moist, rich soils. Its dense, low growth helps prevent the intrusion of weeds and poisonous plants. Clover is useful because its root nodules contain nitrogen-producing bacteria. Its inclusion in the mix will help reduce the need for fertilizing. It is important to choose wild clover rather than one of the farm varieties, which grow very aggressively and can take over an entire paddock.

Even with the right basic mixture of grasses, the amount and quality of grazing produced will vary according to a number of natural factors. These include soil type, rainfall, wind and altitude. Soil should be

■ BELOW
Grazing cattle with horses, or in rotation, helps control worms and weeds.
■ BELOW LEFT
Droppings must not be allowed to accumulate in the paddock. If they cannot be picked up regularly, they should be harrowed.

tested for its suitability to sustain grass. For example, if it is acidic it will need to be treated with lime (horses must be kept off the grazing until the lime has been washed in by rain).

The best grazing is produced on well-drained land. The installation of underground drainage is expensive but it may be essential where ground is so badly drained that it is both unproductive and easily poached by a horse's feet. Where drainage exists it is important to maintain it. Check ditches regularly, and remove any blockages which prevent water from running away freely (remember that blocked ditches on neighbouring land can prevent the free run of water from your paddock). Check all pipes leading into and out of ditches and repair as necessary.

Ideally the horses' droppings should be removed frequently as this will help to control worm infestation. Where removal is not practical, for example on large acreages, the droppings should be harrowed regularly. This should be done during warm, dry weather (which will spread out the droppings and kill the larvae). Another aid to worm control is the grazing of cattle either with the horses or in rotation. The larvae will be destroyed in the cattle's digestive system. Cattle and sheep will also help keep paddocks tidy by eating the rougher herbage. Sheep do less damage to wet ground than cattle.

Harrowing in the spring helps to pull out dead growth and make room for new, and a field should always be harrowed before the application of fertilizer. Rolling will help to firm the soil and repair poached areas. Weed control is also best carried out in spring as soon as new shoots appear. Persistent weeds should be dug out and burnt before they seed.

Pasture needs to be rested periodically. If you have nowhere else to put your horse, divide off the paddock into two or more sections. Rest one portion, graze horses in another and, if possible, graze cattle or sheep in a third.

THE STABLED HORSE

Well-designed stabling is vitally important to the
horse's health and safety, whether the horse lives in
most of the time, whether he is kept on the combined
system (that is part stabled, part out at grass) or
whether he is stabled only occasionally.

▮ OPPOSITE **All stables should have horse-proof fastenings on
the outside of the doors.**

▮ ABOVE **Roughened concrete provides a suitable surface for a
busy stableyard.**

Stables

Care must be taken with the positioning and construction of stables. This applies equally to a single stable and to a large yard. Stables should be sited so that cold north and east winds cannot blow in and should be positioned on well-drained ground. When planning new stabling, various factors should be taken into consideration. These include the supply of water and electricity as well as vehicular access. It is preferable, too, to build stables near a house, in order to deter thieves.

The most popular type of stable is the loosebox, or box stall. These are usually made of wood, concrete blocks or brick and may be roofed with wood (protected by waterproof felt), tiles, slates or heavy-duty corrugated plastic. Metal should never be used for stabling because it is hot in summer and cold in winter; it is also likely to cause injuries to the horse. A loosebox must be large enough for the occupant to be able to move about, roll, lie down flat and get up again in comfort and absolute safety. A horse standing 16hh and over needs a loosebox measuring at

■ BELOW
Good airy barn stabling provides a suitable alternative to looseboxes, especially in a hot or very cold climate. The disadvantages are the ease with which disease can spread and the fire risk.

least 12 feet x 14 feet (3.7m x 4.3m); a horse up to 16hh, 12 feet x 12 feet (3.7m x 3.7m), and a 14hh pony, 10 feet x 12 feet (3m x 3.7m). A stable of 8 feet x 8 feet (2.4m x 2.4m) is adequate for small ponies.

The roof should be sloped and fitted with effective guttering and downpipes. A high ceiling or roof is essential to prevent the horse hitting its head. If the stable has a ridge roof, the eaves should be no less than 7 feet 6 inches (2.25m) above the ground and the top of the roof should be from 12–15 feet (3.7–4.5m) high. The lowest point of a single-planed roof should be no less than 10 feet (3m) high.

Wooden kicking boards, to a height of at least 4 feet (1.2m), provide added strength and security. The stable floor should slope slightly towards the rear of the box (to aid drainage) and the surface must be hard-wearing and non-slippery. Roughened concrete is most often used. It may be covered with a special rubber material to give better purchase. Drains inside the stable are best avoided as they tend to become blocked with bedding and can also trap a horse's hoof.

For safety, the stable door must give plenty of clearance – it should be at least 4 feet (1.2m) wide and 7 feet (2.1m) high for a horse. It should be made in two halves, opening outwards, and the top half should fasten back securely for the free circulation of air and to enable the horse to see out. Only rarely is the weather so severe that it is necessary to close both halves of a stable door. The top edge of

▌ OPPOSITE TOP
A well-built block of brick stables. The overhang gives extra protection to horses and humans from extremes of weather.

▌ OPPOSITE MIDDLE
Note the protective strip on the top of the doors and the kick-over bolts at the bottom.

▌ BELOW
The inside of a barn complex. With kit and equipment conveniently to hand, this type of stabling is popular with humans though it can be a boring environment for horses.

▌ BELOW
A converted container makes a poor and potentially dangerous home for a horse. Metal is cold in winter and hot in summer and the horse could easily injure himself on the makeshift door.

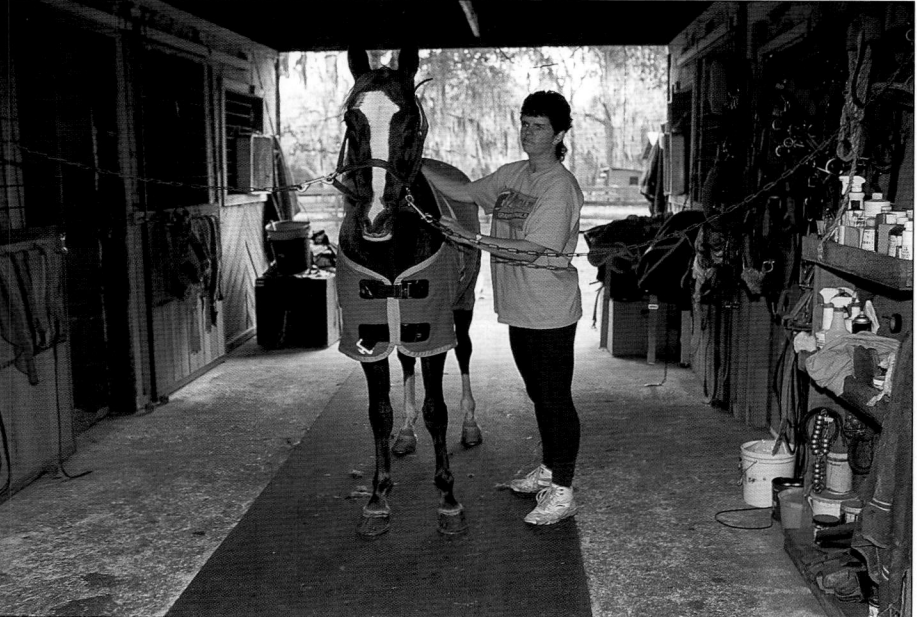

SAFETY CHECKLIST

- Provide adequate fire extinguishers (water and foam)/fire hose/sand buckets in the stable area – your local fire prevention officer will advise on suitable precautions. Have fire extinguishers serviced regularly.

- Ensure that all electrical wiring is protected with suitable conduits to prevent interference by horses and rodents.

- Ensure that all light fittings are out of reach of the horse.

- Fit waterproof switches, well out of reach of the horse.

- Keep stable fixtures and fittings to a minimum: two rings, one to tie up the horse, one (if required) for a haynet; water bucket or automatic waterbowl; manger.

- Make regular checks for protruding nails, screws, splinters etc.

- Make regular checks of all door bolts and hinges and keep them oiled.

- Fit protective grilles to all windows.

- Keep all drains clean.

- Cover open drains in the stable yard area with strong grids.

the bottom door should be securely fitted with a protective strip of metal to prevent the horse chewing the wood, and the door should have a horse-proof bolt at the top and a kick-over bolt at the bottom.

The stabled horse needs a constant supply of fresh air, so good ventilation is essential. The open top door and high roof help provide this. What the horse does not need is a draughty environment. Windows, which help ventilate and light the stable, are usually positioned on the same side of the box as the door to prevent draughts. If they are to provide maximum air and light, they should not be obscured by the top door, which tends to be the case with some stabling. Windows must be fitted with protective grilles. Additional ventilation can be provided by means of ventilation cowls in the roof, or louvre boards in the eaves. Additional light may be provided by a window in the wall opposite the door. If this is also used for ventilation, it must be above the height of the horse's head to prevent cross-draughts.

Internal stabling, where lines of looseboxes are contained within a larger building (which can be an existing barn or purpose built), is popular in some countries and is particularly useful in areas which experience extremes of heat or cold. Correctly constructed, such stabling will be warm in winter and cool in summer, but care must be taken to provide good ventilation – infectious diseases are more likely to spread in this type of stabling arrangement. Doorways and centre aisles must be wide enough to enable horses to move about without banging themselves – sliding stable doors are often the best in this situation as they do not protrude into the gangways when open. The running channels must always be kept clean.

Another way of keeping horses under cover is the yard system, where a number of horses are given the run of a large barn or a partially covered area. The yard system is labour saving, since the horses can be kept on deep litter; and horses enjoy being together with the freedom to wander about. Care must be taken, however, to choose horses who get on with each other, otherwise biting and kicking will occur.

BELOW
Wheat straw is less palatable than oat or barley straw and is therefore the most suitable for horses.

BELOW LEFT
Deep straw, well banked up the sides of the stable, provides the horse with a safe, comfortable bed.

Bedding

An ample supply of bedding encourages the horse to lie down to rest, thus taking unnecessary strain off the legs and feet; it reduces the likelihood of injuries such as capped hocks when the horse does lie down; it allows the horse to roll in comfort and protects him from injury when he does so; it reduces the jarring effect on the legs and feet that may result from standing for long periods on hard flooring; it prevents the horse from slipping up; it encourages him to stale (male horses, particularly, are usually very reluctant to stale on a bare floor); it provides warmth and insulation from draughts and it helps to keep the horse and his rugs clean.

There are a number of types of suitable bedding, all of which have pros and cons. **Straw** has traditionally been the most popular – and economical – and many people still prefer it since it makes arguably the warmest, most comfortable bed and allows free drainage. It is normally easily available though it may become scarce in wet years. Wheat straw is the best for horses, being less palatable than barley or oat straw, both of which are also likely to contain awns which can get into a horse's eyes or irritate the skin.

Straw has the advantage of being much easier to dispose of than some other forms of bedding: it can be burnt (in a safe place, well away from stabling, hay stores, etc) or contractors may collect it for use as mushroom compost. The main drawback of straw is that it may be dusty or contain fungal spores, which can cause an allergic reaction in some horses, leading to respiratory problems. This in turn can affect the horse's work performance because he will not be able to take in enough oxygen. Coughing is often the first sign of problems in this respect.

It can sometimes be difficult finding a supply of small straw bales, too,

BELOW
Good-quality wood shavings are a useful alternative
to straw though they provide a rather less warm
bed. They are also more difficult to dispose of.

particularly if you live in an area where there are few horse owners and therefore not much demand for the old type of bale. Straw is best bought in small bales because they are easier to handle. The large ones, weighing half a tonne or more, are difficult to manoeuvre and often present storage difficulties, especially for someone keeping horses on a small scale. It will take about four small bales to put down a good, thick straw bed in an average sized loosebox and upwards of half a bale a day to maintain the bed, the exact quantity depending on the amount of time that the box is occupied.

Aside from straw, **wood shavings** are probably the most popular form of bedding nowadays. Correctly managed, they provide a clean, hygienic bed which will not be eaten by the horse. Shavings do not have spores and, provided they are dust free (having been passed through a dust extractor by the suppliers), they can be a good alternative to straw for horses with any sort of respiratory problem.

They are packed in strong plastic bags and it is therefore possible to store shavings outside, provided there has been no damage to the wrappings in transit. Shavings do have their share of disadvantages, however. They are difficult to dispose of – being slow rotting they cannot be spread on the land – and bales are fairly heavy to handle. Shavings are also much heavier to handle when wet than straw. There is also the possibility of foreign bodies, such as sharp fragments of wood or nails, being present – though this should not be a problem with good-quality shavings. Some horses' skin may be irritated if the shavings are from wood which has been treated with chemicals and foot problems sometimes occur.

Unlike straw, which traps pockets of air, shavings pack down closely. A bed of shavings is therefore less warm than a straw bed and rather less comfortable to lie on, particularly as it is less stable than straw and more prone to exposing bare patches of floor. A shavings bed will use approximately three bales per week.

Aubiose is a fairly new and entirely natural product made from the hemp plant. It is proving particularly beneficial for horses with dust allergies and has the advantage of being exceptionally absorbent: four times more absorbent than wood shavings and twelve times more than straw. The bed is more expensive than other forms of bedding to put down initially, an average stable requiring some eight bales, but thereafter it is economical to maintain as it requires only half to one bale a week. When the bed is first laid it needs dampening with a hose or watering can to help it settle and activate its sponge-like properties.

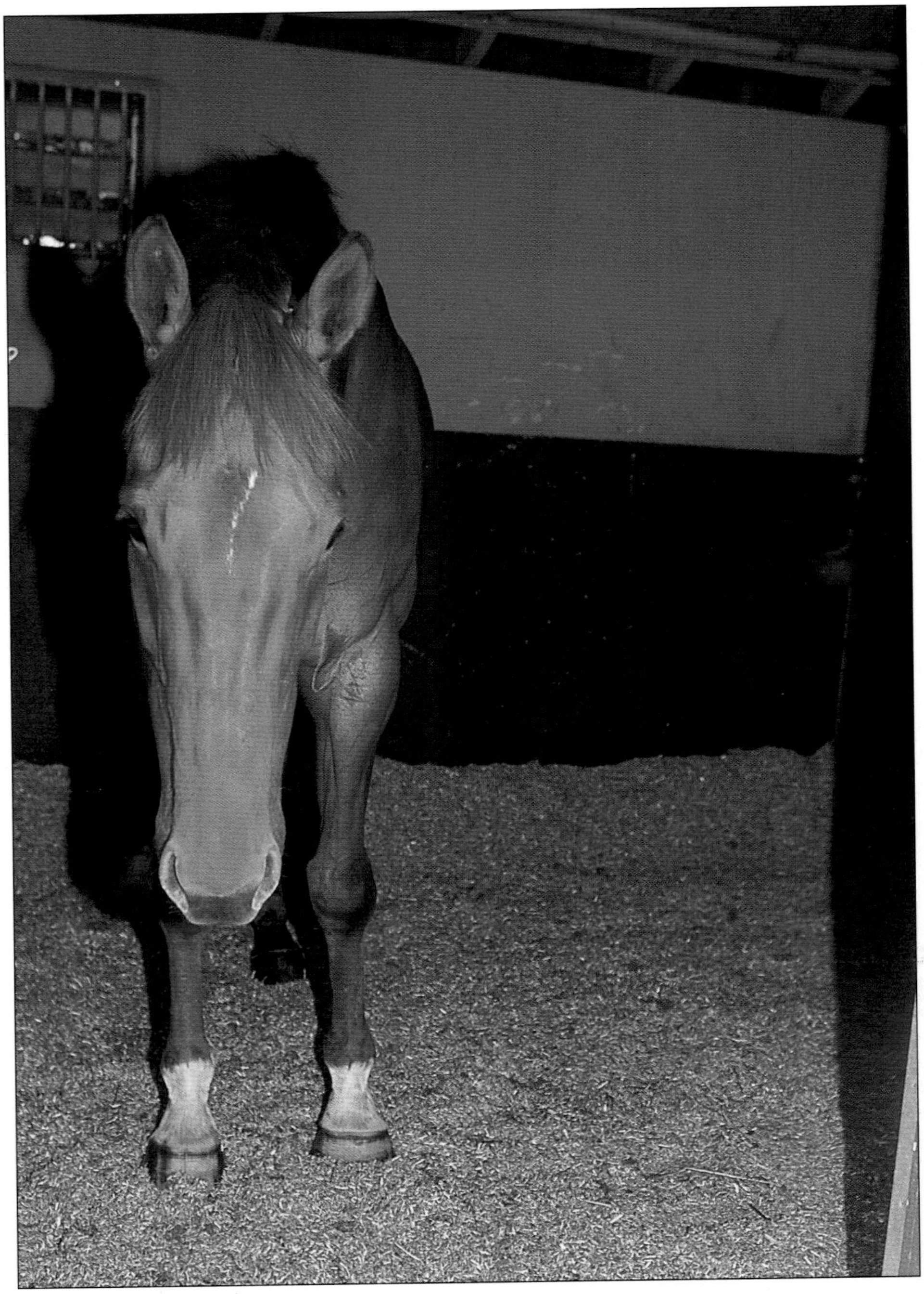

Aubiose works by soaking up liquids in a small area at the base of the bed, in much the same way as cat litter. The top layers of the bed remain dry. It is a labour-saving form of bedding since mucking out consists simply of frequent removal of droppings and a light raking over to keep it level. It is recommended that the saturated bedding should be removed every five to ten days, depending on the horse. It is also suitable for use with the deep litter system.

Another big plus for Aubiose is the fact that it rots down to a valuable compost within five to six weeks and is therefore easy to dispose of. Its only disadvantage, apart from the initial cost, is that it is very free flowing (the particles are smaller and softer than shavings) and so it is not so easy to bank up the sides of the bed.

Shredded paper provides the most dust-free bed of all and is, as a result, often used for horses with allergies to straw or respiratory problems. It is also increasingly used for high-performance horses, such as eventers or racehorses, whose lungs need to be kept as free as possible of dust. Paper is cheaper to buy than shavings but on the other hand a deeper bed is required because it becomes saturated more quickly than either shavings or straw. On the plus side, it is light and easy to handle and

provides a really warm bed. On the minus side it is often made from printed paper and this may cause staining of the horse's coat, particularly with greys, which causes extra work for the owner or groom. It is also difficult to control a paper-bed muck heap when it is windy. Again the bed will need around three bales per week.

Peat moss may be used for bedding in areas where it is easily available . Like shavings, it is usually sold in plastic-covered bales. It, too, has its good points and its bad points. It provides a comfortable bed, is not palatable and should be reasonably easy to dispose of.

However, its main advantage over other forms of bedding is one of safety: it will not burst into flames in the event of a fire. On the other hand it is expensive, heavy to handle, needs frequent mucking out and forking over to prevent it becoming soggy and compacted and is so dark in colour that it is difficult to identify the wet areas.

Rubber matting can be used for bedding purposes but, apart from the fact that it is totally dust free when used on its own, it has more minus points than plus ones. It certainly does not look very attractive and, more important, provides

■ OPPOSITE

Hemp is a relatively new type of bedding for horses. It is exceptionally absorbent. Rather expensive initially, it is economical (and easy) to manage thereafter.

■ BELOW

Rubber matting is dust free, long lasting and labour saving but affords little comfort unless other bedding is used on top.

■ BOTTOM

Paper, being dust free and warm, is ideal for bedding down horses with respiratory problems. Printed paper can cause coat stains, especially on grey horses.

little warmth or protection from draughts. It does not absorb wet and if it is used without a covering of other bedding material, the droppings will be scattered about by the horse, who will then lie in them and, as a result, tend always to be dirty. There is little to prevent a horse becoming cast (the banked-up sides of conventional beds help in this respect). When used on its own its chief advantage, apart from being dust free, is its low-cost maintenance: after the initial outlay there is no more bedding to purchase and the matting should last for a number of years. Mucking out can be done by hosepipe, and is both quick and easy.

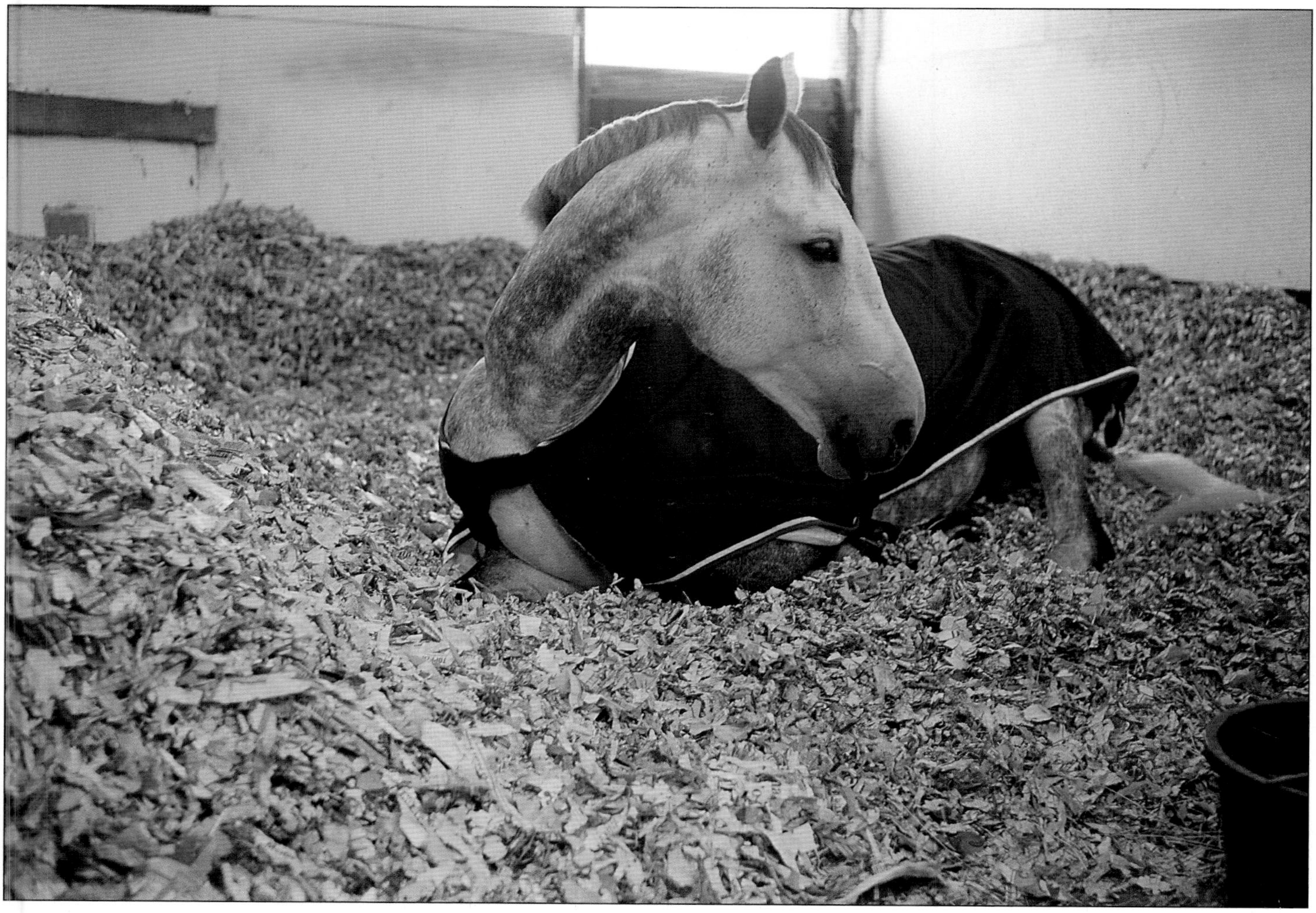

197

Management of Beds

Good management of beds is essential to keep the horse's environment healthy and to keep both the horse and his rugs as clean as possible. Stables can either be mucked out every day or you can adopt the deep litter or semi-deep litter system. The horse should be tied up during mucking out or, preferably, removed from the stable altogether. This protects him from any dust which may be disturbed while the bedding is being moved about and also makes the job easier.

Daily mucking out entails the removal of all droppings and soiled bedding. The best system is to take up the bed completely to allow the floor to dry while the horse is out. This is less of a chore with lightweight bedding materials such as straw and paper than with something heavier such as shavings.

You will need a wheelbarrow or a muck sheet, a fork and a strong yard broom with hard bristles. For mucking out a straw bed many people use a four-pronged fork for lifting droppings, but the same job can be accomplished with a three- or even a two-

pronged fork. Much depends upon the skill of the wielder – the fewer prongs, the lighter the fork, the less tiring the job and the faster you can work. For mucking out shavings you will need a shavings fork, which has more prongs set closer together. The advantage of using a muck sheet is that you do not normally need a shovel. Most of the soiled litter can be forked or swept on to it and any remnants can be hand lifted, provided you wear protective gloves. When a shovel is required, it should be large and lightweight.

The muck sheet or wheelbarrow is positioned across the doorway and visible droppings collected and placed on/in it. The bedding is cleared away from one corner of the box (usually the one on the same side as the door and furthest from where the horse is tied up, though if the box is large enough the other corners may be used in rotation to ensure that all corners of the floor are dried out regularly). The floor in that corner is then swept clean. The corner is used to stack all

the clean bedding – the squarer and neater the better since it will take up less room. All the droppings and wet straw are placed in the wheelbarrow or on the muck sheet and the entire floor is swept clean. Finally, a thin layer of the clean bedding is scattered across the box as standing litter. This will prevent the horse from slipping but will facilitate the drying of the floor. Assuming that the horse will stay tied up to be groomed and then exercised, the box can be left with the bed up for some time, which will help ensure that the floor – the sides as well as the centre – dries out before the bed is put down again.

An alternative, though not quite so satisfactory, method is to clear the bed completely from one wall of the box each day, thus ensuring that each bank of bedding is turned on a regular basis.

When putting down the bed again the existing bedding should be used to provide a good, deep covering to the entire floor area (right up to the door, to prevent draughts) and new bedding used to bank up the sides (with a straw bed if a

LEFT
A selection of mucking out tools: wheelbarrow, five-tined fork, shovel, shavings scoop, broom and skip. A wheelbarrow is more cumbersome to use than a muck sheet.

ABOVE
The horse should be tied up during mucking out and setting fair. (Note that, for safety, coats should be fastened while you are working with horses.)

■ RIGHT
A muck heap sited in a three-sided bunker is easier
to manage and to keep tidy than a free-standing one.

■ BELOW
Position the muck heap where there is good
drainage and easy access – for large vehicles as well
as wheelbarrows.

horse has a tendency to eat it, new straw should be covered with a layer of the used bedding which will be less palatable). Banked sides keep out draughts, help protect the horse from injury when he is rolling or lying down and may help prevent a horse becoming cast (that is stuck with his legs in such a position that he cannot get up again).

To keep the bed as clean as possible, droppings should be picked up regularly throughout the day in a container known as a skip or skep, which may be made of metal, plastic or rubber. At evening stables the bed should be set fair, that is straightened out and put tidy for the night, care being taken to bank the sides well and ensure that the entire floor area is evenly covered.

To keep a horse on deep litter the stable needs to be large (in a small one the bed will quickly become sodden) and well ventilated. This system saves time as it involves the daily removal of the droppings only, not the wet bedding underneath. The old bed is left undisturbed and covered with fresh bedding each day. This type of bed needs careful management and is better suited to horses who are out by day as this enables the bedding to dry out more. A deep litter bed is warm in winter and may stay down for as long as six months. However, if it begins to build up too high or to smell it must be completely removed. The box should be thoroughly dried out before a new bed is started. Woodwork will tend to deteriorate more quickly with this type of bed because of the dampness in the lower layers.

A good compromise is the semi-deep litter system, whereby the droppings and the worst of the wet bedding are removed daily and the whole box given a complete muck out once a week or once every few weeks. This works well with shavings beds. With any deep-litter system, frequent removal of droppings is essential.

Management of the muck heap is also important. For convenience it should be sited reasonably close to the stables, with a dry, level approach and easy access for large vehicles. It should be downwind of the stables. A muck heap can be free-standing or contained in a three-sided bunker – breeze blocks are particularly suitable for this purpose – which makes it easier to keep the heap tidy. Make sure that there is adequate drainage away from any paths or driveways.

During mucking out the entire stable floor should be swept clean and, if possible, allowed to dry before the bed is put down again.

The sides of the bed should be banked well up the stable walls to help keep out draughts and to prevent injury when the horse lies down.

A skip is used for the periodic removal of droppings during the day. Skips may be made of plastic, metal or rubber.

Feeds

The horse is a herbivore, that is an eater of plants and especially grass and herbs. Left to live a totally natural life, the horse will spend some twenty hours out of every twenty-four grazing, slowly moving from place to place in his search for satisfying food. Horses are what are known as trickle feeders: they have comparatively small stomachs in relation to the size of their large intestines and need to top up with food at regular intervals. In the wild they put on condition when food is plentiful and lose it when it is not. The unnatural conditions imposed upon horses by man – the lack of constant access to grass and the need to burn up energy by working – mean that they must be fed suitable alternatives to grass if they are to thrive. Feeding horses is a complex subject. Like humans, horses are individuals and vary a good deal in the type and quantity of food they need to maintain health and fitness. Basically, however, the domesticated horse's diet consists of roughage, or bulk food, and concentrates.

ROUGHAGE

The usual way to feed roughage is in the form of hay, which is simply dried grass. There are two types of hay: seed hay and meadow hay. **Seed hay** is suitable for horses in hard work, because it is usually more nutritious than meadow hay. It is taken from grasses specifically sown as an annual crop, which will include top-quality plants such as rye grass and timothy. **Meadow hay** is cut from permanent pasture and is softer to the touch and often greener in colour than seed hay. It contains a greater variety of plants than seed hay (some of which may be of inferior quality) and is usually less nutritious and therefore more suitable for animals in light work.

A newer way of feeding bulk is in the form of **haylage**, which is grass sealed in plastic bags. It comes in different nutritional levels and is particularly

Seed hay (left) and meadow hay (right)

Crushed oats

Bruised barley

Flaked maize

suitable for horses with respiratory problems. Haylage may be mixed with hay or replace it altogether as the horse's bulk feed.

Chaff or **chop** is hay, either alone or mixed with one-third proportion of oat straw, which has been chopped into small pieces by passing it through a chaff cutter. It may be added to concentrates to encourage mastication and aid digestion.

CONCENTRATES

Food such as oats and barley are known as concentrates. These are the energy-giving foods which, when fed in the correct balance with the roughage, enable the horse to perform the work required of him without losing condition.

Oats have always been considered the ideal cereal for feeding to horses. The fibrous husk covering the rich seed encourages chewing and helps prevent the horse from eating too quickly, which can seriously disrupt his digestive system. The one drawback is that oats have a low calcium-to-phosphorus ratio and the horse's diet should therefore contain a calcium supplement to balance the minerals in the roughage. Oats may not be suitable for feeding to all equine animals, however, as they can have a heating effect, making them difficult to control. Oats should be lightly rolled and used within two or three weeks thereafter, otherwise they lose nutritional value.

Barley has a higher energy value than oats but is lower in fibre. It may be fed cracked, rolled, flaked (heat treated) or micronized. It may also be fed as a mash, which is prepared by pouring boiling water over flaked barley and allowing it to cool before feeding. Whole barley should never be fed unless it has first been cooked to soften it, otherwise it is too indigestible. It should be covered with boiling water and allowed to simmer for several hours until the grain has split, swollen and become soft.

Bran

Linseed (which must be boiled before feeding)

Soaked sugar beet

Molassed chop

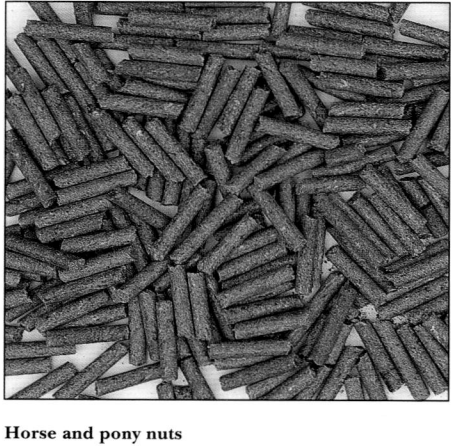

Horse and pony nuts

Coarse mix

Maize is high in starch but low in protein and fibre. It is usually fed flaked or micronized. It can be very heating and should be fed only in small amounts.

Bran, a by-product of wheat, is high in fibre and often fed to horses who are off work or on a low-protein diet. It may be fed dry in small quantities, mixed with the horse's other feed, or as a mash. This is made by putting the bran, together with a handful of salt, in a bucket, pouring boiling water over it (not so much that the mash is sloppy), covering and allowing it to steam and cool.

Linseed, the seed of the flax plant, is rich in oil and often fed to improve the condition of the horse's coat. It is poisonous (it contains prussic acid) if not first boiled. The linseed is covered with cold water and

soaked overnight. The following day more water is added (about 4 pints/2 litres to 2–3oz/110g of linseed) and the mixture is brought to the boil and simmered for several hours. When the resultant jelly has cooled it may be added to a bran mash or to the horse's ordinary feed.

Sugar beet is a highly digestible source of energy and fibre. It has a good calcium-to-phosphorus ratio and may be used to correct the imbalance of those elements in cereals. Sugar beet pulp (the remains of the root vegetable after the sugar has been extracted) comes in cube form or shredded. Before feeding it is essential to soak it for at least twelve hours using at least double the amount of water to pulp. Cubes may require soaking for longer in more water. If it is not adequately soaked,

it will swell up in the horse's stomach, with potentially fatal results.

Molasses is a by-product of sugar. Dark and sticky in appearance and very palatable, it may be added in small quantities to the feed to supply energy, improve the condition of the coat and to tempt fussy feeders.

Concentrates which come in cube form or as coarse mixes are known as **compound feeds**. They are made from a variety of ingredients and are scientifically prepared to provide a balanced diet. Specially formulated compound feeds are available for foals, brood mares, competition horses, and so on. They are particularly useful for the novice horseman as a good-quality compound feed takes much of the guesswork out of feeding.

Feeding

To work out a suitable feed ration for your horse you must take into consideration his size, his age, his type and the amount and nature of the work he is doing. Feeding is both a science and an art. Science tells us much about the principles of feeding and the nutritive value of the various feedstuffs but horses are all individuals and ultimately the proof of the pudding is in their appearance and performance. You can learn to judge the correct, healthy condition for a horse of a particular breed, age, size and build doing a particular job of work by studying similar animals to your own which are being used for similar purposes (perhaps at your riding school or in local competitions).

The ratio of bulk feed to concentrates will vary according to the nature and amount of work the horse is required to do. A horse in light work does not require a great deal of energy-giving feed (it will merely serve to make him a "hot" ride). On the other hand a horse such as a hunter or an eventer needs more energy-giving feed and less bulk. For a horse in light work (doing up to about six hours a week hacking and light schooling) and for

The following is an approximate guide to total food requirements based on height (but bear in mind that it is only approximate, since horses vary a good deal in build and a finely made animal may require less food than a heavyweight doing the same amount of work):

Height	Daily feed requirement
Under 12hh	14 – 16lb (6.3 – 7.2kg)
12 – 13hh	16 – 18lb (7.2 – 8kg)
13 – 14hh	20 – 22lb (9 – 10kg)
14 – 15hh	22 – 24lb (10 – 11kg)
15 – 16hh	24 – 26lb (11 – 12kg)
over 16hh	26 – 28lb (12 – 12.5kg)

To find a more accurate yardstick it is customary to measure feed requirements against the horse's body weight (the horse requires a total daily intake of about 2-2.5 per cent of its body weight). The best way to check his weight is to use a weighbridge. Failing that you can estimate his weight by using the following formula:

$$\frac{\text{Girth}^2 \times \text{length (in inches)}}{300} = \text{weight in lbs}$$

NB Measure the girth round the largest part of the barrel at the moment when the horse has breathed out; measure the length from the point of the shoulder to the point of the buttock.

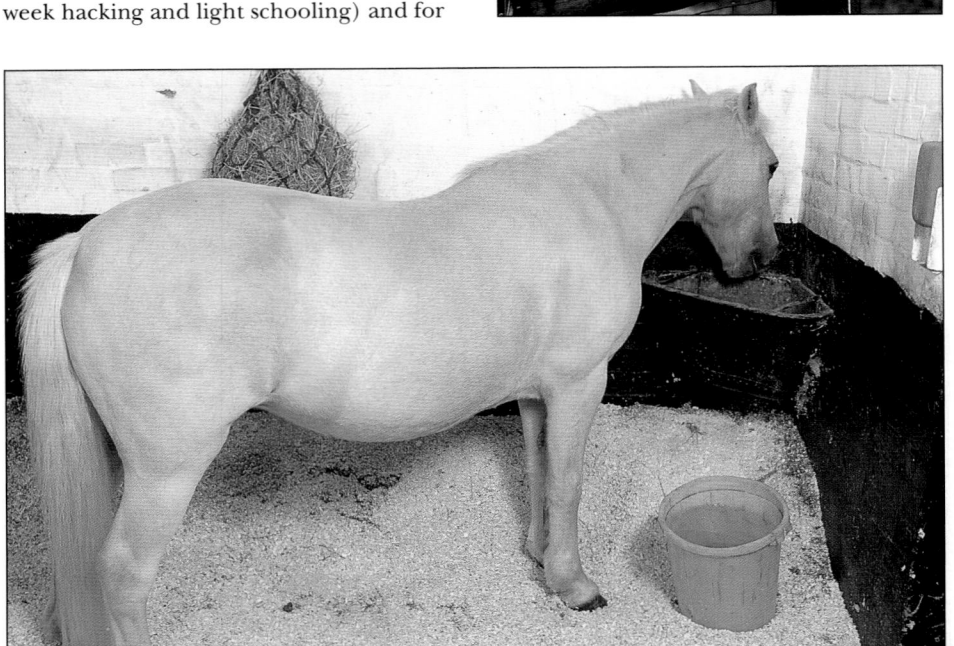

▌ TOP LEFT
Some barn-type stabling incorporates swinging feed bowls. They are labour saving in large yards with a lot of horses to feed.

▌ ABOVE LEFT
Hook-on plastic mangers are useful for feeding horses kept at grass.

▌ LEFT
A large corner manger is a suitable way to feed the stabled horse. Mangers must be cleaned out regularly.

GOLDEN RULES OF FEEDING

☛ Feed nature's way: little and often – the horse has a small stomach in relation to its size.

☛ Divide the concentrate ration (preferably mixed with chaff or other small roughage) into three or four feeds a day – never give more than 4lb (1.8kg) of concentrates in one feed.

☛ Feed at the same times each day.

☛ Wash mangers regularly with clean water.

☛ Never leave uneaten feed in the manger – if your horse regularly fails to eat up, either you are overfeeding or there is something wrong with him or the feed.

☛ Never feed directly before exercise – allow up to two hours for digestion.

☛ Never feed immediately after work – allow an hour for the horse to recover.

☛ Never make sudden changes to a horse's diet – introduce new feedstuffs gradually over a period of at least a week.

☛ Feed hay after concentrates and give the bulk of the hay at night.

☛ Never leave a horse for longer than eight hours without food.

☛ Always ensure that the horse has clean, fresh water available.

☛ Have the horse's teeth checked regularly – sharp edges must be rasped down to enable him to chew his food efficiently.

☛ Worm the horse regularly.

☛ Keep feed in clean, dry, rodent-proof bins, and hay in a waterproof feed shed, protected from damp ground.

☛ Add variety to the feed by giving succulents such as sliced apples and carrots (sliced lengthways to prevent choking), especially if the horse is a shy feeder.

most ponies the ratio should be 30 per cent concentrates to 70 per cent bulk. For a horse in medium work (doing up to ten hours work a week, including up to two hours schooling a day, some dressage, show jumping and hacking) the ratio should be 50 per cent concentrates to 50 per cent bulk. For a horse in hard work (more than ten hours a week, or including fast work such as hunting, eventing or endurance riding) the ratio should be 70 per cent concentrates to 30 per cent bulk. These are general guidelines and all horses are different, but however hard he is working the horse should never receive less than 25 per cent bulk by weight.

Horses and ponies living out at grass during the winter require the same amount of food as stabled horses in order to maintain their health and condition during bad weather. During the spring and summer (assuming that the weather is fine) good-quality grazing should provide enough nutrition for ponies and coldblooded horses doing no more than an hour or two of light work, though it is best to check their weight regularly to make sure. During the winter, grazing will do no more than provide maintenance. In severe weather it will not even do that and the horse will lose condition if he does not receive supplementary feeding.

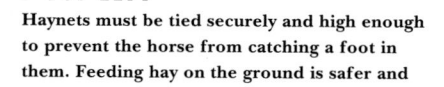

▌ **TOP LEFT**
Haynets must be tied securely and high enough to prevent the horse from catching a foot in them. Feeding hay on the ground is safer and more natural.

▌ **LEFT**
Horses should have access to salt, to counteract any deficiency in their diet. A salt lick is a convenient way of providing it.

▌ **FAR LEFT**
Soaking hay in clean water for a few hours before feeding helps prevent horses inhaling mould spores.

Water

Water makes up approximately 60 per cent of an adult horse's body weight, the exact percentage depending on his age and condition. It is present in all his body fluids and is vital for the correct functioning of the blood, the digestion and the excretion process. A horse can survive for several weeks without food but only for a few days without water.

The quantity of water required by a horse on a daily basis varies according to his diet, the prevailing weather conditions, his work load and his general health. A stabled horse may drink in the region of eight gallons (37 litres) of water a day, although the amount may be as little as five gallons (20 litres) or as much as ten (40 litres). A horse at grass may drink less than a stabled horse because of the moisture content in the grazing. A horse will drink more when the weather is hot and humid or when he sweats as a result of hard work. A sick horse may be reluctant to drink.

It is vital for the stabled horse to have access to a constant supply of fresh, clean water, the only exception being before hard, fast work. Horses are extremely fussy about the water they drink and will go thirsty rather than drink dirty or tainted water.

Water for the stabled horse may be provided either in buckets or by means of an automatic water bowl. The advantage of using buckets is that you can easily check the amount of water the horse is drinking. Water buckets should be large and strong – heavy-duty rubber is the most resilient. Plastic buckets, though convenient because they are light to carry, are not the safest as they tend to split and can cause injury. Metal buckets are stronger but they, too, might cause injury to a restless horse.

Buckets should be positioned in a corner of the stable, not right by the door but not too far from it, either, so that they are easy to reach for refilling. The handle

should be positioned away from the horse. Many horses can be trusted never to knock a bucket over, even when it is empty. Others get into the habit of playing with theirs. Some are just naturally clumsy and will knock a bucket over when moving about the box. Water buckets can be fixed to the wall with clips or, if the stable is roomy enough, stood in a rubber tyre.

During the day water buckets should be checked and refilled regularly. Water should be replaced rather than topped up to ensure a fresh supply. At night a big horse will need two buckets so that there is no possibility of his going short. Buckets should be scrubbed out regularly with clean water.

Automatic drinking bowls, connected to the water supply and controlled by a small ballcock, are popular in large yards because they are labour saving. However, they do have several disadvantages. Compared with buckets they are quite small and may not permit a horse to enjoy a deep drink. Unless they are fitted with a plug (which should be recessed into the bottom out of the way of the horse's teeth) they are difficult to clean. Also, it is not possible to judge at a glance how much a horse is drinking. Since water consumption, like food consumption, is an indication of the horse's state of health, this is not ideal. It is, however,

■ BELOW
An automatic drinking bowl provides an alternative to buckets. The bowl must be checked frequently to ensure that the water supply is operating correctly.

■ BELOW
The stabled horse must have constant access to clean water. A large horse will need two buckets.

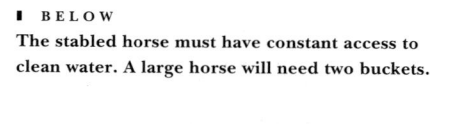

GOLDEN RULES OF WATERING

☛ Always provide the stabled horse with a constant supply of clean water.

☛ Always water before feeding.

☛ Never work a horse hard immediately after a long drink.

☛ After hard work (such as hunting or cross-country) give a horse a small quantity of water – about half a gallon (2.5 litres) every quarter of an hour until he is satisfied.

☛ When giving electrolytes (minerals to replace those lost during strenuous exercise) always offer plain water as well.

☛ Keep all water utensils clean.

☛ Check automatic water bowls every day.

possible to install drinkers fitted with a meter which overcomes this problem. All projecting fixtures in a stable are a potential source of injury to the horse and a water bowl is no exception. Conversely, there is every possibility of a bowl being damaged by the horse. Drinking bowls must be rigorously checked every day – a blocked supply will cause the horse great distress while an overflowing bowl with swamp his bedding. Precautions must be taken when fitting pipes so that they cannot freeze in winter.

Daily Care

Horses must be kept fit and healthy if they are to perform the work required of them. Keeping them that way requires daily care and attention. It is the responsibility of the owner to ensure that the horse has sufficient regular exercise of the right type and to learn how to recognize the signs of ill-health. Every horse, whether he is kept stabled or at grass, should be checked over carefully every day to ensure that he is well, sound and has no injuries or fresh lumps or bumps. Horses are creatures of habit. They thrive on a regular routine and therefore should be visited, fed, exercised and so on, at the same times each day. Some common equine ailments and minor injuries can be dealt with by the competent horseman, others will need veterinary attention. The owner must judge when to seek expert advice, bearing in mind that the sooner treatment begins, the better the chance of a cure. Regular visits from the farrier are also an essential part of horse care. There was never a truer maxim than "no foot, no horse".

Exercise

The horse needs daily exercise for the maintenance of health and, like all athletes, when he is in work he needs additional exercise to build up and maintain condition.

Where fitness of the horse is concerned exercise is always linked to feed. A horse who is kept at grass, provided the paddock is not very small, has the opportunity to

STABLE "VICES"

Being cooped up in a stable for some twenty-two hours out of every twenty-four is unnatural and boring and may lead to a horse developing bad habits, or stable "vices". These include wood chewing, box-walking (aimless walking round and round the stable), crib-biting (in which the horse takes hold of the manger or the top of the door or some other convenient object with his teeth and swallows air) or weaving (in which he stands, usually with his head over the door, and sways from side to side). Virtually all stable vices can do harm to the horse in one way or another. All can be avoided if the horse is not allowed to become bored and frustrated.

take all the gentle exercise he needs to stay healthy. Space and the freedom to move around at will are an intrinsic part of the horse's everyday life in the natural state so the bigger his paddock the nearer it is to his natural environment and the more contented he will be.

However, the totally grass-fed horse will not be fit to do anything other than light work in summer. By keeping the horse in a stable it is possible to monitor his food intake and gradually build up his physical fitness to enable him to carry out the work required of him. But because the stabled horse is deprived of his freedom for part, if not all, of the day a good exercise regime is essential if he is to be happy and healthy and not become unmanageable.

If possible, all stabled horses should spend part of the day turned out at grass in addition to their normal work routine. There is a danger of fit horses doing themselves harm when turned out, so it is essential to have safely fenced paddocks and to fit protective boots to guard against accidents. If for some reason it is not possible to give the stabled horse his usual exercise (for example in bad weather when it may be impossible to ride on the roads), he should be turned out for a time each day or at the very least led out and allowed to eat some grass. Another alternative to ridden exercise is to work the horse on the lunge.

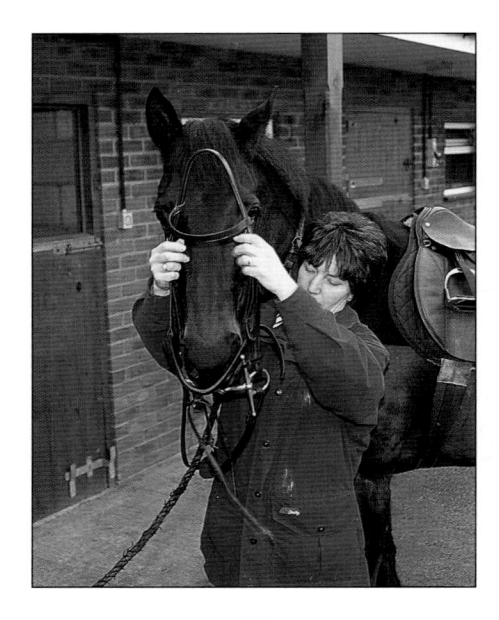

■ RIGHT
For exercise purposes
a simple snaffle bridle
and general purpose
saddle are usually
adequate.

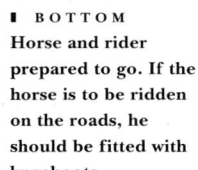

■ BOTTOM
Horse and rider
prepared to go. If the
horse is to be ridden
on the roads, he
should be fitted with
kneeboots.

Before being exercised or worked the horse should be given a quick grooming to make him neat and tidy. Stable stains should be sponged off and all remnants of bedding removed from his mane and tail. His feet should be picked out and his shoes checked.

An all-purpose saddle is suitable for general hacking out and roadwork. A numnah will protect the saddle from grease and dirt from the horse's coat and will also be more comfortable for his back.

Keeping a bridle for everyday use will minimize the wear and tear on the bridle you use for "best", e.g. for showing or competing. The bitting and bridling arrangement will depend on the horse. Most can be hacked out safely in a snaffle with a cavesson noseband. If you do need a little more control, you may prefer to fit a Grakle or flash noseband. Whether or not you use a martingale will again depend on the horse and how difficult or otherwise he is to control.

When exercising on the roads it is advisable to fit the horse with kneeboots – fitted correctly they will not impede his action. It is all too easy for a horse to slip up on tarmac and injure his knees, yet it is surprising how few people take this simple precaution. Brushing boots are another useful means of protecting the horse's legs.

A clipped horse in winter will need an exercise sheet to keep his loins warm. This is placed under the saddle to prevent it slipping back. It should be fitted with a fillet string, which passes under the tail to prevent it blowing up in the wind.

You can exercise two horses at the same time by riding one and leading one, in which case the led horse should wear a bridle and you should lead him either by the reins or on a leather lead rein run from one bit ring, through the other and into your hand. Never lead a horse on a lunge rein which could easily become tangled, and never wind a lead rein or reins round your hand. The ridden horse must always be between the led horse and the traffic and you should always ride on the same side of the road as the direction of the traffic. Avoid riding and leading on roads where there is anything but light traffic and never ride and lead unless the horses are traffic-proof and well behaved. For maximum control the led horse's head should be at or just behind the ridden horse's shoulder.

For more serious work – schooling, dressage, jumping and so on – the horse should wear the saddle and bridle most suited to that activity and protective boots or bandages. For jumping, fit his shoes with appropriate studs to prevent slipping.

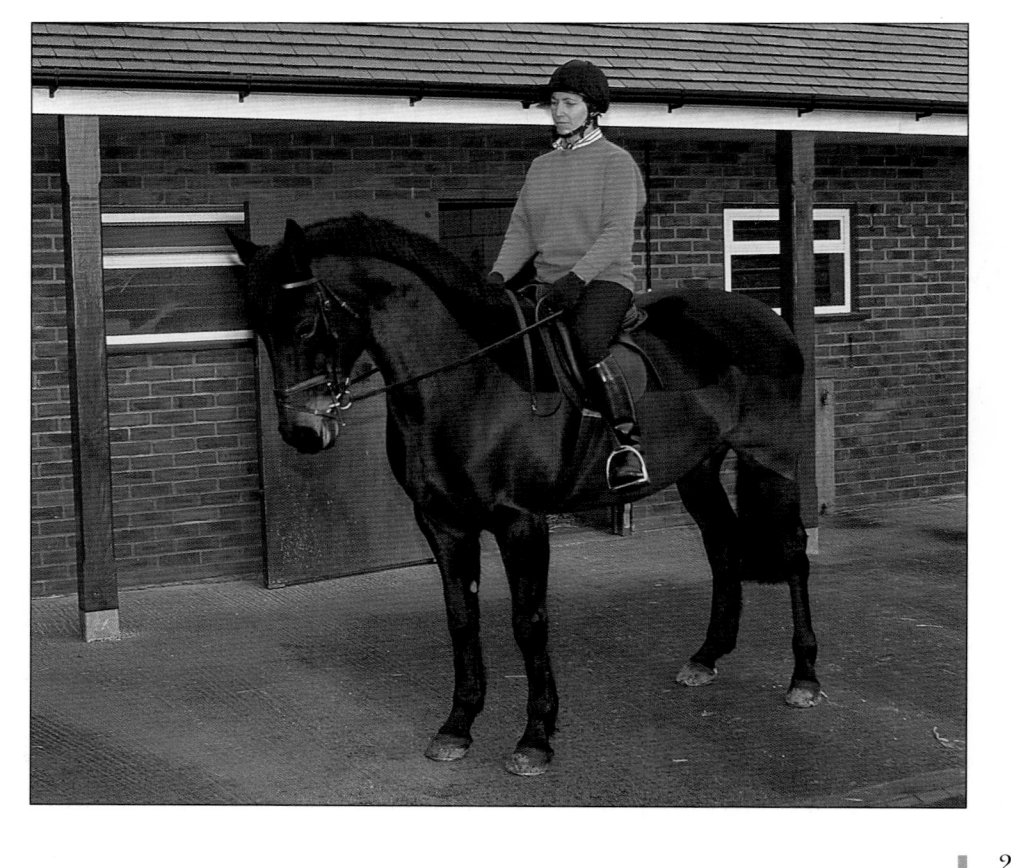

Fitness

Broadly speaking the fitness training of the horse can be divided into three distinct stages. First, there is a period of slow work designed to strengthen him up in readiness for more serious work. Second, there is the build up designed to bring him to the necessary fitness for most everyday riding activities. And third, there is the fine tuning required to bring him to a peak for physically demanding pastimes such as regular hunting, show jumping, eventing or racing.

FIRST STAGE

The period of slow work is vital and should never be rushed. The tried and tested way to make horses fit, and to prevent strains and sprains when they begin serious work, is roadwork. When the horse is first ridden after a period of rest,

he must have walking exercise only. Three-quarters of an hour a day is sufficient to begin with if the horse has been out at grass. Gradually, over a period of **two or three weeks** (preferably longer if the horse is ultimately going to be asked to do a lot of hard, fast work), this can be increased to an hour and a half to two hours a day.

Although this is slow work, the horse must not be allowed to slop along any old how. He should be kept going forward,

straight and in a good rhythm in order to start the process of building up muscles in the right places. The exercise route should be varied as much as possible to keep the horse alert and interested and he should have a day off each week to allow him to relax.

Trotting can begin during weeks **three to four**. To begin with the horse should walk for about thirty minutes before starting to trot. This will give his muscles time to warm up. His exercise period

LEFT
Hillwork builds up muscle, particularly in the hindquarters, and improves the horse's lung and heart capacity.

BOTTOM
Hacking out makes a welcome break from school work for both horse and rider.

▌ LEFT
By week five the horse
should be fit enough
to start a little
gymnastic jumping.

▌ BELOW LEFT
Serious schooling can
begin when the horse
has been in work for
about six weeks.

should also finish at walk, in order to cool
him off. The trot should be controlled and
rhythmic and in the early stages the
periods of trot should be short and
interspersed with longer periods of walk.
As the days progress and the horse begins
to feel fitter, the periods of trot can be
made longer. The pace must always be
controlled: trotting flat out on the roads
(or any other hard surface) jars the
horse's legs and can lead to injury. Uphill
trotting is better than trotting on the flat
because it reduces the strain placed on the
front legs. At all times when trotting the
rider should change the diagonal
regularly and, when trotting uphill, keep
the weight forward.

During **week four** some periods of
schooling on the flat can be introduced.
They should be no longer than about
twenty minutes and cantering should be
kept to a minimum. To encourage the
horse to relax and to continue the
building-up process, he should be taken
for a hack afterwards.

Week five can see the introduction of a
little hillwork, one of the finest ways of
building up muscle. Hacking and flatwork
should continue.

By **week six** he should be ready for
a canter work-out, in which he should
be allowed to stride on but without
going into a wild gallop. As with
trotting, uphill cantering is the most
beneficial.

SECOND STAGE

Once the first stage in the fitness
programme is completed the horse will be
in a fit state to begin more serious work.
Work on the flat, incorporating suppling
exercises such as serpentines and circles,
should be introduced. The schooling
sessions should be kept short to begin with
but may be gradually increased in length
as the horse becomes more toned up.
Gymnastic jumping exercises over grids
and on circles and elements of circles will
all help to improve his athleticism.

THIRD STAGE

The type of fitness required in a
particular horse is always governed by
the type of work required of him. For
example a show jumper needs the
muscular power to clear big fences but is
never required to gallop flat out for a
prolonged period. On the other hand the
three-day eventer needs great stamina and
endurance to be able to cope with the
demands placed on him.

Getting the horse fit for sports which
require speed and endurance involves
longer periods of canter work. Canter
work must be introduced gradually and
should always be carried out on good
ground to reduce the risk of injury. Short
periods of canter are sufficient to begin
with. Later, periods of long, steady
cantering may be used to bring the horse
to a high degree of fitness. Only rarely is
the occasional really fast galloping
necessary, as for instance with the fine
tuning of a racehorse or three-day event
horse. The main thing to remember is
that the faster the pace the more chance
there is of injury occurring.

Even when the horse reaches peak
fitness for the activity required of him, he
should be allowed regular periods of
relaxation if he is not to become sour –
hacks in the countryside or spells at liberty
in the paddock. During a rest day after
strenuous work the horse will appreciate
being led out for a bite of grass.

The Healthy and the Unhealthy Horse

Recognizing signs of ill-health in the horse is all part of good horse management. The experienced horseman can tell at a glance when something is not quite right with an animal in his or her care. Learning to recognize the warning signs means an early diagnosis which, in turn, means a better chance of successful treatment.

A change in the horse's eating habits is often the first indication of something being amiss with his health: if a normally good feeder loses his appetite, be suspicious. A change in behaviour is also a reliable early-warning signal. For instance, if a normally bright, alert horse suddenly becomes listless, it may well be the first sign of a health problem. Any form of nasal discharge, coughing or a dull "staring" coat are also indications of ill-health. A change in the consistency and frequency of the horse's droppings may also mean that all is not well.

All owners should learn to check their horse's temperature, pulse rate and respiratory rate so as to know when to call for veterinary help.

The normal temperature of the healthy horse is around 101.5° Fahrenheit (38°C). You should learn to take your horse's temperature by practising while he is healthy so that you will be capable of making a fast, accurate reading should the

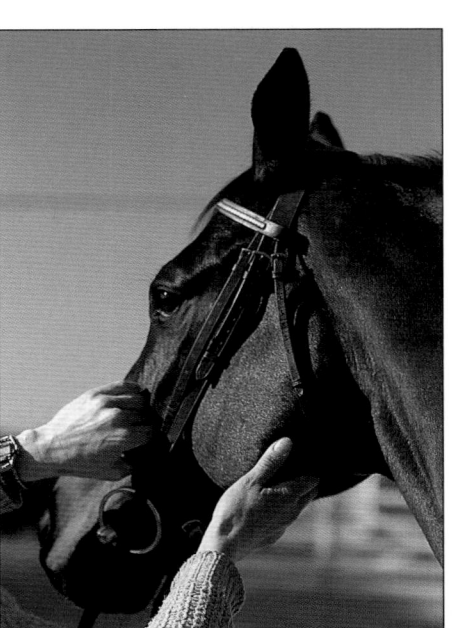

The horse's pulse is to be found along the edge of the lower jaw. In the healthy horse the heart rate is about 40 per minute.

need arise. The temperature is taken with a clinical thermometer which is inserted into the rectum and held there for about one minute. It is best to hold the horse's tail steady to prevent him swishing it and possibly dislodging the thermometer.

At rest the healthy horse has a heart rate of about 40 per minute. If the heart rate exceeds 60 per minute, there is definitely something wrong with the horse. To count the heart rate you need a stethoscope but failing that it is possible to count the horse's pulse rate by resting a finger over the artery situated about halfway along the bottom edge of the lower jaw. Locating the pulse will take a certain amount of practice.

In the healthy horse at rest the respiratory rate can vary from about eight to sixteen breaths a minute. To count the respiratory rate watch the horse's flanks.

Like humans, some horses have heart murmurs or faulty heart rhythms. If a heart abnormality is only present when

the horse is resting and disappears when he begins to work, there is usually no cause for alarm.

Problems with the limbs manifest themselves in various ways. Often the slightest suspicion of heat or a tiny swelling may be an indication of a serious tendon problem. Actual lameness can be detected by watching the horse as he is trotted both away from you and towards you. Watch for a sinking of the hindquarters or a nod of the head as one foot hits the ground (it will be the other limb which is causing the pain). When acquiring a new horse take note of any scars or bony enlargements so that you can distinguish new problems from old conditions or injuries.

All horses carry a worm burden which must be controlled by regular worming if it is not to cause serious damage to their health. Your veterinary surgeon will advise on a suitable worming programme.

In young horses a raised temperature and cold-like symptoms such as a nasal discharge may indicate an infestation of ascarids. These are quite large worms which can cause colic. In the adult horse the main danger comes from the large red worm, or *Strongylus vulgaris*, whose immature larvae burrow into the small arteries in the intestinal wall. The damage

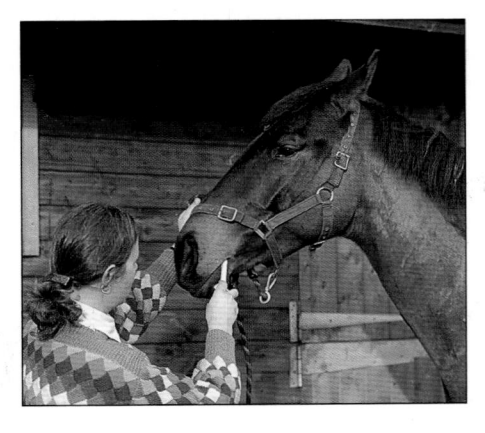

All horses carry a worm burden and require regular worming. The usual method of worming is to administer an oral paste.

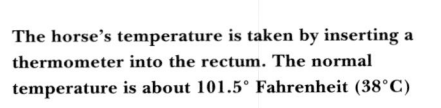

The horse's temperature is taken by inserting a thermometer into the rectum. The normal temperature is about 101.5° Fahrenheit (38°C)

they cause to the walls of the blood vessels may result in a blood clot. An infestation of *Strongylus vulgaris* can cause colic and anaemia. It may also disrupt the normal movement of the bowels.

If the horse is seen rubbing his tail, he may be suffering from pin worms, which inhabit the rectum.

Cream-coloured eggs attached to the horse's hair, particularly on the legs, during summer are the eggs of the horse bot, a fly whose larvae are able to penetrate the skin and migrate to the horse's stomach. If the infestation is severe, bots can produce ulceration of the stomach wall and may affect digestion.

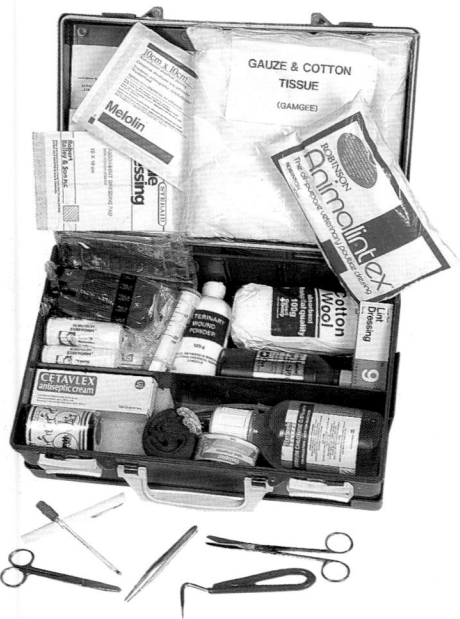

Every horse owner should have a well-stocked equine first-aid kit readily available at all times.

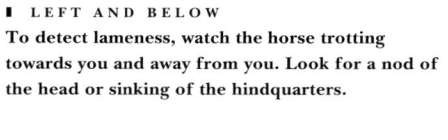

■ LEFT AND BELOW
To detect lameness, watch the horse trotting towards you and away from you. Look for a nod of the head or sinking of the hindquarters.

Common Ailments

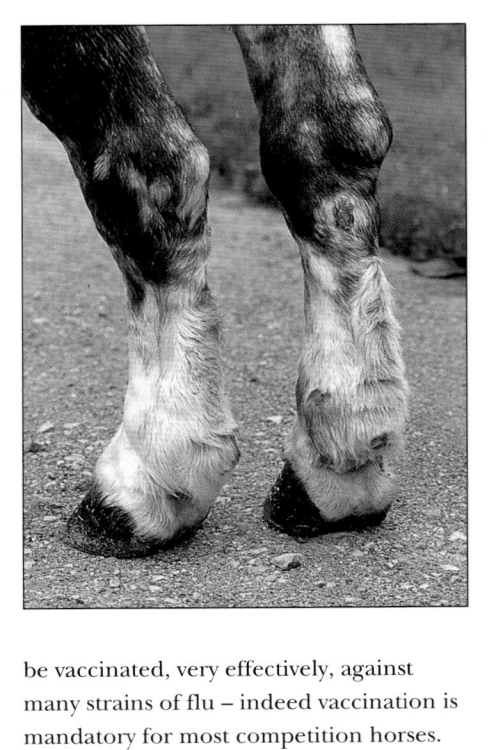

Azoturia, also known as set fast or tying-up, is a stiffening up of the large muscles of the back and hindquarters. It results from the accumulation of large amounts of lactic acid. It is not always possible to determine the reason, though too much food combined with too little exercise is a common cause. The horse begins to sweat up and has difficulty in moving forwards. The muscles feel hard to the touch and the horse will clearly be in pain. Dark, red-coloured urine may be passed. The horse should be rugged up and not moved. The veterinary surgeon should be called. He or she may prescribe drugs to relieve the pain and inflammation.

In **chronic obstructive pulmonary disease** (COPD) the airways to the horse's lungs become, as the name suggests, chronically obstructed. COPD is the result of an allergic reaction to fungal spores, for instance in the horse's hay or bedding. Symptoms include a nasal discharge followed by a cough. The horse's ability to perform hard work diminishes and in time his respiratory rate at rest increases. Treatment includes rest, fresh air, antibiotics and clean stabling with dust-free bedding and spore-free feed.

Equine influenza occurs in two main strains with numerous subtypes; a serious respiratory disease, it can prove fatal. Symptoms include a horse going off his feed, a raised temperature and general cold-type symptoms. Antibiotics may help and the horse must be rested. Horses can be vaccinated, very effectively, against many strains of flu – indeed vaccination is mandatory for most competition horses.

Grass sickness is a painful and fatal disease affecting the horse's nervous system. It is typified by loss of condition, muscle twitching, difficulty in swallowing and a green nasal discharge. In an acute case the horse may die in a few days. Others linger for weeks or months. Its cause is uncertain and it is more common in some regions than others.

Mud fever is a bacterial infection of the skin which affects the legs and/or lower body. It is most often seen on the lower legs. Raw areas develop which ooze serum and then form scabs. At the back of the pasterns and heels cracks often develop in the skin. The condition is most often seen in skin exposed to very muddy or very dry, dusty conditions. Skin with white hair is most susceptible. The best way of preventing mud fever and cracked heels is to protect the skin, when dry, with a barrier cream. Treatment involves clipping the hair from the affected area, regular washing (with antiseptic shampoo) and removal of scabs, careful drying and the use of antibiotic ointment.

COLIC

Colic is abdominal pain which may occur for a number of reasons, such as a sudden change in diet, migrating worm larvae, impaction of the intestines or, in rarer cases, a twisted gut. Signs of colic include the horse standing and looking round at, or trying to kick, its flank, sweating and/or repeated lying down and rolling.

The horse should be put in a stable on a deep bed to guard against injury if he wants to lie down and roll and the vet should be called. He or she may administer pain-relieving or relaxant drugs and/or a lubricant, depending on the type of colic. If a twisted gut is diagnosed, immediate surgery is essential to save the horse's life. Potentially life-threatening attacks of colic are accompanied by a high temperature (above 103° Fahrenheit/39°C) and raised pulse rate (above 60 per minute).

Rain scald is a skin infection caused by the same bacterium as mud fever. It occurs on the upper surfaces of the body. Like mud fever it is treated with antiseptic shampoos and the removal of the scabs which harbour the bacteria.

Ringworm is a fungal infection of the skin and hair. It occurs as small crusty, hairless patches and is infectious. An affected horse should, therefore, be isolated. Ringworm is treated with special antibiotic skin washes which should also be used on the horse's tack to kill off all traces of the infection. The stable should also be treated. Careful control is required as ringworm can affect humans, too.

Strangles is an infection of the lymph glands under the jaw caused by the bacterium *Streptococcus equi*. Affected horses have difficulty in swallowing and the glands under the jaw become swollen. The temperature may rise to as high as 106° Fahrenheit (41°C) and there is a nasal discharge. Infected horses must be kept warm and given soft food. Antibiotics

may help. The abscesses in the glands should be treated with hot fomentations – once they burst the horse's condition usually improves. The pus from burst abscesses is highly contagious and horses affected by the infection should be isolated. A policy of strict hygiene must be adopted to prevent the spread of the infection on clothing and equipment. Abscesses which burst internally are very serious since they can cause pneumonia.

Sweet itch is a skin irritation caused by hypersensitivity to the bites of midges and is therefore found chiefly during the spring and summer. It usually occurs along the mane and the base of the tail, which become inflamed and sore. The irritation is such that the horse will often rub out all the mane and tail hairs at the affected places, making the skin raw. A susceptible horse or pony will suffer from sweet itch annually and must be protected from midge bites by being stabled at dusk and dawn when the insects are most active. Benzyl benzoate is used to sooth

the sore areas and helps to repel the midges. Fly repellents will also help and mosquito netting should be fitted over open windows and doors while the horse is stabled. Special sheets that cover the entire neck and body give useful protection.

All horses should be vaccinated against **tetanus** and given a booster injection every other year. Tetanus is caused by a bacterium found in the soil and may enter the horse's system via a wound, especially a deep puncture wound. Typical symptoms are stiffness of the muscles, twitching, the horse standing in a stretched-out manner and, as the disease progresses, overreaction to sudden noises or movements. Eventually the horse is unable to stand and death occurs when the breathing muscles become affected. Some horses do recover from tetanus since the infection can be halted by the use of antibiotics and antitoxin. Early diagnosis is essential and the horse will need to rest in a quiet, dark stable.

Common Injuries

Back injuries, either to the bones or muscles of the back, are often the result of falls. Treatment involves rest and the use of anti-inflammatory drugs. Faradism (stimulation of the muscles by electricity), massage and laser therapy may also help.

A **capped elbow** – the term used for a bursal enlargement at the point of the elbow – is usually caused by the horse's shoe striking the elbow when he is lying down. The swelling is soft and is hot and painful when it first appears. A **capped hock** is a similar injury, caused by the horse striking his hock against something hard like the wall of his stable (perhaps through the use of too little bedding) or the partition in a horsebox (hock boots should be fitted to guard against this, particularly if the horse is a bad traveller). Unless the condition causes lameness or there is an infection, it will not require treatment. In the case of a capped elbow the horse should be fitted with a "sausage boot" (a protective ring) on the pastern. This protects the elbow while it is healing.

An **overreach** is an injury to the heel or the back of the tendon of the front legs

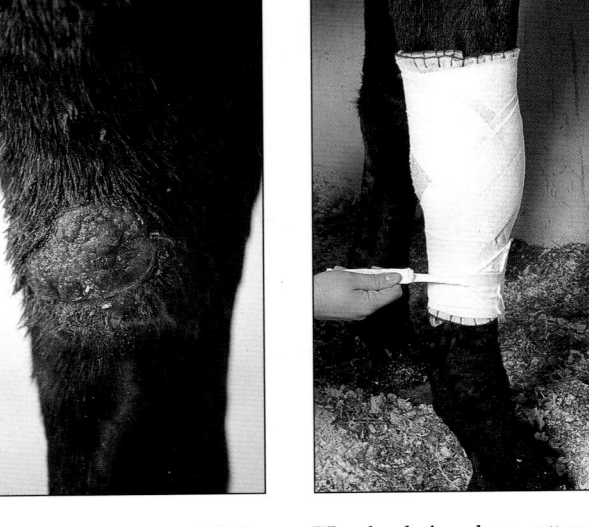

■ LEFT
Wounds must be thoroughly cleaned and then treated with ointment or powder. Leg wounds tend to heal less well than wounds to the body where the skin is looser.

caused by the horse striking itself with the toe of its own hindfoot. Overreaches should be carefully cleaned. An antibiotic dressing will help guard against infection. Overreaches can be serious – there is often extensive bruising – and are often slow to heal.

Splints are bony swellings found between the splint bones and the cannon bones. Although splints are most commonly found on the inner side of the forelegs, they can occur on either side of the leg and on the hindlegs. Splints often appear when a young horse first begins work. Conformation is a contributing factor. In many cases splints are associated

FIRST-AID KIT

The horse owner's first-aid kit should include:

- ☛ Disinfectant – for washing wounds.

- ☛ Skin swabs – small swabs impregnated with disinfectant for cleaning wounds where there is no clean water supply.

- ☛ Wound cleansing cream or liquid.

- ☛ Wound ointment or powder.

- ☛ Wound dressings.

- ☛ Crêpe bandages.

- ☛ Adhesive bandages.

- ☛ Gamgee tissue.

- ☛ Cotton wool.

- ☛ Cold packs.

- ☛ Poultices.

- ☛ Thermometer.

- ☛ Scissors (sharp, but with rounded ends for safety).

- ☛ Fly repellent.

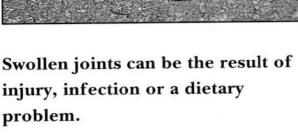

Swollen joints can be the result of injury, infection or a dietary problem.

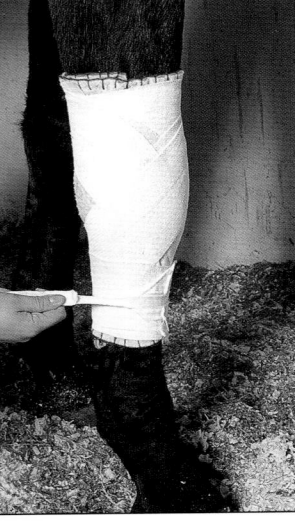

Fibrous tissue known as proud flesh may form a permanent blemish which will require surgical removal.

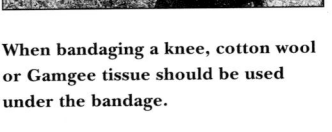

When bandaging a knee, cotton wool or Gamgee tissue should be used under the bandage.

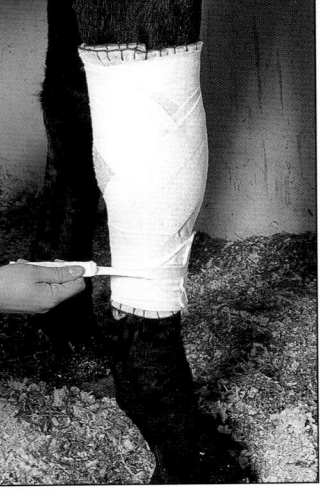

The correct way to bandage a hock.

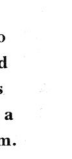

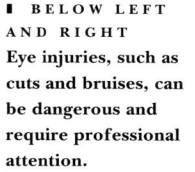

■ **LEFT**
Infra-red helps to relax muscles and soothe pain. This horse is enjoying a spell in a solarium.

■ **BELOW LEFT AND RIGHT**
Eye injuries, such as cuts and bruises, can be dangerous and require professional attention.

■ **BOTTOM**
Stimulation of the muscles by electricity (Faradism) is useful in the treatment of back injuries.

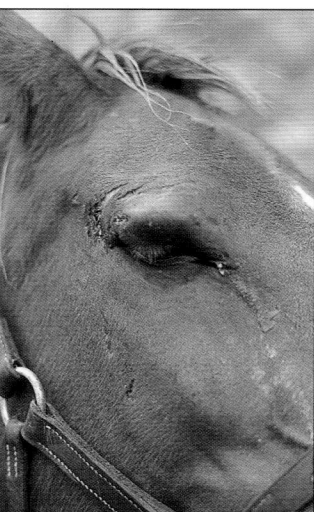

with poor foot and limb balance, in which case corrective shoeing often helps. Lameness may result, in varying degrees, while the splint is forming but often the pain associated with splints disappears in time. In the case of persistent lameness, the leg should be X-rayed to eliminate any possibility of a fracture.

Because of the strain put on the legs when galloping and jumping, **tendon injuries** are all too common in horses, particularly in the forelegs. The superficial and deep flexor tendons, which run down the back of the cannon bones, the suspensory ligament, which is immediately behind the lower part of the cannon bone, and the check ligament, situated below the knee, are all at risk. Tendon and ligament injuries are the result of sudden stress, which causes the fibres to tear. The injury causes pain, followed by heat and swelling. Cold is the most important part of the treatment: ice packs or, in an emergency, a pack of frozen peas, should be applied to the site of the injury as quickly as possible. Ice packs should be replaced frequently and the limb should be bandaged firmly, though not too tightly, for support. Laser treatment may help to reduce the swelling. The oldest – and best – treatment for all strains and

sprains is rest. A leg which has suffered a serious tendon injury is more likely to stand up to future work if the horse is given a period of twelve to eighteen months off. The veterinary surgeon can determine, by using a scanner, when a tendon injury has healed.

Horses suffer all types of **wounds** as a result of falls, accidents in the field and stable, and bites and kicks from other horses. Some, such as grazes, heal quickly provided they are kept clean and dry. Others can cause serious problems. **Puncture wounds** are often the most dangerous since bacteria may be carried deep into the wound. Although it is impossible not to notice a large, jagged laceration accompanied by a copious flow

of blood, it is easy to overlook a deep puncture wound simply because the wound to the skin is small and insignificant looking. It is important to ensure that such wounds heal from the inside out – poulticing may be necessary to draw out infection.

All wounds should be cleaned, if possible, with cold water though it should be remembered that continuous washing will not stop a wound from bleeding. The application of a pressure pad (such as a clean handkerchief) will help control the flow of blood while you are waiting for veterinary help. Large wounds may need stitching. If there is any doubt about the horse's vaccination status, he must be given a tetanus injection. If a wound needs covering to keep it clean, medicated gauze should be used as it will not stick to the wound. Wounds on the body, where the skin is loose, heal better than leg wounds which tend to develop proud flesh as they heal. Proud flesh is fibrous tissue, projecting beyond the level of the skin surrounding the wound and often forming a permanent blemish. The veterinary surgeon may advise using caustic preparations to arrest its development or it may need to be removed surgically.

Poulticing and Cold Treatments

The application of heat by means of a poultice helps to repair injury by stimulating the blood supply to the affected area. Heat also has a "drawing" effect, and will help to bring any pus to the surface.

Poultices may be made with kaolin, or specially impregnated padding can be bought. To make a hot kaolin poultice the tin of kaolin, with the lid loosened, is placed in a pan of boiling water for several minutes. When the kaolin is hot (no hotter than can be borne on the back of your hand) it is spread over a piece of lint, covered with gauze and applied to the injured area. To keep the heat in, polythene or aluminium foil is then wrapped over the gauze, followed by a piece of Gamgee tissue and the poultice is held in place with a bandage.

The poultice should be changed at least twice a day. All the kaolin must be removed from the wound before a new poultice is applied, otherwise the drawing effect of the new poultice will be lost. The main drawback of kaolin is that it is messy

to put on and remove. This problem can be overcome if you use ready-made poultices consisting of kaolin enclosed in a thin envelope of polythene.

Gamgee-type tissue impregnated with chemicals with drawing properties is also available. This must be activated by soaking in warm water. Like the envelope type of kaolin poultice it is easy to apply though it does leave a residue on the skin

which must be cleaned off before another poultice is applied.

Bran may be used to poultice the horse's foot in the case of problems such as a septic foot or corns. Boiling water is poured on to one or two scoops of bran to form a crumbly, not excessively wet, mixture. Test the bran for heat on the palm of the hand before applying it to the foot. The bran may be applied in a foot poultice boot, which is strapped on to the foot, or it may be placed in polythene and sacking and secured in place with a bandage. Horses sometimes try to eat bran poultices so it is advisable to add a little disinfectant to the boiling water to act as a deterrent. The poultice should be left on for twelve hours.

Tubbing is used for some foot wounds, which may require more regular applications of heat. Hand-hot water is placed in a non-metal bucket or tub and the horse's foot placed in it. Horses who are unwilling to cooperate by immersing their foot should be encouraged by having hot water gently splashed on their leg.

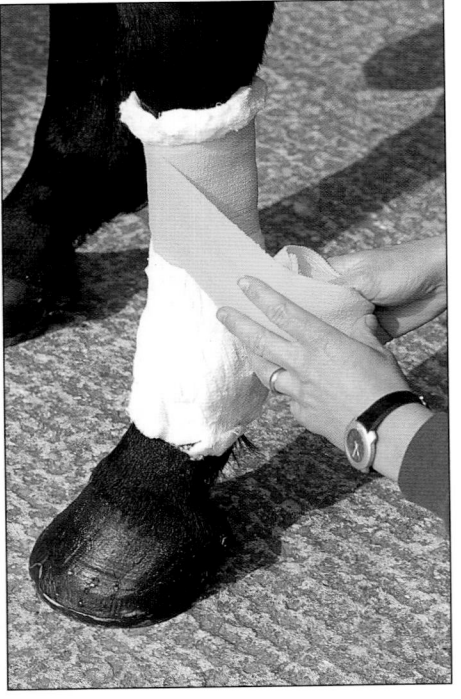

▪ **TOP**
Three types of equine boot designed to keep dressings in place on the horse's foot. Alternatively sacking, secured by a bandage, may be used.

▪ **FAR LEFT**
Gamgee-type tissue, impregnated with chemicals, makes an effective poultice. It is soaked in warm water before application.

▪ **LEFT**
Poultices should be removed at least twice a day. Any residue must be cleaned off the horse's skin before re-poulticing.

■ LEFT
Inhalants are
sometimes used when
horses have respiratory
tract problems. The
bag containing the
inhalant is fitted like a
nosebag.

■ BELOW
Hosing with cold water
helps to reduce the
swelling and heat
which accompany most
leg injuries.

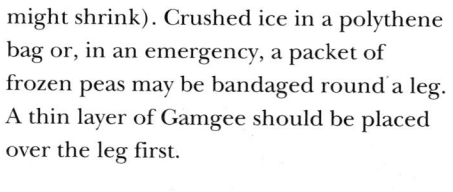

■ BELOW LEFT
Another effective
method of applying
cold treatment: a
hosepipe attached to a
"hose boot".

■ BELOW RIGHT
Hot or cold tubbing
can be carried out by
standing the horse's
foot in a bucket –
always providing he
cooperates!

Epsom salts and antiseptic may be added to the water. Tubbing lasts for about twenty minutes and should be carried out at least twice a day.

Where cold treatment is required as opposed to heat, there are various methods. Cold water may be applied with a hose for regular periods of about ten minutes. The horse should be accustomed to the feel of the water by starting at ground level and then gradually working it up the foot and leg. The legs should be bandaged between hosing sessions. Where suitable facilities are available the hose can be bandaged to the horse's leg. He should be given a haynet to keep him occupied. Walking or standing a horse in a river or in the sea is equally beneficial.

Specially designed flexible packs, which retain their cool temperature for quite a long time, can be obtained. They are cooled in a freezer and bandaged into place. Special bandages are available, too. These are designed to absorb water and are flexible enough to be applied even when the water is frozen. Another way to apply cold to a leg is to soak bandages in cold water (care must be taken to remove them before they start to dry out as they might shrink). Crushed ice in a polythene bag or, in an emergency, a packet of frozen peas may be bandaged round a leg. A thin layer of Gamgee should be placed over the leg first.

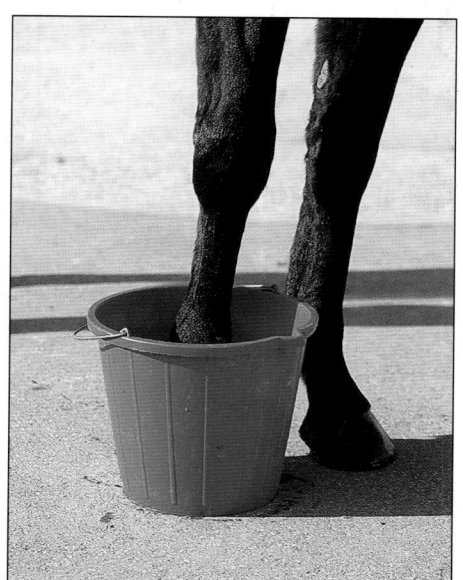

Anatomy of the Foot

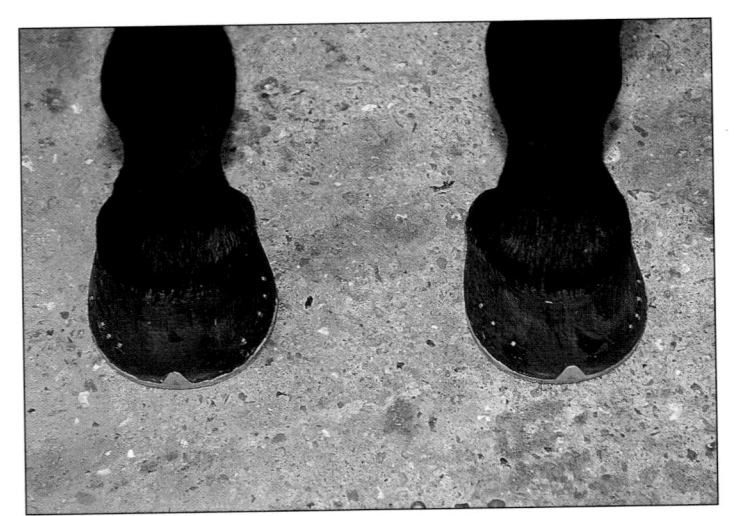

Lameness in horses occurs far more often in the foot than in any other part of the limbs. This is not surprising considering the amount of strain put upon the feet of domesticated horses required to pull heavy loads or carry a rider, particularly at fast speeds or over jumps.

The term foot is used to describe the hoof – the dense horny covering – and all the structures contained inside it. The external, insensitive part of the hoof comprises the wall (the outer, protective layer of the foot); the sole (a plate of hard horn just under an inch (2cm) thick; the frog (a wedge-shaped mass of soft elastic horn), and the periople (a thin layer of epidermis between the hoof wall and the skin).

The function of the sole is to give protection to the sensitive inner structures and to help support weight. The frog performs the same functions as the sole as well as providing grip and acting as a shock absorber. The periople controls evaporation from the underlying horn.

The internal part of the hoof comprises the sensitive laminae, the sensitive sole, the sensitive frog, the perioplic corium and the coronary corium.

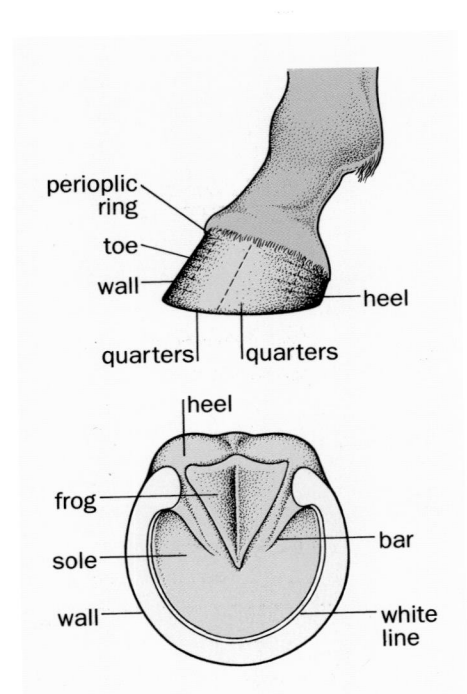

Laminae are interlocking leaf-like structures which attach the hoof to the pedal bone. Hundreds of sensitive (or primary) laminae dovetail with thousands of horny (secondary) laminae which grow outwards from the interior of the wall of the hoof.

The sensitive sole, which is attached securely to the lower surface of the pedal bone, is a thin layer of tissue which corresponds to the horny sole and supplies it with nutrition.

The sensitive frog supplies nutrition to the digital cushion on which it is moulded. This cushion is a wedge-shaped fibro-elastic pad situated in the hollow behind the heels. It has an important part to play in reducing concussion by expanding when the foot takes weight.

The perioplic corium or ring situated just above the coronary corium (coronary body) supplies nutrition to the periople. The coronary corium, a thick structure situated above the sensitive laminae, lies in the coronary groove and supplies nutrition to the wall of the hoof.

On the ground surface of the sole, where the sole meets the wall, is a narrow band of soft plastic horn known as the white line. This white line is of great importance to the farrier because it indicates the position of the sensitive structures of the foot and the thickness of the wall, thus helping determine where nails can be driven into the wall to hold shoes in place without encroaching on the sensitive areas.

The Role of the Farrier

Horses have been shod with metal shoes for over two thousand years and although it is impossible to say for certain who first had the temerity to try nailing a shoe to the horse's hoof, it is widely assumed to have been the Celts and the Gauls.

The need to protect the feet arose when man began to use the horse as a beast of burden and for riding. The unnatural wear and tear inflicted upon the feet of the domesticated horse results in the hooves being worn down more quickly than they are renewed – this would not occur in the horse's natural state. The damage caused to the hoof is worse when travelling over hard, rough ground or in a wet environment. The latter leads to the growth of softer horn, which wears away more quickly. This explains why horses in dry, hot climates, which promote the growth of hard horn, can often do a considerable amount of work unshod without any ill effects.

The role of the farrier is of vital importance, since the horse cannot work adequately if his feet are painful. It is the farrier's job to ensure that the horse's feet are not only well and securely shod but are also correctly trimmed. The horn of the hoof is constantly growing and fitting a metal shoe to the hoof prevents excess growth being worn down naturally, as is the case with the unshod horse. The average monthly growth of horn is around ¼–⅜ inch (5–9mm) and the horse needs to have his feet trimmed about every four or five weeks, depending on the rate of growth. If his old shoes are not worn, they may be refitted – these are known as "removes".

Shoes may be fitted either hot or cold. The advantage of hot shoeing is that it ensures a better fit because the shoe can be finely adjusted to fit the foot (the shoe must always be altered to fit the foot, not vice versa). The shoe is heated in the furnace and held against the prepared hoof (which is insensitive) for a short

time. The imprint it leaves indicates to the farrier any necessary adjustments required. Once these have been made the shoe is plunged in cold water before being nailed on to the foot.

It is important to remember that horses who are unshod, perhaps because they are resting, still need regular attention from the farrier. Being confined in a paddock is not the same as being free to roam in search of food, and the horse's hooves will not wear down as they would in the wild.

The farrier's work is very skilful. He must be able to trim the hoof, and drive nails into the insensitive part of the hoof wall, with great precision. One slip, and the result will be a lame horse. Nor is farriery simply about the routine trimming and re-shoeing of horses. It also involves skilled remedial shoeing, which calls for a detailed knowledge of the anatomy of the horse's limbs, including the bones, the joints, the muscles, the vascular system and the nervous system. Defective action, caused by less than perfect conformation or injury, can be greatly improved by expert trimming of the foot and the fitting

of specially designed shoes. In these cases, the farrier will work in conjunction with the veterinary surgeon.

At one time it was the practice for the horse to be taken to the farrier for shoeing, which meant that the farrier had all the facilities of a permanent forge on hand. Nowadays it is usually the farrier who has to travel to the horse with a mobile forge, so the onus is on the horse owner to provide him with a suitable working area.

A dry, level surface for the horse to stand on is essential, as is good lighting. In summer, when flies are a nuisance, the horse should be in a shady area, either in a building or under a tree, and it is advisable to have some fly repellent handy.

The horse's feet should be cleaned and dried beforehand and it is the owner's responsibility to ensure that the horse is as well behaved as possible. Most horses will stand quietly. But remember that feeding or moving other horses about while a horse is being shod can make him extremely restive – and the farrier's job that much more difficult.

■ LEFT
In order to make horseshoes, the farrier must be skilled in bending, turning and shaping metal. He uses an anvil specially designed for the purpose.

The Farrier's Tools

The farrier's tools are divided into two categories: forge tools, that is those used while making shoes, and shoeing tools, that is those used while preparing the foot and nailing on the shoe.

Forge tools include the anvil, on which the metal is shaped; various hammers and tongs; the stamp, used for making nail holes in the shoes; the fullering iron, used to make a groove round the edge of the ground surface of the shoe and the pritchel, a steel punch used to finish off the nail holes and also for carrying hot shoes to the horse's foot for fitting.

Shoeing tools include hammer, pincers, trimmer and rasp. The farrier's shoeing hammer, which has a short, curved claw, is used to drive in the nails, to twist off the points of the nails and form the clenches, and to pull out nails.

When removing shoes the farrier uses a buffer (or clench cutter) to cut off the clenches or knock them up before withdrawing the nails.

Pincers are used for raising and levering off shoes and for withdrawing nails. They are also used to turn the clenches. For trimming, a hoof trimmer, cutter or parer is used. This is a tool with a pincer-like head, one side being sharp and the other flat. To remove the overgrown wall of the hoof the flat side is placed on the outside of the wall and the sharp cutting side on the inside.

When removing ragged pieces of frog or loose flakes of sole a drawing knife is used. The searcher, a similar tool but with a thinner blade, is designed for use when cutting out corns or paring away the horn round puncture wounds.

The farrier's rasp is partly coarse, partly smooth (file cut) and has serrated edges. The farrier uses the coarse side to remove excess hoof wall and for the final levelling of the bearing surface of the foot. The coarse side is also used to finish off the clenches. The file cut surface is used to finish off the shoe and to shape the clenches. Using the serrated edges the farrier removes the sharp edge of the wall (to prevent it splitting) after the shoe has been nailed on.

STUDS

Although shoes help to give the horse added grip on grass it is often essential to fit studs in the shoes as well. Studs may be permanent or of the screw-in type (in which case the shoes are provided with screw holes by the farrier). Screw-in studs

1 Having cut off or knocked up the clenches (the turned-over points of the nails), the farrier uses pincers to lever off the old shoe.

2 Excess growth of hoof is removed with a trimmer, which has one flat and one sharp side.

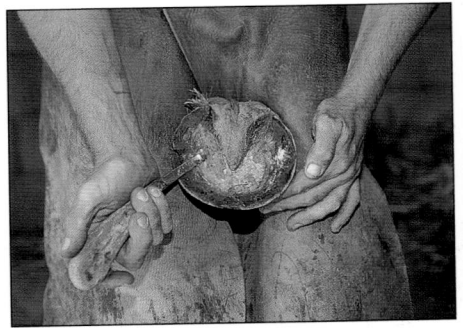

3 A drawing knife is used to lower the hoof wall and remove loose flakes of sole.

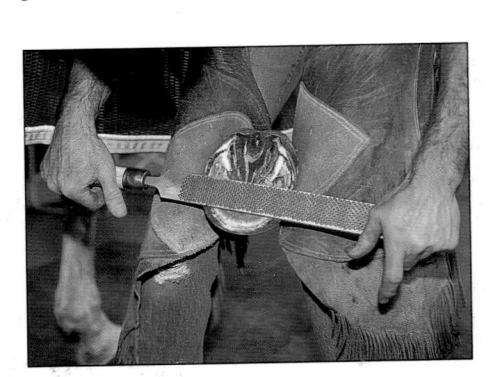

4 The bearing surface of the foot is levelled with a rasp before the shoe is fitted.

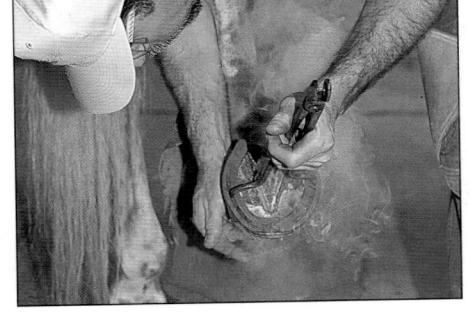

5 Hot shoeing ensures a better fit than cold shoeing and causes the horse no pain.

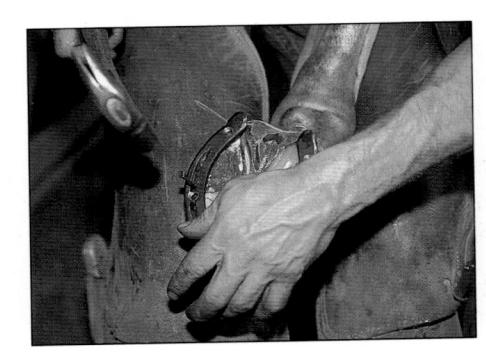

6 Nails are driven into the insensitive wall of the foot to hold the shoes in place.

nail stamp

drawing knife

pincers

clenching tongs

punch

buffer

hoof cutters

rasp

punch

nails

drawing or nailing-on hammer

nail puller

pincers

shoe tongs

turning hammer

▌ ABOVE
The farrier's tools

▌ RIGHT
Screw-in studs are essential for the competition horse. After use they are removed and the holes plugged to protect the threads. A T-tap (centre) is used to clean out the screw holes before inserting the studs.

are best for competition horses because they require different types of studs according to the work they are doing and the state of the ground.

There is a wide range of studs available, varying from small ones for everyday hacking and road work (these are usually made with a tungsten core and are very hard wearing) to large round or square ones suitable for use in soft going and pointed ones which enhance the grip on very firm ground. There are two schools of thought about the fitting of studs: some people fit only one stud on the outside of each shoe. Others believe that this may throw the foot out of balance and so fit one on either side of the shoe.

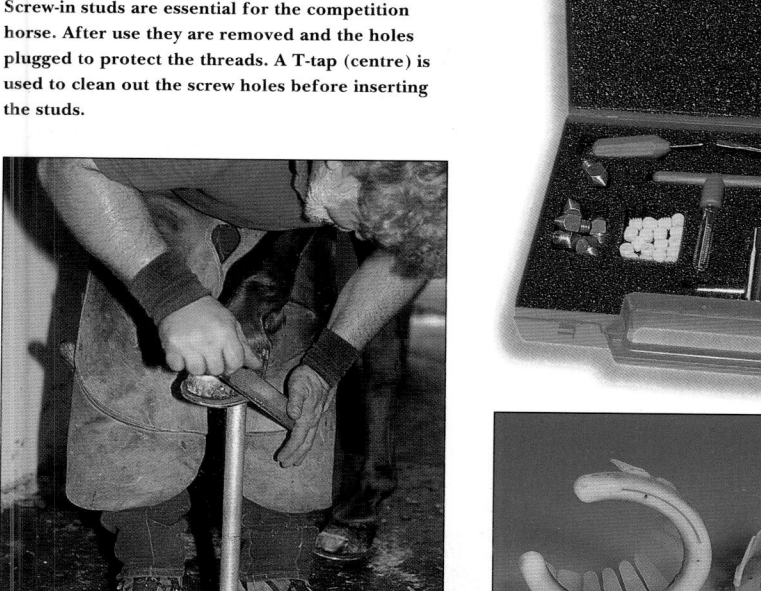

The farrier uses the rasp to smooth the horn and shape the clenches.

Lightweight plastic shoes are a modern alternative to metal ones. They are attached to the hoof with glue.

Studs are screwed into place shortly before the horse competes. The size and shape depends on the ground conditions.

Common Foot Problems

Corns occur most often in the front feet. A corn is a bruise of the sole in the angle between the wall of the foot and the bar (known as the "seat of corn"). Corns are caused by pressure and can be the result of a stone becoming wedged, faulty shoeing or shoes having been left on too long. The shoe should be removed and the discoloured horn pared away. The condition can be complicated by the presence of infection, in which case

poulticing will be necessary. Pressure can be relieved from the area by fitting a shoe on which the ground surface of the heel is lowered so that it does not make contact with the ground.

Laminitis (also known as "founder") is a painful condition resulting from inflammation of the laminae. The feet become hot and the horse adopts a typical leaning back stance in order to take the weight off the front of the forefeet.

Although the pathological cause is not yet completely understood, laminitis is associated with excessive concussion and the presence of inflammatory toxins which damage the blood vessels, particularly those in the feet. It is often the result of faulty diet (over-fat ponies, with overlong feet, kept on too rich pasture are the classic example) although it can also be caused by retention of the afterbirth in the broodmare.

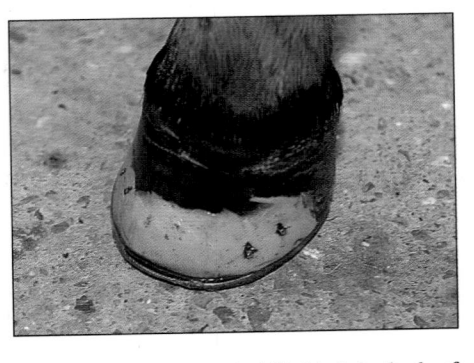

An example of the farrier's skill: this defective hoof has been artificially lengthened.

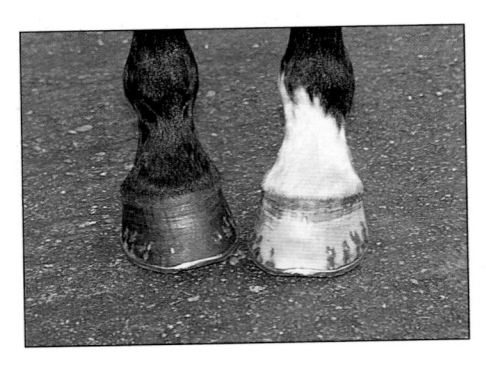

Pigeon toes (those which turn inwards) cause uneven wear on the shoes.

A sandcrack may produce lameness if the sensitive part of the foot is affected.

This leaning back stance is typical of a horse suffering from laminitis. He takes the weight on his heels to relieve the pain. Laminitis is one of the major causes of equine lameness, particularly in ponies.

Veterinary treatment is essential. If diet is the cause, the vet may advise a purgative. The horse should be stabled (standing the horse on sand is said to reduce the pain because it provides support to the feet). The vet may prescribe drugs (including pain killers) and if the horse or pony is overweight, he will advise on a suitable diet.

One of the dangers of laminitis is the possibility of pedal bone rotation. Except in the mildest cases, therefore, when the horse may be gently led out in hand, the horse must be given box rest.

Good foot care is vital. Corrective trimming will help restore the structures of the foot to their normal alignment and will limit the rotation of the pedal bone. Special shoes can also be fitted.

Navicular disease is believed to be the result of poor foot conformation and/or concussion, caused by hard work. Bony changes occur in the navicular bone, a small, shuttle-shaped bone which acts as a fulcrum for the deep flexor tendon before the tendon attaches to the under side of the pedal bone. In most cases both forefeet are affected.

A horse with navicular disease will put his foot on the ground toe-first as he attempts to avoid pressure on the affected area. In the early stages, lameness wears off during exercise but as the condition progresses the periods of lameness both increase and become more prolonged. As

pastern (high ringbone) or around the coronet (low ringbone). It is usually caused by injury. There is heat and swelling and the horse may have a shortened stride and tend to be more lame when turned sharply. Rest may help give relief in less serious cases. Where more serious injury is involved the horse may not become fully sound again, although some horses continue to work if given anti-inflammatory drugs.

of bruising of the toe area or pressure from the toe clip of a shoe. Sometimes it follows laminitis. Treatment involves cleaning out the cavity and filling it with tow. The farrier will be able to trim the foot and shoe it in such a way that further damage is avoided during movement.

A **sidebone** results when the lateral cartilages of the foot become ossified or converted into bone. The ossified

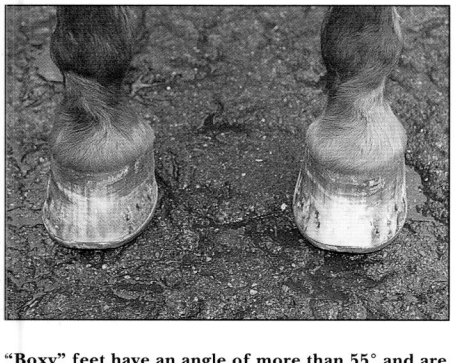

"Boxy" feet have an angle of more than 55° and are associated with upright pasterns.

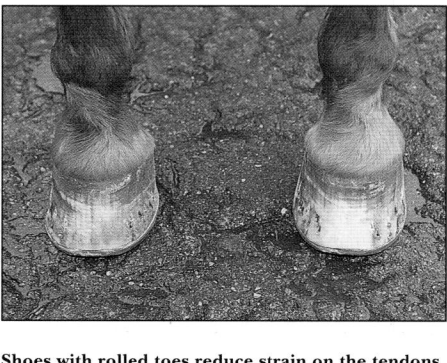

Shoes with rolled toes reduce strain on the tendons and the navicular bone.

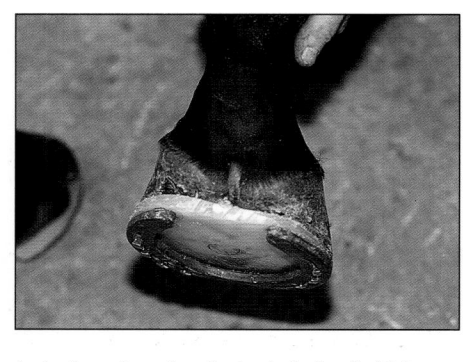

A plastic wedge raises the heel of a hoof which slopes too much.

time goes on, the horse may become prone to stumbling.

Although the condition is incurable, various treatments are employed to help relieve the pain. Corrective shoeing is used to raise the heels and reduce concussion to the navicular area. The horse may be given anticoagulants or anti-inflammatory drugs. Laser and ultrasound treatment may also be beneficial.

Pedal osteitis is inflammation of the pedal bone. It is often the result of jarring but can also develop after an attack of laminitis or following puncture injuries to the sole of the foot. It usually affects both forefeet and the horse will tend to shuffle when he moves. The demineralization of the bone is visible on X-ray. Careful shoeing can bring relief to what is usually an irreversible condition. Laser and ultrasound therapy may be beneficial.

Ringbone is an abnormal bony growth which occurs either at the centre of the

A **sandcrack** is a break in the wall of the hoof and may occur anywhere between the coronet and the ground surface of the foot. Sandcracks may be the result of injury, poor nutrition, an overdrying of the hoof (for instance in very dry weather), too much rasping during the shoeing process or neglect, for example lack of regular trimming by the farrier. Lameness may result if the crack is serious.

The farrier may be able to arrest the progress of a sandcrack by making grooves in the hoof wall to isolate the crack. Metal clips may also be used or, in the case of a deep crack, it may be necessary to fill it with a special bonding substance. Because the crack opens when weight is put on the foot as it is placed on the ground, a shoe with clips may be fitted.

Seedy toe is a condition in which the wall of the foot parts company with the sole at the white line. It may be the result

cartilages can be felt at the junction of the hair and the hoof in the area of the quarter of the foot. Sidebones are usually caused by concussion. Heavy or common-bred horses are the most susceptible. The horse may be lame while the cartilage is ossifying and sometimes lameness persists once the sidebones have developed because of pressure on the wall of the foot. The condition does not normally require treatment other than short-term rest but if lameness persists the farrier may be able to relieve the pressure with corrective shoeing and grooving of the hoof to allow expansion.

Thrush is caused by bad stable management (dirty bedding and failure to pick out the feet regularly). It is easily detected by the evil smell coming from the frog, which is moist and may have a black discharge. The affected area of the frog must be opened out to expose it to the air and treated with antiseptics.

Equipment

When man first began to ride horses, his only piece of equipment was a rudimentary bridle. It was a very long time before the invention of the saddle and longer still to the arrival of the stirrup. By contrast, the array of equipment available to the modern horse owner is quite staggering: such a diverse range of bits that whole books have been devoted to their usage; saddles of every conceivable shape and size; boots and bandages to protect most parts of the horse's anatomy; rugs to keep him warm and dry, and a plethora of "gadgets" designed to control him – the majority of which would not be necessary if man made a better job of schooling the horse in the first place! For everyday riding purposes, certain items of basic equipment will suffice: a bridle, saddle, a few essential items of horse clothing. The important thing is that they should fit correctly and be well cared for, in which case they will last for many years. For the rider, the popularity of horse sports has led to the development of special clothes for each and every occasion. Everyday riding clothes should be neat, comfortable and, above all, safe. Riding is a risk sport and no short cuts should be taken in this respect.

Bridles and Saddles

The minimum basic equipment, or tack, required for the ridden horse is a saddle and bridle. He will also need a headcollar or halter and lead rope.

The simplest means of controlling a horse is by means of a snaffle bridle. There are many varieties of **snaffle bit**. The mildest is the unjointed type which acts principally on the bars of the mouth, that is the portion of the lower gums where there are no teeth. A jointed snaffle is more severe because it exerts pressure

■ **LEFT**
The double bridle employs two bits, a curb and a bridoon (snaffle). It should only be used by the experienced horseman.

■ **PREVIOUS PAGE OPPOSITE**
The hackamore or bitless bridle works by leverage. It, too, should only be used by the experienced rider.

■ **PREVIOUS PAGE**
A horse wearing a driving bridle. The blinkers prevent the horse being distracted by things alongside or behind him.

■ **BELOW, LEFT TO RIGHT**
A bitless bridle or hackamore; a leather headcollar; a snaffle bridle with flash noseband; a snaffle bridle with cavesson noseband and running martingale.

■ **BOTTOM LEFT**
Numnahs are comfortable for the horse's back. They must be kept clean – the washable type are best.

on the corners of the mouth as well. A snaffle may be loose-ring or eggbutt (the latter prevents the lips being pinched). The choice, as with all bits, depends very much on the horse and it may be necessary to try a number of different bits until you find the one which suits the horse best. Snaffles may be made of stainless steel, which is easy to clean and very hard-wearing, rubber, plastic or nylon. A horse with a very sensitive mouth will often go better in a non-metal bit.

The **bridle** consists of a headpiece and adjustable cheekpieces, to which the bit is attached, a throatlatch to prevent the headpiece slipping forward over the ears and a browband to prevent it slipping down the neck. There may also be a noseband. Most bridles are made of leather. Narrow leather looks best on a quality horse such as a Thoroughbred,

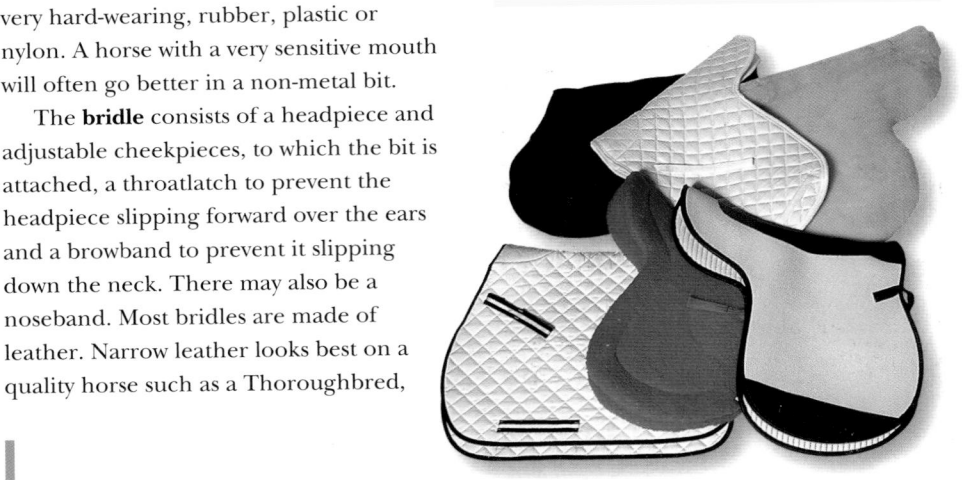

wide leather suits a heavyweight horse.

Various designs of **noseband** may be used. The widely used cavesson is fitted largely for appearance's sake – many people feel that a horse looks "undressed" without one. Other nosebands are designed to give added control over the horse, mainly by preventing him from evading the action of the bit by opening his mouth and crossing his jaws.

A **martingale** (a strap passing from the girth, between the horse's front legs, and attached to some part of the bridle) is used primarily to prevent a horse from raising his head above a certain level. A **bitless bridle** or **hackamore** may be used on a horse which is difficult to bit adequately, or one who has some problem with his mouth or teeth. The bridle works by pressure and leverage on the horse's nose and chin groove. The longer the

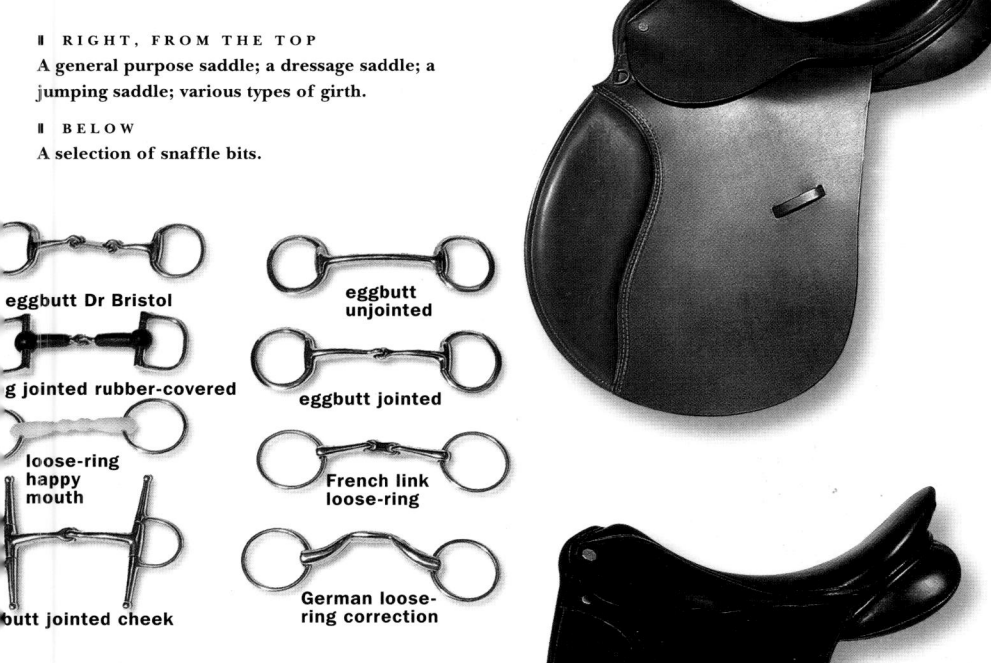

eggbutt Dr Bristol

g jointed rubber-covered

loose-ring
happy
mouth

butt jointed cheek

eggbutt
unjointed

eggbutt jointed

French link
loose-ring

German loose-
ring correction

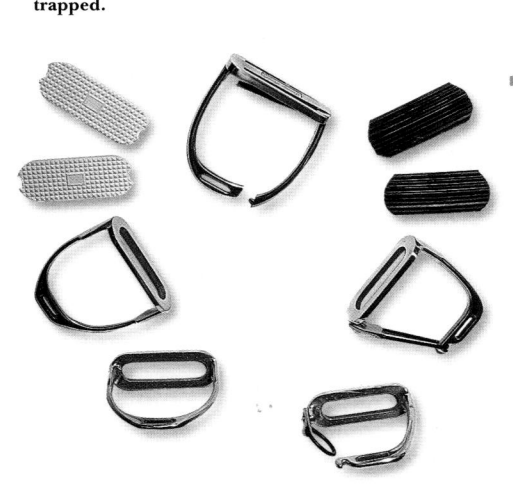

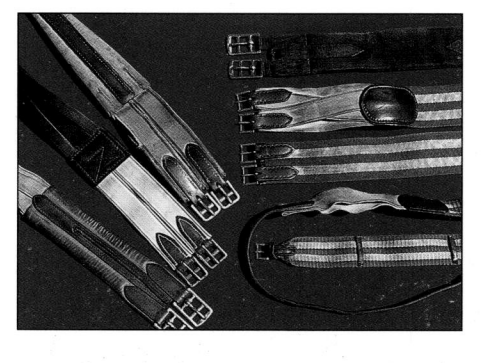

cheeks of the bridle the more severe its action. A bitless bridle should only be used by an experienced rider – the braking power provided can be tremendous, but it is much less easy to make turns than with a conventional bridle.

Saddles, like bridles, have traditionally been made of leather, though nowadays cheaper, synthetic ones are also available. All saddles are built on a tree, or frame, made of laminated wood, with inset springs for added resilience, or of plastic.

For everyday use an all-purpose saddle is suitable, being designed as its name suggests for general riding. For riders specializing in dressage or show jumping there are saddles designed for the job. The dressage saddle has a deeper seat and straighter flaps than the all-purpose saddle, allowing the rider to use a longer length of stirrup and to have more of the leg in contact with the horse's side. The jumping saddle is made on a longer tree and has forward-cut flaps to enable the rider to ride with short stirrups and to adopt the necessary forward position.

Stirrup irons should be made of stainless steel for strength and must be large enough to allow a gap of about ½ inch (1.5cm) on each side of the rider's boot. Good quality **stirrup leathers** are essential for safety.

It is vital that the saddle fits both the horse and the rider. It must not impede the action of the shoulders and there must be no pinching of the withers or pressure on the spine. The rider's weight should be evenly distributed on the large muscles on either side of the spine. An incorrectly fitted saddle will result in a sore back. The rider's shape and length of leg must also be taken into consideration as it is impossible to ride well on an uncomfortable saddle.

The saddle is held in place by a **girth** or girths, the design of which will depend on the horse's conformation, the type of saddle and the type of work being done. Girths were traditionally made of leather, but today they are also available in synthetic materials.

A **numnah,** or saddle pad, fitted under the saddle, affords greater comfort to the horse than the leather lining of the saddle. The numnah should be made of natural fibre which will absorb sweat. The centre must be tucked up well into the channel of the saddle to prevent pressure on the spine. Numnahs must be washed regularly – dirt can cause a sore back.

To guard against the saddle slipping back the horse may be fitted with a **breastplate.** The leather hunting breastplate has straps which are attached to the D rings of the saddle. The racing breastplate, also known as the Aintree type, is a broad band of web or elastic which passes round the horse's breast and fastens to the girth straps.

Rugs

Regular grooming deprives the stabled horse of the natural protection of grease and dirt which, in the wild, accumulate in his coat and help to keep him warm. In winter clipping removes even the natural protection of a woolly coat. It is most important, therefore, that the stabled horse is provided with rugs and blankets, the amount depending on the individual horse and the prevailing weather conditions.

The traditional type of stable rug or night rug is made of hard-wearing jute, lined with wool. It fastens round the horse's chest and should be kept in place with a roller rather than a surcingle, which can cause pressure on the spine. A roller is a broad strap, padded where it lies on the horse's back (with a clear channel for the spine) and fastened with two strong buckles. Leather rollers are very hard wearing though they are heavier than the webbing variety. If necessary a breast strap can be fitted to prevent the roller sliding back. Wither pads fit under rollers and are designed to give added protection from pressure. All rollers should be regularly

checked, particularly the stitching, as they take a great deal of strain when the horse gets up or down and when he rolls.

Stable rugs also come in a range of modern materials, which are lighter to handle than jute and may be fitted with self-righting straps (that is they will return to the correct position on the horse even if he rolls), which eliminate the need for a roller.

For added warmth a blanket or blankets may be fitted under the stable rug. The traditional type is the Witney blanket, made of wool and coloured gold with red and black stripes. To prevent the

blanket slipping back it is positioned high up the horse's neck. The corners are then turned up to the withers. The rug is placed on top, the front of the rug fastened and then the folded part of the blanket is turned back over the top of the rug and the roller fitted on top of both the blanket and the rug. A cotton sheet may be placed under the blanket to keep it clean (blankets do not usually wash well). Where no roller is used it is difficult to keep a blanket in place and better to use a specially designed quilted liner under the rug for extra warmth.

Day rugs are usually made of wool

▌ LEFT
A lightweight stable rug with fitted surcingles which eliminate the need for a roller.

▌ RIGHT
New Zealand rugs are ideal for horses when turned out in cold or wet weather. A carefully designed system of leg straps ensures that the rugs stay in place even if the horse rolls.

RUG CARE

- Check all fastenings regularly and have worn stitching repaired – leather straps with buckles are the strongest type of fastening and the easiest to use.

- Keep all leather fastenings soft and pliable and all buckles and clips oiled.

- Give all rugs, blankets and sheets a daily shake and, if possible, an airing.

- Give all washable rugs and sheets a regular wash in a safe washing powder (some horses are sensitive to biological powders) and dry well before re-using or placing in storage.

- Give jute rugs a regular brushing – scrub thoroughly as necessary.

- Give woollen rugs and blankets a thorough, regular brushing – have them dry cleaned as necessary.

- Check the stitching and buckles on rollers regularly.

- Clean the outside of New Zealand rugs with a hose and brush – detergents may damage the waterproofing – and scrub the linings.

- Have New Zealand rugs reproofed as necessary.

- Protect stored rugs from moths.

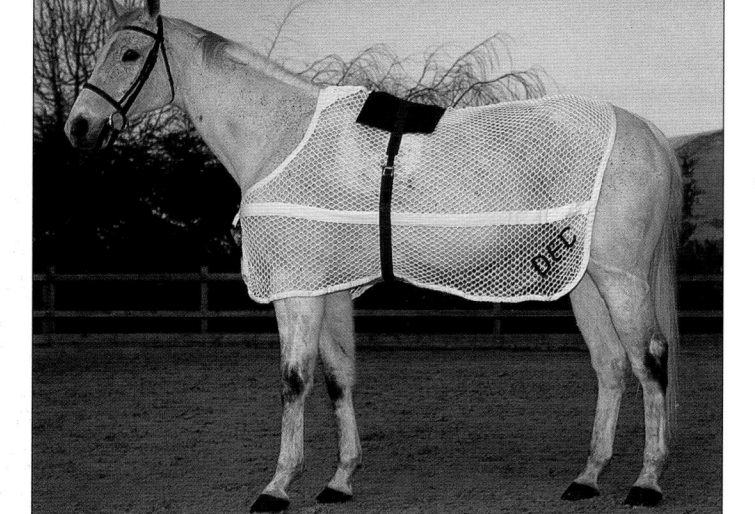

▌ RIGHT
A string rug is useful to help dry off a wet horse. Note the surcingle fitted over a back pad to prevent pressure on the spine.

(different weights are available for use in winter and summer) and are most often kept for use on special occasions such as at shows and other public appearances.

Cotton sheets are suitable for use in summer when they will give protection from flies and also help to keep the horse clean. Cotton mesh or string rugs are used to help dry off a sweaty or wet horse. In cold weather a sheet may be placed over the top to prevent chilling. All sheets should be kept in place with a surcingle, preferably fitted over a back pad. Light cotton coolers, which cover the horse from just behind the ears to the top of the tail, are useful in hot climates to protect the horse from both sun and flies.

When travelling, the horse should always wear rugs made of a breathable material to ensure that moisture can escape should he become sweaty.

Horses who are turned out for part of the day and some who live out permanently will need a New Zealand rug. New Zealand rugs are warm, waterproof and windproof. They may be made of heavy canvas (which can cause pressure sores) or lighter weight modern weatherproof materials. To give adequate protection the rug must be well shaped and come well down the legs and over the quarters. Some rugs have tail flaps and neck covers for added protection in really bad weather. Correct fit is essential to enable the horse to move about freely. New Zealand rugs are fitted with a system of leg straps and many are self-righting. All straps must be kept clean, soft and supple to prevent chafing of sensitive areas such as the insides of the legs.

For exercise purposes the horse may need a paddock sheet to keep his loins warm. A paddock sheet (so named because they are traditionally used on racehorses) does not have a front fastening but is fitted under the saddle, usually with the corners turned back. A fillet string passing under the tail helps prevent the rug blowing about on a windy day. Paddock sheets are usually made of wool or cotton but they are also available in waterproof materials. A fluorescent sheet is an excellent safety device for use when riding on the roads.

Waterproof rugs and sheets are particularly useful at shows and competitions for keeping tack and other rugs dry. Since most waterproof materials do not "breath" care must be taken that the horse does not sweat up when wearing this type of rug. Remember, too, that noisy materials can startle horses.

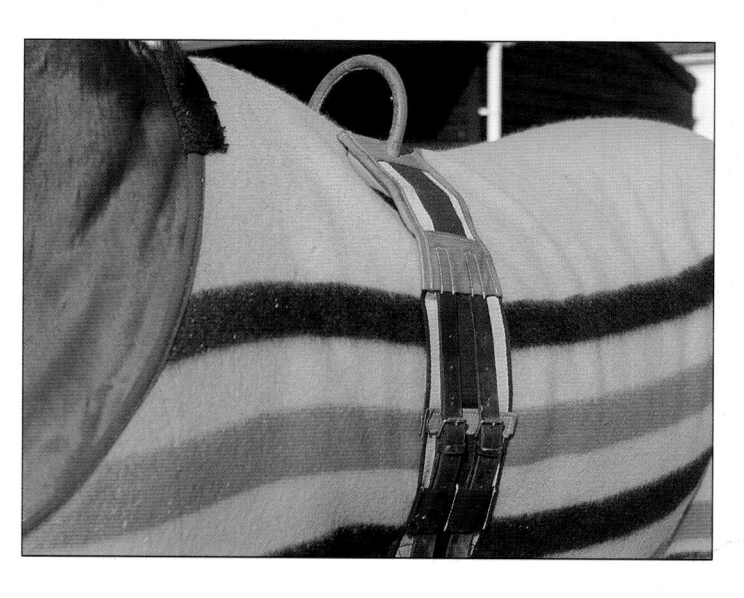

▌ RIGHT
The leather covered metal hoop on this anti-cast roller helps to prevent the horse from rolling over in his box and becoming cast (stuck). The roller should be fitted over a back pad.

Bandages

Leg bandages may be used to give protection, support or warmth, as required. Exercise bandages are made of crepe or stockinette and may be used instead of boots to give protection and support to the tendons. They are about 3–4 inches (8–10cm) wide and should be put on over a layer of Gamgee or other suitable padding.

Bandaging the legs is a skilled task and should not be attempted by the novice horse owner except under expert guidance. Exercise bandages must be applied tightly enough to prevent them slipping and becoming unfastened – which can be dangerous when a horse is working – but not so tight that they cause undue pressure on the tendons or restrict the circulation. They must be applied with even pressure and are best secured with needle and thread. Tape may be used but

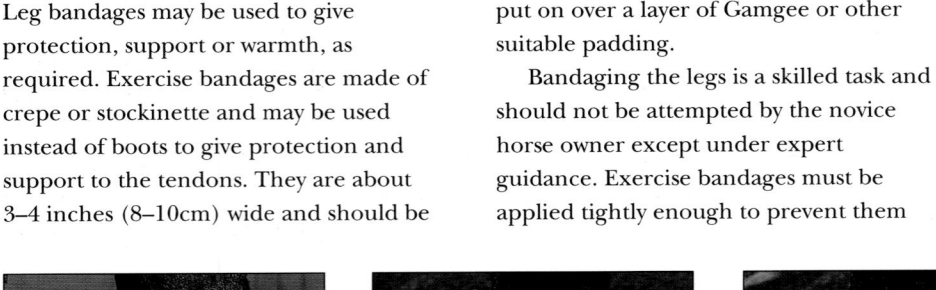

1 Before applying exercise bandages, first wrap the leg in a layer of Gamgee tissue or other suitable padding.

2 Start bandaging at the top, leaving a flap loose as shown. Exercise bandages are made of stretch material.

3 Turn down the flap and bandage over it, overlapping two-thirds of the width of the bandage at each turn.

4 Always apply nearside leg bandages in an anti-clockwise direction and offside ones in a clockwise direction.

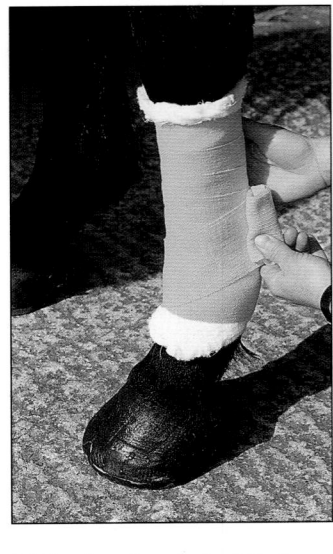
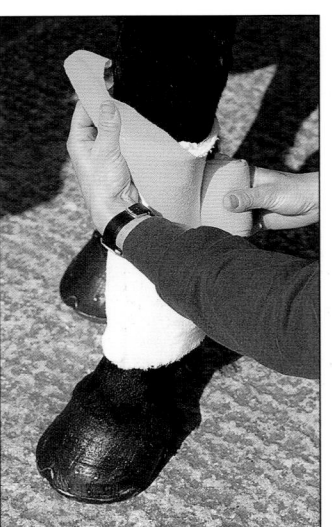
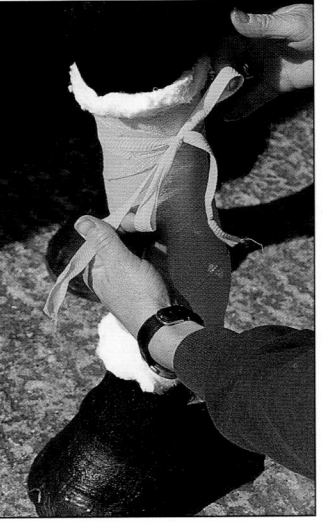
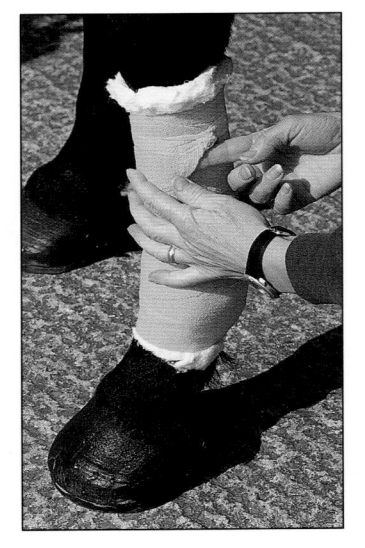

5 Bandage down to the fetlock joint and up again, keeping an even pressure at each turn.

6 Fasten the tapes on the outside of the leg – never at the back or the front.

7 Tie (or sew) the tapes securely, making sure that they are no tighter than the bandage.

8 For neatness and safety, tuck away any loose ends of tape. Exercise bandages should be firm but not overtight.

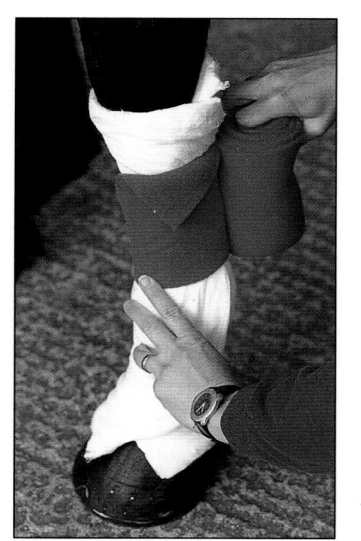

1 Stable bandages are wider than exercise bandages and are fitted over longer pieces of Gamgee for warmth.

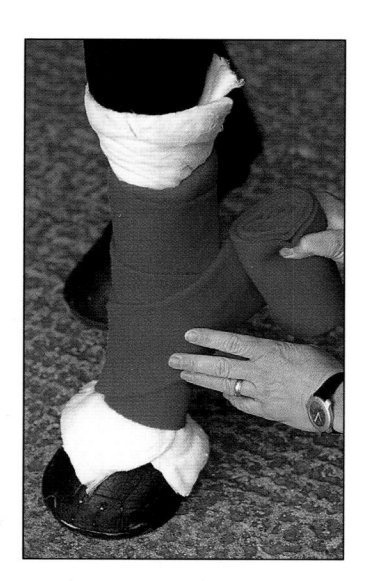

2 The bandage is put on less firmly than an exercise bandage. There must be no wrinkles.

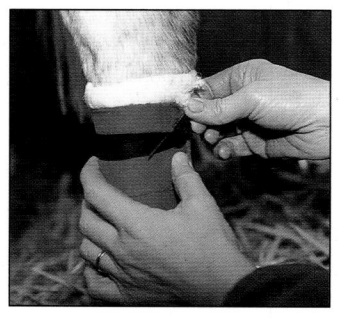

3 Bandage right down to the coronet, overlapping half the width at each turn.

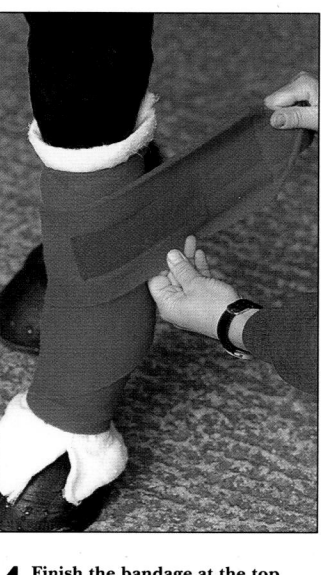

4 Finish the bandage at the top, just below the knee or hock.

5 Velcro is a quick and convenient method of fastening stable bandages.

■ **RIGHT**
Sewing the tapes of a bandage in place is the most secure way of finishing off.

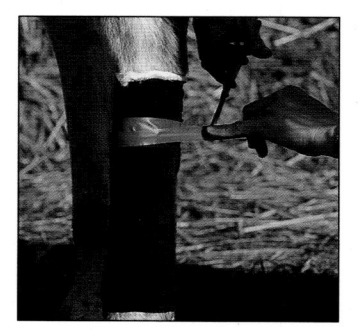

■ **RIGHT**
As an alternative to tieing or sewing the tapes, strong adhesive tape may be used to hold the bandages in place.

When a horse has a leg injury it is usual to bandage the opposite leg with a support bandage (that is an exercise-type bandage) since the horse will be putting more weight and so more strain on this leg while the injury repairs.

SAFETY CHECKLIST

☛ Ensure that the legs are free of dirt and sweat before applying bandages to protect them from being rubbed sore.

☛ Keep bandages clean – avoid washing them in biological powders as some horses are sensitive to them.

☛ Apply bandages over a layer of Gamgee or other padding.

☛ Apply bandages with even pressure.

☛ Apply bandages in an anti-clockwise direction on the nearside legs and clockwise on the offside.

☛ Sew or tape exercise bandages in place with the same pressure as the bandage.

☛ Do not fit exercise bandages too low – they will interfere with the horse's movement and will tend to slip down.

☛ Always tie tapes, when used, on the outside of the legs, never on the inside or at the back or front.

☛ Never apply a bandage to one leg without also bandaging its opposite number.

☛ Remove and replace stable bandages at regular intervals.

care must be taken that it is not applied tighter than the bandage itself, otherwise it will cause pressure on the tendons.

Exercise bandages should be fitted low enough to afford protection to the sesamoid bones at the rear of the fetlock but not so low that they restrict the movement of the fetlock joint.

For competition purposes self-adhesive bandages are often used nowadays. These tend to exert more pressure than the non-adhesive variety so great care is required when fitting them.

Stable bandages are designed to keep a horse's legs warm, particularly if he has

had a full clip. The bandages are usually about 4½ inches (11cm) wide and are traditionally made of wool although nowadays they are also available in several other materials, including the thermal variety. They should be fitted over a layer of Gamgee or similar padding and must not be applied too tightly, otherwise they will restrict the circulation. The tape fastenings should always be tied on the outside, never on the back of the tendon and care must be taken not to make them too tight. To ensure the horse's comfort, stable bandages should be removed and reapplied at least twice daily.

Boots

Boots of various types may be fitted to protect the horse's legs from injury during exercise and competition. Some horses are apt to knock one leg with another during work because of a conformational irregularity. Young horses are especially vulnerable to injury because they are less well balanced when being ridden than older, more experienced ones; also tired horses, for example those nearing the end of a cross-country course, may become less well co-ordinated. Ground conditions will also affect the horse's legs, hard going making it more likely that the horse will jar himself and deep, muddy going making overreaches more likely.

Boots may be made of leather, with strap fastenings, or from synthetic materials such as PVC and Neoprene, which are easier to clean. These usually have quick-adjusting Velcro or clip fastenings.

Knee boots, consisting of a padded leather kneecap, should be fitted when exercising on the road where it is all too easy for a horse to slip up. The top, elasticated strap should be fastened just tight enough to keep the boot in place, the lower one should be loose so as not to impede the horse's action.

Brushing boots may be fitted on the forelegs and/or hindlegs to prevent injury caused by one leg knocking against the other. This is known as "brushing". Brushing usually occurs on or in the region of the fetlock joint. If the horse knocks his own legs higher up, for example just under the hock, it is known as "speedy cutting".

Overreach boots are fitted to prevent injury to the heels of the forelegs from the toes of the hindlegs. They are bell-shaped and usually made of strong rubber or Neoprene. Those made with "petals" (overlapping sections) give the best protection as they do not invert during use. Boots which are fitted with a strap are much easier to put on and take off than

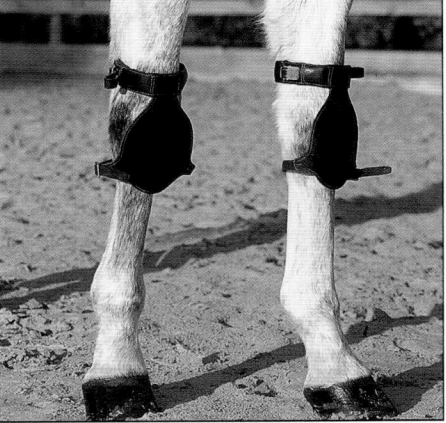

Open-fronted leather tendon boots protect the tendons from being struck by the toes of the hindfeet – a potentially dangerous injury.

Many modern boots are fitted with quick-release clips or Velcro which are easier to put on and take off than traditional buckles and straps.

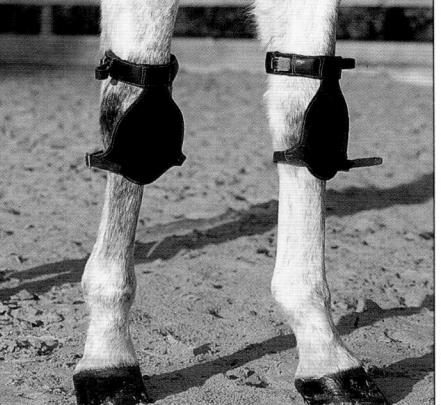

Kneeboots are a wise precaution when exercising on the road. The type of boot illustrated is known as a skeleton kneeboot.

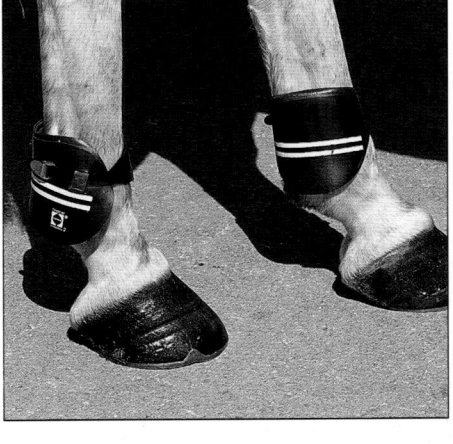

Fetlock boots protect the joints from injury caused by brushing – that is the horse hitting one leg with its opposite number. They come in varying depths.

the old type of pull-on boots.

Tendon boots give a limited amount of support to the tendons and protect them from injury. They are used as an alternative to bandages for fast work and jumping. They come in a variety of designs and materials for both fore and hindlegs.

▌ LEFT
Petal-type overreach boots are easy to fit and do not invert in use. Damaged "petals" can be replaced. They protect the heels of the forelegs.

Travelling Equipment

■ BELOW LEFT AND BOTTOM
Specially designed travelling boots may be used or the horse may wear bandages with knee and hock boots. Note the poll guard to protect his head.

The horse should always wear protective clothing when travelling. His most vulnerable parts are his legs, particularly the coronets – which he might easily strike into with his other feet if he is suddenly thrown off balance – and his poll. To guard against injury if he throws his head up he should wear a poll guard – a piece of padded leather which is fitted to his headcollar.

Specially designed travelling boots give protection to the horse's entire lower legs, including the knees, hocks and coronets. They usually fasten with Velcro and are quick and easy to put on and take off. Alternatively the legs can be protected with travelling bandages applied over suitable padding, such as Gamgee. The Gamgee should cover the coronets and the bandages be applied evenly and not too

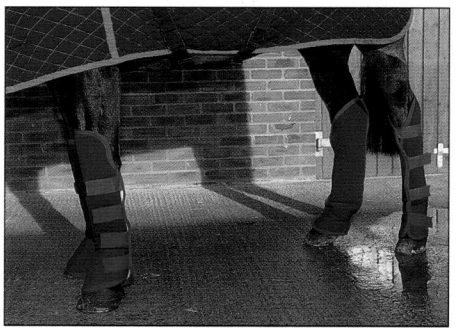

tightly. Overreach boots may be fitted and kneeboots should also be used.

Hock boots will protect a horse who is inclined to kick during travelling. The horse may object to hock boots the first time he wears them so they should be fitted a few times in the stable first until he becomes accustomed to them.

To prevent his tail becoming rubbed he should wear a tail bandage and tail guard. The latter fastens round the tail (over the bandage) and is attached to the roller of the rug. Depending on the weather, the horse should wear a sheet or rug. He should be kept warm but not be allowed to become sweaty. Frequent checks should be made during travelling to ensure that he is neither too hot nor too cold.

The horse should be travelled in a leather headcollar with a lead rope, preferably one that is attached with a quick-release mechanism in case of emergencies. You will have more control over the horse if you slip a snaffle bridle (without a noseband) over the headcollar during loading and unloading and lead him on the reins and the headcollar rope rather than just on the rope.

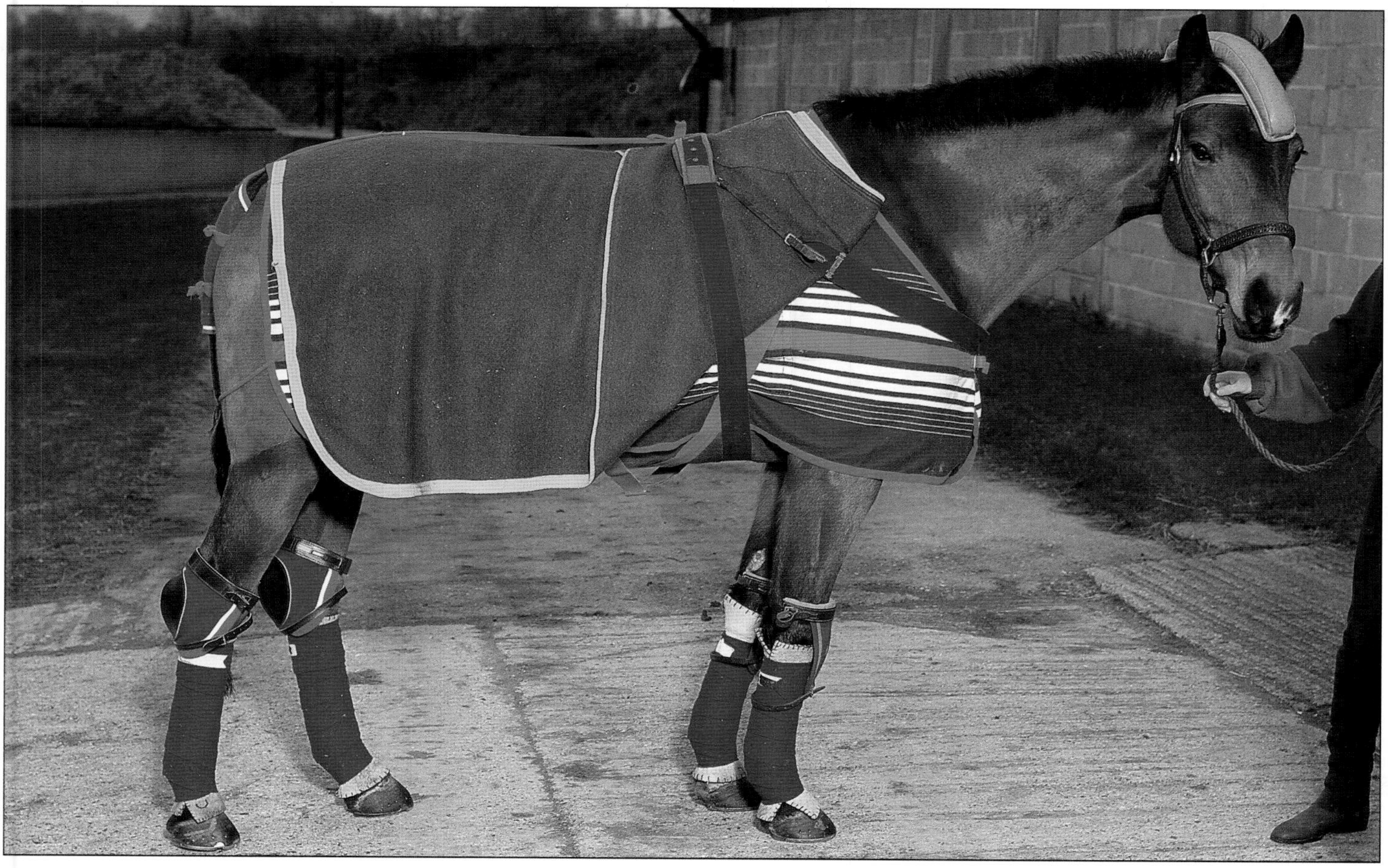

Clothes

When working with horses, whether you are on the ground or riding, safety is the keynote. Horses are big, strong animals and there is always an element of danger, however calm and placid they might normally be. Therefore care should be taken even when choosing clothes for mundane, everyday chores such as mucking out.

Neat clothing which is well fitting without being too tight is the easiest to move around in. A long-sleeved shirt with a sweatshirt or sweater, depending on the weather, and a pair of comfortable trousers, jeans or jodhpurs are ideal for stable work. Avoid overtight trousers as they make bending down difficult. Dark colours will stay looking smart longer. Long sleeves are preferable to short ones since they give some protection from nips from equine teeth. Sleeveless suntops and vests should definitely be avoided.

Footwear is of great importance since a misplaced hoof can do a great deal of damage to a human foot. "Trainers" give little protection, nor do most rubber boots, though sturdy Wellingtons are as good as anything for mucking out, particularly if you wear thick walking-boot socks inside. At other times a pair of leather jodhpur boots will probably afford the best protection and will certainly enable you to move more quickly than when wearing Wellingtons. Some boots are now fitted with protective toecaps.

Coats and body warmers, when worn, should be kept fastened – a flapping coat can frighten a nervous horse and there is also the danger that it might become caught up on some "foreign body". Some horses are nervous of noisy waterproof fabrics, so avoid wearing them around the stables.

Long hair should be tied up, again to avoid the possibility of scaring a horse or becoming caught up. This is particularly important in windy weather. Avoid wearing jewellery: rings, earrings,

noserings and the like can all cause nasty injuries if they become caught up.

Most well-trained horses are safe to lead about, in and out of their stables, down to the paddock, etc. But if you have any doubts whatsoever about a horse's good behaviour (when handling a young horse, for example) take precautions: wear a hard hat, correctly fastened, in case he rears up and strikes out, boots to protect your feet and a pair of gloves.

▎ **ABOVE**
A sweatshirt, breeches, boots and a hard hat make a suitable outfit for everyday exercise.

▎ **LEFT**
Neat, workmanlike clothes enable you to carry out daily chores in comfort and safety.

Safety Gear

Riding has always been and always will be a risk sport. But modern safety equipment is constantly improving and everyone who rides should ensure that they wear the best available protective gear, which includes hat, body protector and boots.

The most vulnerable part of the rider is the head and it is irresponsible to get on to a horse, or to lunge or long rein or otherwise handle an unpredictable young

■ LEFT
Fluorescent clothing is a wise safety precaution when riding on the roads. The message on the tabard helps to alert drivers.

SAFETY CHECKLIST

☞ Wear a correctly fitting hard hat with the chin strap fastened at all times when mounted.

☞ Replace a hat that has been subjected to impact in a fall – it may not give sufficient protection next time.

☞ Always ride in your own hat – a borrowed hat is unlikely to fit you correctly.

☞ Wear safe footwear at all times when mounted.

☞ Always use the correct stirrup iron size – about 1 inch (2.5cm) wider than your boot – to prevent your foot becoming stuck.

☞ Wear fluorescent garments – hat cover, tabard/body warmer etc – fitted with retro-reflective strips when riding on the roads and fit your horse with similar high visibility leg bands.

☞ Avoid riding on the roads in poor visibility and after dark.

☞ Never ride in jewellery.

☞ Always fasten tiepins horizontally or at an angle, never vertically.

☞ Always ride with your coat fastened.

☞ Never take off a coat or sweater while mounted – while you are taking your arms out of the sleeves you will have no control over the horse should he make an unexpected move.

☞ If you have less than perfect eyesight, wear soft contact lenses if possible. If not, seek your optician's advice on the safest type of spectacles.

---

horse, without wearing a **hard hat** securely fastened with a **chin strap**. Your country's national federation (for example in Britain the British Horse Society, in the United States the American Horse Shows Association) will advise on the most up-to-date safety standards. The **jockey skull**, or **crash hat**, is generally considered to give maximum protection and is therefore recommended (and obligatory under the rules of most sports) for all riding which involves fast work or jumping. The **chin harness** must be correctly adjusted and fastened at all times. It may be worn on the point of the chin, with a chin cup, or under the chin, whichever is most comfortable. The alternative is the traditional **hunting cap** which must have a soft peak (a hard peak can cause facial, head or neck injuries in a fall). All riding

hats should be correctly fitted (many retailers are trained in hat fitting).

Body protectors are designed to protect the torso and the shoulders in the event of a fall. They should fit well, feel comfortable and not restrict the rider's movement.

Riding boots and **jodhpur boots** are designed to prevent the foot from sliding right through the stirrup iron or otherwise becoming caught up in the iron in the event of a fall – a potentially fatal situation. They have smooth soles and a clearly defined heel. Leather boots afford the best protection from knocks, for example when riding across country, but rubber ones fashioned in the same style are suitable for everyday riding. Wellington boots, trainers and other boots or shoes with ridged soles and little or no heel should never be worn for riding.

■ LEFT
A body protector should be worn when jumping fixed fences and by people needing special protection (for example, an older person with more brittle bones).

■ LEFT
A jockey skull or "crash hat", with a correctly adjusted chin harness, gives the head maximum protection. It is fitted with a silk cover.

Riding Clothes

By and large all riding clothes are designed for comfort and protection. Only with the odd item of equipment (such as the top hat for dressage) is clothing dictated by fashion.

Most riding clothes are based on hunting attire, which evolved over a long period and led to the design of an entire outfit which would give protection from wet, cold and the many knocks experienced when travelling at speed across country. Long leather boots keep the feet and lower legs dry and give maximum protection from painful encounters with gateposts or other fixed objects. Breeches keep the upper legs warm and dry and protect the insides of the knees from chafing against the saddle. A well-fitting jacket made of a good stout tweed or twill gives warmth and a certain amount of waterproofing while at the same time affording complete freedom of movement – essential for all riding, but particularly for jumping and riding at speed. Gloves keep the hands warm and dry and give a secure grip on the reins. A hunting tie or stock helps protect the neck in the event of a fall. A hard hat, correctly secured with a chin harness, protects the most vulnerable part of all, the head.

For everyday riding there is a wealth of suitable clothing to choose from which is both cheaper than more formal attire and suited to frequent immersion in the washing machine. **Jodhpurs**, which extend down the leg to the ankle, and are usually worn with short, elastic-sided leather jodhpur boots, are cooler in summer than breeches and long boots. They come in a range of materials, from lightweight cotton suitable for hot climates to thermal material for wear in extremes of cold. Instead of jodhpur boots, jodhpurs may be worn with **half-chaps**, which cover the leg from below the knee to the foot, or with full **chaps**, which extend up to the thigh.

Close-fitting **riding trousers** are also suitable for everyday wear. Like jodhpurs,

▌ **LEFT**
Everyday riding clothes should be neat and safe. Dark colours are more practical than the light shades worn with traditional hunting dress.

▌ **BELOW LEFT**
Chaps are a good alternative to boots. This rider is prepared for roadwork – note the fluorescent tabard and the horse's protective boots.

they come with "strappings" – reinforcements at the knee and thigh. Some garments are also fitted with an inset seat panel made in an extra-grip material.

Rubber **riding boots** are a cheaper alternative to leather ones, though they can be cold in winter, when an inner sole

or an extra pair of socks may be required.

Casual **riding coats** such as waxed or quilted jackets, blousons and body warmers are fine for everyday riding and may be worn with a shirt and/or sweatshirt or sweater. Modern waterproof materials are light and comfortable to wear and the more expensive ones have the advantage of being "breathable". Waterproofs come in a range of lengths and may have added features such as storm collar and cuffs, fleecy lining and pommel flap. Noisy waterproof materials should be avoided as horses tend to be frightened of them, particularly on a windy day.

There are **gloves** for every occasion, specially designed for the rider. Special features include reinforced rein fingers, pimple palm grips and lycra inserts for extra flexibility.

Clothes for Competition

▌ LEFT
Correct dress for top-level dressage includes a top hat, tail coat and waistcoat.
▌ BELOW
Most riding gear, for women as well as men, is based on clothes developed for the hunting field.
▌ BOTTOM LEFT
The clothes worn for endurance riding are less formal than in other competitive sports.

For most forms of competitive riding it is usual to wear a riding coat with breeches and boots, a shirt with a collar and tie or collarless shirt with a hunting tie or stock. The rules of some sports also stipulate the wearing of spurs. A hat is obligatory and although the bowler hat (derby) is still seen in show classes and the top hat in dressage, the trend is more and more to the safer type of hunting cap and, even more so, the jockey skull. The latter is usually worn with a dark-coloured silk cover.

For cross-country riding the jacket is replaced by a sweater or shirt, according to the weather, which may be in the rider's own colours, as may the hat silk.

Endurance riding is one area where tradition holds less sway, partly because the sport is of fairly recent origin (at least in an organized competitive way) and also because at the higher echelons riders are not only in the saddle for very long periods but also spend some of the time on their feet, running alongside their horses to give them a breather. Breeches and boots would be too hot and uncomfortable so this is the one sport where runningshoes are permitted. However, as a safety precaution, riders are required to use enclosed-type stirrup irons to prevent their feet slipping right through.

Grooming

Regular grooming is an essential part of good horse management. It is not simply a question of making the horse look smart. Far more important is the fact that thorough brushing helps keep the horse healthy by removing accumulated dust, dead skin and hair and helping to keep the pores open and clean. During hard work the horse's skin excretes waste matter in the form of sweat. It is important that the skin and coat are kept clean to enable this system to work efficiently. A good, strenuous grooming also serves as a massage, improving the horse's muscle tone. In addition, grooming helps to keep the horse's tack and rugs clean, which in turn prevents sores. While the stabled horse needs daily grooming both before and after exercise, the grass-kept horse requires far less attention. Although the areas under the saddle and bridle must always be cleaned before tacking up, only the worst of the mud or grease should be removed elsewhere for appearances' sake. Horses and ponies who live out need the natural grease and dirt in their coats to help keep them warm and dry. This is particularly important in winter.

Grooming Kit

The **dandy brush** has long, stiff bristles and is used for removing dried mud and stable stains (where the horse has lain in its droppings or wet bedding) from the legs. It is too harsh to use on the horse's body or on the mane and tail.

The **body brush** has shorter, finer bristles than the dandy brush and may be used on the horse's entire body (and legs). It has a loop for the hand (leather or canvas are the most comfortable). The best body brushes have a leather back which is less likely than wood or plastic to hurt the horse if you inadvertently knock him with it while grooming. Leather, being softer and flexible, also sits more comfortably on the hand.

The body brush is cleaned after every few strokes by drawing the bristles across the teeth of the **metal curry comb**. The metal curry comb should never be used on the horse.

For dampening down the mane and tail the **water brush** is used. This usually has a wooden back and has softer bristles than the dandy brush.

Two **sponges** are required, one for cleaning the eyes and nostrils, the other for use on the dock and the gelding's sheath. The sponges should never be interchanged (having two different colours prevents them being muddled up). They should be washed out after each use.

The **hoof pick** is a vital piece of equipment, used for cleaning out the horse's feet. The end of the pick should be blunt to prevent damage to the foot. Hoof picks are easily dropped and lost in the bedding. It is a good idea to tie a piece

▌ RIGHT
The grooming kit should include trimming scissors, thinning scissors and mane combs for use when trimming the heels, and when pulling the mane and tail.

▌ PREVIOUS PAGE OPPOSITE
Quarter marks put the finishing touch to a show pony.

▌ PREVIOUS PAGE
Grey horses, like this Percheron, take more keeping clean than dark-coloured horses.

▌ CLOCKWISE FROM LEFT
Body brush and metal curry comb; dandy brush; water brush; rubber and plastic curry combs; 'cactus' cloth.

of brightly coloured twine to the handle to make it easier to locate.

A **stable rubber**, usually made of cloth, is used, slightly dampened, to give a final polish to the horse's coat. A piece of chamois leather or jute sacking is equally effective for this purpose.

A **rubber** or **plastic curry comb**, which like the body brush is fitted with a loop for the hand, may be used for removing dried mud from the coat. Care must be taken when using it on bony areas such as the legs.

A **sweat scraper** is used to remove excess water from the horse's coat after washing him down. It consists of a blade of rubber attached to a metal frame with a handle. Again care must be taken not to knock the bony parts of his body.

Also in the grooming kit will be a **metal mane comb** which is not actually required for the grooming process but for use during trimming the mane and tail. The mane comb may have thick, widely spaced teeth or thin, closer ones.

All grooming tools should be kept tidily in a container designed for the purpose. Brushes should normally be kept bristle-side up (the bristles will last longer that way). They should be kept clean by regular washing. Since hot water may soften the glue which holds bristles in place, the whole brush should be plunged into cold water after cleaning and stood bristle-side down while it dries (this is particularly important for wooden-backed

brushes as the wood will deteriorate if it is left wet for long periods). All other items of grooming equipment should also be kept scrupulously clean.

For **wisping** – a form of massage involving a rhythmic thumping of the muscles of the neck, shoulders and quarters – a pad is required. Traditionally wisping was carried out with a hay wisp, made by twisting a rope of hay into a firm pad. Nowadays special pads are obtainable, often made of leather.

Sometimes the horse may need to have his mane and tail washed and occasionally his whole body. Buckets, sponges, an appropriate horse shampoo (if necessary), sweat scraper and towels will be required.

Electric groomers, which operate like a household vacuum cleaner, are useful for removing grease and dirt particularly from a horse who has not been clipped. Because of the noise horses must be introduced to them carefully and the tail should always be plaited up out of the way to avoid the possibility of the hair becoming caught up if the groomer has a rotating brush. An electric groomer is not suitable for use on the horse's head. While electric groomers are useful for removing dust and dirt, they do not provide the same massaging effect as a good hand grooming.

▌ RIGHT
A good hoof pick is an essential item of equipment. The one on the left is fitted with a brush which is used after the pick to remove remnants of dirt from the feet.

Grooming Technique

The stabled horse needs a thorough grooming every day. This is best carried out after exercise when the horse is warm. The pores of the skin will be open and grease and dirt will be easier to remove. The horse should be tied up during grooming.

Each **foot** should be picked up and carefully cleaned out with the hoof pick. The pick should be used from the horse's heel towards the toe to avoid damaging the frog. Dirt from the feet should be placed in a skip, not in the horse's bed.

The body brush is used to clean the horse's entire **body,** starting with the neck and working down to the shoulders and the front legs, along the body, over the hindquarters and down the hindlegs. Use the brush – in the left hand for the nearside, in the right hand for the offside

– with brisk, firm strokes and after every few strokes clean the bristles on the metal curry comb, which is held in the other hand. Periodically the dirt should be tapped from the curry comb. This should be done in the doorway or just outside the stable, not into the bedding. Care should be taken when grooming not to bang the horse's bony projections, for example those of the hips and legs, and the brush should not be used with too much pressure over the loins. Having completed

one side, move round to the other side of the horse and repeat the process.

The body brush is also used to clean the **head,** which should be done very gently. The horse should not be tied up for this, in case he pulls back. The headcollar should be fastened round his neck, leaving his nose free.

Brush out the **mane** and **tail** with the body brush, taking care not to break the hairs. The tail should be held away from the horse's body with your free hand and

■ LEFT
A very sweaty or dirty horse may be washed down provided he can be dried quickly to prevent chilling. Excess water is removed with a sweat scraper.

1 Grooming begins with picking out the feet. The hoof pick shold always be used from the heel towards the toe.

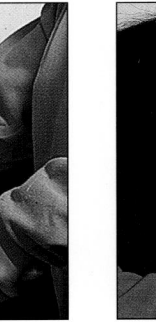

2 Remnants of dirt may be removed from the area round the frog with a brush.

3 The hoof wall should be kept clean – a stiff brush may be used to remove mud and other forms of dirt.

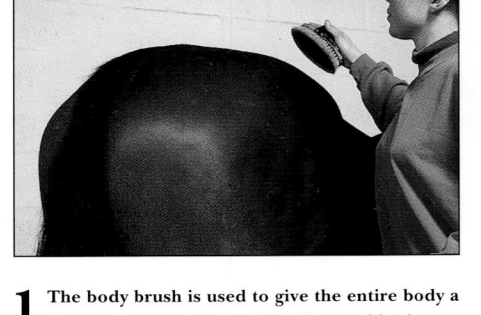

1 The body brush is used to give the entire body a thorough grooming. It should be used in the direction of the lie of the coat.

2 The curry comb is held in the spare hand and used for cleaning the body brush – never use it on the horse.

3 The dock should be sponged each time the horse is groomed. Use a different sponge from the one used for the eyes and nose.

  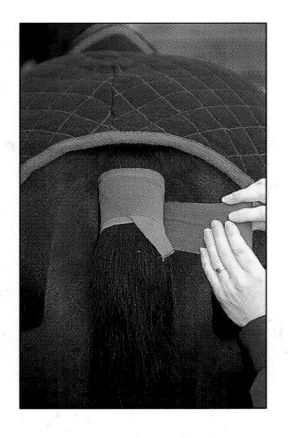 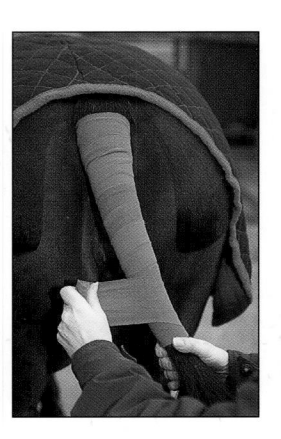 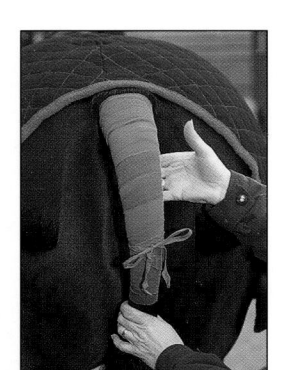

1 Tail bandages are made of elasticated cotton and are about 3 inches (8cm) wide and 10 feet (3m) long.

2 The bandage is started high up, as near as possible to the top of the dock.

3 A loose flap is left at the top and then turned down and bandaged over. This helps prevent slipping.

4 The bandage is applied down the length of the dock and up again. It should not be fitted too tightly

5 The bandage is secured with tapes and the dock should be eased into its natural shape.

brushed out a lock at a time. Any tangles should be teased out with the fingers. A very muddy tail will need washing. To finish off the mane and tail, dip the bristles of the water brush in clean water (not the horse's drinking water) and go lightly over the mane to "lay" it down smoothly. Do the same to the top hairs of the tail. A pulled tail should be bandaged for an hour or so afterwards to keep it tidy.

Use a damp sponge to clean the horse's **eyes** and **nostrils** and another for the **dock.** In the case of geldings the **sheath** will need sponging out once every couple of weeks or so to remove the greasy discharge which accumulates and can cause the horse discomfort. Special solutions can be obtained for this purpose or you can use a mild soap and warm water. Use the same sponge that is used for cleaning his dock. The easiest time to give him a thorough clean in this area is when he is staling. Do it carefully and gently – and beware of being kicked should the horse object. If you are unable to catch the moment when the horse is staling, clean out the sheath by gently inserting the sponge inside it and cleaning all round. Rinse the whole area several times and dry off with a towel.

The finishing touch to the whole grooming process is applied by running a damp stable rubber or other cloth over the entire coat to add a final polish. Wisping with a hay wisp or pad, when done, takes place after regular grooming since its purpose is not to clean but to **massage.** The pad or wisp is applied in

GROOMING TIPS

☛ Never try to groom a sweaty horse – walk him about until he is dry.

☛ Never try to brush off wet mud – either hose it off or let it dry first.

☛ To dry off a wet horse in the stable cover him with a sheet or rug made of "breathable" material or put a layer of straw along his back and quarters with a rug over the top (this is known as "thatching").

☛ To remove dried mud use a dandy brush or rubber curry comb but not too roughly – it may be necessary to remove mud from sensitive areas of skin, such as inside the hindlegs, with your hand.

☛ In cold weather keep a clipped horse warm during grooming by turning his rugs back and forward (as when quartering) rather than removing them altogether.

☛ Give all rugs and blankets a thorough shaking every week – it is pointless to put dusty rugs back on to a clean horse.

☛ Never stand directly behind a horse.

☛ Never sit or kneel on the floor to reach the lower parts – always squat or bend so that you can move quickly if he does.

☛ Keep a watchful eye open for any skin injuries or tell-tail lumps or bumps, particularly on the legs, which could warn of impending soundness problems.

☛ With the grass-kept horse clean the area under the saddle and brush off the worst of the mud for appearances' sake but do not attempt regular, thorough grooming.

much the same way as a brush, but with a firmer thump (though not too hard). It is used on the large muscular areas of the horse (the neck, shoulders and quarters). It is said to improve the circulation and muscle tone. It should never be used on the more tender areas, such as the loins, nor on the bony areas, such as the legs.

A thorough grooming will take from half to three-quarters of an hour, depending on the initial cleanliness of the horse's skin and coat – and the strength and endurance of the groom! Grooming is most effective if you stand a little away from the horse in order to put your weight behind the brush.

A less comprehensive type of grooming called **quartering** is used to prepare the horse in the morning for exercise. Its purpose is to remove any surface dirt accumulated during the night and to make the horse generally presentable. Quartering involves unfastening his rugs, turning them back over his loins and giving his front half a quick brush over, then turning his rugs forward and doing the same to his hind end. Any stains and bedding marks should be removed, if necessary by using a damp sponge or water brush. The damp areas should be dried off with a stable rubber or a towel. The mane and tail should be brushed through and all traces of bedding removed. The feet should be picked clean and the eyes, nostrils and dock sponged. Quartering takes between ten and twenty minutes, depending on the horse's size and how dirty he is.

Types of Clip

In winter horses grow a thick coat to protect them from the weather. A horse with a thick coat who is required to do anything other than light work will sweat excessively and, as a result, be very uncomfortable, lose condition and run the risk of catching a chill if he is not carefully dried off after exercise. Clipping off the thick winter coat of the stabled horse removes these problems and also makes it easier to keep the horse clean and looking smart. A clipped horse must be kept warm with blankets and rugs. A clipped horse who spends some time out at grass will need a waterproof New Zealand rug.

There are different ways of clipping a horse or pony, depending on the work he is required to do and the type of coat he grows. A **full clip** involves removing the coat from the entire body and the legs. A thick-coated horse may be given a full clip when he is first clipped and then at subsequent clippings have his legs left unclipped. Leaving the hair on the legs affords some protection from knocks. The full clip is usually only used for horses in very fast work, such as racing, or sometimes for a show horse being prepared for early spring shows.

The most usual clip for other horses doing hard work is the **hunter clip** which involves leaving the hair on the legs and the area under the saddle. Again the reason for leaving legs and saddle patch unclipped is to provide protection. Care must be taken to dry off the saddle patch thoroughly after work.

As its name suggests the **blanket clip** involves leaving an area of the horse's back, loins and quarters unclipped (and also the legs). The hair is removed from the neck, shoulders and belly and all or part of the head. A blanket clip is suitable for a horse doing a fair amount of medium to hard work.

Horses who are kept out, and stabled horses not in hard work, may be given a low **trace clip,** which consists of removing the hair from the underside of the neck, between the forelegs, the belly and the upper part of the hind legs. Medium and high trace clips, which involve removing more of the body and neck hair are suitable for stabled horses in steady work.

With the **chaser clip** the hair is removed from the head, the lower part of the neck, the chest, the belly and the upper part of the hindlegs. The clip finishes just behind the ears. It is often used on steeplechasers (hence its name). Many Thoroughbred horses have fine coats which may not require total removal even when they are in hard work.

There are various other partial clips suitable for the grass-kept horse used only for light work such as occasional hacking. These include the **bib clip** and the **apron clip.** In the bib clip the coat is removed only from the jowl, down the underside of the neck down to and including the front of the chest. In the apron clip an area above the forelegs and extending back under the girth area of the body is also removed. These areas, together with the flanks and the inside of the hindlegs, are usually the first to become sweaty. A tough animal, such as a native pony, could probably live out without rugs after having a bib or apron clip though in very adverse weather he might need to be rugged. When clipping the hair from the hindquarters an inverted V is left at the top of the tail. The unclipped leg hair is sloped at the top from front to back.

The horse's head is a particularly vulnerable spot because of its thin covering of skin and hair. Many people leave the head unclipped or simply clip the lower half which effectively removes the hair from the sweatiest part (i.e. the jowl) while leaving the top half with protection from the weather. Many horses dislike having their heads clipped at all. This can be caused by a number of reasons, from fear of the sound or feel of the clippers to painful conditions such as toothache or an ear infection.

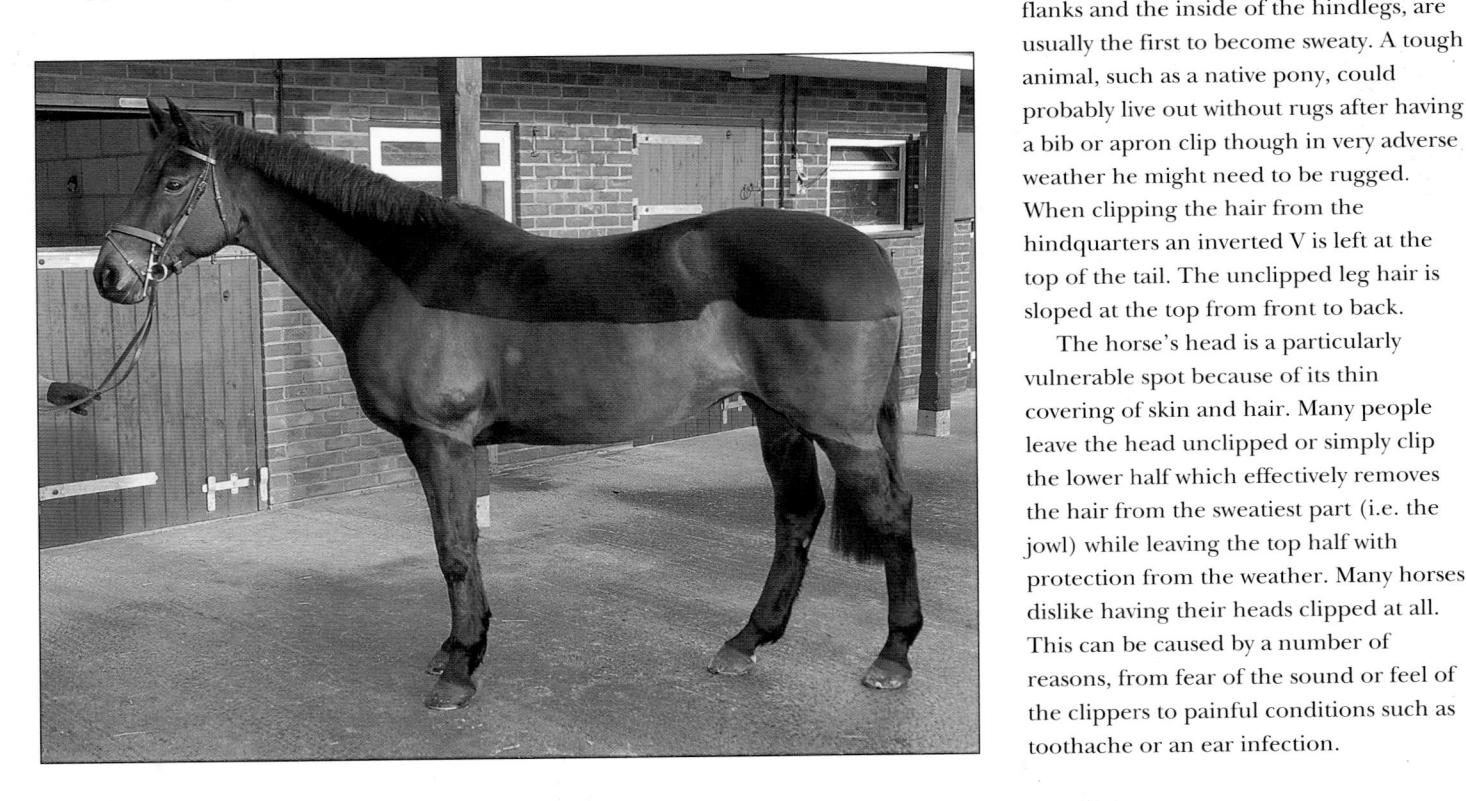

■ ABOVE
This horse has been blanket clipped. The clipping lines should be carefully marked on the horse beforehand, using chalk or a damp bar of saddle soap.

■ ABOVE RIGHT
The area above the tail is finished off in a neat V shape. Care must be taken not to cut into either the mane or tail hair.

■ LEFT
The Irish clip involves removing the hair from the belly and chest and part of the shoulders and neck. This horse has had his head clipped, too.

■ OPPOSITE PAGE
A trace clip is suitable for stabled horses not in hard work. The body and neck may be clipped higher or lower depending on the amount of work the horse is doing.

■ LEFT
For the horse in hard work the hunter clip is most suitable. A full or part saddle patch (as here) should be left to protect the back.

Clipping and Trimming

Clipping horses is hard work and can be dangerous. It should never be carried out alone. The beginner should learn the techniques by watching an expert at work. If in doubt, find someone else to clip your horse, at least to begin with so that you can find out how he behaves.

Having decided on the type of clip, all lines (for example the leg lines and saddle patch) should be marked on the horse's coat with chalk or a damp piece of saddle soap. To mark the saddle patch put the horse's usual saddle on his back, without its fittings, make sure it is in the position where it lies when he is being ridden, and draw round it. It is better to make the saddle patch a little larger than it will finally need to be to make allowance for any mistakes when clipping the edges. A badly positioned saddle patch will spoil the look of the horse.

Start clipping at the front of the horse, on the neck or shoulder, and work your way backwards section by section. The clippers should be used against the lie of the coat (broadly speaking from the back of the horse towards the front) with long, sweeping strokes. Each stroke should be parallel to the one above or below it and should slightly overlap the previous one.

Take care when clipping the top line of the neck not to cut into the mane. Clip a short bridle path out of the mane just

RIGHT
Essential clipping and trimming equipment: electric clippers, electric and battery driven trimmers, spare clipper blades, oil, small brush (for cleaning clogged blades) and screwdriver (for changing fuses if necessary).

behind the ears where the headpiece of the bridle lies. This does not need to be very long: 2 inches (5cm) is adequate.

After the neck and shoulders clip the body and finally the hindquarters. Be particularly careful when clipping awkward places such as the delicate skin below the stifle and the folds between the front legs. The stifle skin should be held with your spare hand to straighten out the folds. An assistant should hold each foreleg up and forward in turn to stretch the folds of skin. Holding up a foreleg will also help prevent a horse from fidgeting or kicking. When clipping between the hindlegs be particularly watchful in case the horse does try to kick out. Keeping hold of his tail will help to prevent this.

The most difficult part of the horse to clip well is the head. If a horse is really frightened of having the clippers near his

head it is far better to leave it unclipped. If the horse's head is to be clipped, first remove the headcollar. If he will not stand still without some form of restraint a halter is easier to work round with the clippers than a headcollar. Where you start will depend very much on the horse but the cheeks are probably the best place. Rest the clippers, switched off, against the cheekbone for a few moments until the horse becomes used to their presence. Then if he does not object switch on and work carefully over both cheeks, underneath from the chin to the throat, up over the front of the head and over the forehead. Because the head is so bony the clippers should be used as lightly as possible to reduce vibration. Be particularly careful when working near the eye.

Some people clip off the horse's whiskers round his muzzle but since these

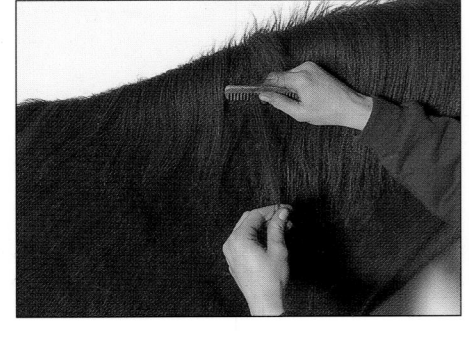

The mane is shortened and thinned by means of pulling, using a mane comb. Remove only a few hairs at a time to prevent soreness and damp the mane down afterwards.

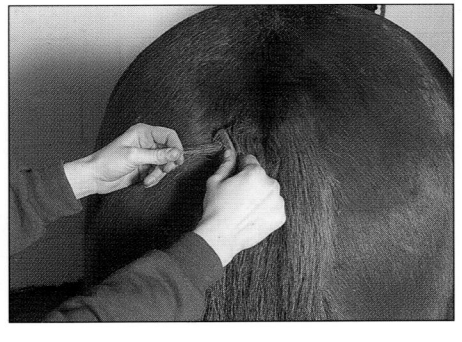

To neaten an untidy tail, pull hair from the sides and centre of the dock, preferably when the horse is warm and the pores are open.

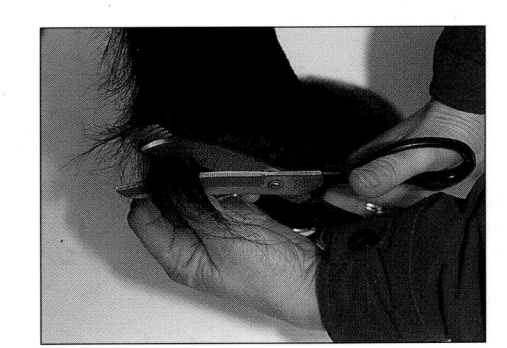

A mane comb and sharp, round-ended scissors are used to trim excess hair from the pasterns and fetlocks of unclipped legs. Take care not to leave "steps" of hair.

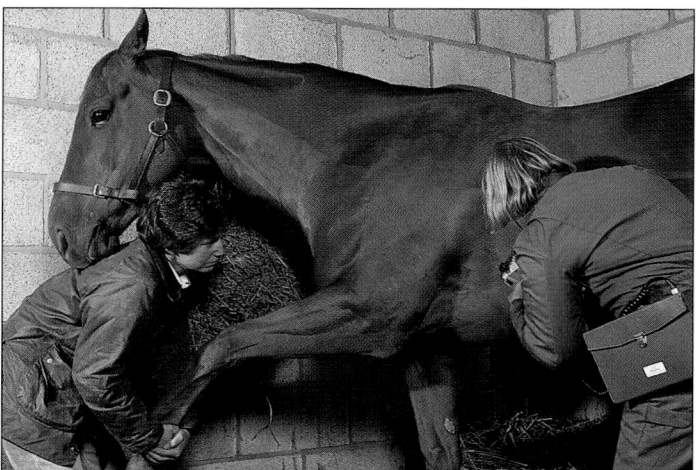

■ RIGHT
Holding up a foreleg
smooths out skin
creases and also stops
the horse fidgeting.

■ MIDDLE RIGHT
Proceed carefully and
gently when clipping
the head.

■ BOTTOM RIGHT
Holding the tail helps
prevent a horse from
kicking. The tail is
bandaged to keep it
clear of the clipper
blades.

CLIPPING AND TRIMMING TIPS

☛ During clipping feel the underside of the blades every few minutes – if they are becoming hot, switch off and allow them to cool down before continuing.

☛ During clipping clean and oil the blades every ten to fifteen minutes.

☛ During clipping keep the horse warm by throwing a rug over the clipped areas – a cold horse will fidget more than a warm one.

☛ Always clip in good light conditions – start in the morning.

☛ Never try to clip a sweaty or dirty horse.

☛ For the best results do not clip until the horse's winter coat has "set" (i.e. is fully grown) – usually mid-autumn.

☛ To gauge the correct position and angle of leg lines measure one hand's width from where the foreleg joins the chest (for the V) and two hands' widths below the elbow; measure four hands' widths below the top of the stifle on the hindleg and two hands' widths above the point of the hock.

☛ Accustom a nervous horse to the feel of clippers by running hand clippers (i.e. non-motorized ones) over him.

☛ Have clippers serviced, and the blades reground, regularly.

☛ Ask your veterinary surgeon to administer a sedative to a horse who is really dangerous to clip.

☛ Pull manes and tails when the horse is warm, either on a hot day or after exercise – the hair will come out more easily while the pores are open, which is easier for you and more comfortable for the horse.

☛ Pull hair, whenever possible, from the underside of the mane – this will encourage it to lie flat.

are used as sensors it is preferable, and kinder, to leave them alone.

To trim the ears, hold each one in turn and run the clippers along the outside edge only. Never try to clip the hair from inside the ear as the horse needs this as protection from insects and dirt. Never clip the eyelashes. Be careful when clipping the top of the head not to cut into the forelock.

If the horse's legs are left unclipped it will probably be necessary to trim his fetlocks and pasterns to make him look tidy. Use a mane comb and scissors (with rounded ends for safety) to remove excess feather, taking care not to create "steps" of hair but to leave a smooth line. Trim any thick hair from around the coronet.

If the horse's head is left unclipped, long hairs around the jaw may also be removed with scissors and comb. Scissors may be used to trim the long hairs from the edge of the ears.

Manes are kept neat by means of pulling, which involves plucking out strands of hair until the mane is the desired length and thickness. If the horse finds this too uncomfortable, it is possible to tidy up the mane with a thinning comb but never be tempted to use scissors which will give a very unsatisfactory result. Pulling can usually be achieved if you take your time and do only a small section of the mane at a time, spreading the whole job over a number of days.

An untidy tail can also be improved by pulling out some of the hairs from the top of the dock. Hair should be removed from the sides and, to a lesser extent, from the

centre. As with the mane, it is best to remove a few hairs each day to prevent soreness. After pulling, the tail should be dampened with a water brush and bandaged to make the hair lie flat (do not leave the bandage on overnight). A pulled

tail will need regular pulling if it is to keep its neat shape. A horse who lives out during the winter should not have his tail pulled – the hair at the top of the dock is there to protect him from rain and snow. To trim the bottom of the tail, raise the horse's dock to the position where he carries it when he is on the move. With your other hand hold the hair at the bottom of the tail and then cut off the hair to the required length. The end of the tail should be parallel to the ground when the horse is moving.

Final Touches for Turnout

Plaiting, or **braiding, the mane** makes the horse or pony look smart, particularly if he has an untidy mane and is to appear in public. In some showing classes it is expected that the horse will be plaited. In others, such as those for Mountain and Moorland ponies and Arabs, the mane is never plaited. It is easier to plait a mane that has been pulled – a very thick, uneven mane will result in ugly, untidy plaits.

The mane hair is divided into equal bunches, each of which is dampened and then plaited, turned under and secured close to the crest of the neck, either by sewing with thread or with rubber bands. Sewn plaits are the most secure and are therefore more suitable for the horse engaged in lengthy periods of work such as hunting or eventing. Rubber bands are suitable for sports such as show jumping, where the mane does not need to remain plaited for long.

The plaits need to be fairly tight to look tidy and stay put, but beware of plaiting too tightly. If you do, it can cause the horse discomfort, particularly if he is required to stretch his neck a lot, for example when he is doing fast work or jumping.

A horse's appearance may be greatly improved by clever plaiting: making the plaits in the dip of the neck bigger than

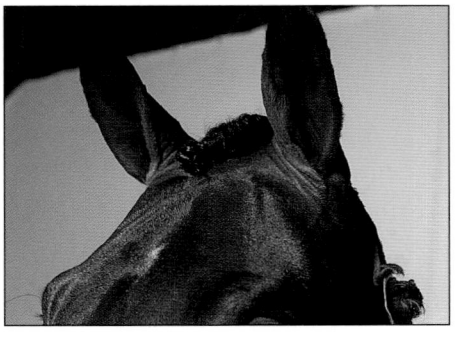

A plaited forelock gives the head a neat appearance. Plaits should be tight enough to prevent them dropping out but not so tight that they cause the horse discomfort.

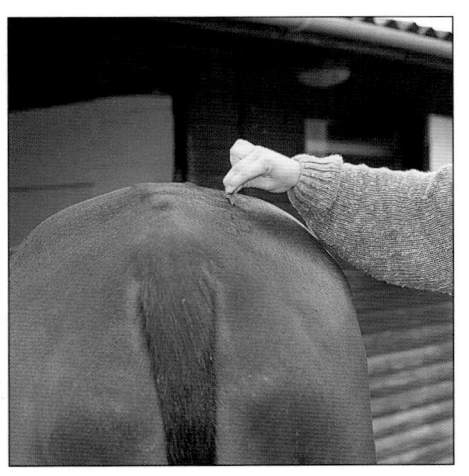

Quarter marks add the finishing touches to a well-groomed horse or pony. A chequered pattern may be made with a mane comb and stencil.

the others will help disguise a ewe neck; a small number of plaits will make a long neck seem shorter; conversely, a short neck will look longer if the mane has lots of small plaits. The appearance of a horse with a very untidy mane can be improved if the mane is hogged, or clipped off altogether. A hogged mane looks best on a horse of fairly heavy build, such as a cob – in Britain cobs are always shown with a hogged mane. Manes grow quickly and will need re-hogging every few weeks.

Plaiting, or **braiding, a tail** looks complicated but is not too difficult once you have had a little practice. For successful plaiting the tail must have long hair at the top – it is not possible to plait a pulled tail. The hair must be clean, well brushed and dampened before plaiting begins. When the plait is complete it should be carefully dampened with a sponge and then protected with a tail bandage. To avoid damaging the plait the tail bandage must be removed by unwinding, not by sliding it down.

In very muddy conditions, for instance when riding across country in wet weather, it may be more comfortable for the horse to have his tail put up so that it cannot become clogged with mud. To put up a tail, start plaiting from the top in the usual way. When you reach the end of the dock,

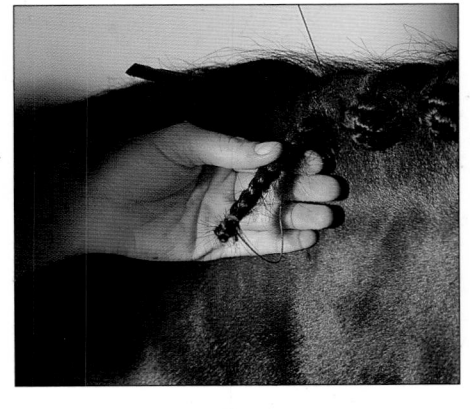

1 Plaiting a mane using needle and thread: the end of each plait is secured with thread.

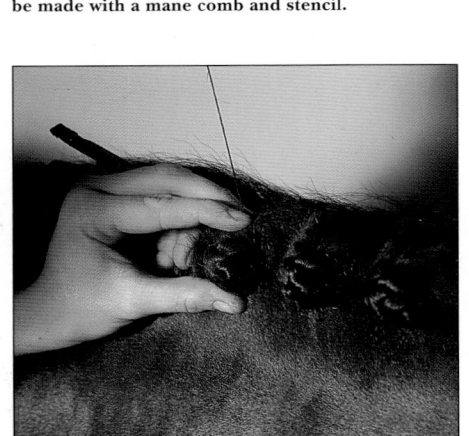

2 The plait is folded or rolled up until it is close to the crest and stitched firmly.

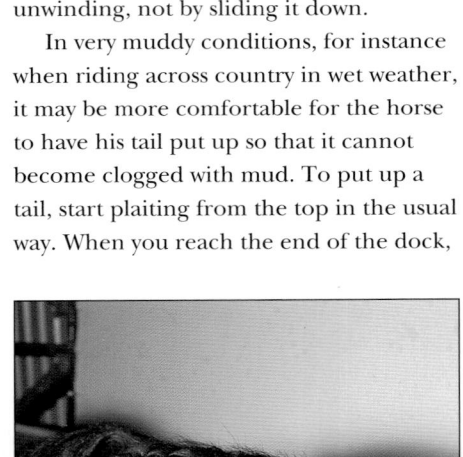

3 Finished plaits should be the same size. Using larger or smaller plaits can help disguise a poorly shaped neck.

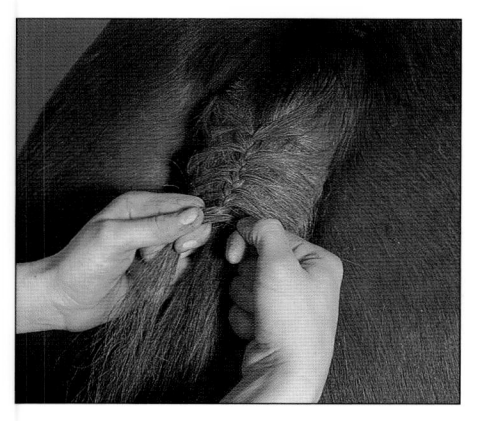

1 To plait a tail begin high up, using one bunch of hair from each side and one from the centre.

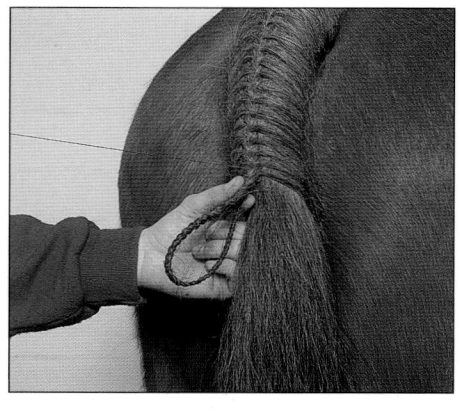

2 Plait down to the end of the dock, using thin bunches of hair from alternate sides.

3 At the end of the dock, stop adding side bunches and continue plaiting the long hair.

divide the rest of the tail into three and continue plaiting to the end of the long tail hairs. The bottom of the plait should be secured with a thick rubber band or needle and thread. The plaited tail is rolled up under the dock and carefully sewn to hold it in place.

For smart occasions, such as showing and racing, the horse's coat may be decorated with **quarter marks.** These are applied on the hindquarters and may be drawn in with a comb, a brush, or by means of brushing over a plastic stencil. All three methods involve producing a pattern by brushing patches of the coat in different directions.

There are various other "tricks of the trade" which will enhance the appearance of a show horse. Chalk may be brushed into white leg markings. It is also useful for disguising any dirty marks on a grey coat, particularly those acquired during travelling, when there is no time to wash and dry the horse before his class. A little baby oil or Vaseline may be rubbed around the eyes and nostrils – this will accentuate the quality of the head. Human hairspray may be used to help control an unruly mane. The horse's coat may be given a final polish with coat gloss, which is specially made for the purpose.

■ RIGHT
The end of the plait is secured with needle and thread, tucked under and sewn in place to give a smart appearance.

Index

Page numbers in *italic* refer to the illustrations

A

abscesses, strangles, 215
advertisements, buying horses, 174
ailments, 214–15
Aintree breastplates, 229
Akhal-Teke, (the Turknen), *10, 11, 24, 108–9, 108–9*
albinos, 17
Alter Real, 93, *93*
American Horse Shows Association, 237
American Shetland Pony, 153, *153*
Andalusian, 19, 24, 26–7, *26–7*
Anglo-Arab, 30–1, *30–1*
Appaloosa, 158–9, *158–9*
apron clip, 246
Arab, 1, 2, 19, 22–3, *22–3*, 129
Ardennais, 33, 42–3, *42–3*
Ariègeois, 38, *38*
ascarid worms, 212
Asiatic Wild Horse, 11, 20, *20*
Assateague Pony, 21
Aubiose bedding, 196
Australian Stock Horse, 124–5, *124–5*
automatic water bowls, 204–5, *205*
azoturia, 214

B

baby oil, 251
back:
  conformation, 14
  injuries, 216, *217*
bandages:
  knees, *216*
  leg, 232–3, *232–3*, 235
  stable, 233
  tail, 235, *245*
Barb, 19, 24–5, *24–5*
barbed wire, 183
barley, 200, *200*
barn stabling, *192*, 193, *193*
Bashkir, 94, *94*
bedding, 194–5, *194–5*
  management, 198–9, *198–9*
Belgian Draught, 33, *33*, 43, 63
bib clip, 246
bitless bridles, 228–9, *228*
bits, 228, *229*
blanket clip, 246, *247*
blankets, 230
blood tests, 176
body brushes, 242, *242*, 244, *244*

body protectors, 237, *237*
body warmers, 236
bone, conformation, 15
boots, 234, *234*
  brushing boots, 209, 234
  fetlock boots, *234*
  foot poultices, 218, *218*
  hock boots, 216, 235
  kneeboots, 209, *209*, 234, *234*, 235
  overreach boots, 234, *234*, 235
  "sausage boots", 216
  tendon boots, 234, *234*
  travelling boots, 235, *235*
boots, riding, 236, *236*, 237, 238
bot flies, 213
Boulonnais, 51, *51*
bowler hats, 239
box stalls, 192
box trees, 187
"boxy" feet, *225*
bracken, 187
braiding manes, 250, *250*
braiding tails, 250, *251*
bran, 201
bran poultices, 218
breastplates, 229
breeches, 238, 239
Breton, 50, *50*
bridles, 209, *209*, 228–9, *228*
brindles, 32
British Horse Society, 237
brooms, 198, *198*
Brumby, 21
brushes, 242, *242*, 243
brushing, 244, *244*
brushing boots, 209, 234
buckets, water, 188, *204*, 204

Budenny, 96–7, *96–7*
buying a horse, 171–7
Byerley Turk, 29

C

"cactus" cloth, *242*
calcium supplements, 200
Camargue, *13*, 21, 40–1, *40–1*
cantering, 211
capped elbows, 216
capped hocks, 194, 216
Caspian Pony, 11, *11*, 129, 150, *150*
cast horses, 199
cattle, in fields, 189, *189*
cavesson nosebands, 209, 228, *228*
chaff, 200
chalk, on white leg markings, 251
chaps, 238, *238*
chaser clip, 246
chest, conformation, 15
'chestnut', 70
Chestnut, 14
chin harness, hard hats, 237, *237*, 238
choosing a horse, 172–3
chop, 200
chronic obstructive pulmonary disease (COPD), 214
clenches, 222, *222*
Cleveland Bay, *8*, 35, 58, 63, 64–5, *64–5*
clipped horses, 209
clippers, *248*
clipping, 230, 246–9, *247–9*
clothes, 236, *236*
  competition clothes, 239, *239*
  riding clothes, 238, *238*

clover, 189
Clydesdale, 33, 63, 72–3, *72–3*
coat:
  clipping, *247*, 246–9, *248–9*
  colours and markings, 16–17, *16*
coat gloss, 251
coats, riding, 236, 238, 239, *239*
Cob, 66, 165, *165*
  Norman Cob, 39
  Welsh Cob, 138–9, *138–9*
cold treatments, 219
coldblood, 19
colic, 215, *215*
colours, 16–17, 155–63
combs, 242, 243
communication, 12–13
competition clothes, 239, *239*
compound feeds, 201
concentrates, 200, 201, 202–3
conformation, 14–15, *14*
Connemara Pony, 146–7, *146–7*
contact lenses, 237
coolers, 231
corns, 218, 224
coronary corium, 220
cotton sheets, 230, 231
cotton-wool, bandages, *216*
cracked heels, 214
crash hats, 237, *237*
creeping red fescue, 189
Criollo, 24, 126, *126*
curbs, *228*
curry combs, 242, *242*, 243, 244, *244*

D

daily feed requirements, 202
Dales Pony, 144, *144*
dandy brushes, 242, *242*
Danish Warmblood, 36–7, *36–7*
Darley Arabian, 29
Dartmoor Pony, *12*, 134–5, *134–5*
Dawn Horse, 10
day rugs, 230–1
dealers, 174
deep litter beds, 199
derby hats, 239
ditches, 189
dock, sponging, 244, 245
domestication, 19
Don, 95, *95*
doors, stables, 192–3, *193*
double bridles, *228*
drainage, fields, 189
drains, stables, 192
draught horses, 19

drawing knives, 222, *222*
dressage clothes, 239
dressage saddles, 229, *229*
drinkers, automatic, 204–5, *205*
droppings:
  mucking out, 198, *199*
  removal from fields, 189, *189*
drying horses, 245
Dutch Warmblood, 52, 91, *91*

E

ears, 13
  trimming, 249
eggbutt bits, 228, *229*
eggs, horse bot, 213
elbows, capped, 216
electric fencing, 182, 183, *183*
electric groomers, 243
electricity, in stables, 193
endurance riding, *173*, 239, *239*
Eohippus, 10, 11, *11*
Equidae, 10, 11
equine influenza, 214
equipment, 227–35
Equus caballus, 10
Equus silvaticus, 11
ergot, 11
evolution, 10–11, *11*
exercise, 208–9, *208–9*
exercise bandages, 232–3, *232*
exercise sheets, 209
Exmoor Pony, 11, *11*, 132–3,
  132–3, 208
eyes, 13
  colour, 17
  injuries, *217*
  sponging, 245

F

facial markings, 16, *16*
Faradism, 216, *217*
farriers, 221–3, *221–3*
feed bowls, *202*
feeding, 202–3, *202*
feeds, 200–1
feet:
  anatomy, 220, *220*
  boots, 234, *234*
  colours, 16
  conformation, 15
  evolution, *11*
  lameness, 220
  picking out, 244, *244*
  poultices, 218
  problems, 224–5, *224–5*
  shoes, 221–3, *221, 222*

tubbing, 218–19, *219*
Fell Pony, 145, *145*
fencing, 182–3, *182–3*
fetlock boots, *234*
fetlocks, trimming hair, *248*, 249
fields, 181–9
  fencing, 182–3, *182–3*
  gates, 184, *184*
  grass management, 189, *189*
  poisonous plants, 186–7
  shelters, 185, *185*
  turning horses out, 208
  water, 188, *188*
fillet strings, 209, 231
fire safety, 193
first aid kit, *213*, 216
fitness training, 210–11, *210–11*
Fjord Pony, 148–9, *148–9*
flash nosebands, 209
flexion tests, 176
floors, stables, 192
fluorescent clothing, *237*
foals, 12
forelocks, plaited, *250*
forks, mucking out, 198, *198*
fossils, 10
Frederiksborg, 26, 34, *34*
French Trotter, 46–7, *46–7*
Friesian, 26, 58, 60, 68, 88–9,
  88–9
frog, 220
full clip, 246
Furioso, 74, *74*

G

galloping, 211
Gamgee tissue, *216*, 218, *218*, 232

gateposts, 184, *184*
gates, 184, *184*
Gelderland, 90, *90*
geldings, 173
genes, 16
girths, 229, *229*
gloves, 236, 238
Godolphin Arabian, 29
Grakle nosebands, 209
grass, haylage, 200
grass-kept horses, 181–9, 203
grass management, 189, *189*
grass sickness, 214
grazing, 200, 203
grooming, 209, 230, 241–51,
  244–5
grooming kit, 242–3, *242–3*

H

Hack, 166, *166*
hackamores, 228–9, *228*
hacking out, *173*, 208, 209, 210
Hackney, 66–7, *66–7*
Haflinger, 130, *130*
hair, rider's, 236
hairspray, 251
half-chaps, 238
Hanoverian, 37, 54–5, *54–5, 58,
  60, 63*
hard hats, 236, *236*, 237, *237*, 238
harrowing fields, 189
hats, 236, *236*, 237, *237*, 238, 239
hay, 200, *200, 203*
haylage, 200
haynets, *203*
head:
  clipping, 248–9, *249*
  conformation, 14

grooming, 244
headcollars, 235
health problems, 212–15
heart abnormalities, 212
heart rate, 212, *212*
heat, poultices, 218
hedges, 183
heels, cracked, 214
hemlock, 187
hemp bedding, 196, *197*
herbivores, 12, 200
herds, 11, 12–13, *12–13*
Highland Pony, *10*, 11, 140–1,
  140–1, 172
hillwork, *210*, 211
hindquarters, conformation, 14,
  15
hocks:
  bandaging, *216*
  capped, 194, 216
  hock boots, 216, 235
hogged manes, 250
Holstein, 27, 37, 54, 56–7, *56–7,
  172*
hoof picks, 242–3, *243*
hooves *see* feet
horse bot, 213
"horse sick" grazing, 189
horses, breeds, 19–127
horsetails, 187
hosing, 219, *219*
Hungarian Half-bred, 76–7, *76–7*
Hunter, 164, *164*
hunter clip, 246, *247*
hunting breastplates, 229
hunting caps, 237, 239

I

ice packs, 217, 219
Icelandic, 80–1, *80–1*
illnesses, 212–15
influenza, 214
infra-red treatment, *217*
inhalants, *219*
injuries, 216–17, *216–17*
Irish clip, *247*
Irish Draught, 82–3, *82–3*
Italian Heavy Draught, 87, *87*

J

jackets, 238
jockey skulls, 237, *237*, 239
jodhpur boots, 236, 237, 238
jodhpurs, 236, 238
joint injuries, 216, *216*
jumping, *211*

jumping saddles, 229, *229*
jumping shoes, 209
jute rugs, 230
Jutland, 35, *35*, 62

K
Kabardin, 98, *98*
Kaimanawa horse, *20*
kaolin poultices, 218
kicking boards, stables, 192
Knabstrup, 36, 162, *162*
knees:
  bandaging, *216*
  kneeboots, 209, *209*, 234, 234,
    235
Konik, 21, *21*, 52

L
labernum, 187
lameness:
  foot problems, 220, 224–5,
    224–5
  signs of, 212, *213*
  splints, 217
  veterinary examination, 177
laminae, 220
laminitis, 224, *224*
laser treatment, leg injuries, 217
Latvian, 103, *103*
lead ropes, 235
leading horses, 209
legs:
  bandages, 232–3, *232–3*
  boots, 234, *234*
  conformation, 15
  flexion tests, 176
  hosing, 219, *219*
  injuries, 216–17
  lameness, 212, *213*, 217
  markings, 16, *16*
  travelling protection, 235
  trimming fetlock hair, *248*, 249
ligament injuries, 217
light, stables, 193
linseed, 201
Lipizzaner, *16*, 17, 26, 34
looseboxes, 192
lunge reins, 209
Lusitano, 92–3, *92–3*

M
maize, *200*, 201
mane combs, *242*, 243
manes:
  brushing, 244–5
  hogged, 250

plaiting, 250, *250*
pulling, *248*, 249
mangers, *202*
Maremmano, 84–5, *84–5*
mares, 12–13, 173
markings, 16–17, *16*
martingales, 209, 228, *228*
massage, wisping, 245
meadow grass, 189
meadow hay, 200, *200*
Merychippus, 10
mesh rugs, 231
Mesohippus, 10, *11*
midge bites, 215
Missouri Fox Trotter, 118–19,
  118–19
molasses, 201
Morgan, 110–11, *110–11*
muck heaps, 199, *199*
muck sheets, 198
mucking out, 198–9, *198–9*
mud fever, 214
Murgese, 86, *86*
muscle injuries, 216, *217*
Mustang, *18*, 21, 24, 122–3,
  122–3

N
nails, shoeing, 222, *222*
navicular disease, 224–5, *225*
neck, conformation, 14–15
New Forest Pony, 137, *137*
New Zealand rugs, *230*, 231, 246
Nez Percé Indians, *17*
night rugs, 230
Nonius, 75, *75*
Noriker, 32, *32*
Norman Cob, 39, *39*
North Swedish, 104, *104–5*

nosebands, 209, 228, *228*
nostrils, sponging, 245
numnahs, 209, *228*, 229

O
oak trees, *186*, 187
oats, 200, *200*
Oldenburg, 27, 58–9, *58–9, 60,*
  63
Orlov Trotter, 100–1, *100–1*
overreach boots, 234, *234*, 235
overreaches, 216

P
paddock sheets, 231
paddocks *see* fields
padlocks, gates, 184, *184*
Paint Horse, 17, 160–1, *160–1*
Palomino, 17, 156–7, *156–7*
paper bedding, 196, *196*
peat moss bedding, 196
pedal bone rotation, 224
pedal osteitis, 225
Percheron, 39, 42, 48–9, *48–9,* 51
periople, 220
Peruvian Paso, 127, *127–8*
petal-type overreach boots, 234,
  234
piebalds, 17, *17*
pig netting, 182
pigeon toes, *224*
pin worms, 213
pincers, farrier's, 222, *222*
Pinto, 17, 160
plaiting manes, 250, *250*
plaiting tails, 250, *251*
plants, poisonous, 186–7
plastic fencing, 183
Pliohippus, 11, *11*

poisonous plants, 186–7
poll guards, 235, *235*
Polo Pony, 167, *167*
ponies, breeds, 129–52
Pony of the Americas, 152, *152–3*
poultices, 218, *218*
privet, 187, *187*
proud flesh, *216*, 217
Przewalski, Colonel N.M., 20
Przewalski Horse, 11, 20–1, *20*
public sales, 174, *174*
pulse rate, 212, *212*
"Punch", see Suffolk
puncture wounds, 217

Q
Quarter Horse, 112–13, *112–13*
quarter marks, *250*, 251
quartering, 245

R
racehorses, 23, 28–9, *209*
rain scald, 215
rasps, 222, *222, 223*
red worms, 212–13
respiratory problems, 194, 195,
  214, *219*
respiratory rate, 212
rhododendron, 187, *187*
riding boots, 236, *236*, 237, 238
riding clothes, 238, *238*
Riding Pony, 151, *151*
ringbone, 225
ringworm, 215
road safety, 209, *237*
roans (red, strawberry, blue), 17,
  28, 33, 42, *43*, 46, 50
rollers, 230, *231*
rolling, 194
roofs, stables, 192
roughage, 200
rubber matting, bedding, 196–7,
  197
rubbers, stable, 243, 245
rugs, 230–1, *230–1*, 235
running martingales, *228*
rye grass, 189, 200

S
Sable Island Pony, 21
saddle patch, unclipped, 246, *247*
  248
Saddlebred, 114–15, *114–15*
saddles, 209, *209*, 229, *229*
safety:
  bandages, 233

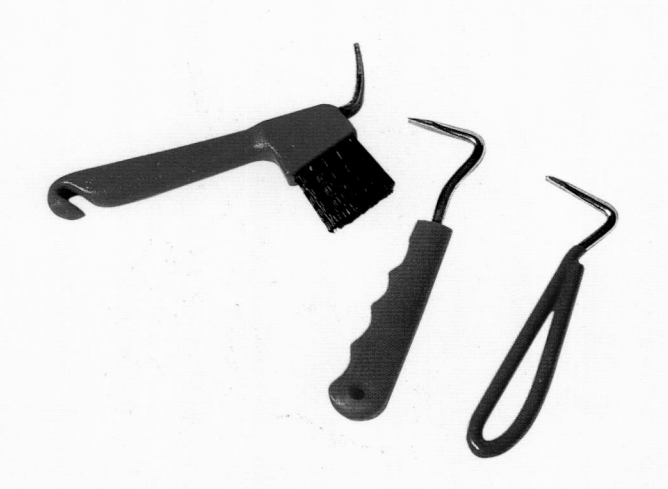

fields, 182
  gates, 184
  poisonous plants, 186
  safety gear, 237, *237*
  stables, 193
  water supply, 188
sales, 174, *174*
salt licks, *203*
sandcracks, *224*, 225
"sausage boots", 216
Schleswig, 35, 62, *62*
schooling, 211, *211*
schoolmaster, 172
screens, field shelters, 185
seed hay, 200, *200*
seedy toe, 225
self-adhesive bandages, 233, *233*
Selle Français, Cheval de, (French
    Saddle Horse), 31, 44–5, *44–5*,
    59
semi-deep litter system, 199
set fast, 214
Shagya, 1, 78–9, *78–9*
shampoo, 243
shavings forks, 198
sheath, sponging, 245
sheep, in fields, 189
sheep netting, 182
sheets, 230, 231, 235
shelters, 185, *185*
Shetland Pony, *13*, 142–3, *142–3*
  American Shetland Pony, 153
Shire, 33, 68–9, *68–9*
shirts, 236, 239
shoes, 209, 221–3, *221–3*
shoulder, conformation, 15
shredded paper bedding, 196, *196*
shrubs, poisonous, 187
sidebones, 225
skewbalds, 17, *17*
skips, 199, *199*
smell, sense of, 13
snaffles, 209, *209*, 228, *228*, 235
soil, fields, 189
sole, 220
Sorraia, 21, *21*, 26, 131, *131*
South German, 63, *63*
"speedy cutting", 234
splints, 216–17
sponges, 242, *244*, 245
Spotted Horses, 17, *17*
Spotted Pony, 163, *163*
spurs, 239
stable bandages, 233, *233*
stable rubbers, 243, 245
stable rugs, 230, *230*

stables, 191–205
  bed management, 198–9, *198–9*
  bedding, 194–5, *194–5*
  construction, 192–3
  mangers, *202*
  water supply, 204–5, *204–5*
stallions, 12–13, 173
Standardbred, 116–17, *116–17*
stirrup irons, 229, *229*, 237
stirrup leathers, 229
stocks, 238, 239
stone walls, *182*, 183
strangles, 215
straw bedding, 194–5, *194*
streams, 188
Streptococcus equi, 215
string rugs, 231, *231*
Strongylus vulgaris, 212–13
studs, shoes, 209, 222–3, *223*
Suffolk, 33, 35, 70–1, *70–1*
sugar beet, 201
surcingles, 230, *230*, 231, *231*
sweat scrapers, 243, *244*
Swedish Warmblood, 34, 37, *52*,
    106–7, *106–7*
sweet itch, 215

T
tails:
  bandages, 235, *245*
  brushing, 244–5
  plaiting, 250, *251*
  pulling, *248*, 249
  putting up, 250–1

tail guards, 235
Tarpan, 11, 21, *21*, 52
temperature, 212, *212*
tendon boots, 234, *234*
tendon injuries, 217
Tennessee Walking Horse, 120–1,
    120–1
Tersk, 99, *99*
tetanus, 215, 217
"thatching", 245
theft, 184
thermometers, 212, *212*
Thoroughbred, *15*, 19, 24, 28–9,
    28–9, 55, 129
thrush, 225
ties, 238, 239
timothy grass, 189, 200
tools:
  farrier's, 222–3, *223*
  grooming kit, 242–3, *242–3*
  mucking out, 198, *198*
top hats, 239, *239*
touch, sense of, 13
trace clip, 246, *247*
Trakehner, 37, 52–3, *52–3*
travelling boots, 235, *235*
travelling equipment, 235, *235*
trees, poisonous, 187
trotting, 210–11
troughs, water, 188, *188*
trousers, 238
trying a horse, 175
tubbing, 218–19, *219*
Turkenmenistan, 108-9

tying-up, 214

V
vaccination, tetanus, 215, 217
Vaseline, 251
Velcro, bandages, *233*
ventilation, stables, 193
veterinary certificates, 175, 176–7
vices, 177
Vladimir Heavy Draught, 102–3,
    102–3

W
waistcoats, *239*
walking, 210
walls, fields, *182*, 183
warmblood, 19
warranties, 175
washing down, *244*
water:
  drinking water, 204–5, *204–5*
  in fields, 188, *188*
  hosing, 219, *219*
water brushes, 242, *242*
waterproof rugs, 231
waterproofs, rider's, 238
weeds, 189
Wellington boots, 236, 237
Welsh Cob, 138–9, *138–9*
Welsh Mountain Pony, 136, *136*
Western riding, 228
Westphalian, 60–1, *60–1*
wheat straw bedding, 194, *194*
wheelbarrows, 198, *198*
whiskers, 248–9
white line, 220
wild horses, 12–13, 20–1, 22–3,
    24
windbreak screens, 185
windows, stables, 193
wisping, 243, 245
wither pads, 230
Witney blankets, 230
wood shavings, bedding, 195, *195*
worms, 189, 212–13, *212*
wounds, 217, *217*, 218

X
X–rays, 176

Y
yard system, stabling, 193
yew, 186, 187, *187*

Z
zebras, *10*

Acknowledgements

The author would like to thank the many individuals and breed societies who kindly provided information for use in the breeds section, particularly: The American Morgan Horse Association, Inc; The American Paint Horse Association, The American Saddlebred Horse Association, Inc; The British Spotted Pony Society; Vivienne Burdon; The Cleveland Bay Horse Society; The Clydesdale Horse Society of Great Britain and Ireland; The Exmoor Pony Society; The Hackney Horse Society; The Haflinger Society of Great Britain; The Highland Pony Society; The Irish Draught Horse Society (GB); Sylvia Loch (author of *The Royal Horse of Europe*, J.A.Allen, 1986); The Lusitano Breed Society of Great Britain; The Palomino Horse Association of America, Inc; The Pinto Horse Association of America, Inc; Valerie Russell; The Suffolk Horse Society; The Walkaloosa Horse Association; The Walking Horse Owners' Association of America, Inc; The Welsh Pony and Cob Society.

We are also grateful to the following for allowing their horses, ponies and stables to be photographed:

BREEDS
Arab – Sariah Arabians, Dorking, Surrey
Barb – Haras Regional de Marrakech, Morocco
Thoroughbred – Mrs M Blackburn, c/o Catherston Stud, Whitchurch, Hampshire
Anglo-Arab – Woodlander Stud, Raglan, Gwent

Danish Warmblood – Catherston Stud, Whitchurch, Hampshire
Ariègeois – Bob Langrish, photographer
Camargue – Laurent Serre, Camargue, France
Norman Cob – Haras National Le Lion d'Angers, Loire, France
Selle Français – Haras National Le Lion d'Angers, Loire, France
French Trotter – Haras National Le Lion d'Angers, Loire, France
Breton – Haras National Le Lion d'Angers, Loire, France
Percheron – Haras National Le Lion d'Angers, Loire, France
Hanoverian – Mrs S Bray, Nuneaton, Warwickshire
Oldenburg – I Brendel, Trenthide, Dorset
Westphalian – Marlow Building Co Ltd, Marlow, Buckinghamshire
Hackney – Georgina Turner, Ipswich, Essex
Shire – Lingwood Shire, Brentwood, Essex
Suffolk – Randy Hiscock, Shaftsbury, Dorset
Icelandic – Edda Hestar, Salisbury, Wiltshire
Friesian – Harrods, London
Gelderland – Mr Luetzow, Wokingham, Berkshire

Holstein – Mr Luetzow, Wokingham, Berkshire
Dutch Warmblood – Mrs C Hughes, Doncaster
Shagya Arab – Sonia Lindsay, Okehampton, Devon
Akhal-Teke – Viscountess Bury, Plumpton, Sussex
Budenny – Mrs Marcus, Beoley, Redditch, Hereford & Worcester (action)
Don – Russian Horse Society, Epsom, Surrey (standing) Mrs June Connolly, Droitwich, West Midlands (action)
Kabardin – Mrs June Connolly, Droitwich, West Midlands
Orlov – George Bowman Jnr, Penrith, Lancashire
Vladmir – Russian Horse Society, Epsom, Surrey
North Swedish – Jan Gyllensten, photographer, Sweden

USA
Morgan – Betty Gray, Orange Lake, Florida
Quarter Horse – Quiet Oaks Farm, Ocala, Florida & Derby Daze Farm, Ocala, Florida
Saddlebred – Boca Raton Equestrian Centre, Del Ray Beach
Standardbred – David McDuffee &

Tom Walsh Jnr, South Florida Trotting Center
Missouri Foxtrotter – Sandy Hart, Winter Haven, Florida
Tennessee Walker – Mrs Carol Worsham, Dunnellon, Florida
Pony of the Americas – Cynthia Bunnell, Eustis, Florida
Palomino – Holmes Quarter Horses, Brandon, Florida
Appaloosa – Classic Acres Farm, Ocala, Florida
Paint – Brooke Hamlin, Ocala, Florida
American Shetland – Caroline Proctor, Ocala, Florida
Mustang – Cindy Bowman, Dunnellon, Florida
Peruvian Paso – Annette Ward, Alachua, Florida

PONIES
Haflinger – Millslade Farm Stud, Bridgwater, Somerset
Exmoor – Mrs J Freeman, Wareside, Hertfordshire
Shetland – Mr & Mrs E House, Bincombe Shetlands, Bridgwater, Somerset
Dales – Mrs B Powell, Farnham, Surrey
New Forest – Shirley Young, Salisbury, Wiltshire
Connemara & Welsh Sec B – Miss S Clark, Dorking, Surrey
Fjord – Mrs Murray, Ottery St Mary, Devon
Caspian – Henden Caspian Stud, Chippenham, Wiltshire
Knabstrub – Mrs Ann Peruzzi-Smith, Diss, Norfolk

STABLE MANAGEMENT
Catherston Stud, Whitchurch, Hampshire
Stretcholt Farm Stud, Bridgwater, Somerset.